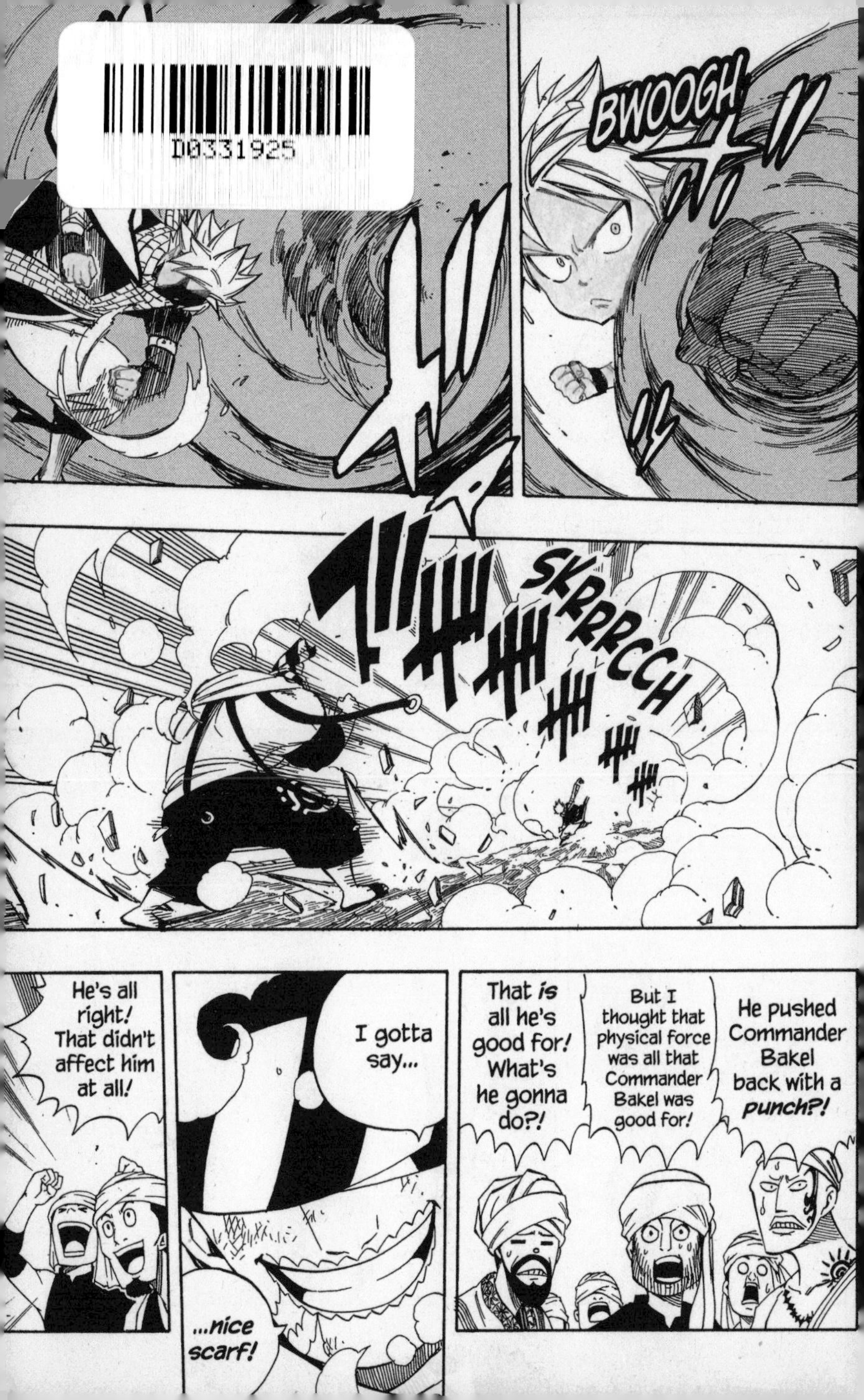
BWOOGH
SKRRRCCH
He pushed Commander Bakel back with a *punch?!*
But I thought that physical force was all that Commander Bakel was good for!
That *is* all he's good for! What's he gonna do?!
I gotta say...
...nice scarf!
He's all right! That didn't affect him at all!

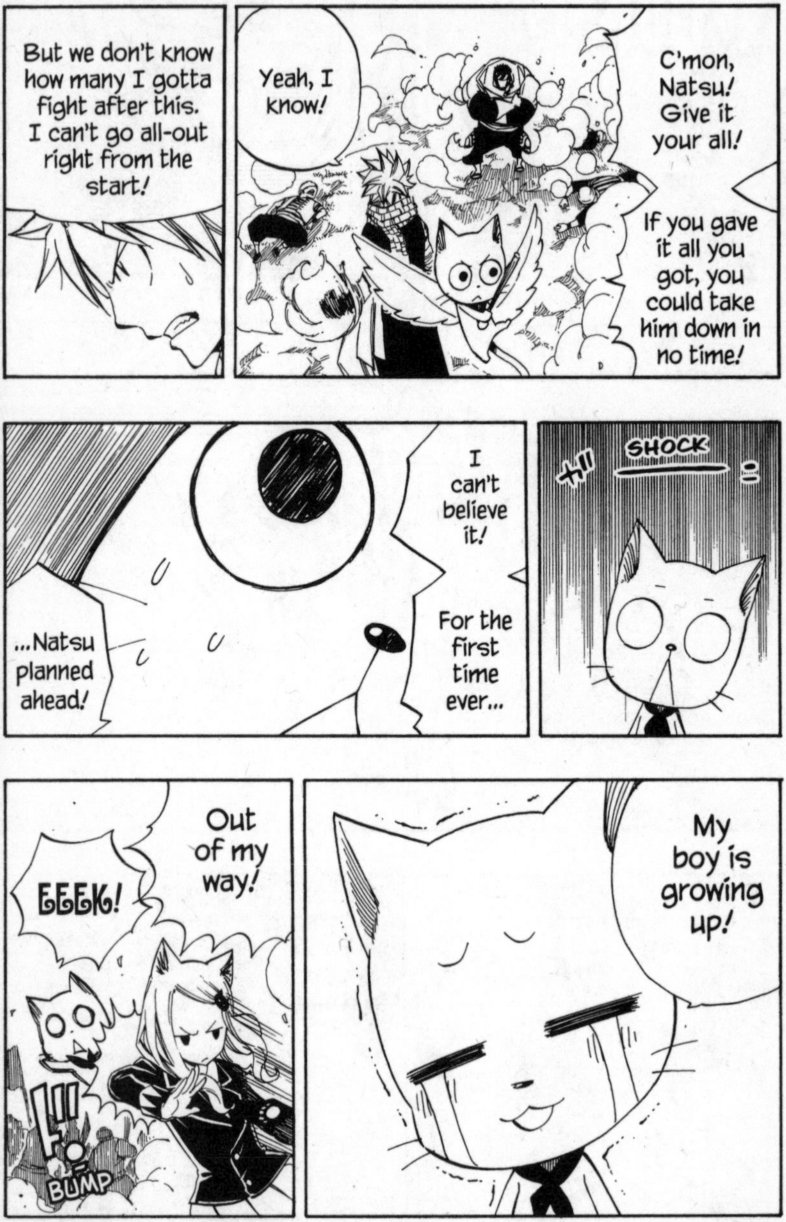
C'mon, Natsu! Give it your all!
If you gave it all you got, you could take him down in no time!
Yeah, I know!
But we don't know how many I gotta fight after this. I can't go all-out right from the start!
SHOCK
I can't believe it!
For the first time ever...
...Natsu planned ahead!
My boy is growing up!
Out of my way!
EEEK!
BUMP

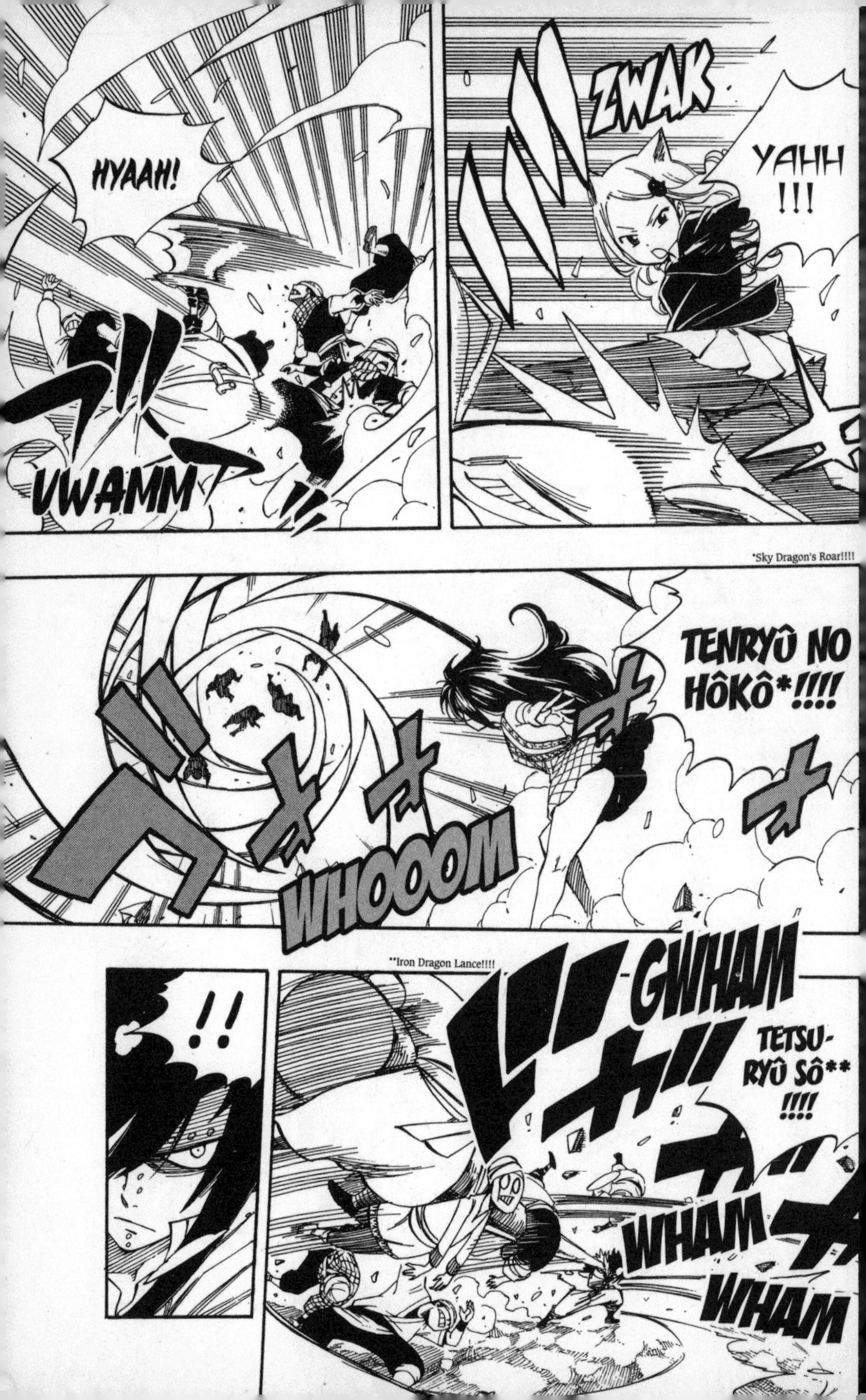
ZWAK
YAHH!!!
HYAAH!
UWAMM
TENRYÛ NO HÔKÔ*!!!!
WHOOOM
GWHAM
TETSU-RYÛ SÔ**!!!!
WHAM
WHAM
!!

*Sky Dragon's Roar!!!!

**Iron Dragon Lance!!!!

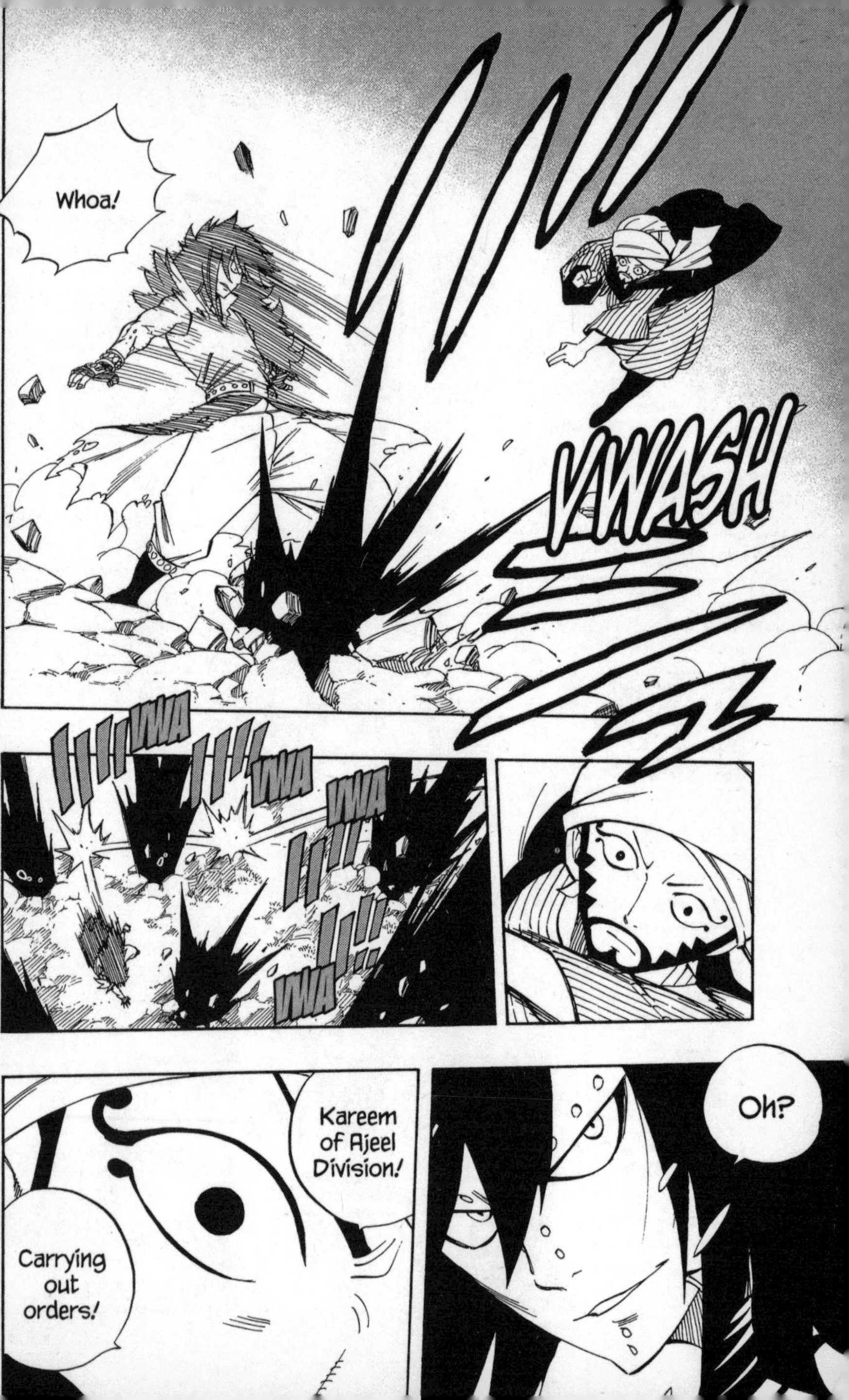
VWASH
Whoa!
VWA
VWA
VWA
VWA
Oh?
Kareem of Ajeel Division!
Carrying out orders!

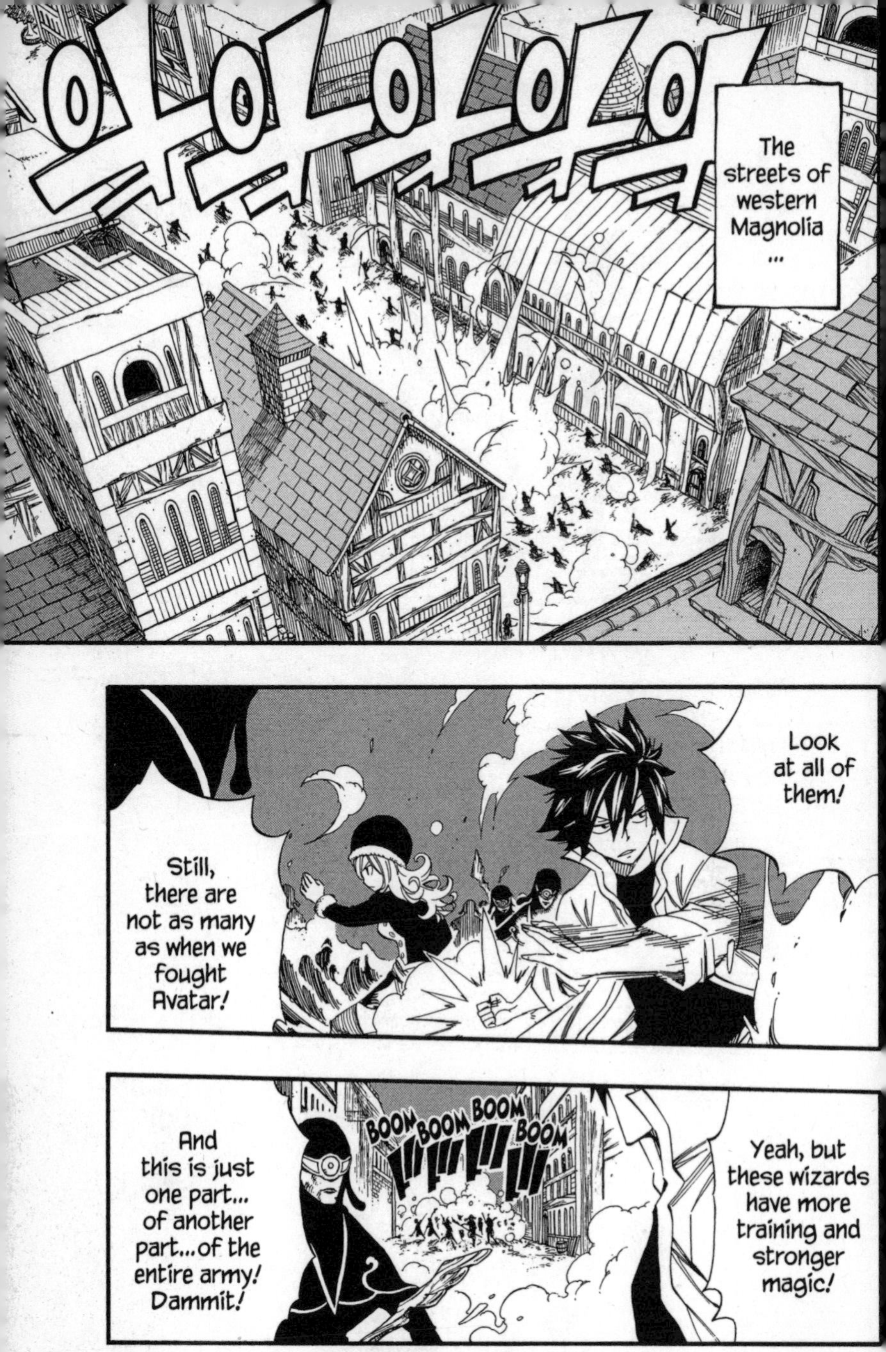
The streets of western Magnolia ...
Look at all of them!
Still, there are not as many as when we fought Avatar!
Yeah, but these wizards have more training and stronger magic!
BOOM BOOM BOOM BOOM
And this is just one part... of another part...of the entire army! Dammit!

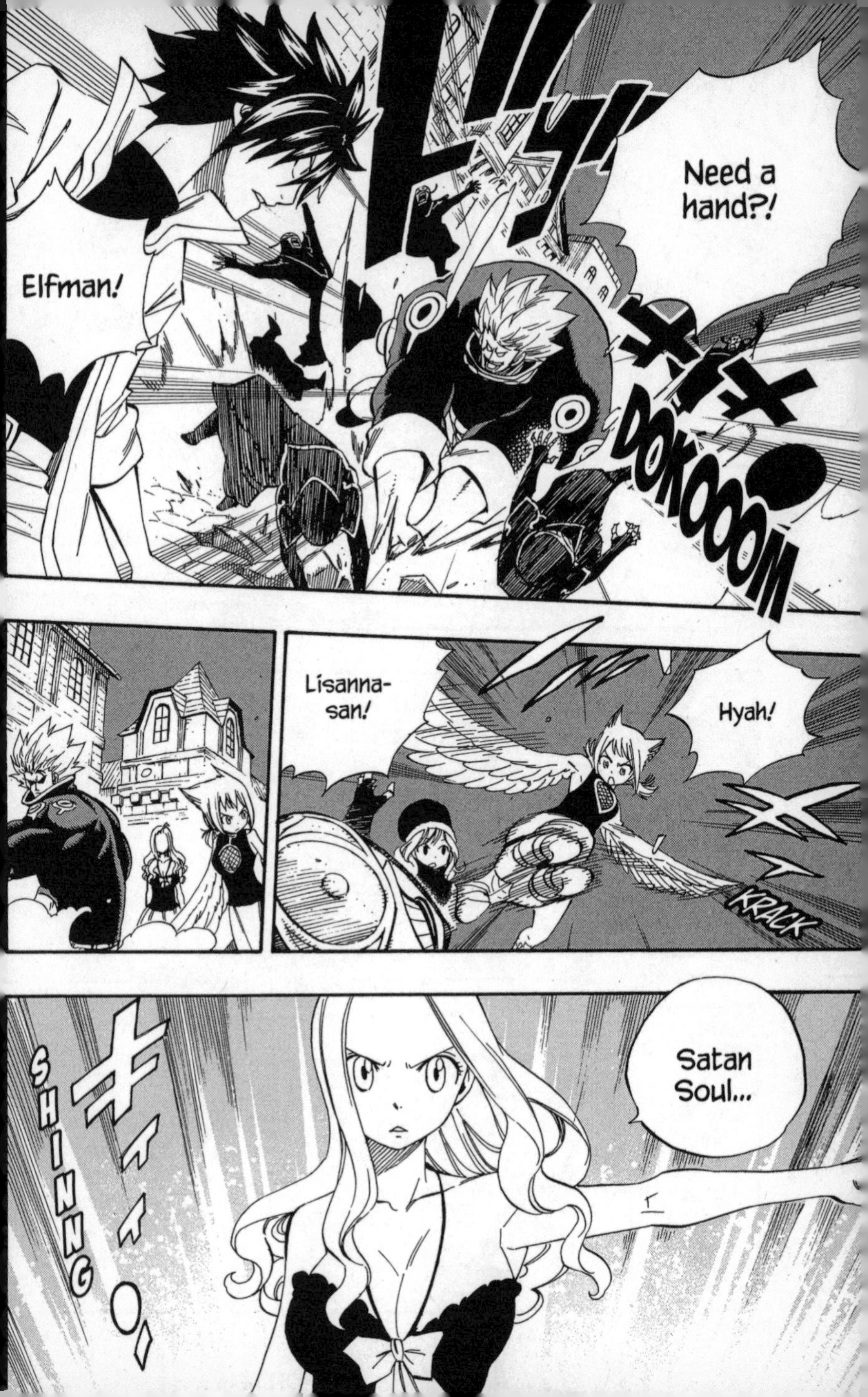
Need a hand?!
DOKOOOM
Elfman!
Hyah!
Lisanna-san!
KRACK
Satan Soul...
SHINNG

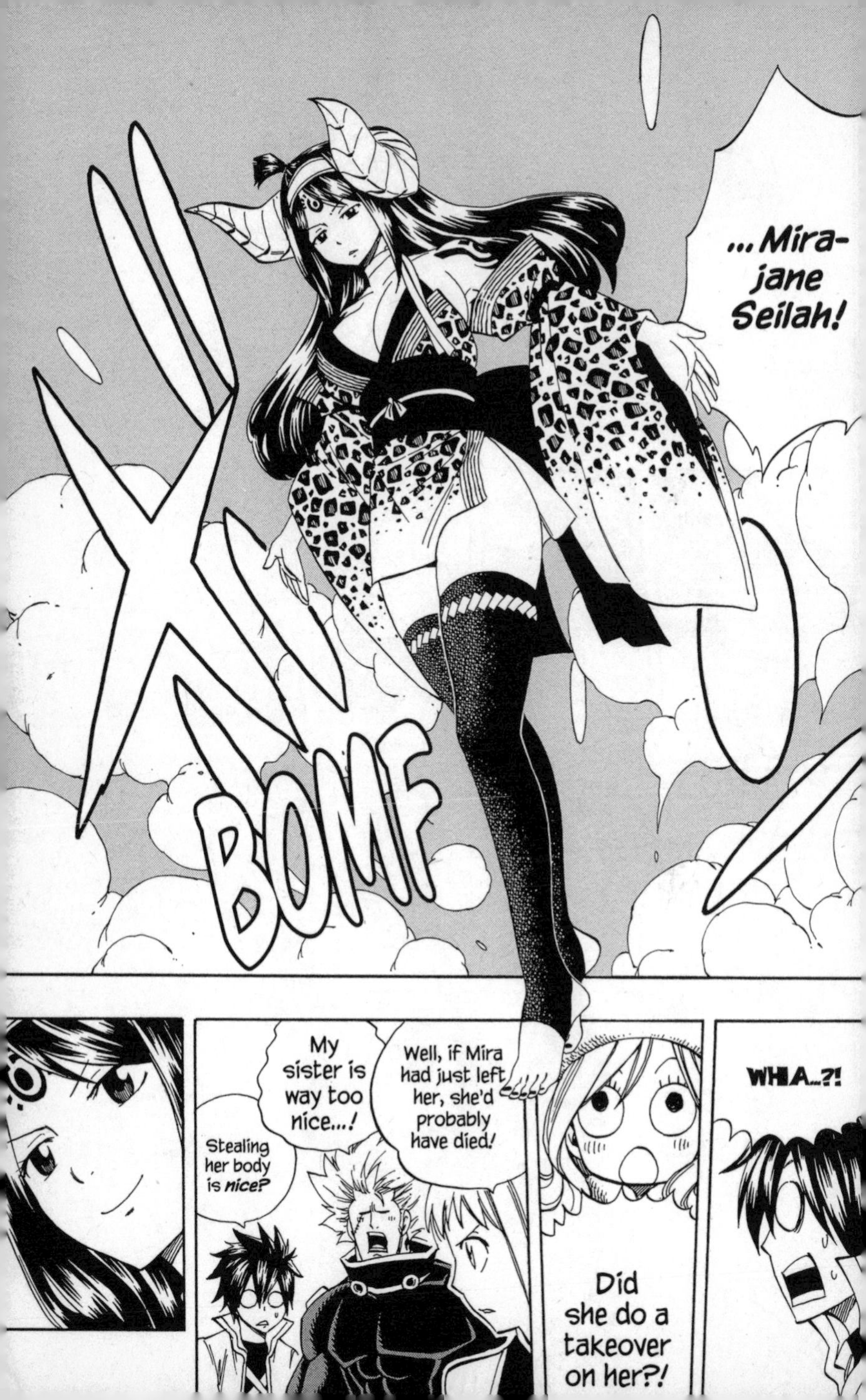

...Mira-jane Seilah!
BOMF
WHA..?!
Did she do a takeover on her?!
Well, if Mira had just left her, she'd probably have died!
My sister is way too nice...!
Stealing her body is *nice?*

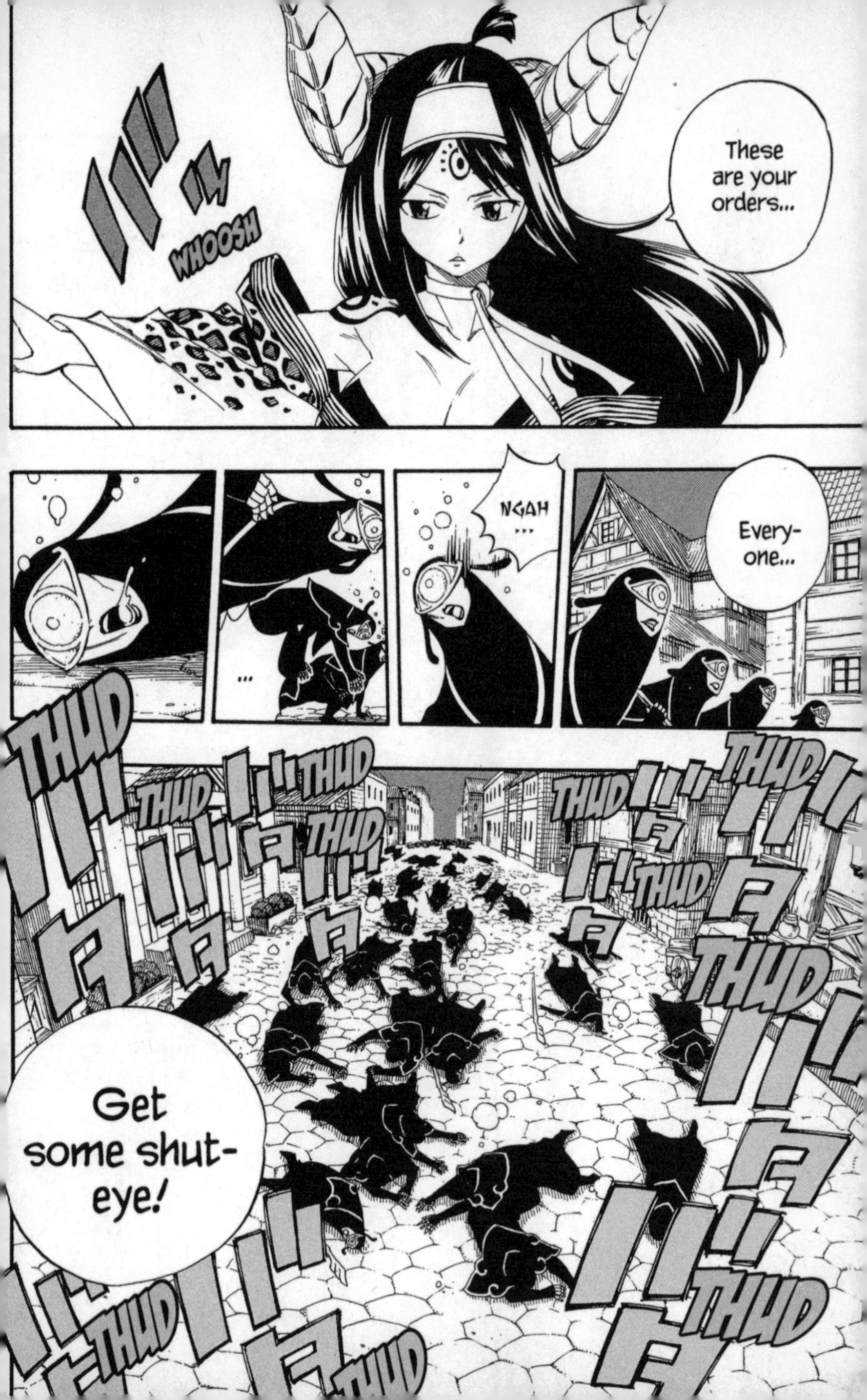
These are your orders...
WHOOSH
Every-one...
NGAH ...
...
THUD THUD THUD THUD THUD THUD THUD
Get some shut-eye!
THUD THUD THUD THUD

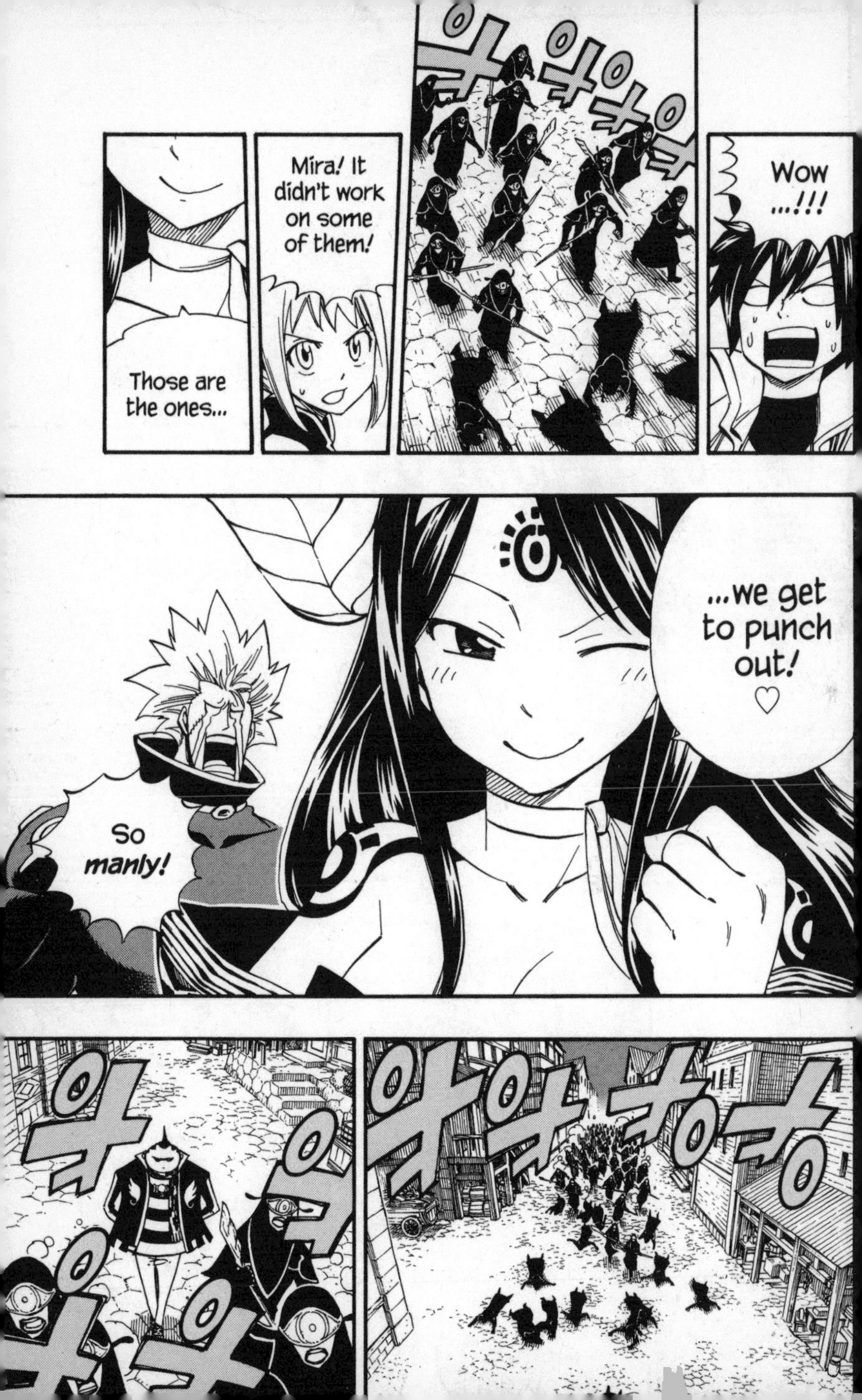
Wow ...!!!
Mira! It didn't work on some of them!
Those are the ones...
...we get to punch out! ♡
So manly!

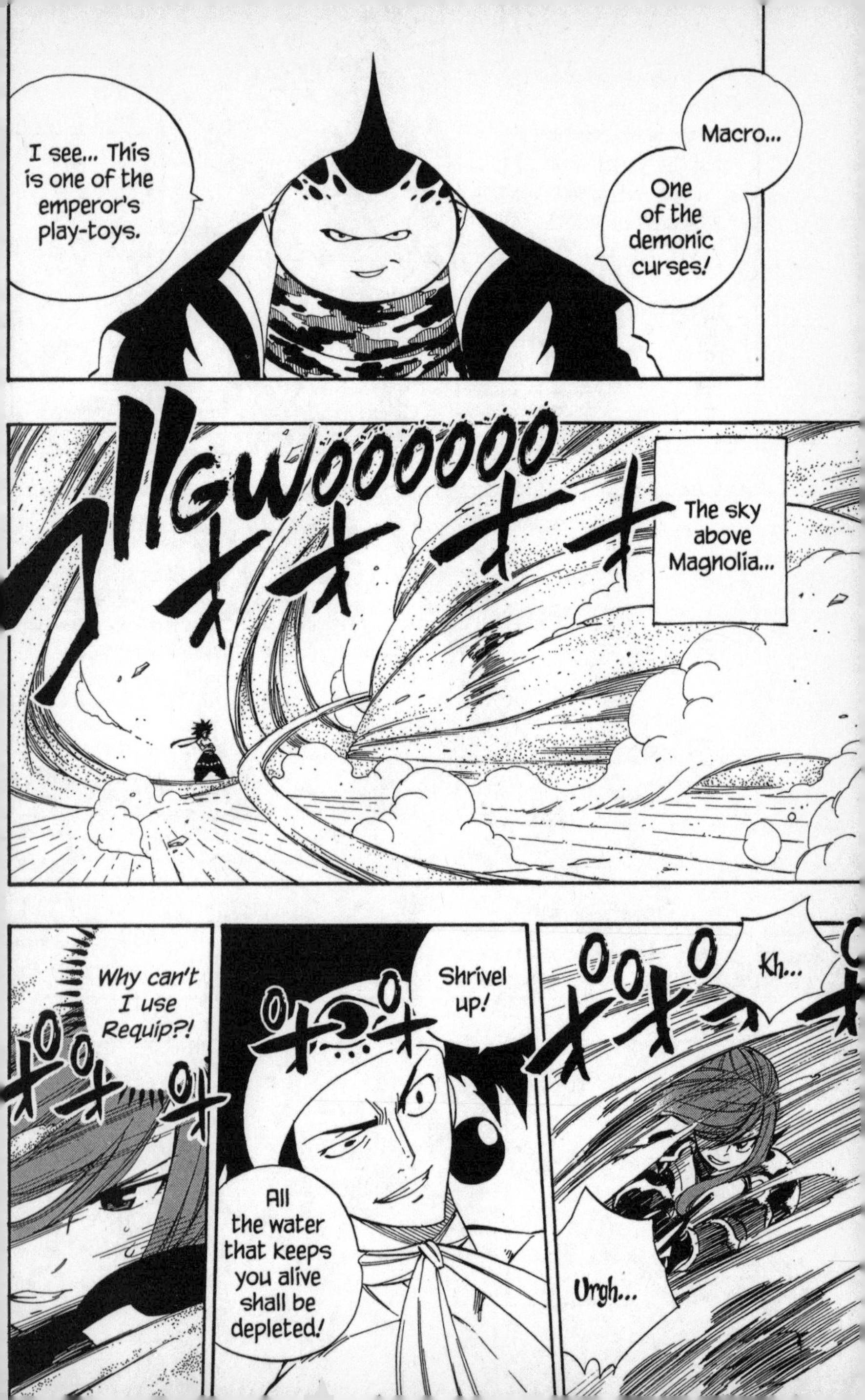
Macro...
One of the demonic curses!
I see... This is one of the emperor's play-toys.
The sky above Magnolia...
GWOOOOOO
Kh...
Urgh...
Shrivel up!
All the water that keeps you alive shall be depleted!
Why can't I use Requip?!

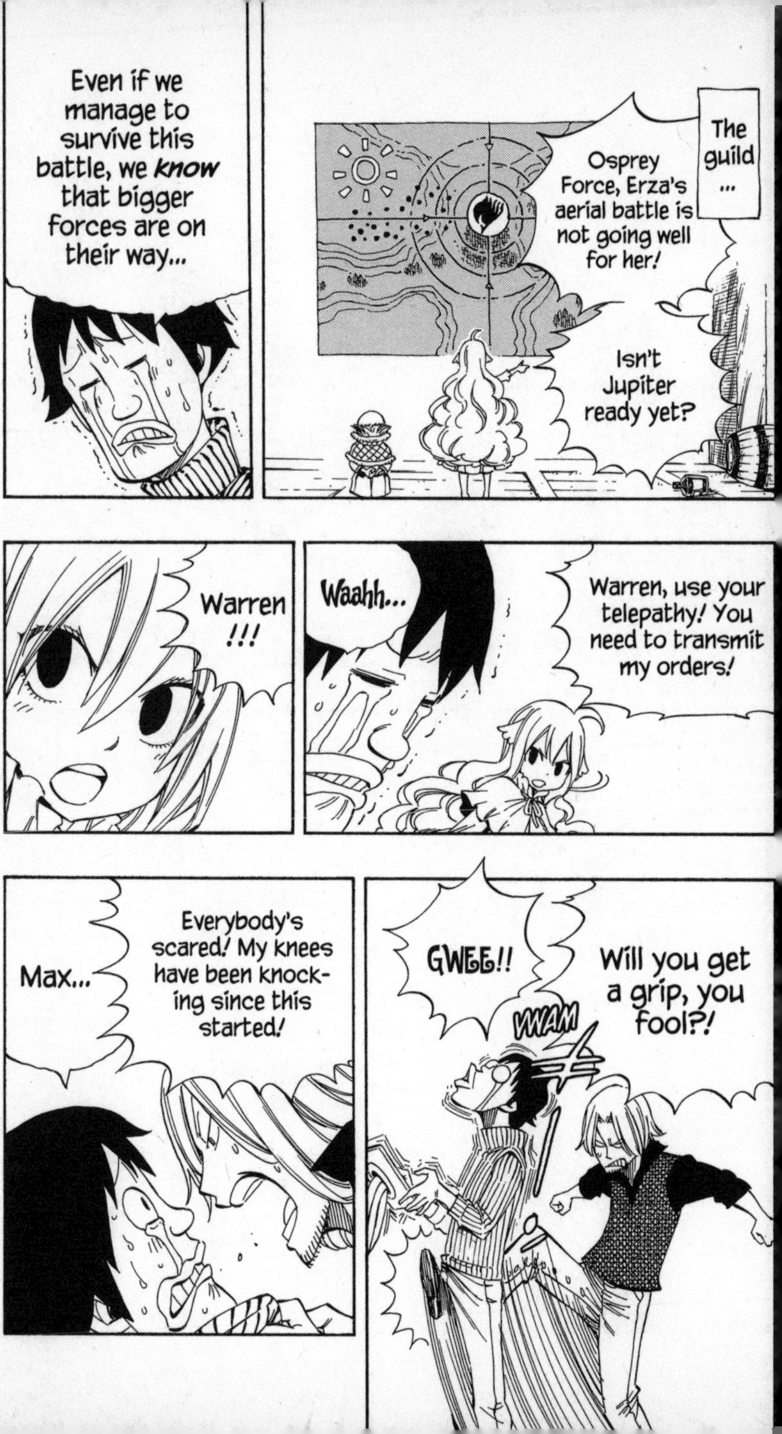

The guild ...
Osprey Force, Erza's aerial battle is not going well for her!
Isn't Jupiter ready yet?
Even if we manage to survive this battle, we *know* that bigger forces are on their way...
Warren, use your telepathy! You need to transmit my orders!
Waahh...
Warren !!!
Will you get a grip, you fool?!
GWEE!!
WAM
Everybody's scared! My knees have been knocking since this started!
Max...

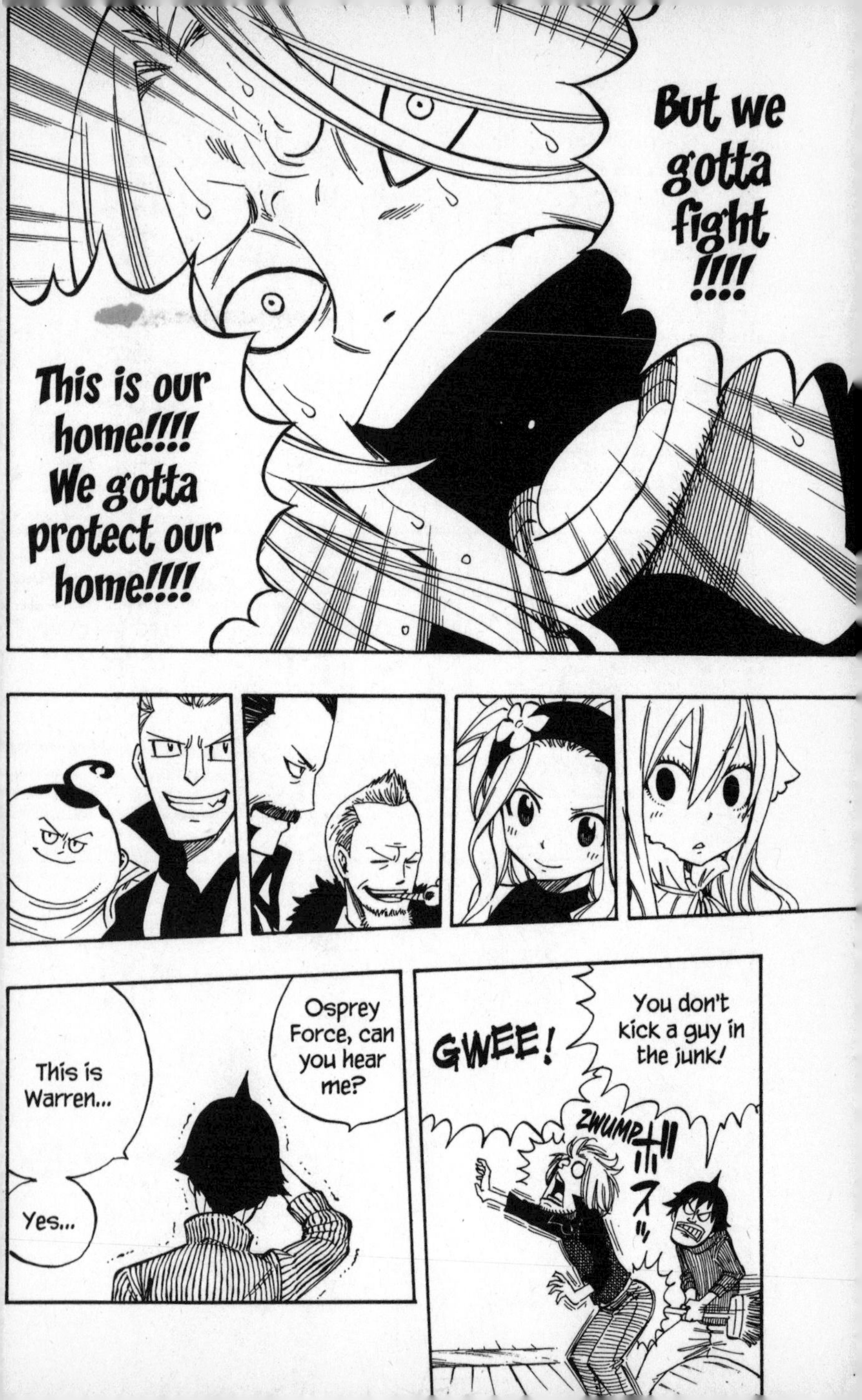
But we gotta fight!!!!
This is our home!!!! We gotta protect our home!!!!
You don't kick a guy in the junk!
GWEE!
ZWUMP!!
Osprey Force, can you hear me?
This is Warren...
Yes...

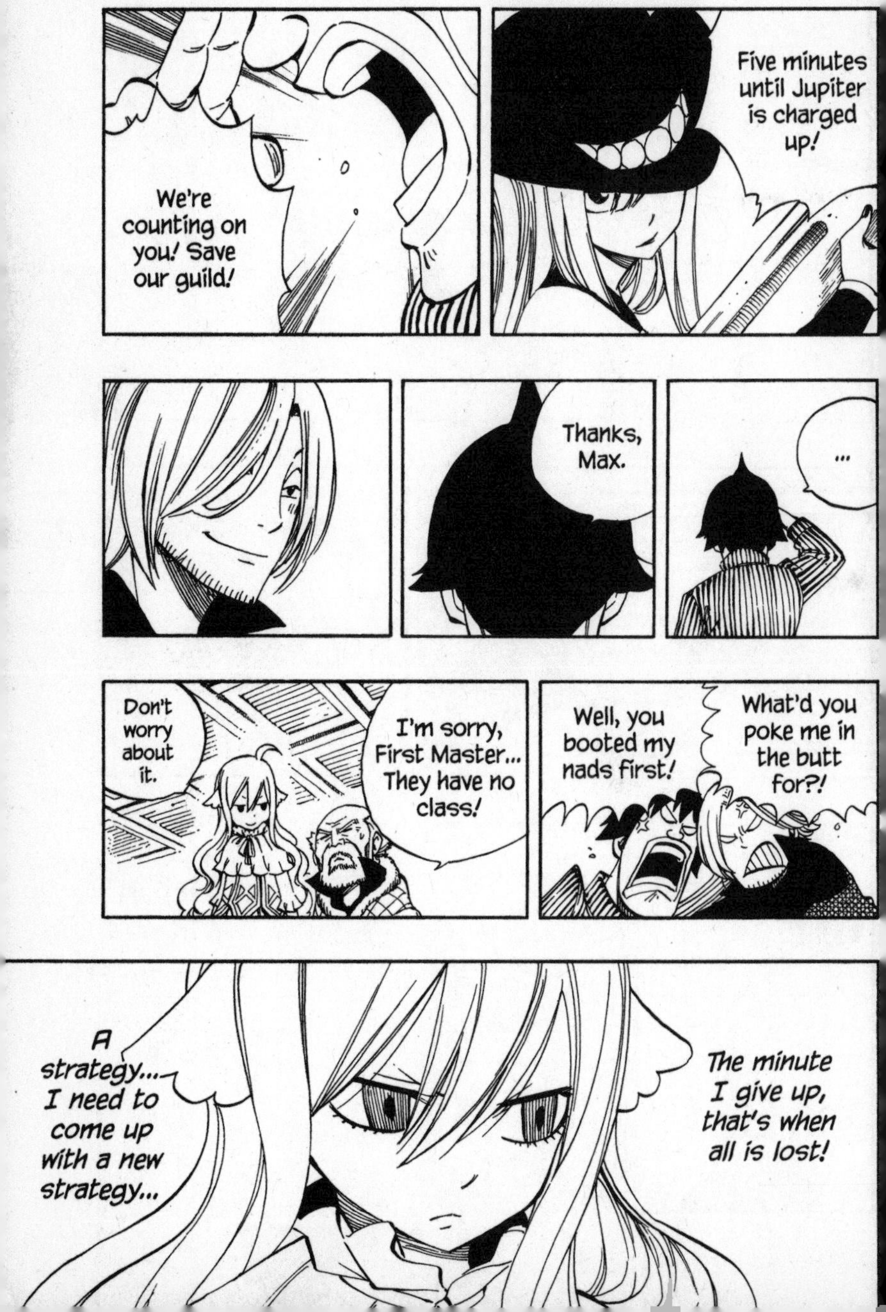
Five minutes until Jupiter is charged up!
We're counting on you! Save our guild!
...
Thanks, Max.
What'd you poke me in the butt for?!
Well, you booted my nads first!
I'm sorry, First Master... They have no class!
Don't worry about it.
A strategy... I need to come up with a new strategy...
The minute I give up, that's when all is lost!

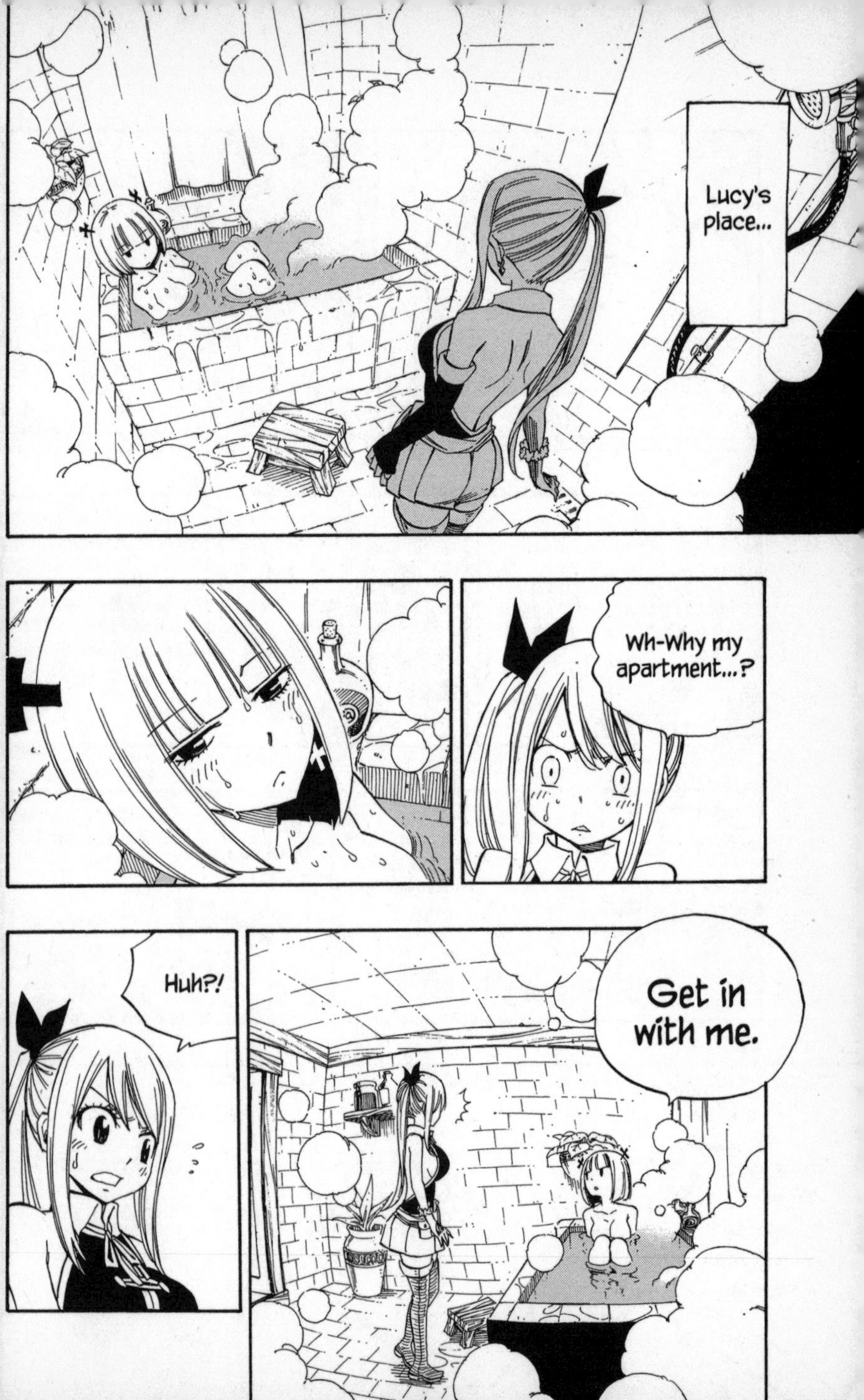
Lucy's place...
Wh-Why my apartment...?
Get in with me.
Huh?!

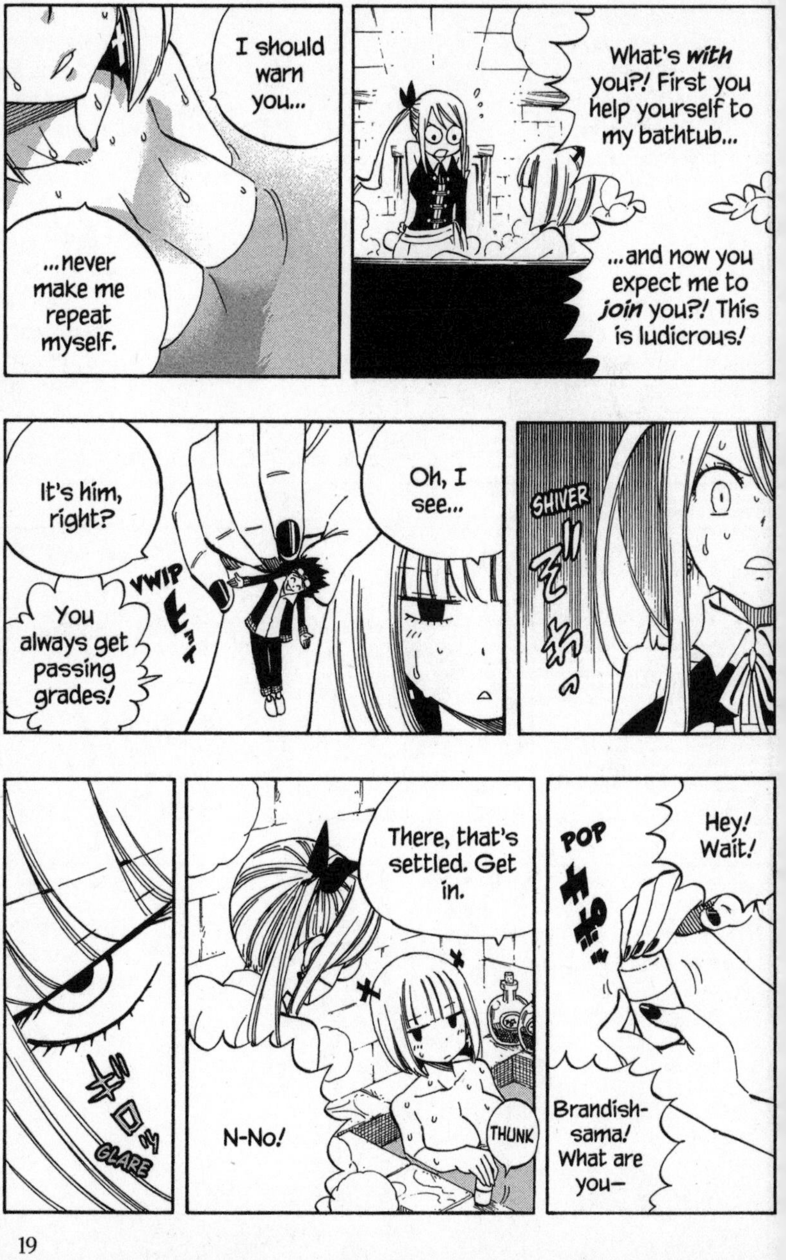
What's *with* you?! First you help yourself to my bathtub...
...and now you expect me to *join* you?! This is ludicrous!
I should warn you...
...never make me repeat myself.
SHIVER
Oh, I see...
It's him, right?
VWIP
You always get passing grades!
Hey! Wait!
POP
Brandish-sama! What are you—
There, that's settled. Get in.
THUNK
N-No!
GLARE

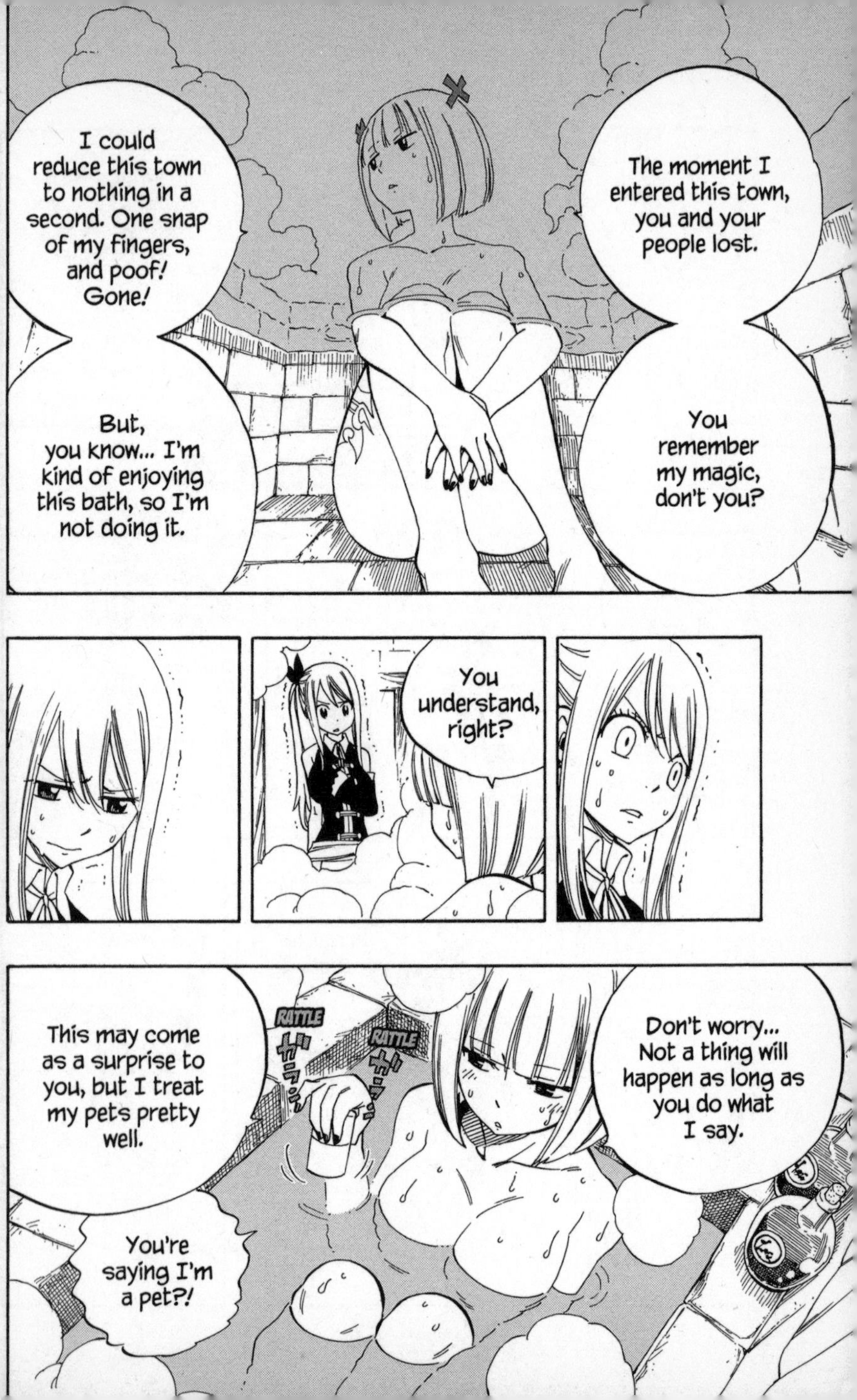
The moment I entered this town, you and your people lost.
You remember my magic, don't you?
I could reduce this town to nothing in a second. One snap of my fingers, and poof! Gone!
But, you know... I'm kind of enjoying this bath, so I'm not doing it.
You understand, right?
Don't worry... Not a thing will happen as long as you do what I say.
RATTLE
RATTLE
This may come as a surprise to you, but I treat my pets pretty well.
You're saying I'm a pet?!

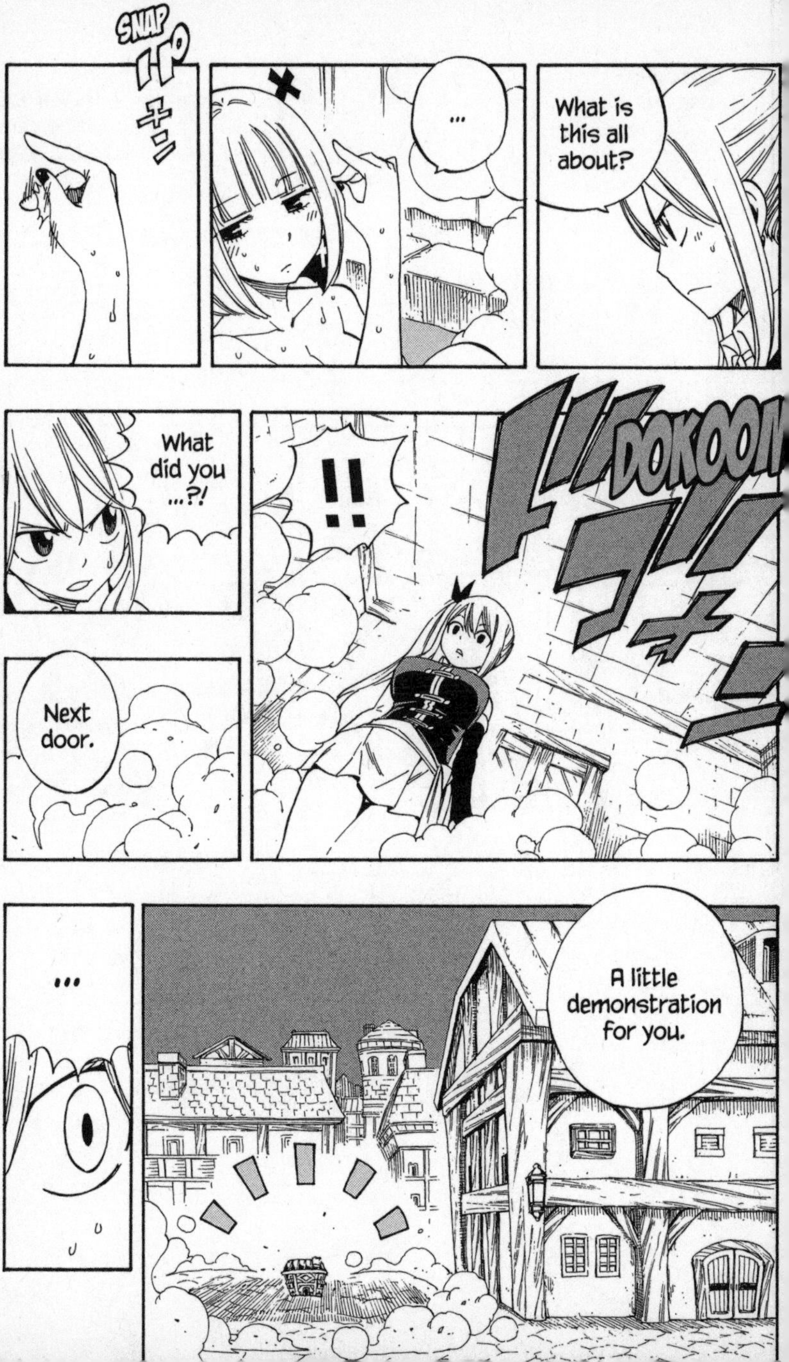
What is this all about?
...
SNAP
DOKOOM
!!
What did you ...?!
Next door.
A little demonstration for you.
...

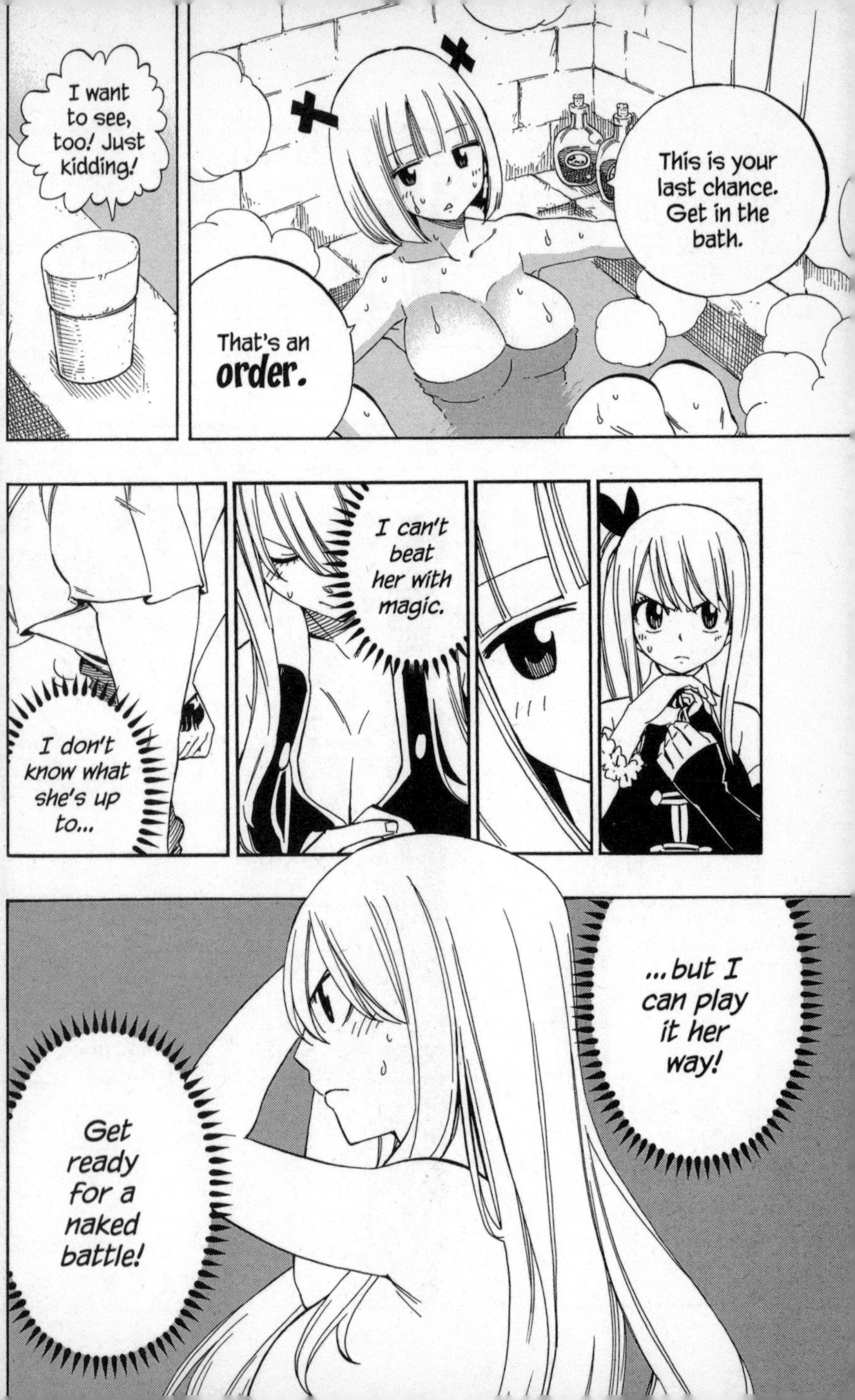
This is your last chance. Get in the bath.
That's an **order.**
I want to see, too! Just kidding!
I can't beat her with magic.
I don't know what she's up to...
...but I can play it her way!
Get ready for a naked battle!

FAIRY TAIL

フェアリーテイル

Chapter 457: Naked Battle

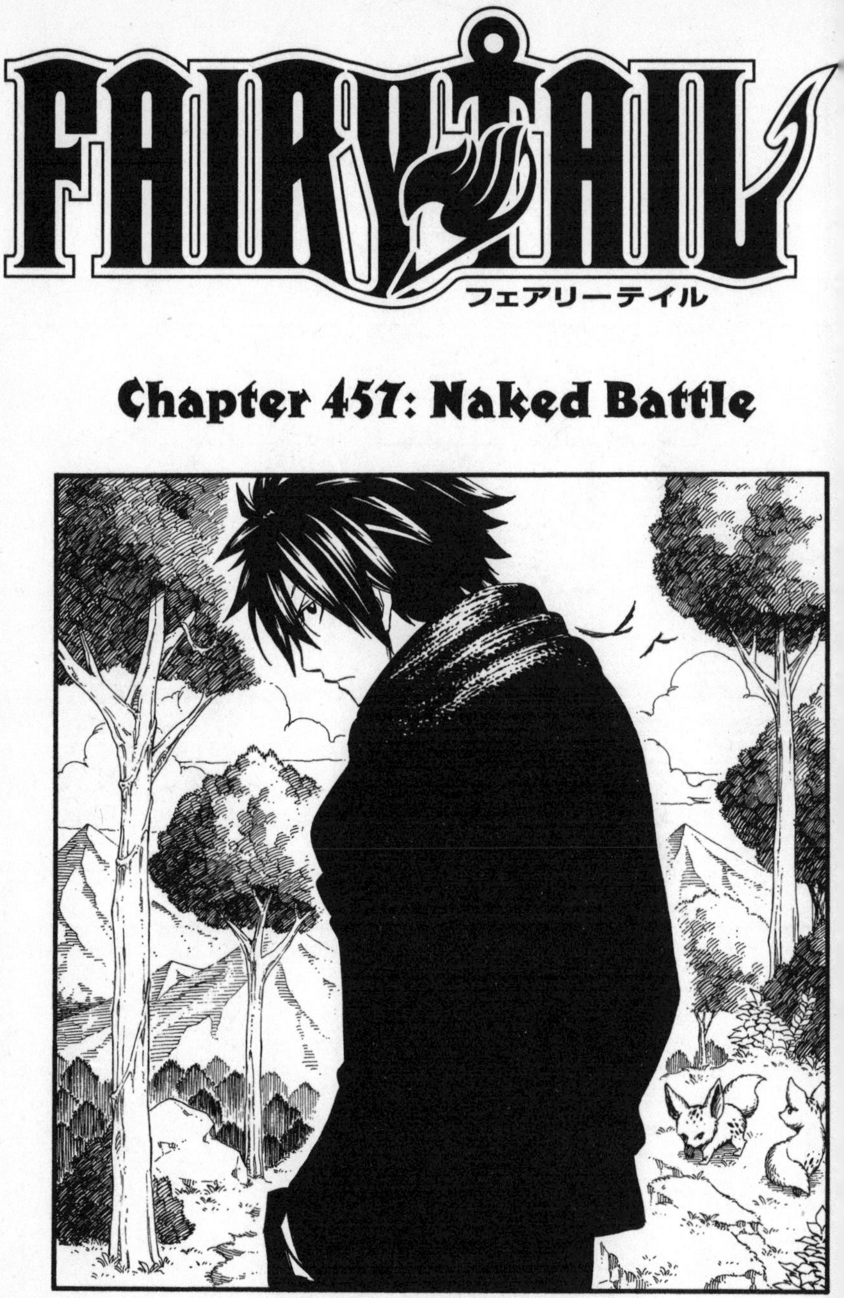

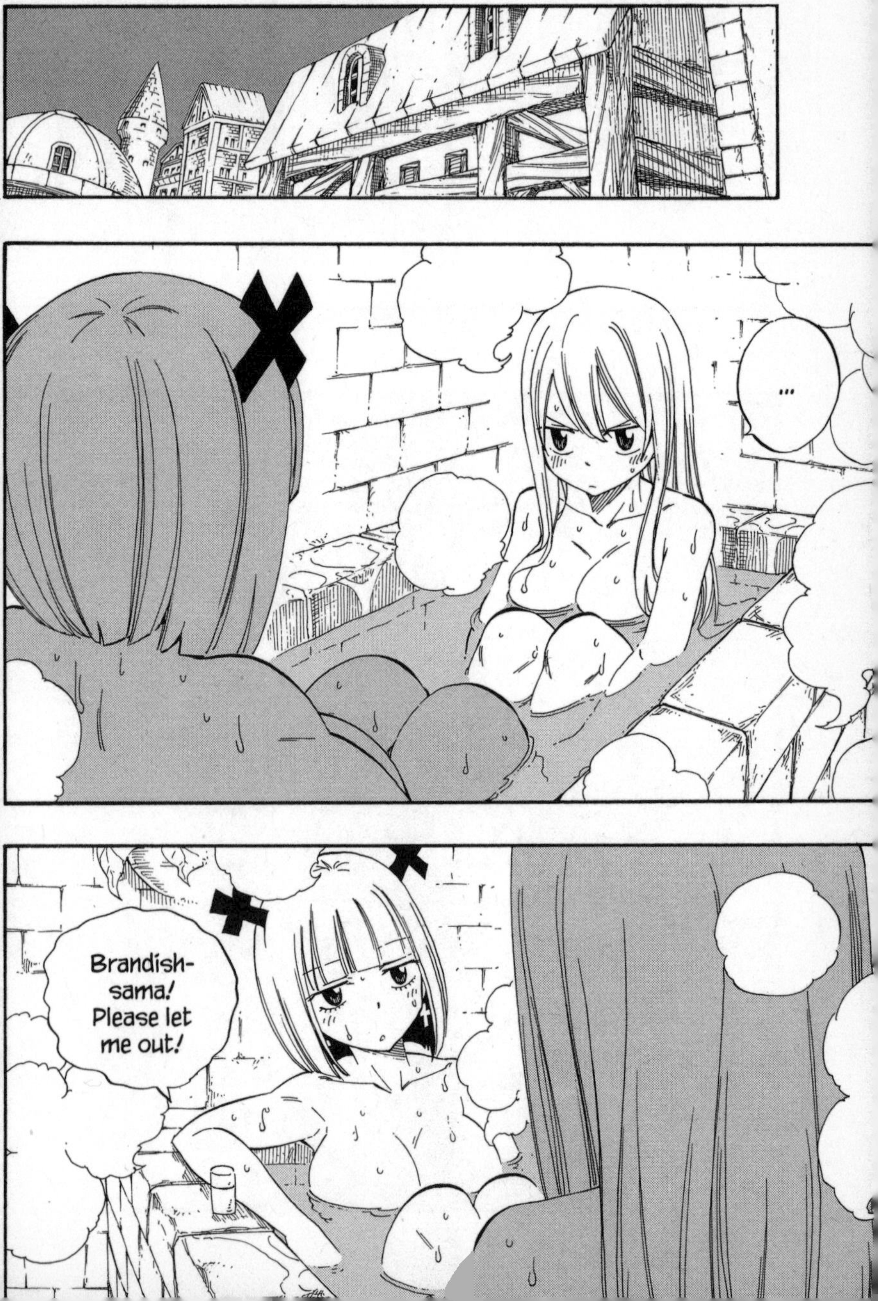
...
Brandish-sama! Please let me out!

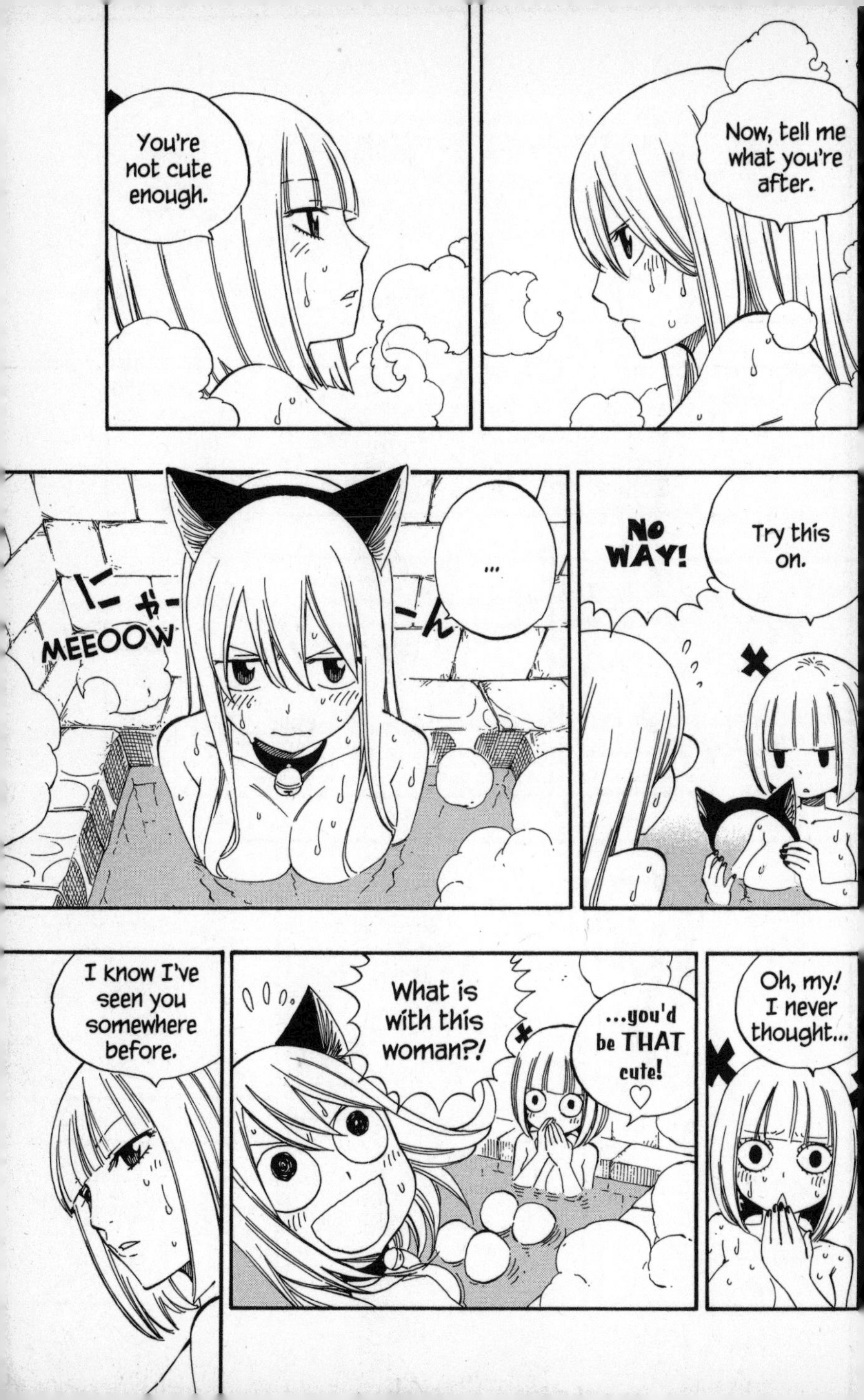
Now, tell me what you're after.
You're not cute enough.
Try this on.
NO WAY!
...
にゃーーん
MEEOOW
Oh, my! I never thought...
...you'd be THAT cute! ♡
What is with this woman?!
I know I've seen you somewhere before.

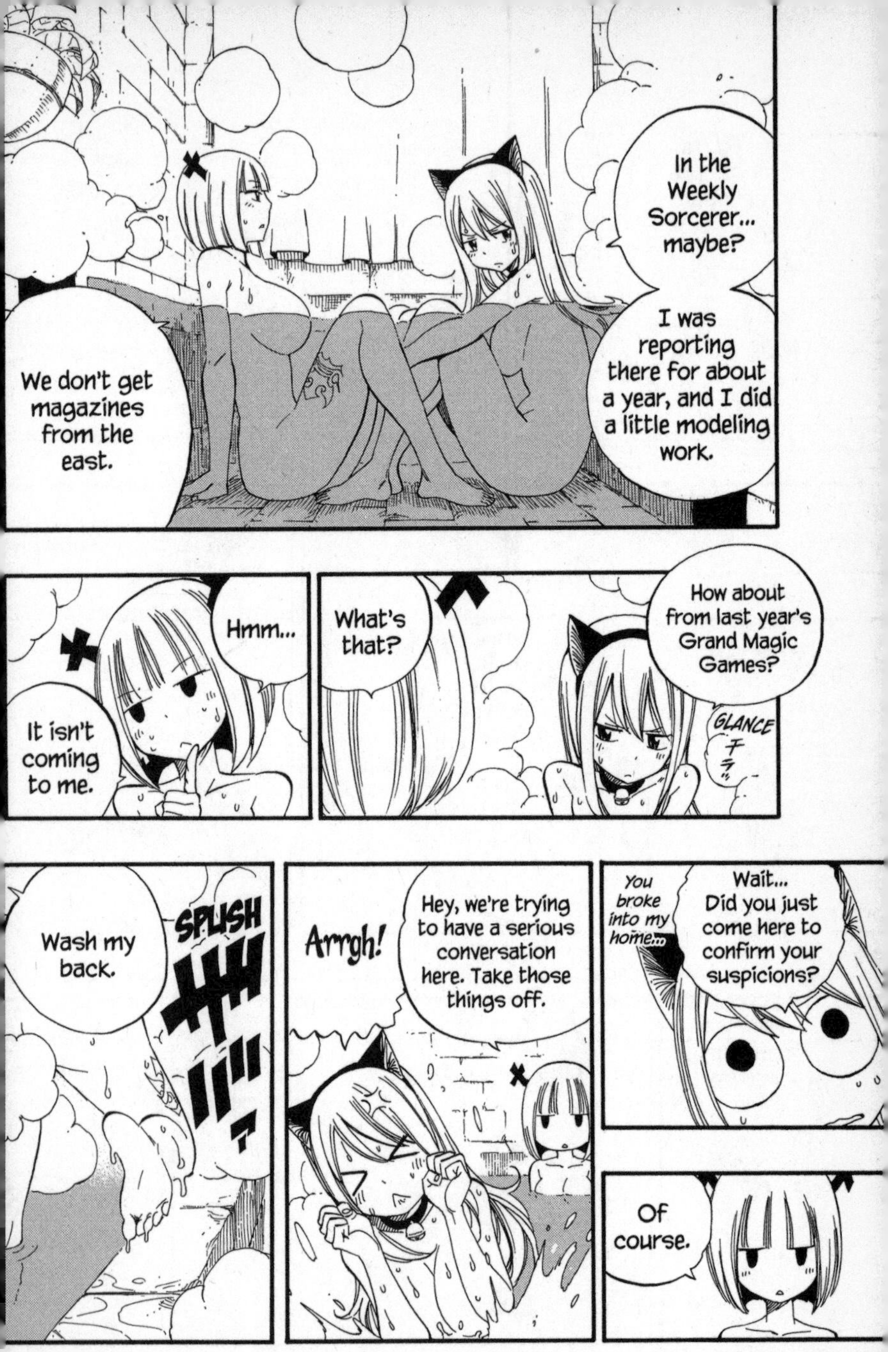
In the Weekly Sorcerer... maybe?
I was reporting there for about a year, and I did a little modeling work.
We don't get magazines from the east.
How about from last year's Grand Magic Games?
GLANCE
What's that?
Hmm...
It isn't coming to me.
Wait... Did you just come here to confirm your suspicions?
You broke into my home...
Of course.
Hey, we're trying to have a serious conversation here. Take those things off.
Arrgh!
SPLISH
Wash my back.

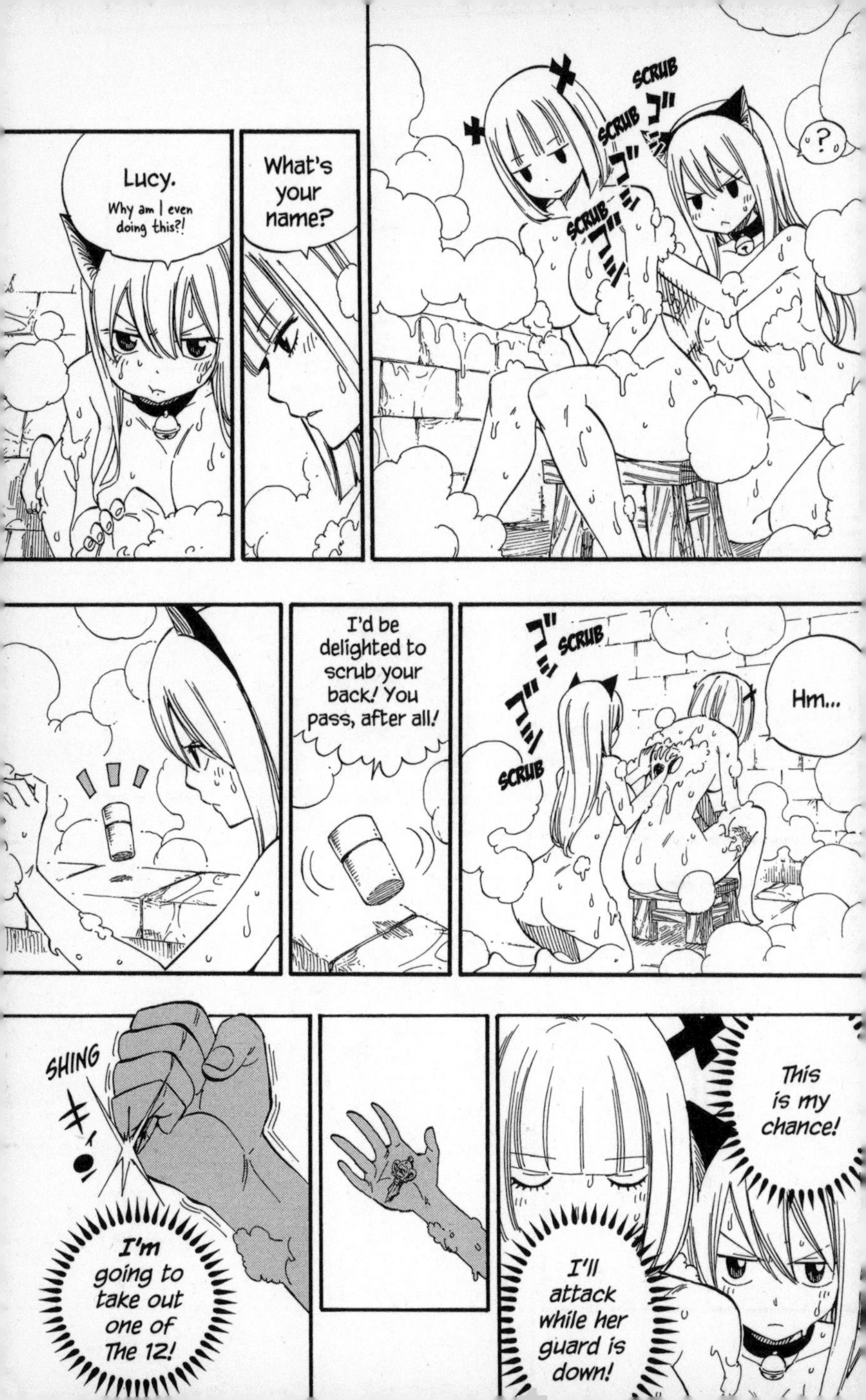
SCRUB
SCRUB
SCRUB
?
What's your name?
Lucy.
Why am I even doing this?!
SCRUB
SCRUB
Hm...
I'd be delighted to scrub your back! You pass, after all!
This is my chance!
I'll attack while her guard is down!
SHING
I'm going to take out one of The 12!

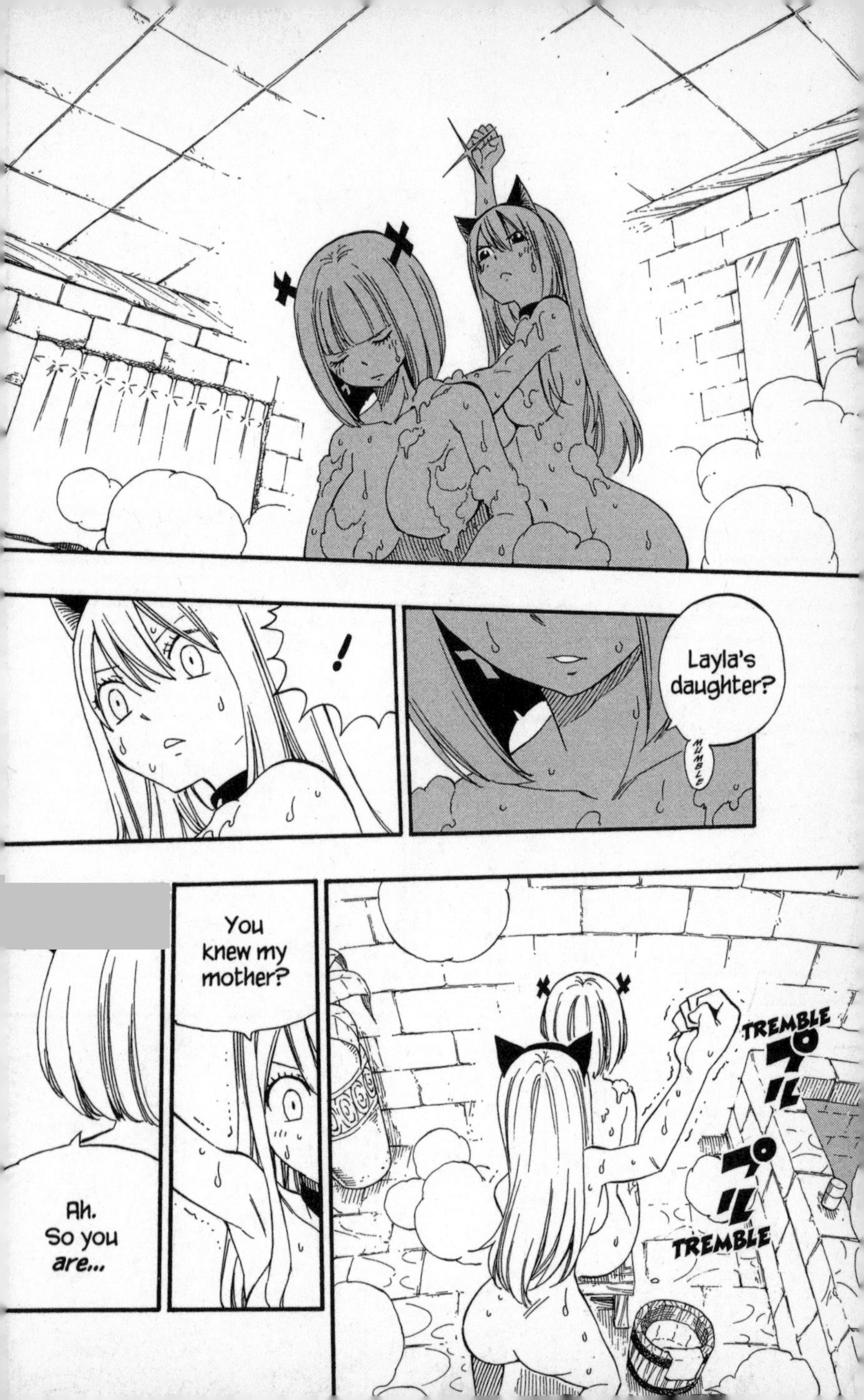
Layla's daughter?
MUMBLE
!
TREMBLE
TREMBLE
You knew my mother?
Ah. So you are...

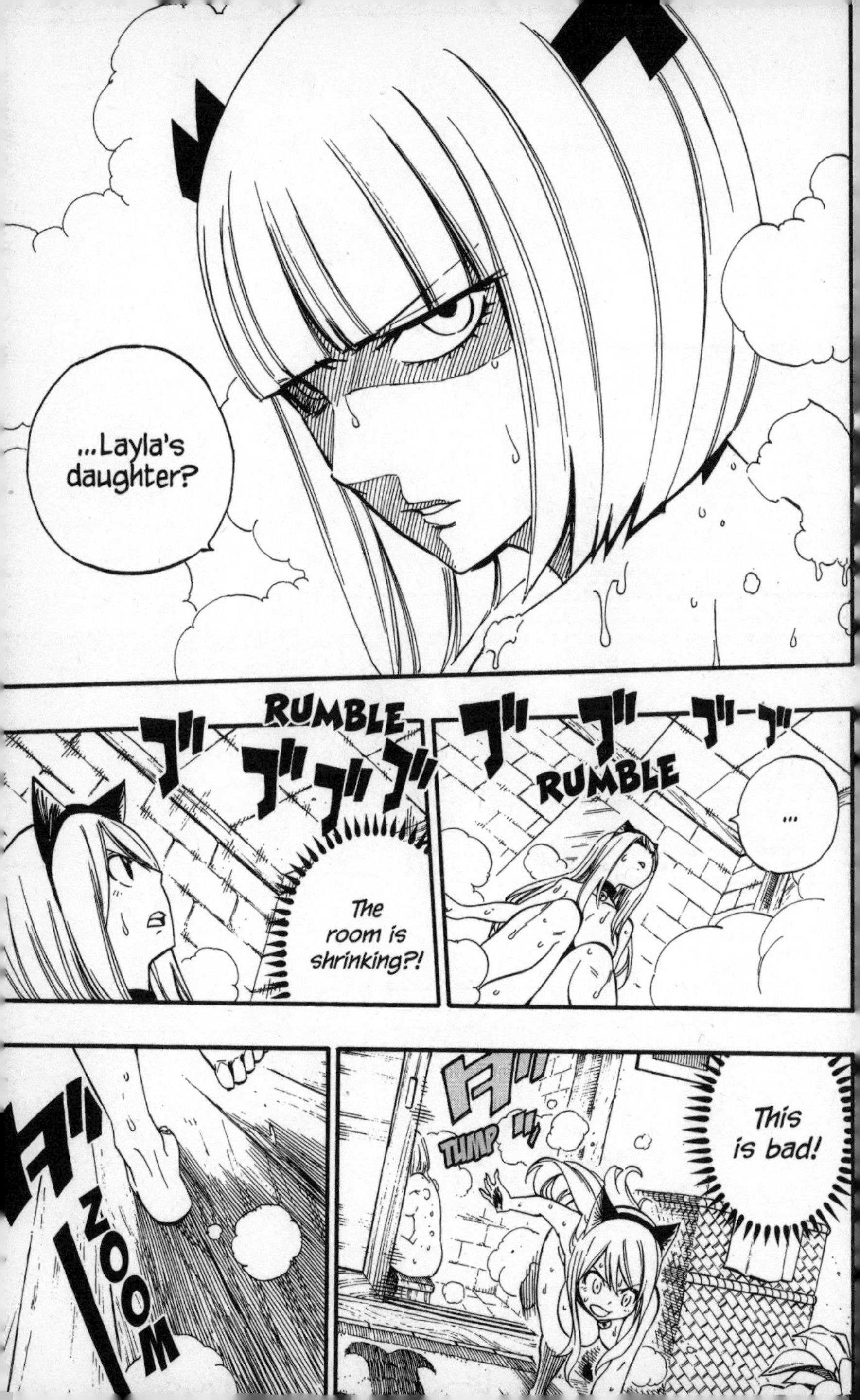
...Layla's daughter?
RUMBLE
...
RUMBLE
The room is shrinking?!
TUMP
This is bad!
ZOOM

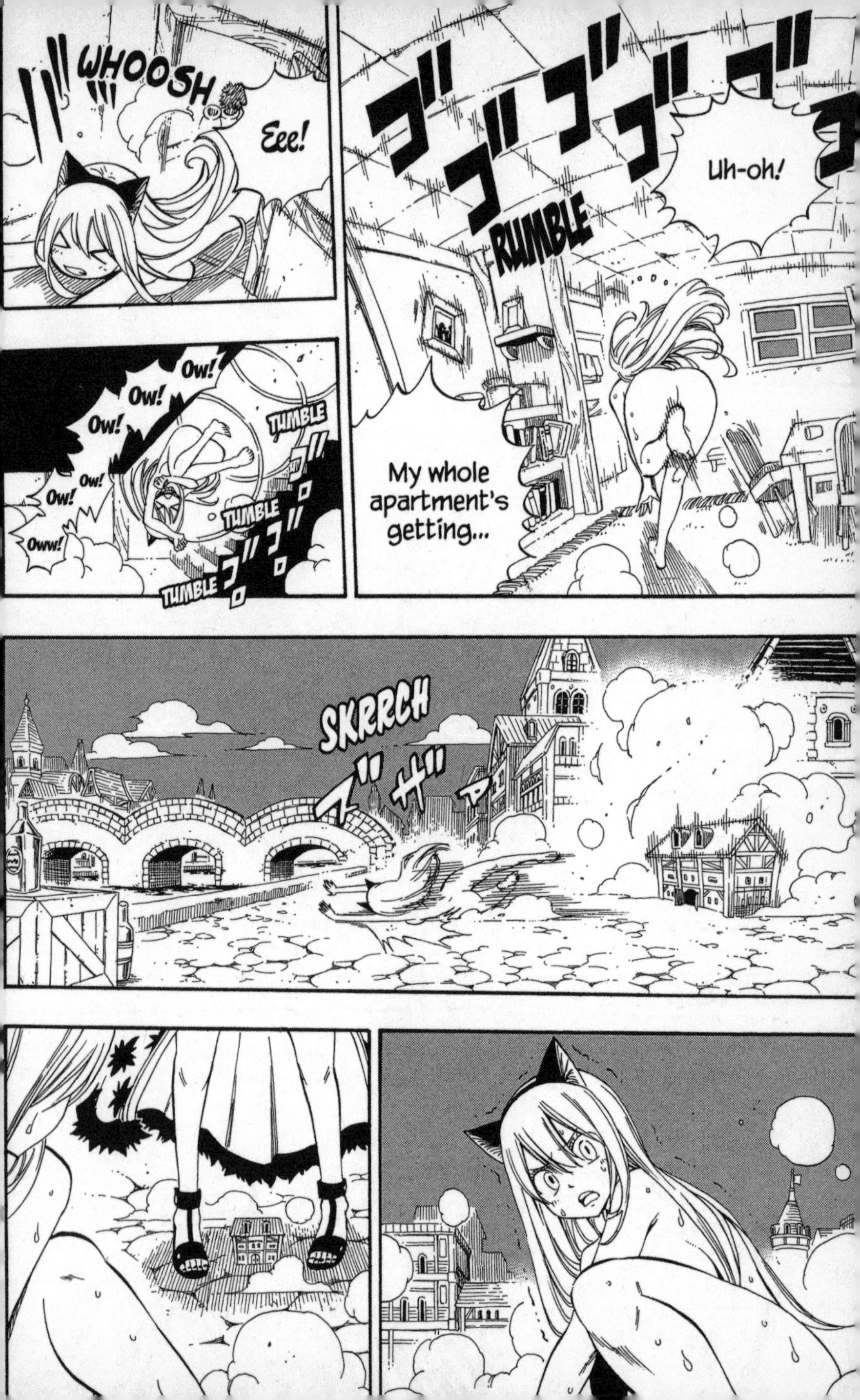
RUMBLE
Uh-oh!
My whole apartment's getting...
WHOOSH
Eee!
TUMBLE
TUMBLE
TUMBLE
Ow!
Ow!
Ow!
Ow!
Ow!
Oww!
SKRRCH

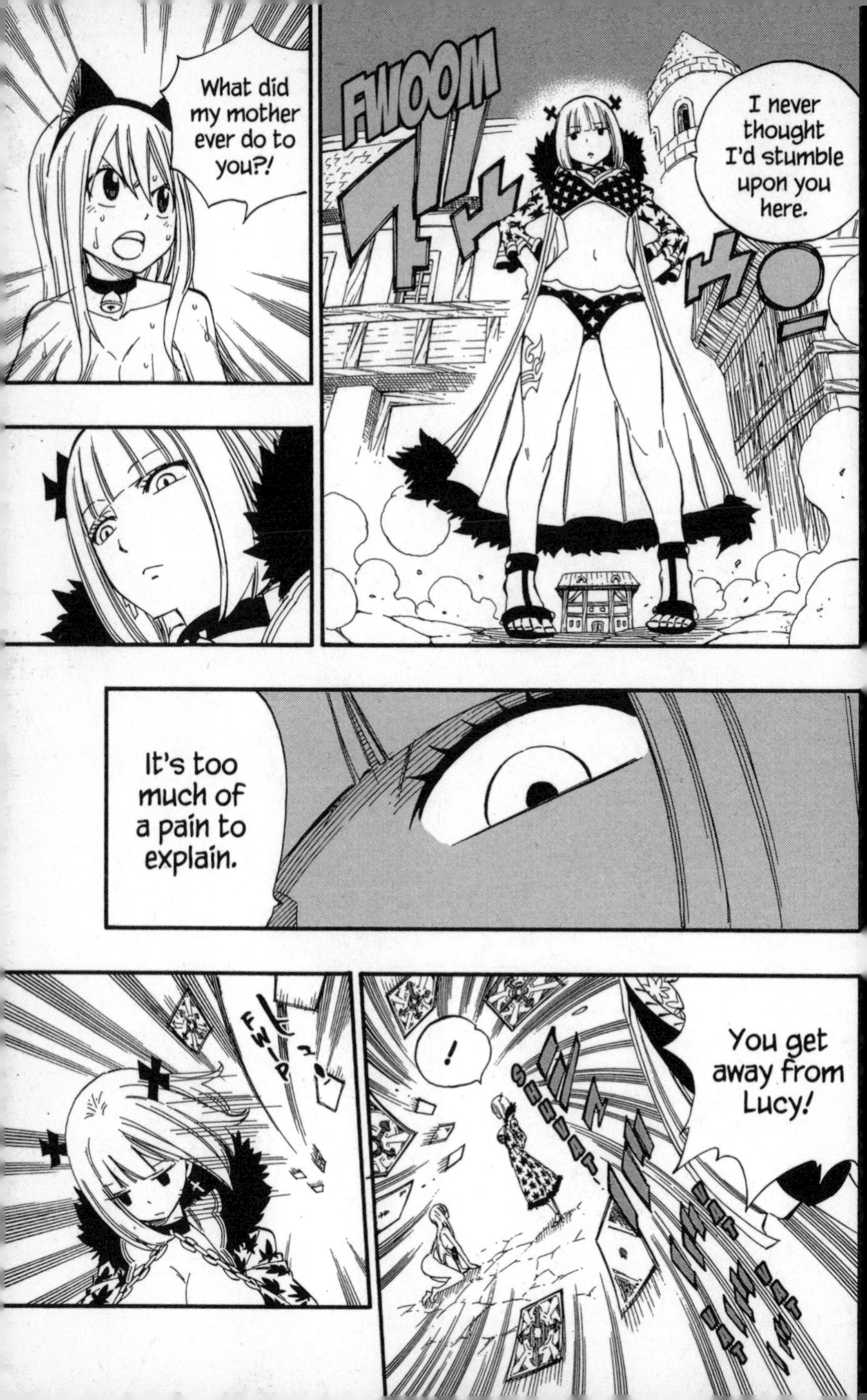
FWOOM
I never thought I'd stumble upon you here.
What did my mother ever do to you?!
It's too much of a pain to explain.
!
You get away from Lucy!
FWIP

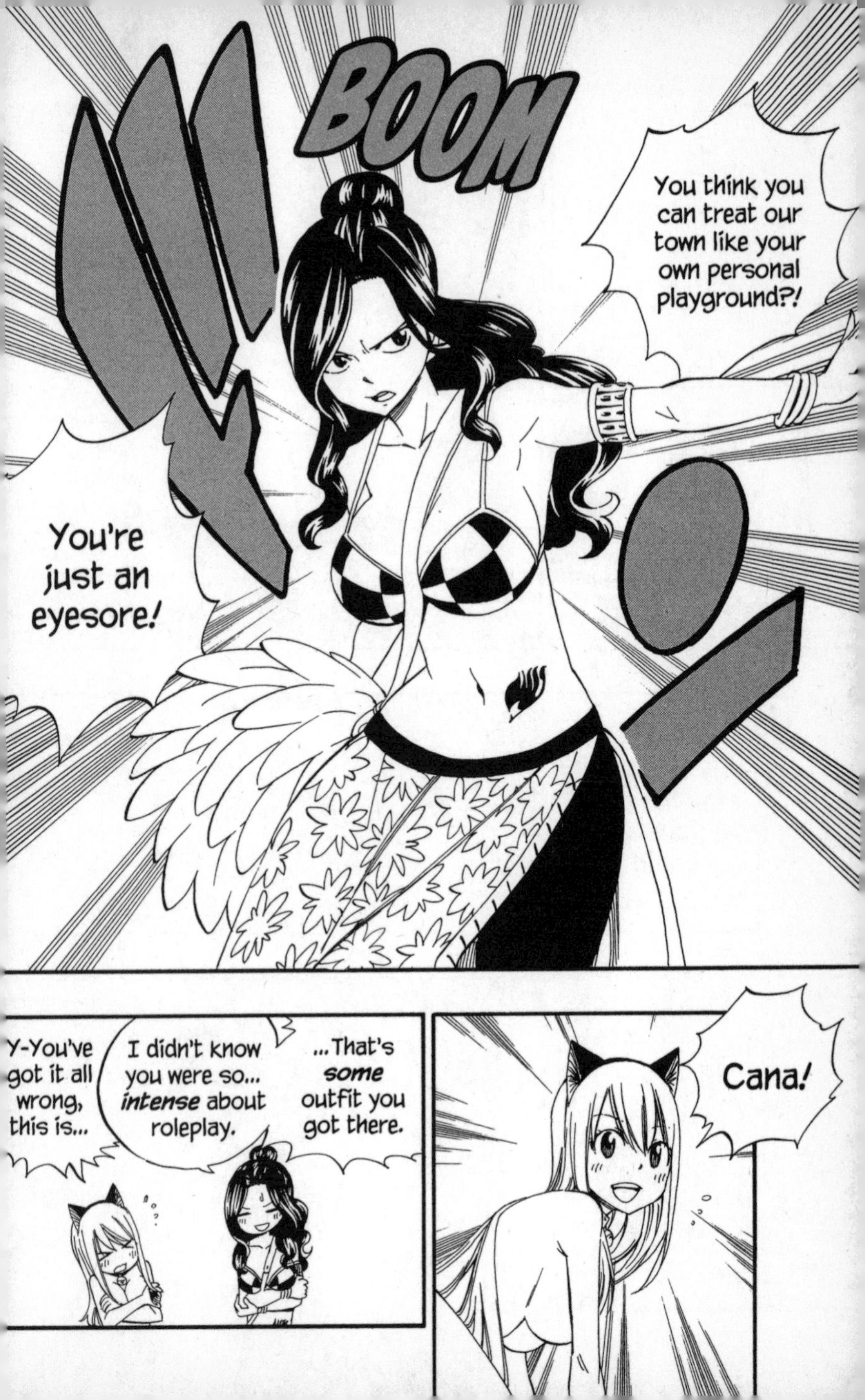
BOOM
You think you can treat our town like your own personal playground?!
You're just an eyesore!
Cana!
...That's *some* outfit you got there.
I didn't know you were so... *intense* about roleplay.
Y-You've got it all wrong, this is...

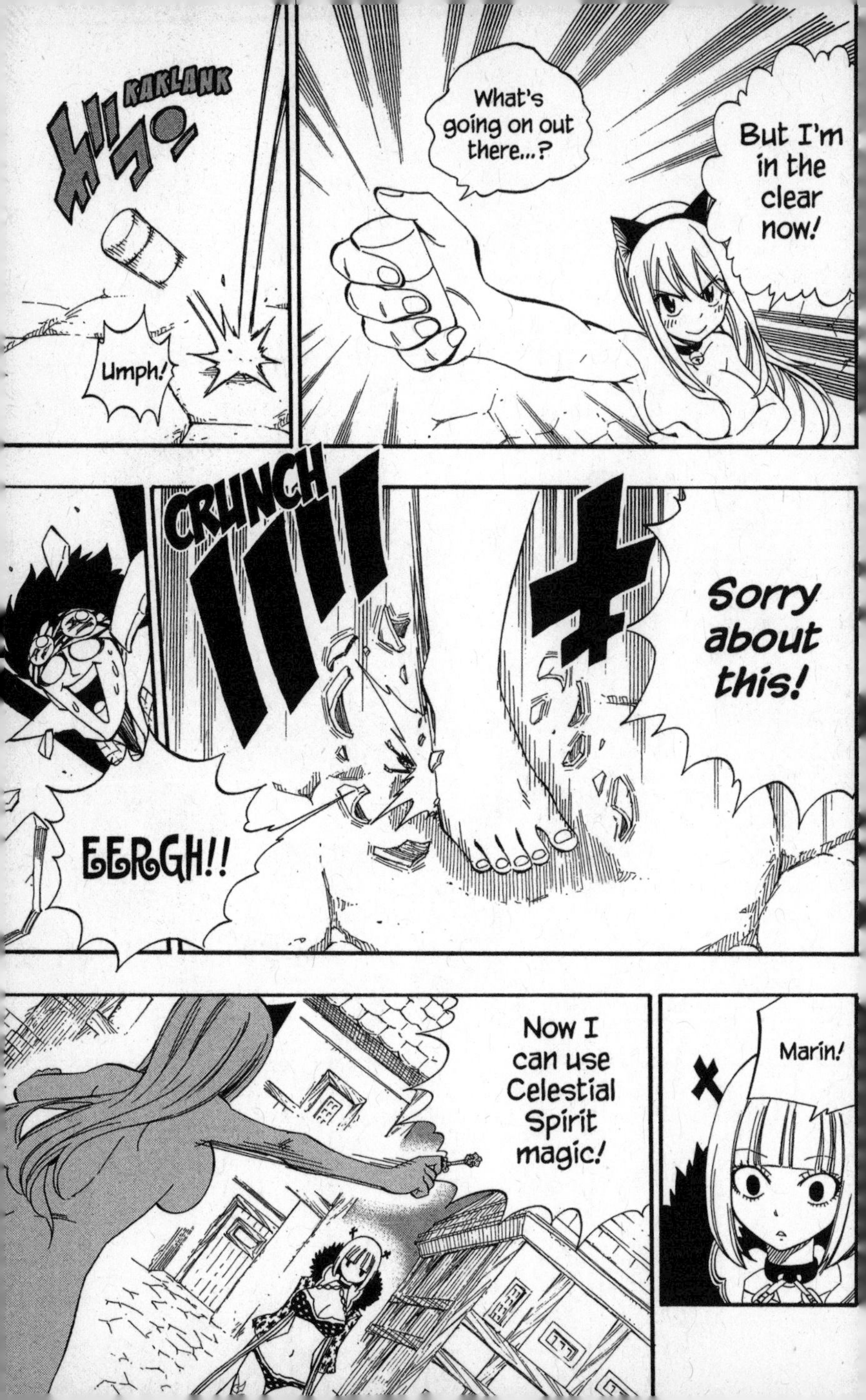

But I'm in the clear now!
What's going on out there...?
KAKLANK
Umph!
Sorry about this!
CRUNCH
EERGH!!
Marin!
Now I can use Celestial Spirit magic!

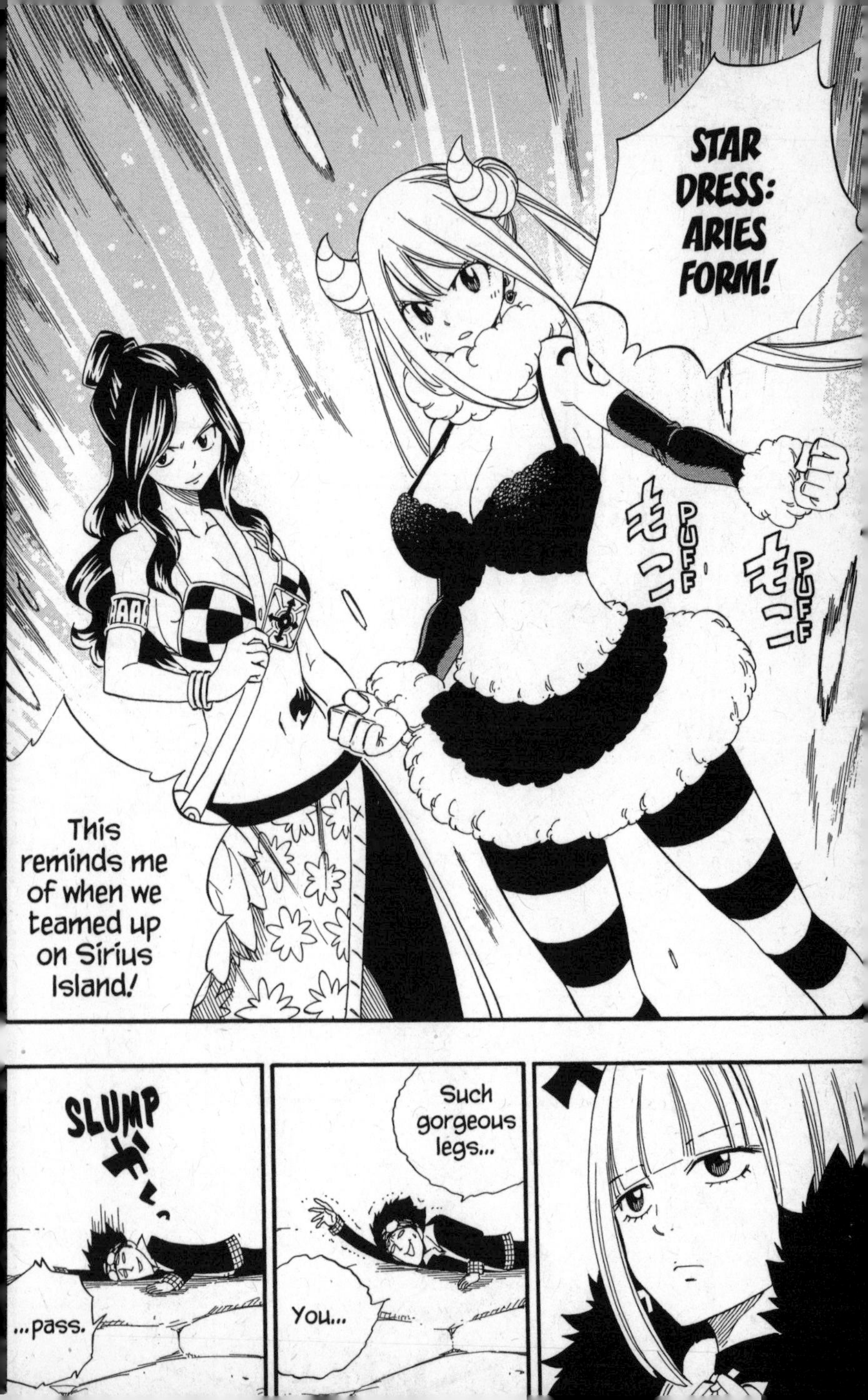
STAR DRESS: ARIES FORM!
PUFF
PUFF
This reminds me of when we teamed up on Sirius Island!
Such gorgeous legs...
You...
SLUMP
...pass.

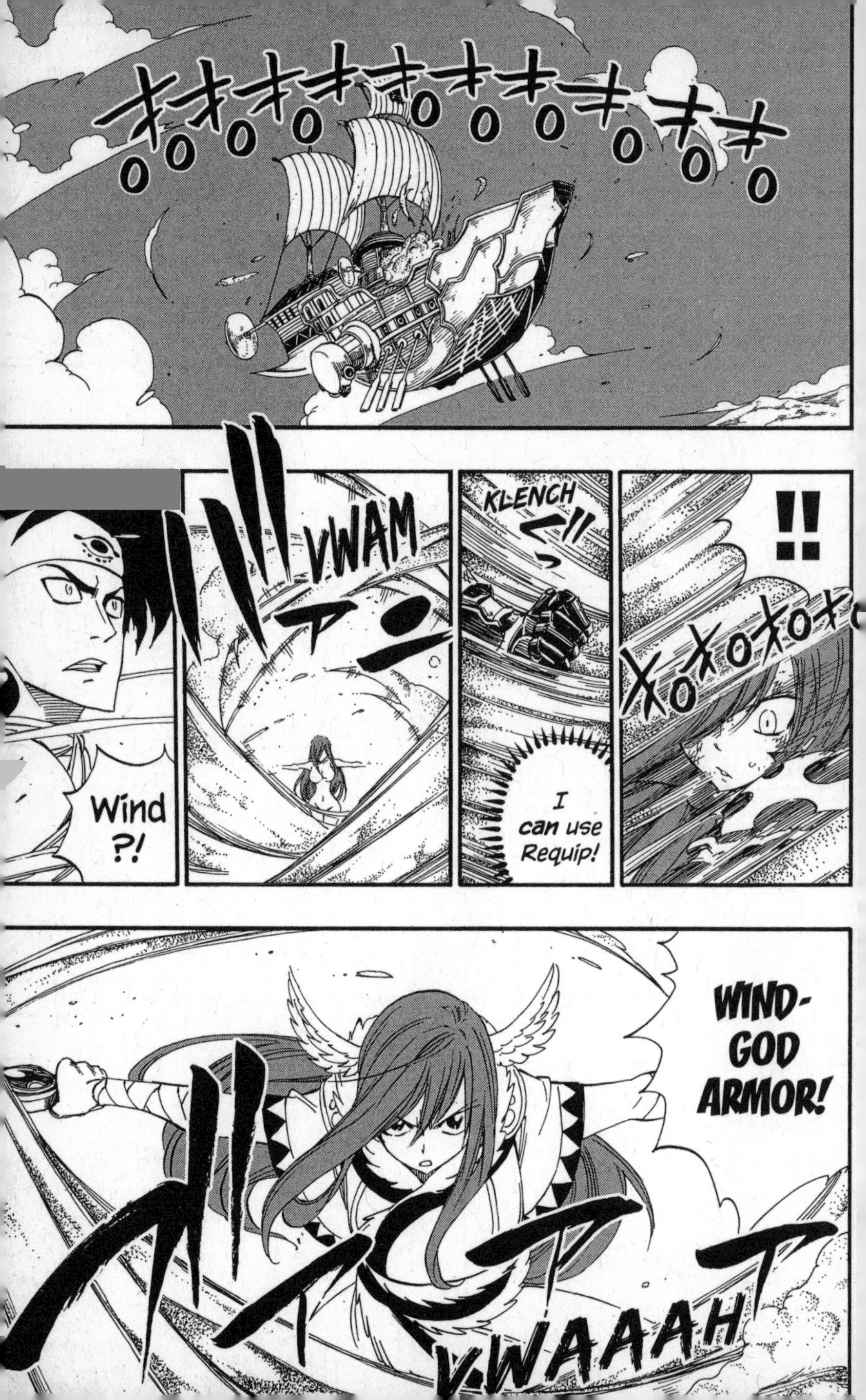
!!
KLENCH
I can use Requip!
V.WAM
Wind ?!
WIND-GOD ARMOR!
V.WAAAH

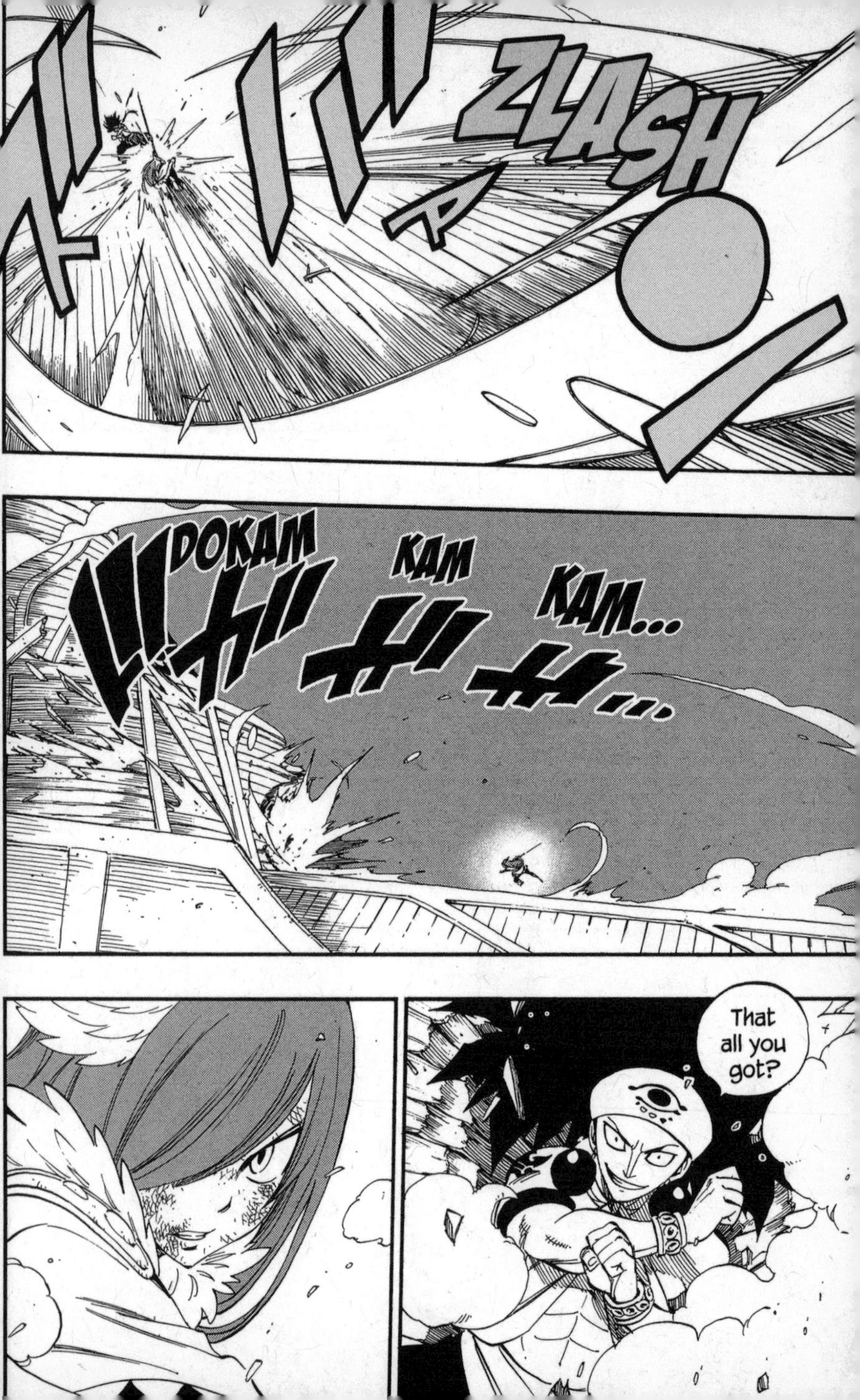
ZLASH
DOKAM
KAM
KAM...
That all you got?

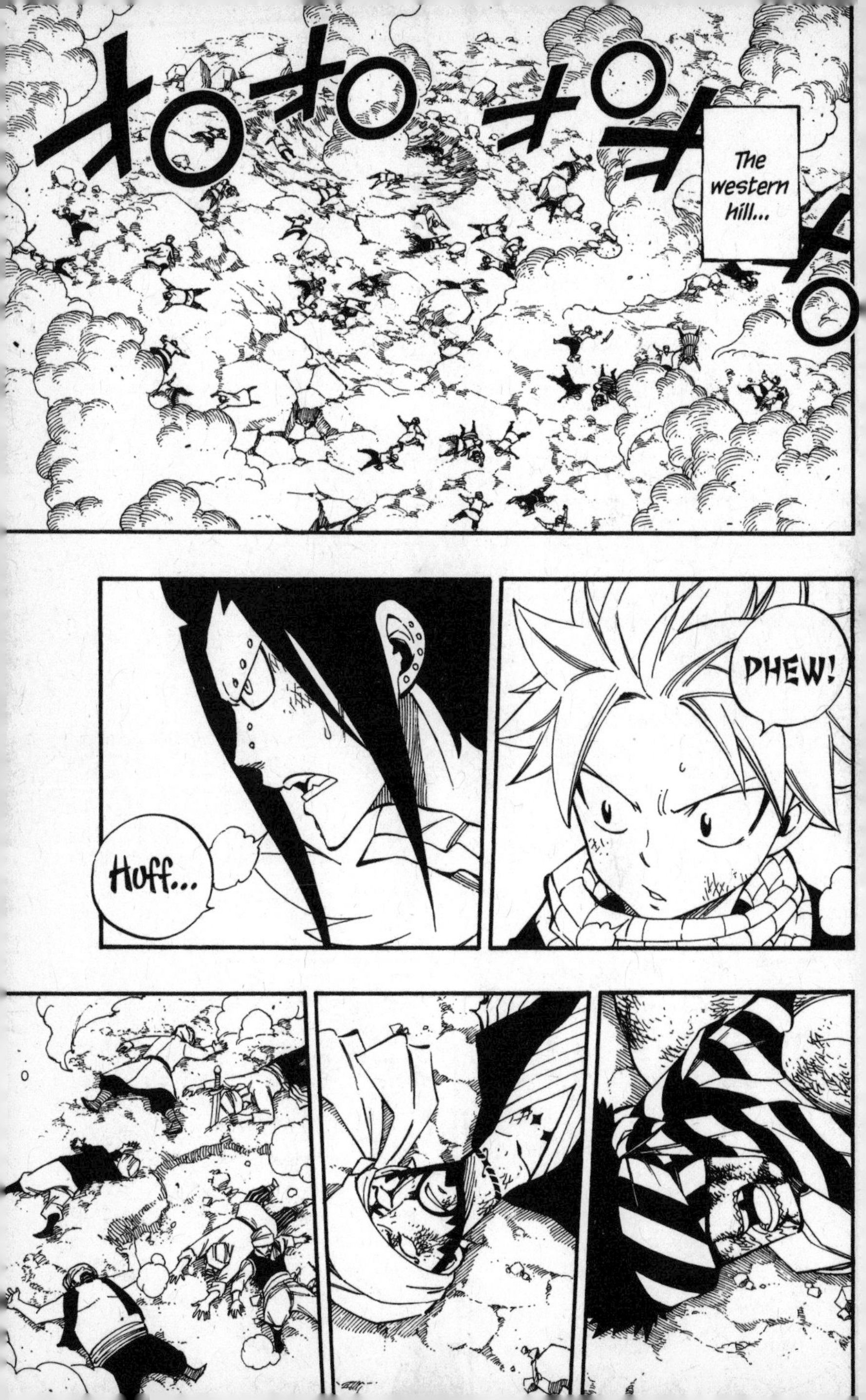

The western hill...
PHEW!
Huff...

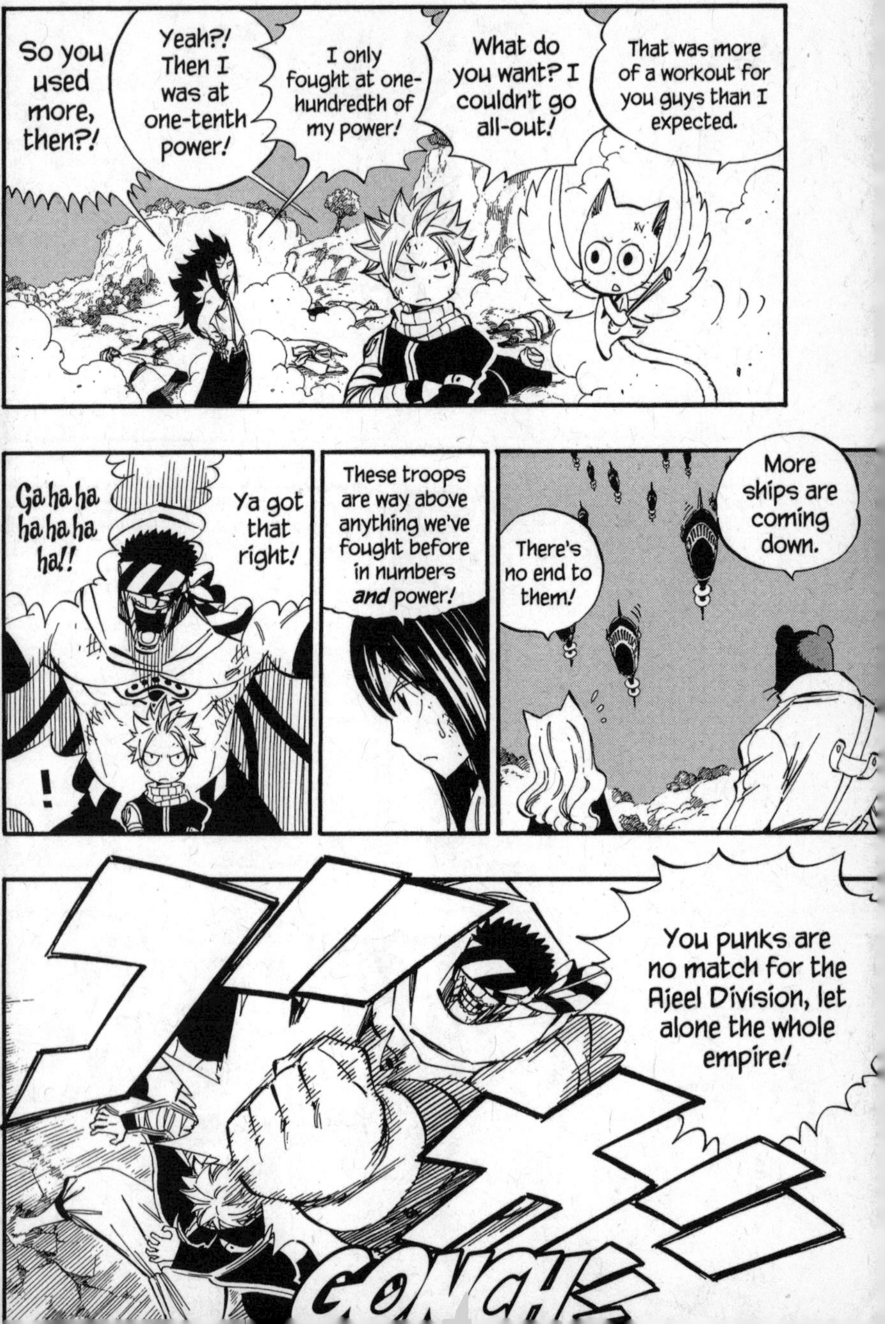

That was more of a workout for you guys than I expected.
What do you want? I couldn't go all-out!
I only fought at one-hundredth of my power!
Yeah?! Then I was at one-tenth power!
So you used more, then?!
More ships are coming down.
There's no end to them!
These troops are way above anything we've fought before in numbers *and* power!
Ya got that right!
Ga ha ha ha ha ha ha!!
!
You punks are no match for the Ajeel Division, let alone the whole empire!
GONCH

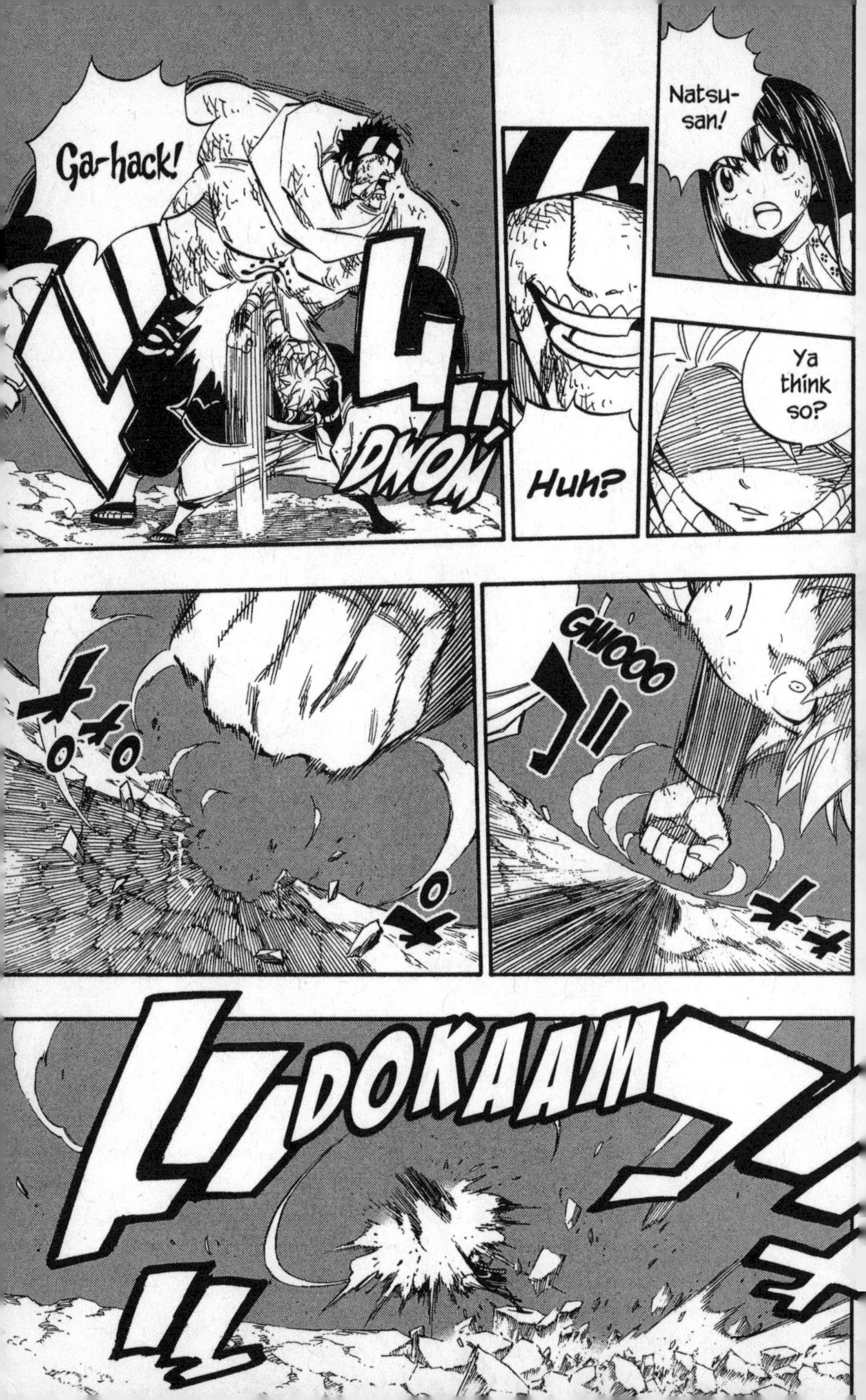
Natsu-san!
Ya think so?
Huh?
Ga-hack!
DWOM
GWOOO
DOKAAM

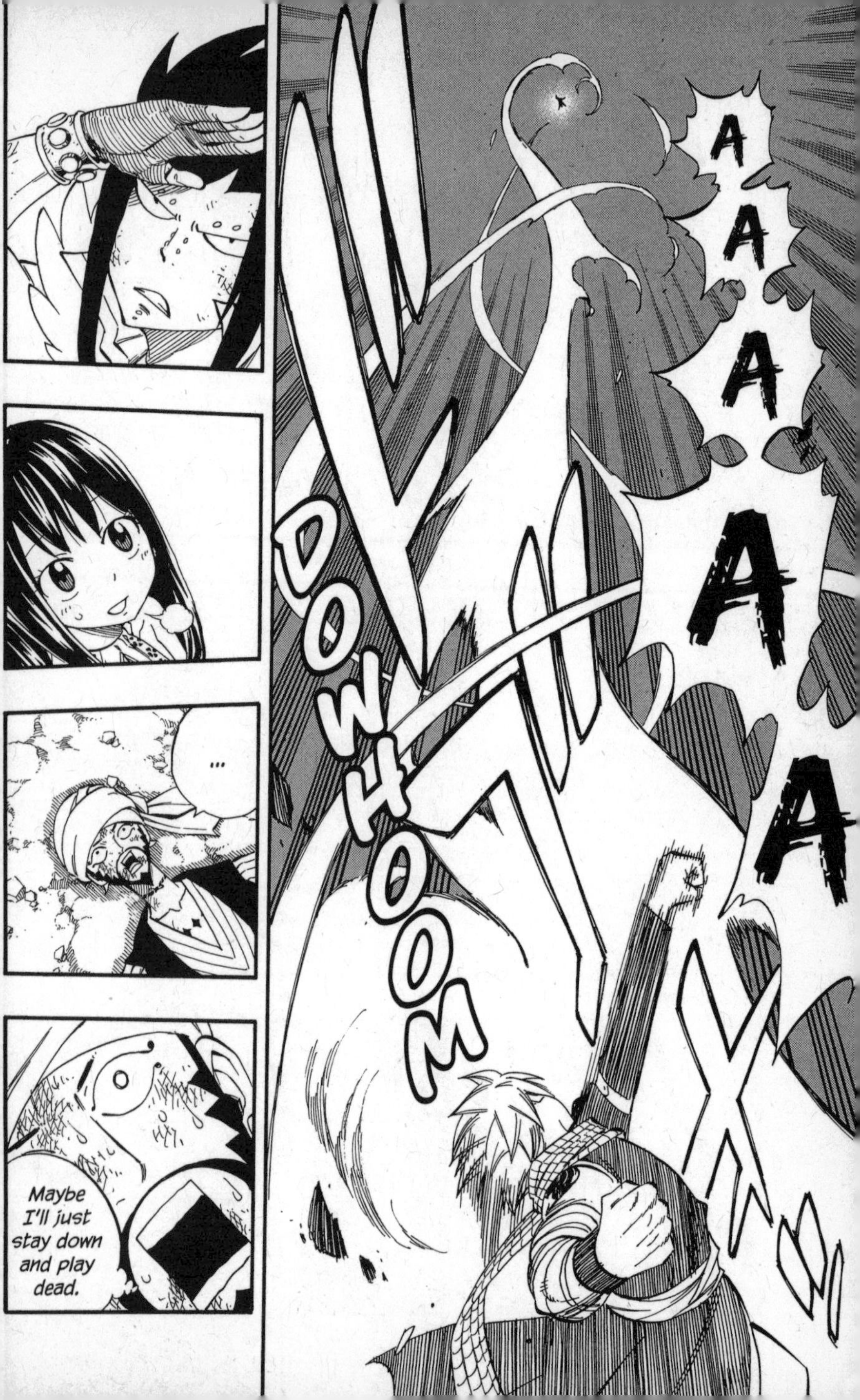
AAAAA
DOWHOOM
...
...
Maybe I'll just stay down and play dead.

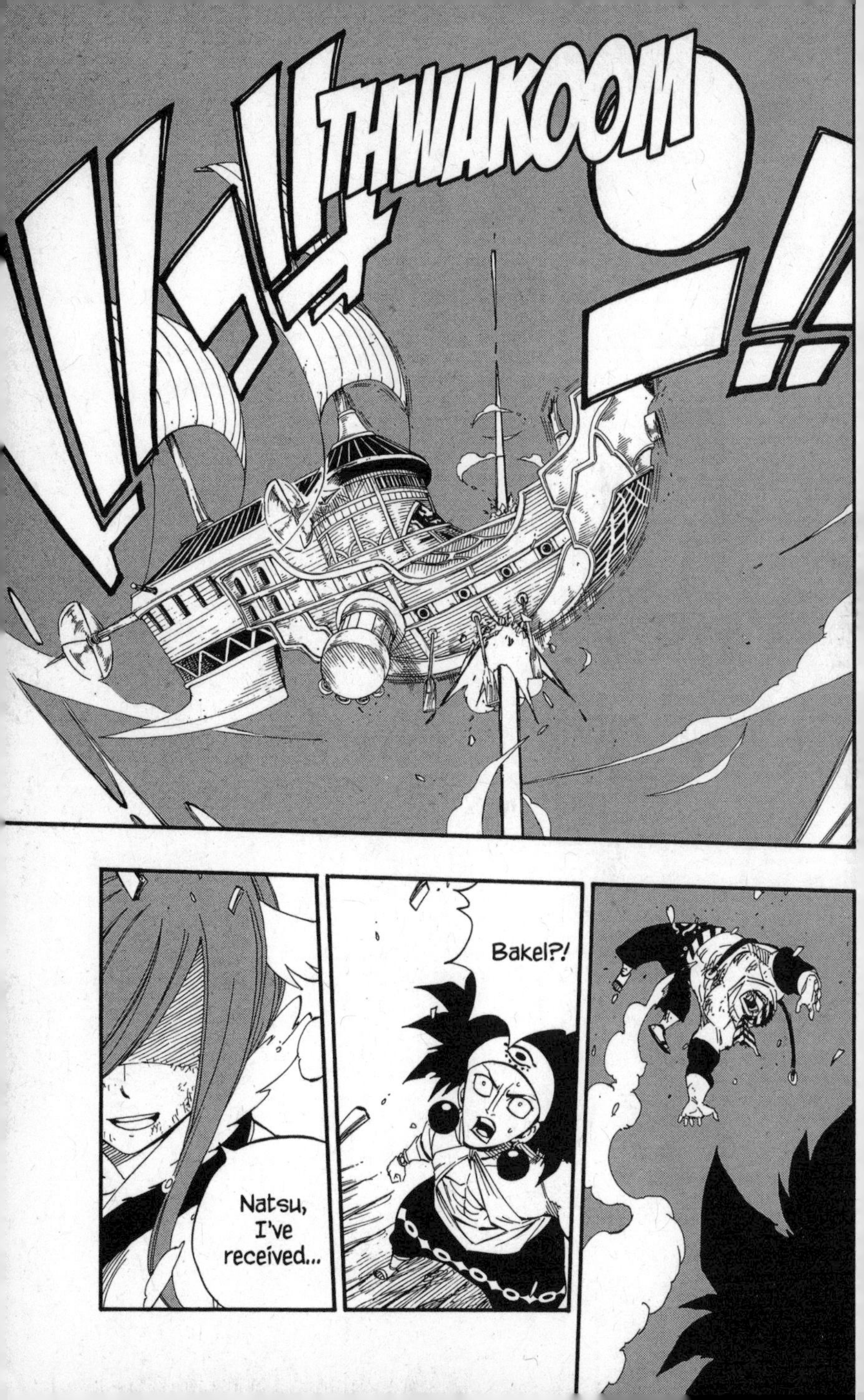
THWAKOOM
Bakel?!
Natsu, I've received...

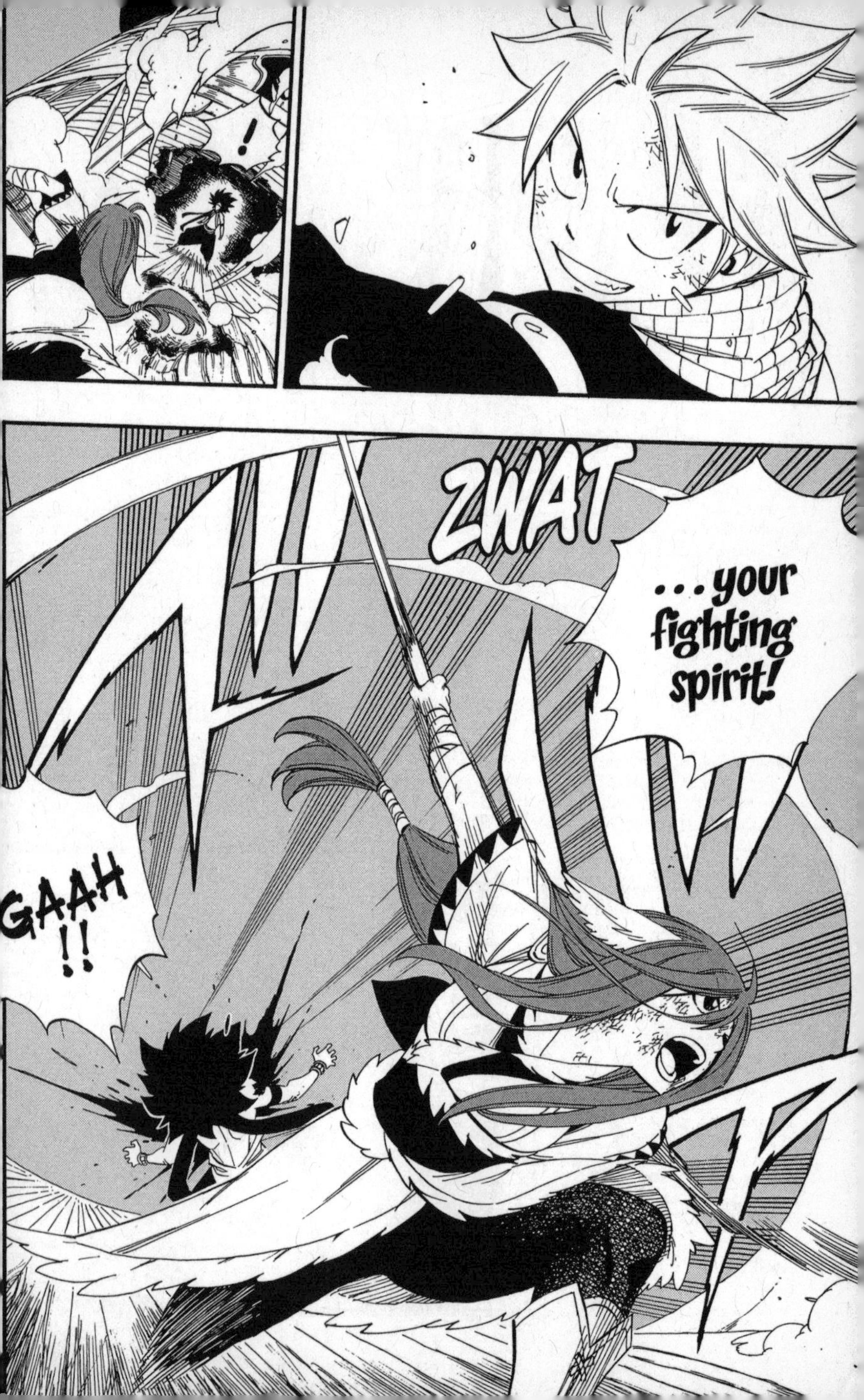
!
ZWAT
...your fighting spirit!
GAAH!!

FAIRY TAIL
フェアリーテイル

Chapter 458: Morning Star

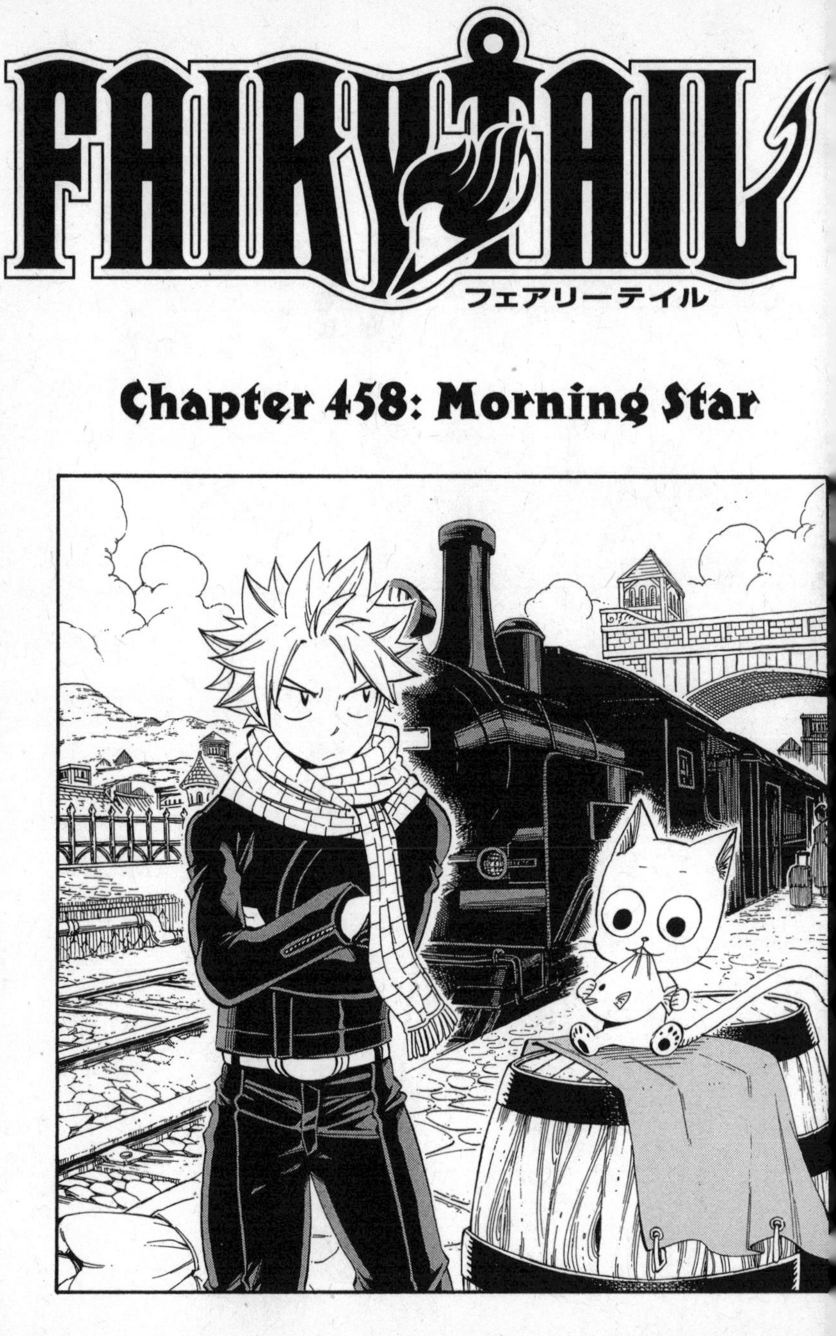

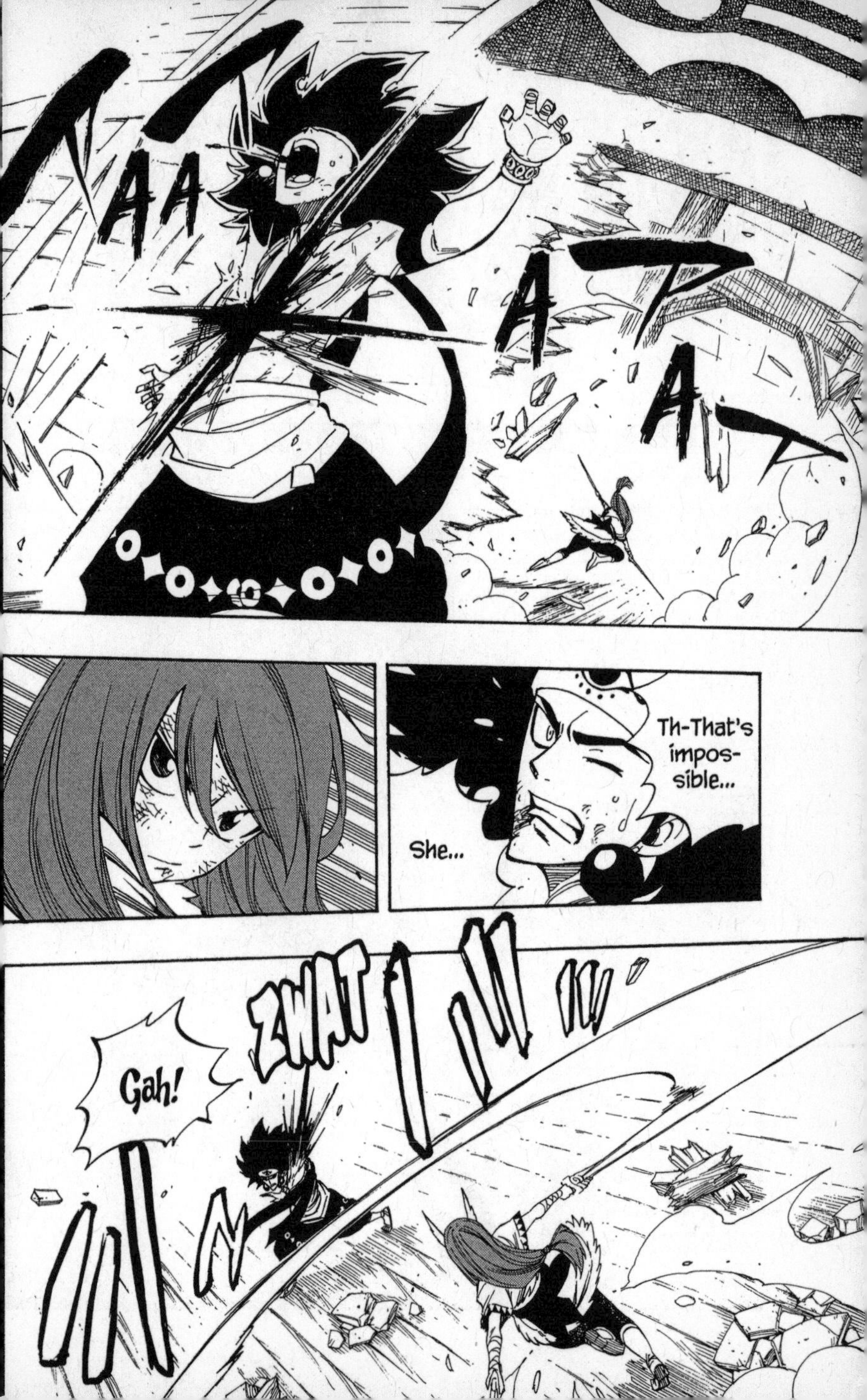
Th-That's impos-sible...
She...
ZWAT
Gah!

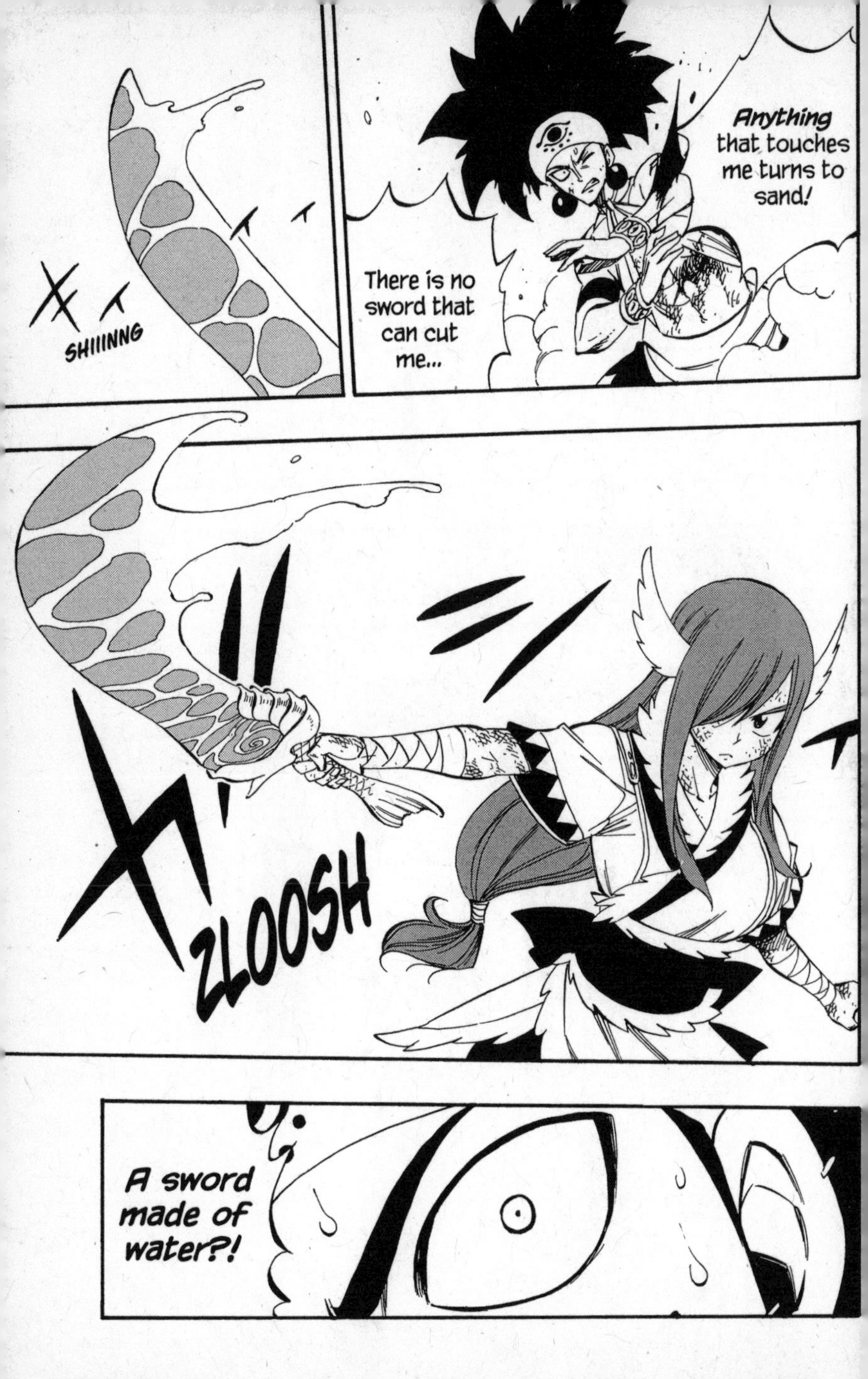
Anything that touches me turns to sand!
There is no sword that can cut me...
SHIIINNG
ZLOOSH
A sword made of water?!

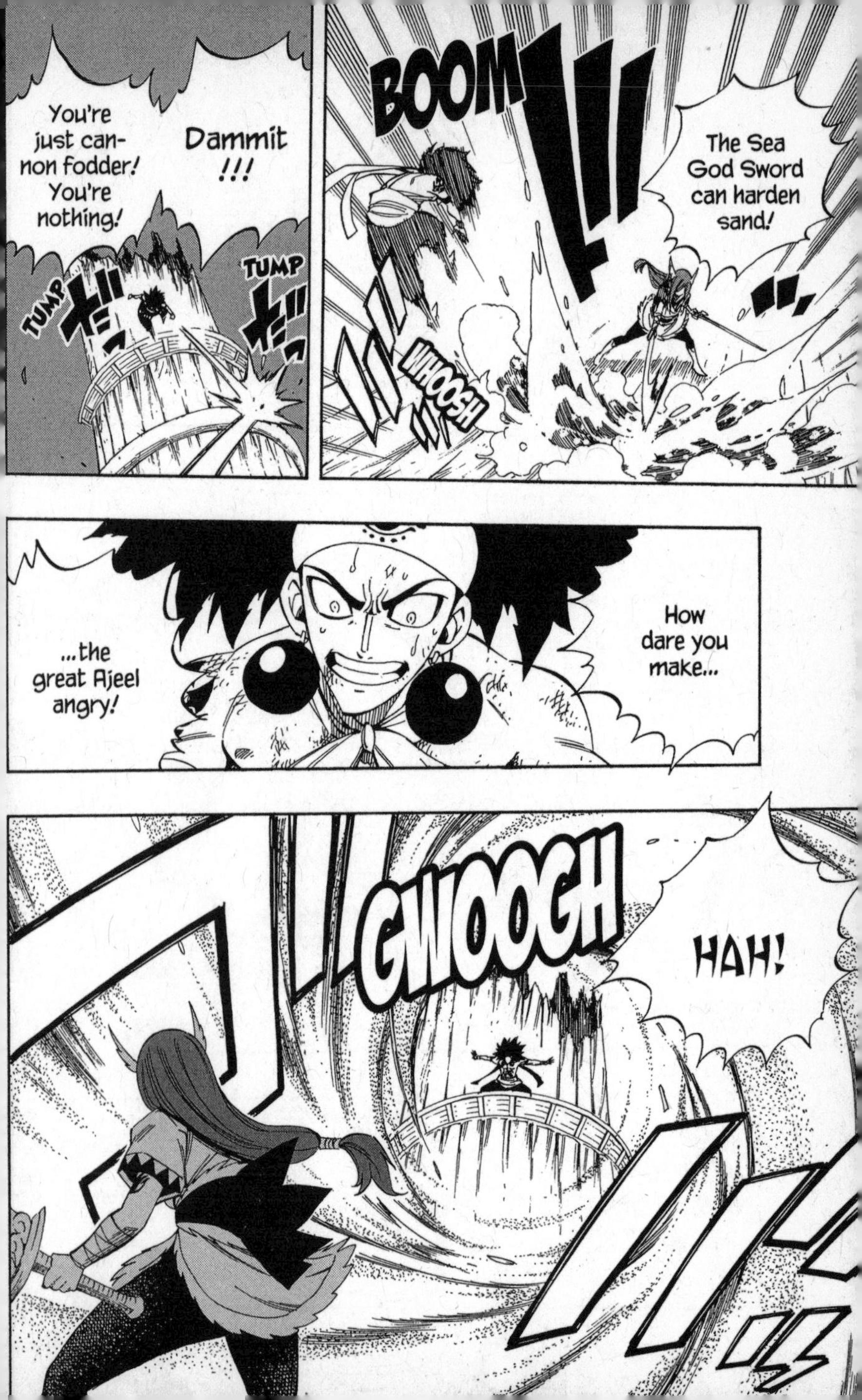
The Sea God Sword can harden sand!
BOOM
WHOOSH
Dammit !!!
You're just can-non fodder! You're nothing!
TUMP
TUMP
How dare you make...
...the great Ajeel angry!
HAH!
GWOOCH

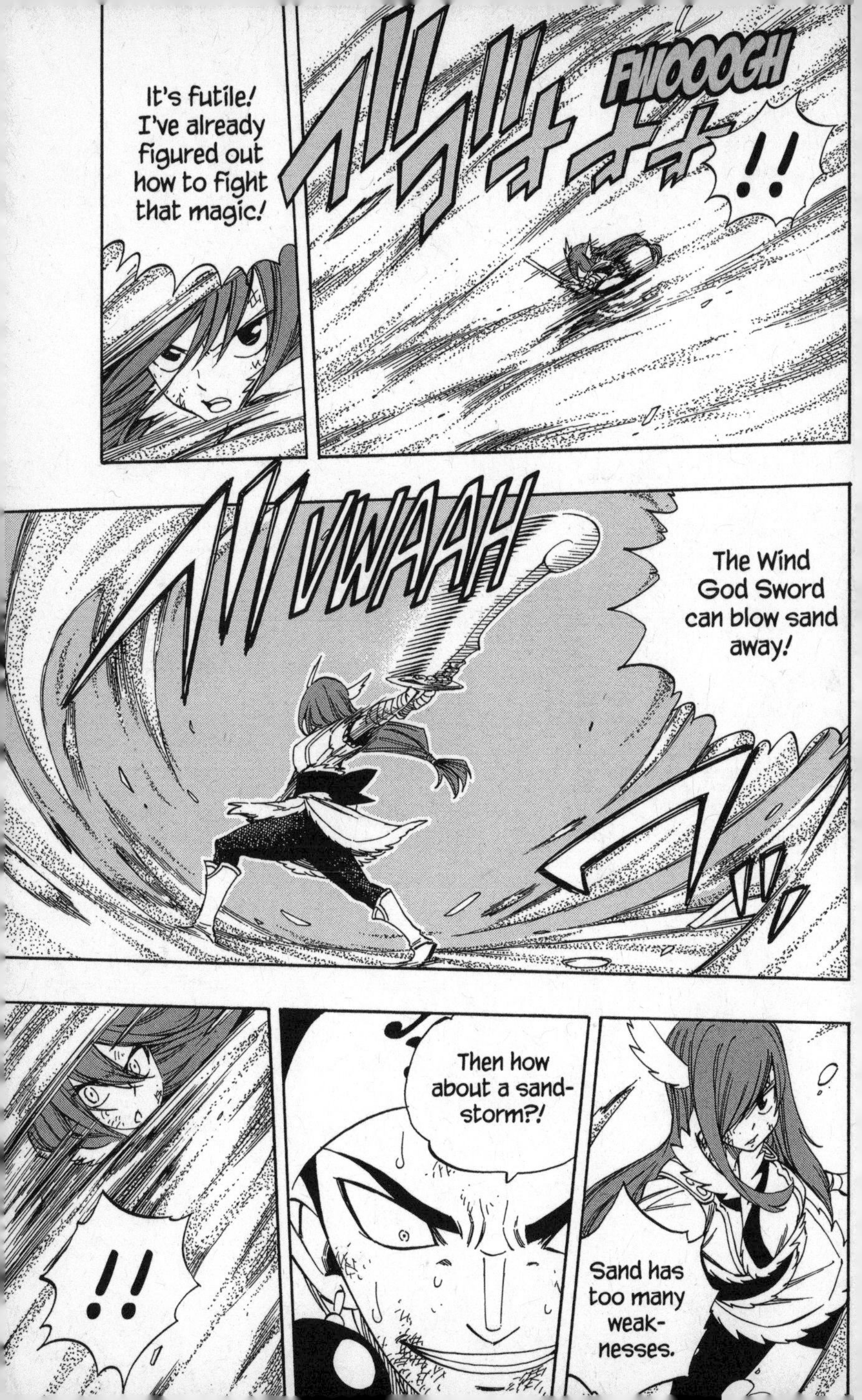
FWOOOGH
!!
It's futile! I've already figured out how to fight that magic!
VWAAH
The Wind God Sword can blow sand away!
Sand has too many weak- nesses.
Then how about a sand- storm?!
!!

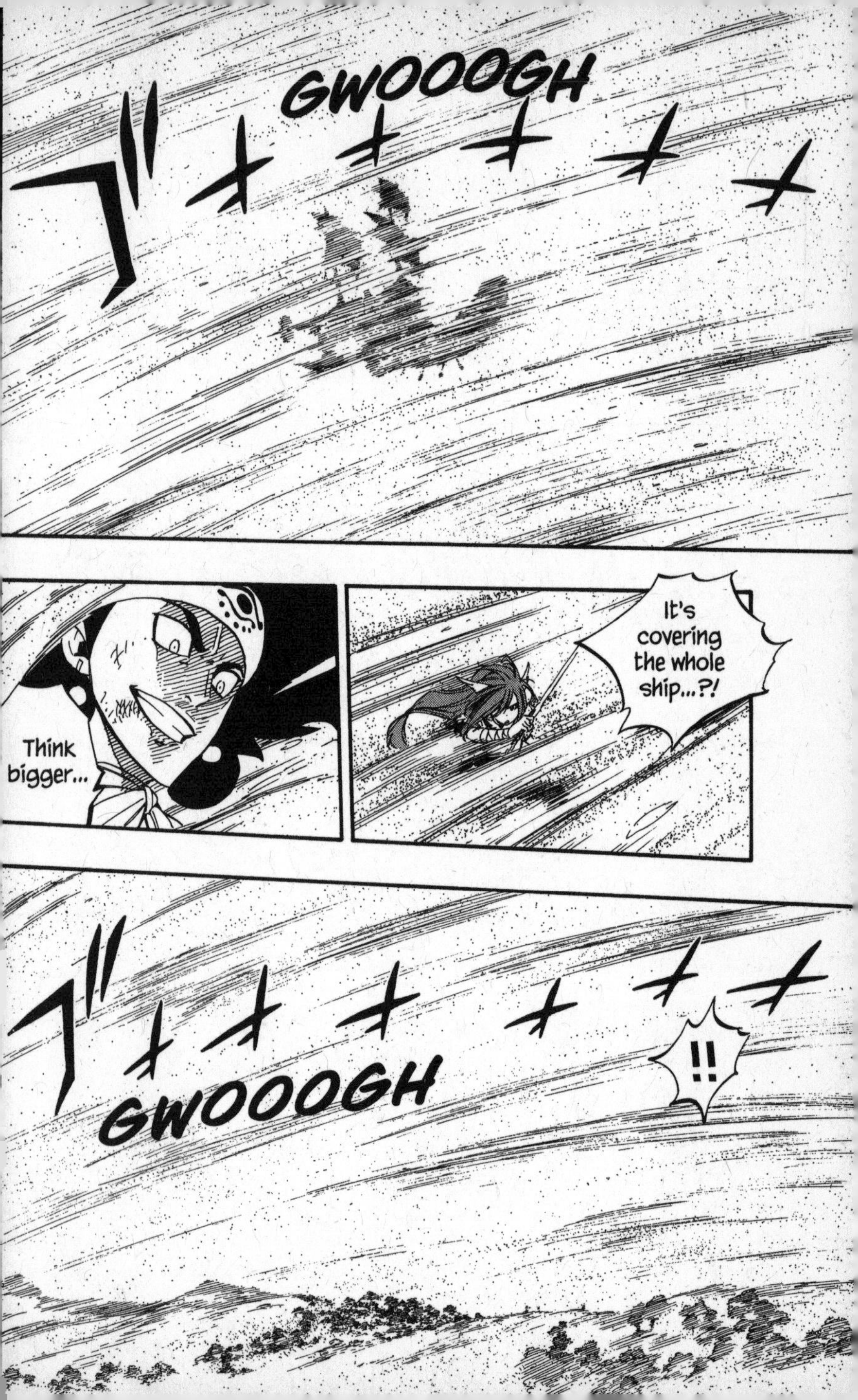

GWOOOGH
It's covering the whole ship...?!
Think bigger...
GWOOOGH
!!

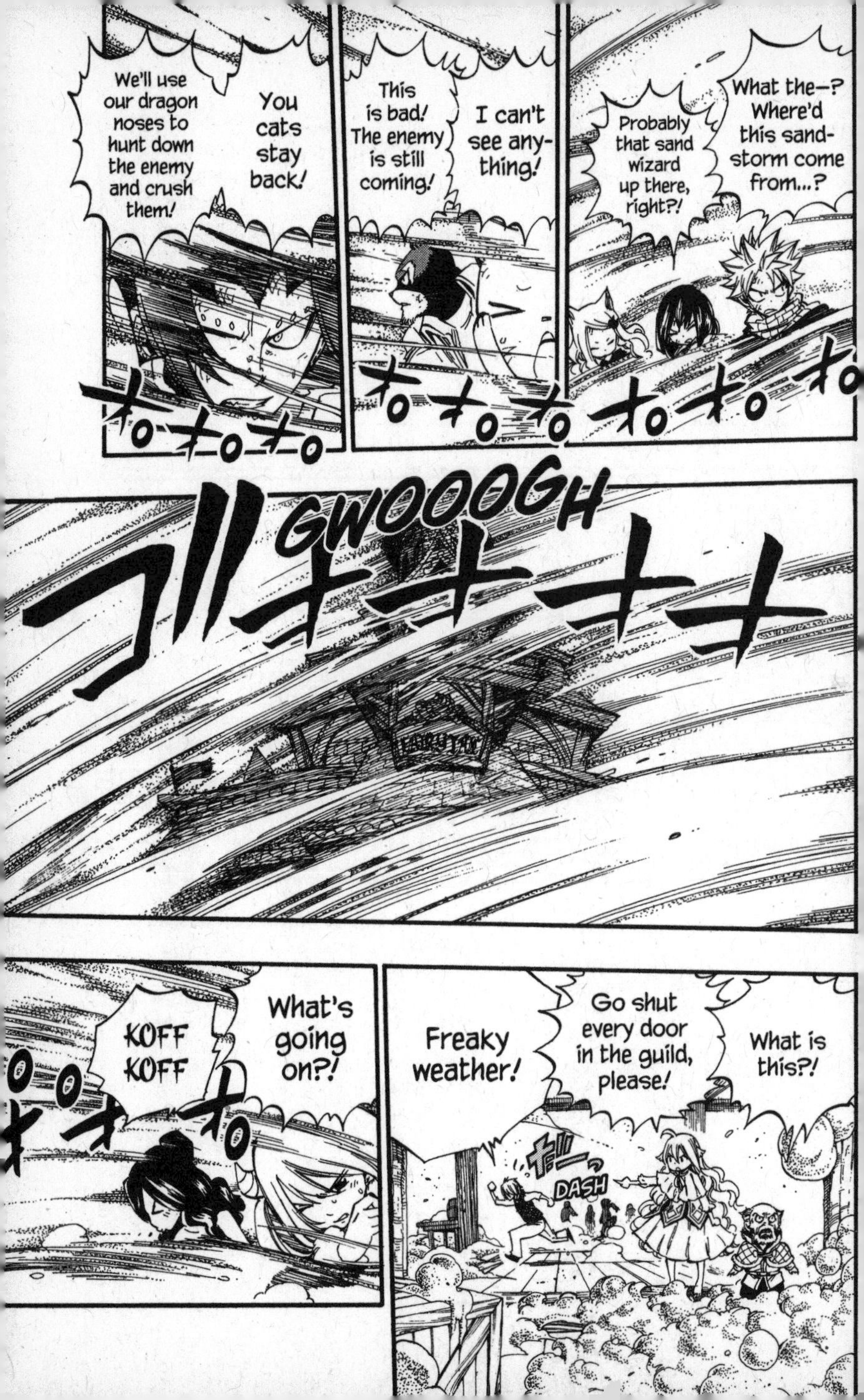
What the—? Where'd this sandstorm come from...?
Probably that sand wizard up there, right?!
I can't see anything!
This is bad! The enemy is still coming!
You cats stay back!
We'll use our dragon noses to hunt down the enemy and crush them!
GWOOOGH
What is this?!
Go shut every door in the guild, please!
Freaky weather!
DASH
What's going on?!
KOFF KOFF

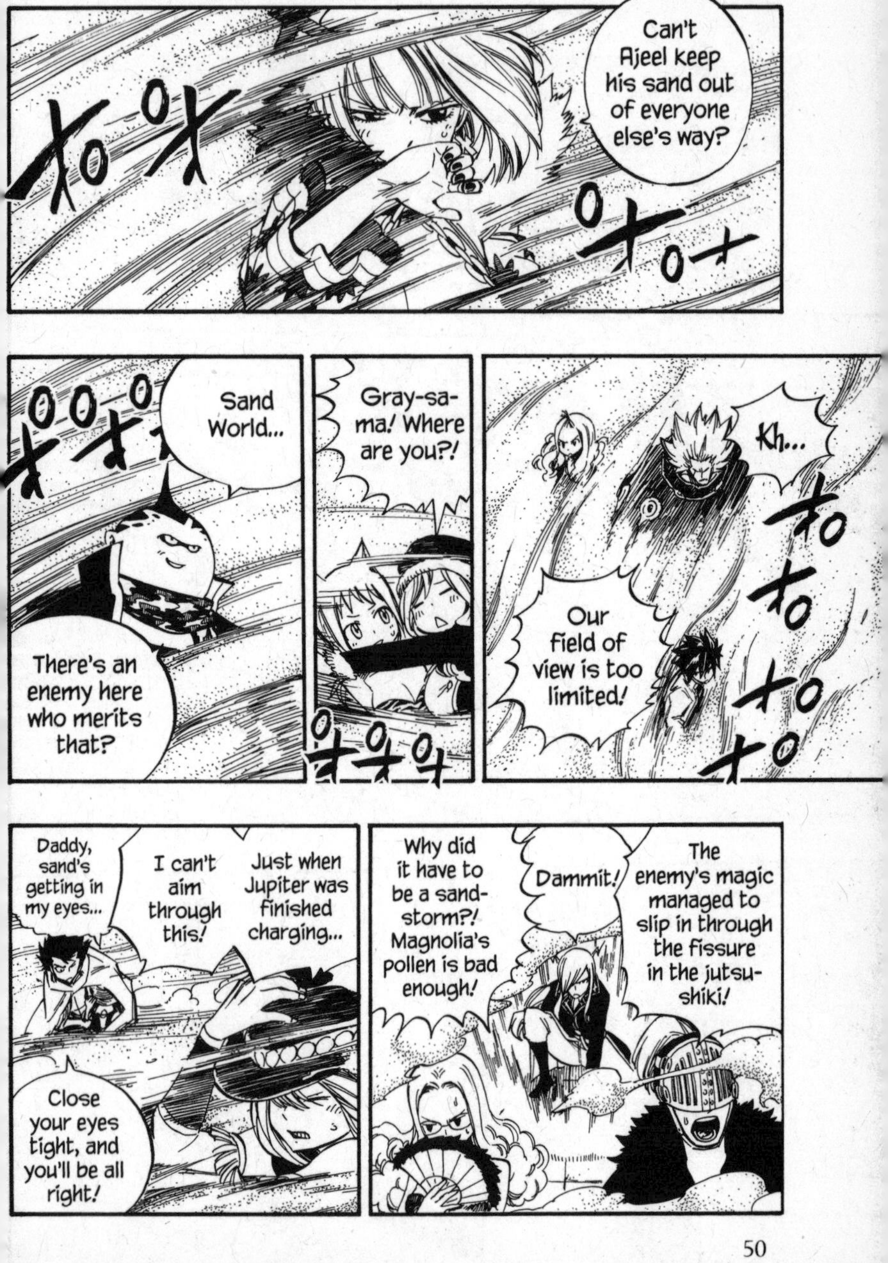
Can't Ajeel keep his sand out of everyone else's way?
Kh...
Our field of view is too limited!
Gray-sama! Where are you?!
Sand World...
There's an enemy here who merits that?
The enemy's magic managed to slip in through the fissure in the jutsu-shiki!
Dammit!
Why did it have to be a sand-storm?! Magnolia's pollen is bad enough!
Just when Jupiter was finished charging...
I can't aim through this!
Daddy, sand's getting in my eyes...
Close your eyes tight, and you'll be all right!

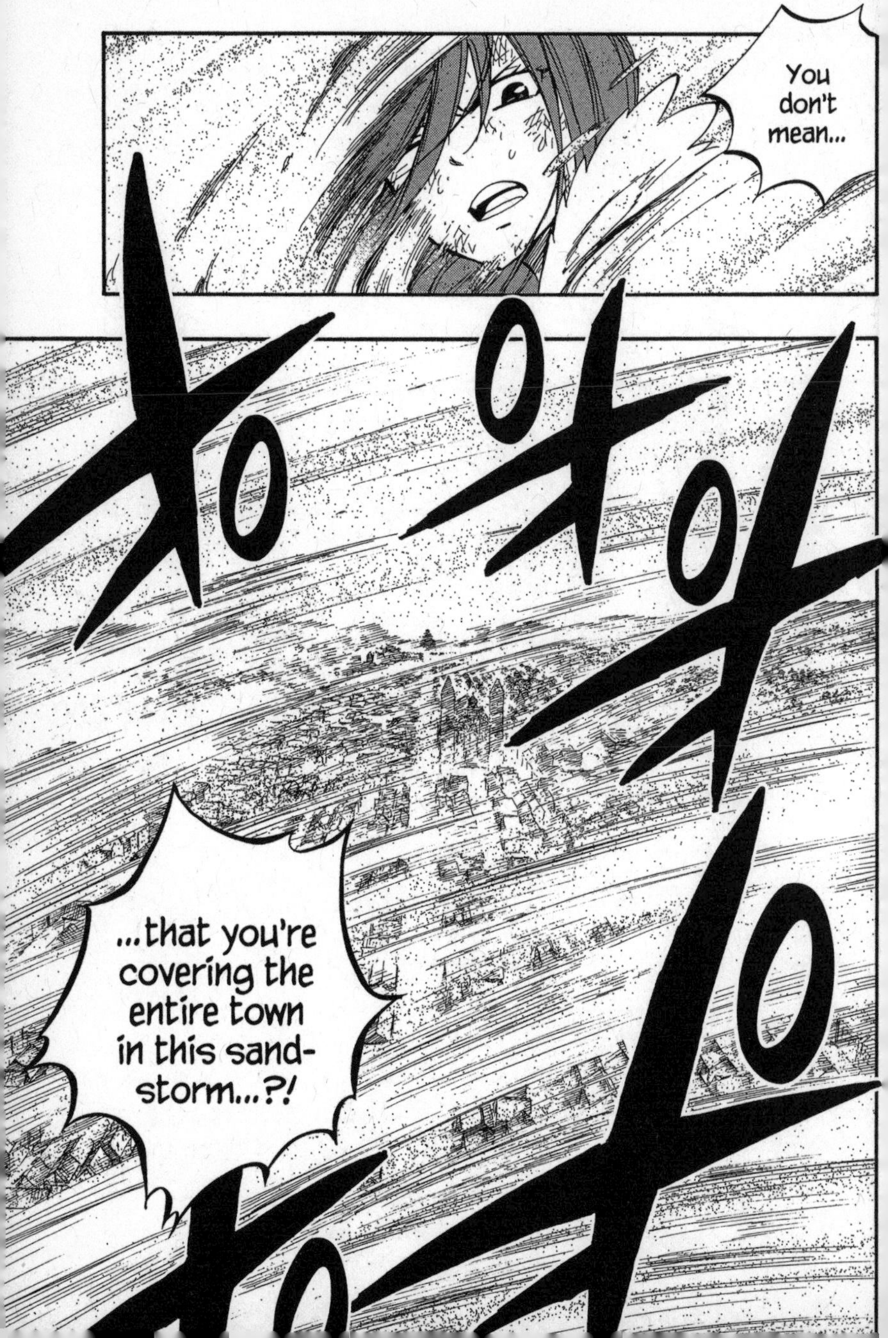
You don't mean...
...that you're covering the entire town in this sand-storm...?!

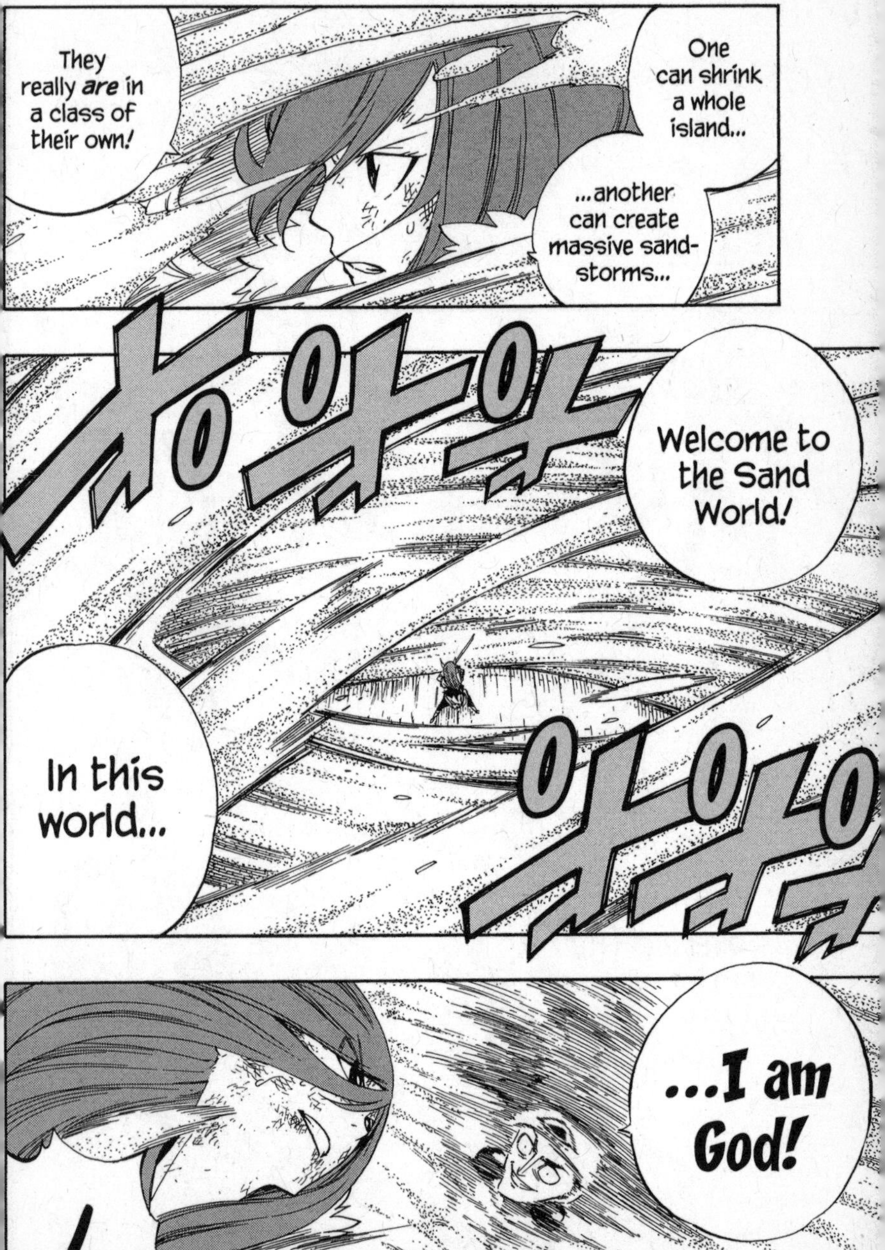
One can shrink a whole island...
...another can create massive sand-storms...
They really *are* in a class of their own!
Welcome to the Sand World!
In this world...
...I am God!
!

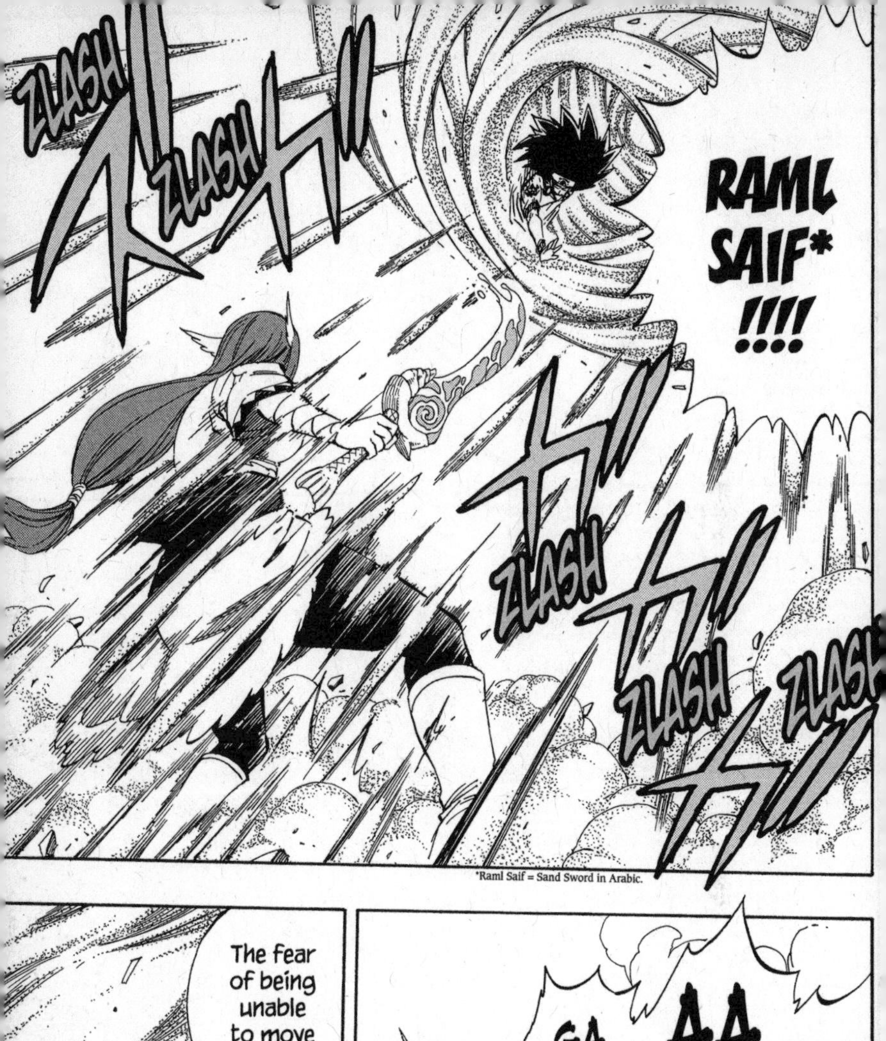
RAML SAIF* !!!!
ZLASH
ZLASH
ZLASH
ZLASH
ZLASH

*Raml Saif = Sand Sword in Arabic.

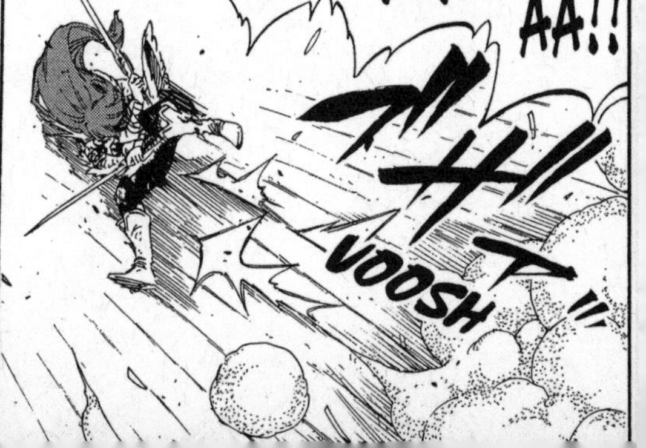
GA AA AA!!
VOOSH!!!

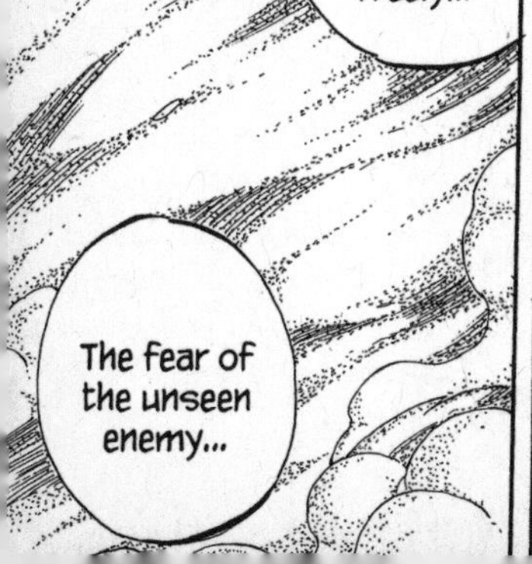
The fear of being unable to move freely...
The fear of the unseen enemy...

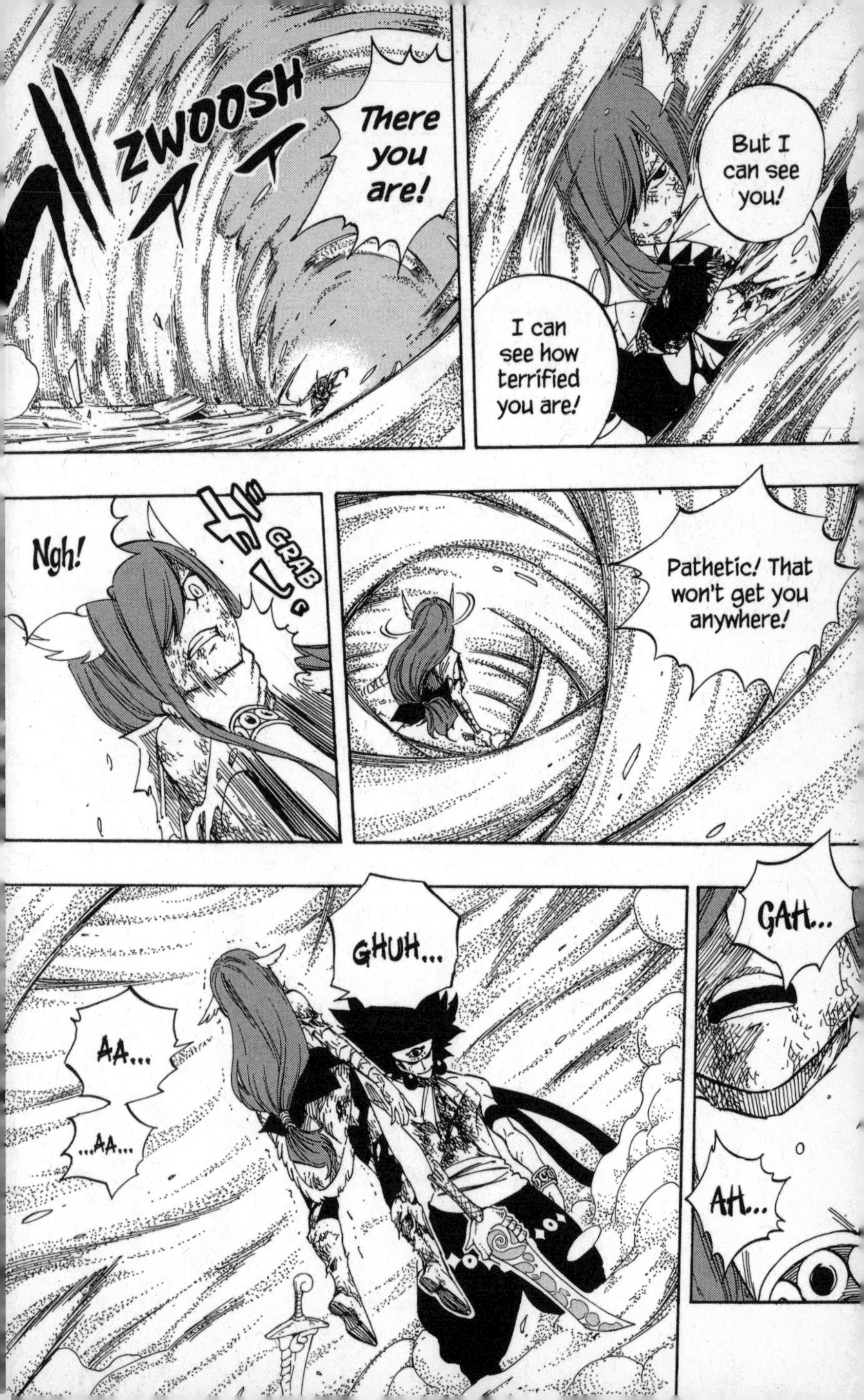
But I can see you!
I can see how terrified you are!
ZWOOSH
There you are!
Pathetic! That won't get you anywhere!
GRAB
Ngh!
GAH...
AH...
GHUH...
AA...
...AA...

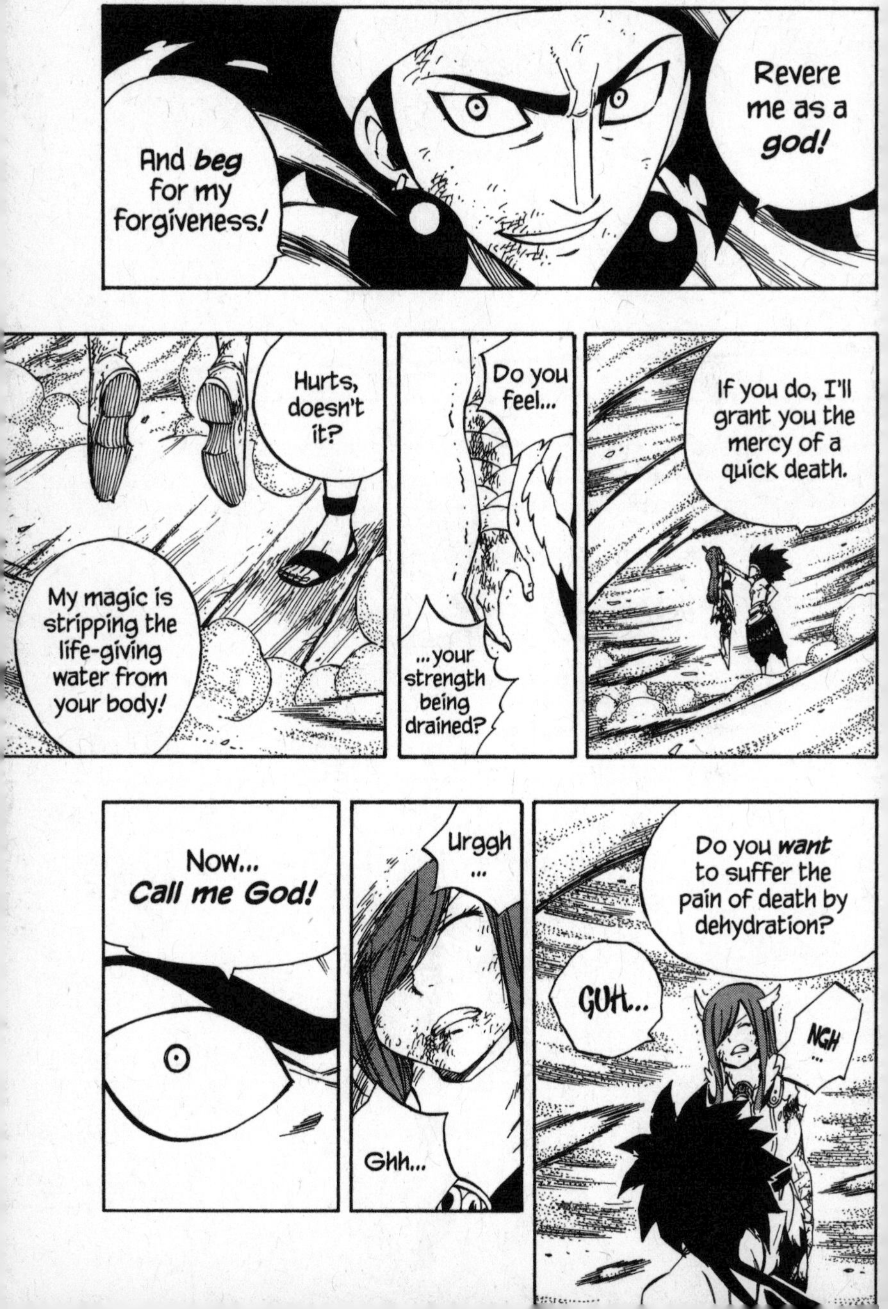

Revere me as a *god!*
And *beg* for my forgiveness!
If you do, I'll grant you the mercy of a quick death.
Do you feel...
...your strength being drained?
Hurts, doesn't it?
My magic is stripping the life-giving water from your body!
Do you *want* to suffer the pain of death by dehydration?
GUH...
NGH...
Urggh...
Ghh...
Now...
Call me God!

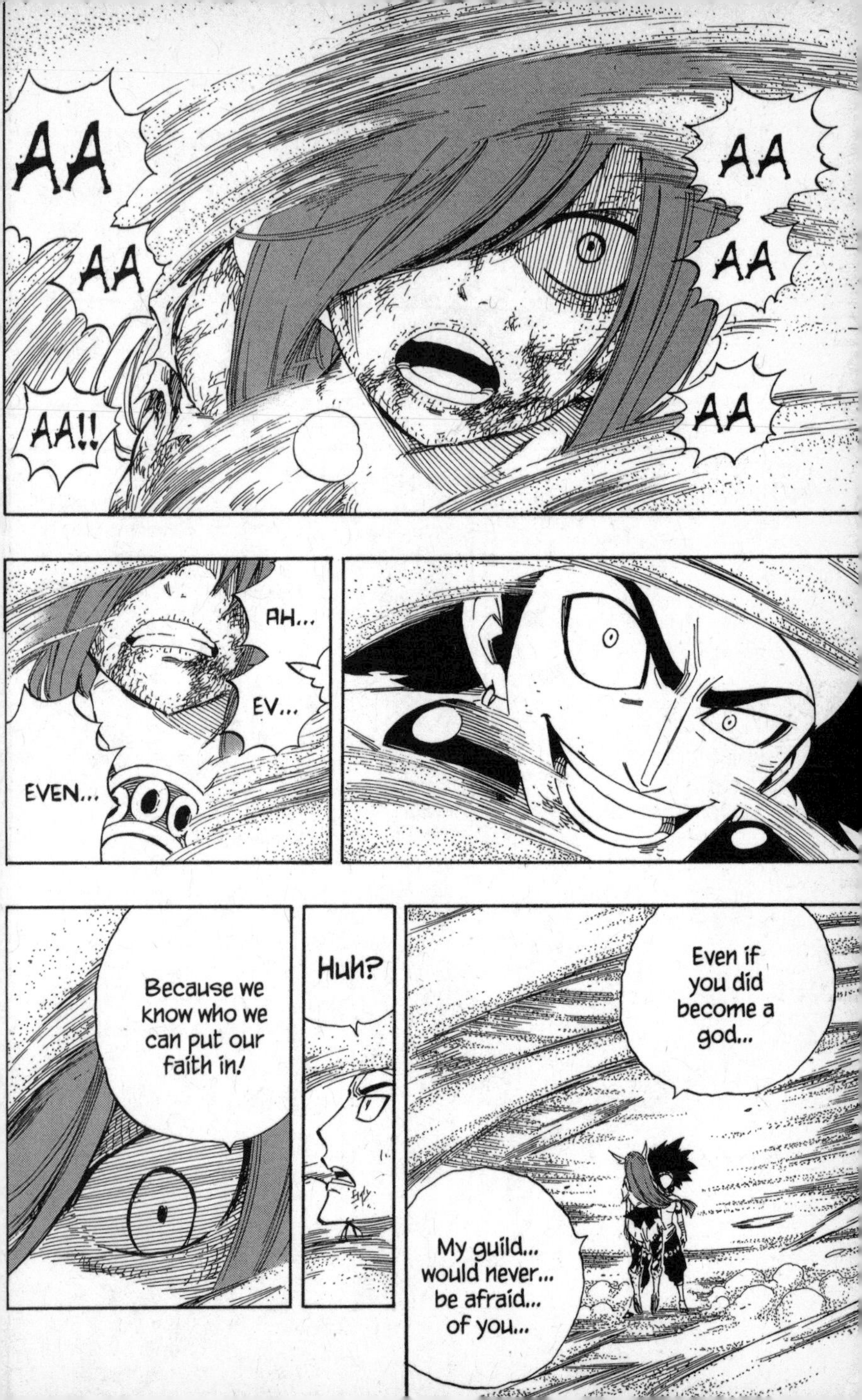
AA
AA
AA
AA
AA
AA!!
AH...
EV...
EVEN...
Even if you did become a god...
My guild... would never... be afraid... of you...
Huh?
Because we know who we can put our faith in!

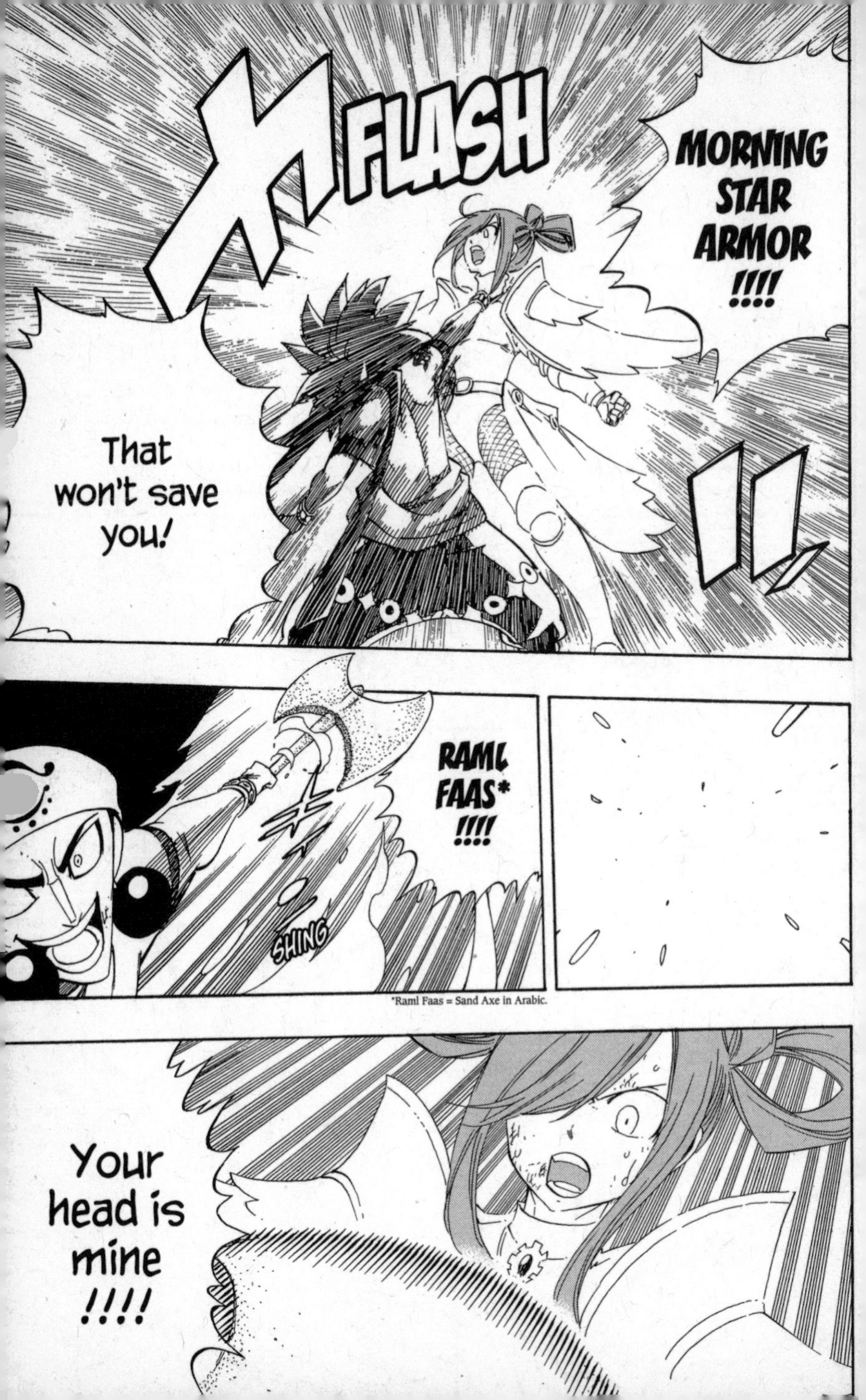
MORNING STAR ARMOR !!!!
FLASH
That won't save you!
RAML FAAS* !!!!
SHING
Your head is mine !!!!

*Raml Faas = Sand Axe in Arabic.

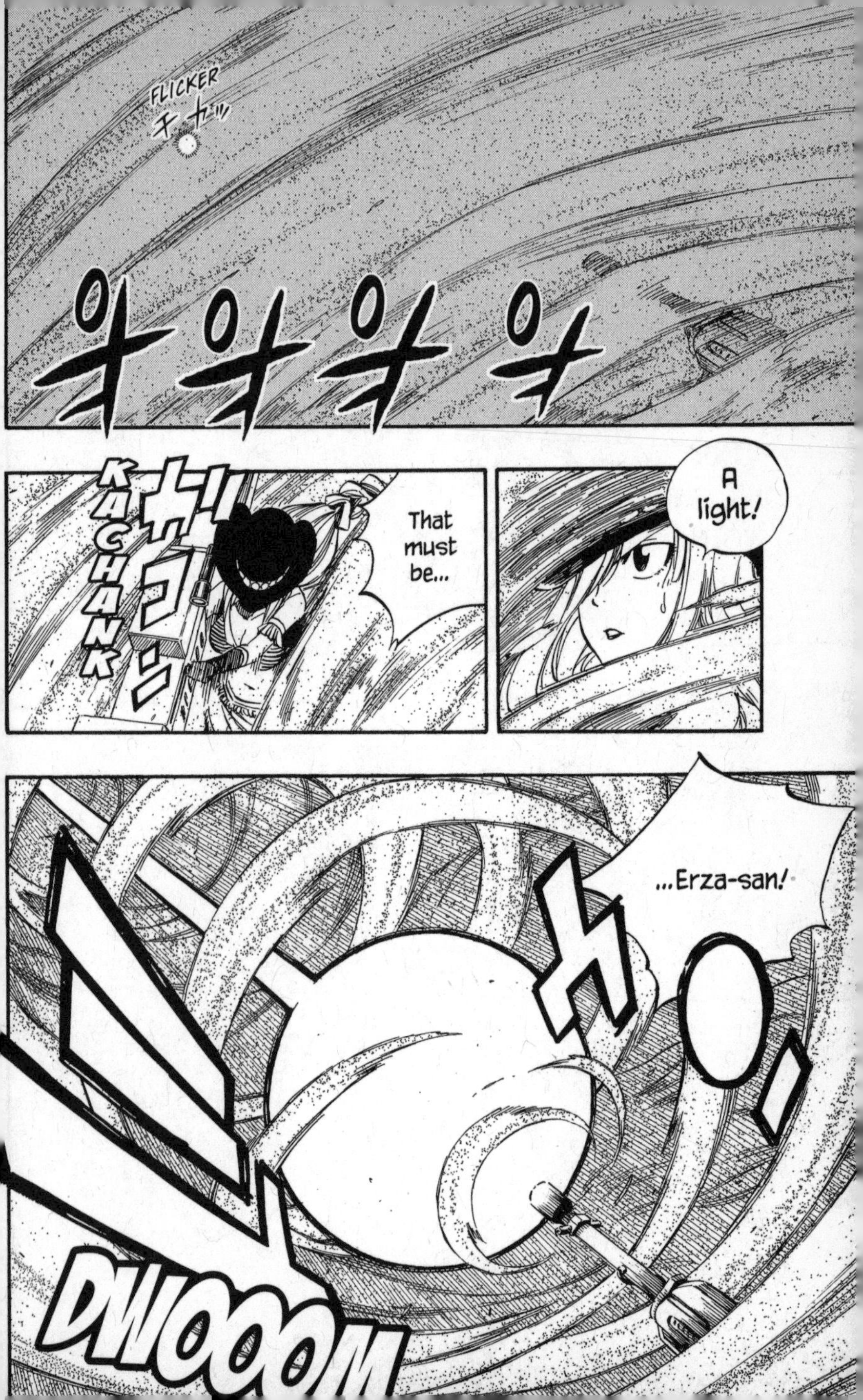
FLICKER
A light!
That must be...
KACHANK
...Erza-san!
DWOOOM

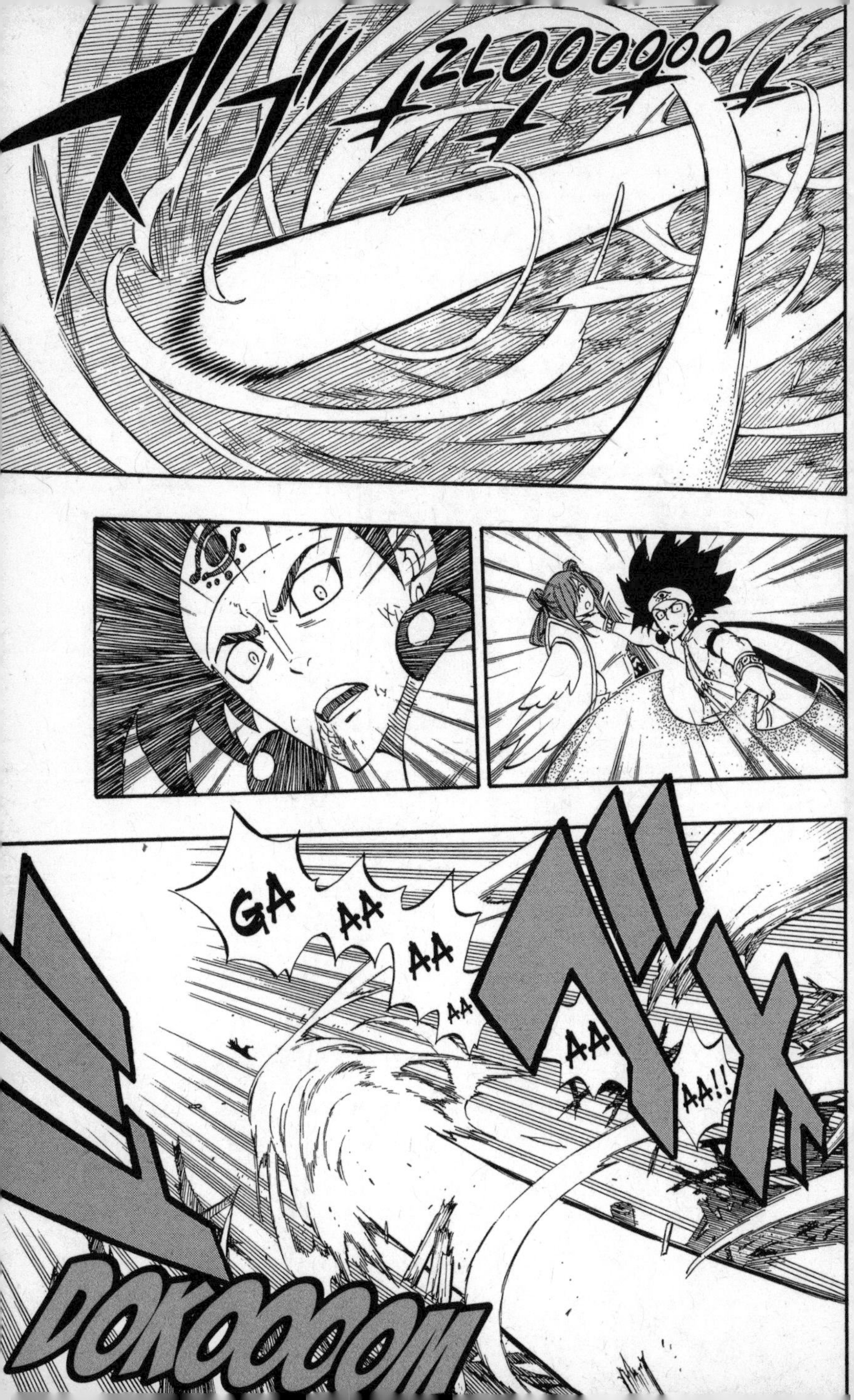
ZLOOOOOO
GA AA AA AA AA AA!!
DOKOOOOM

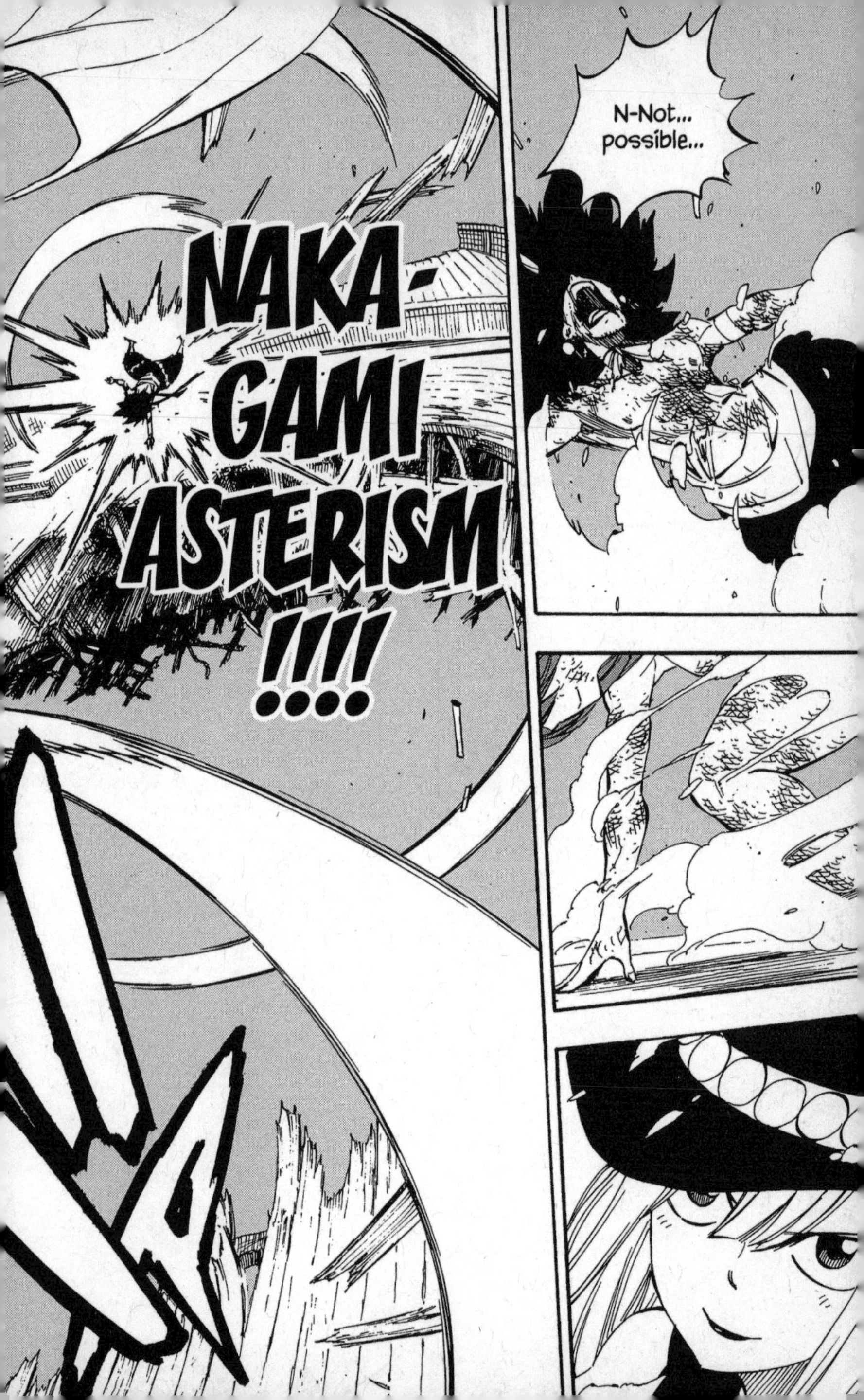
N-Not... possible...
NAKA-GAMI ASTERISM !!!!

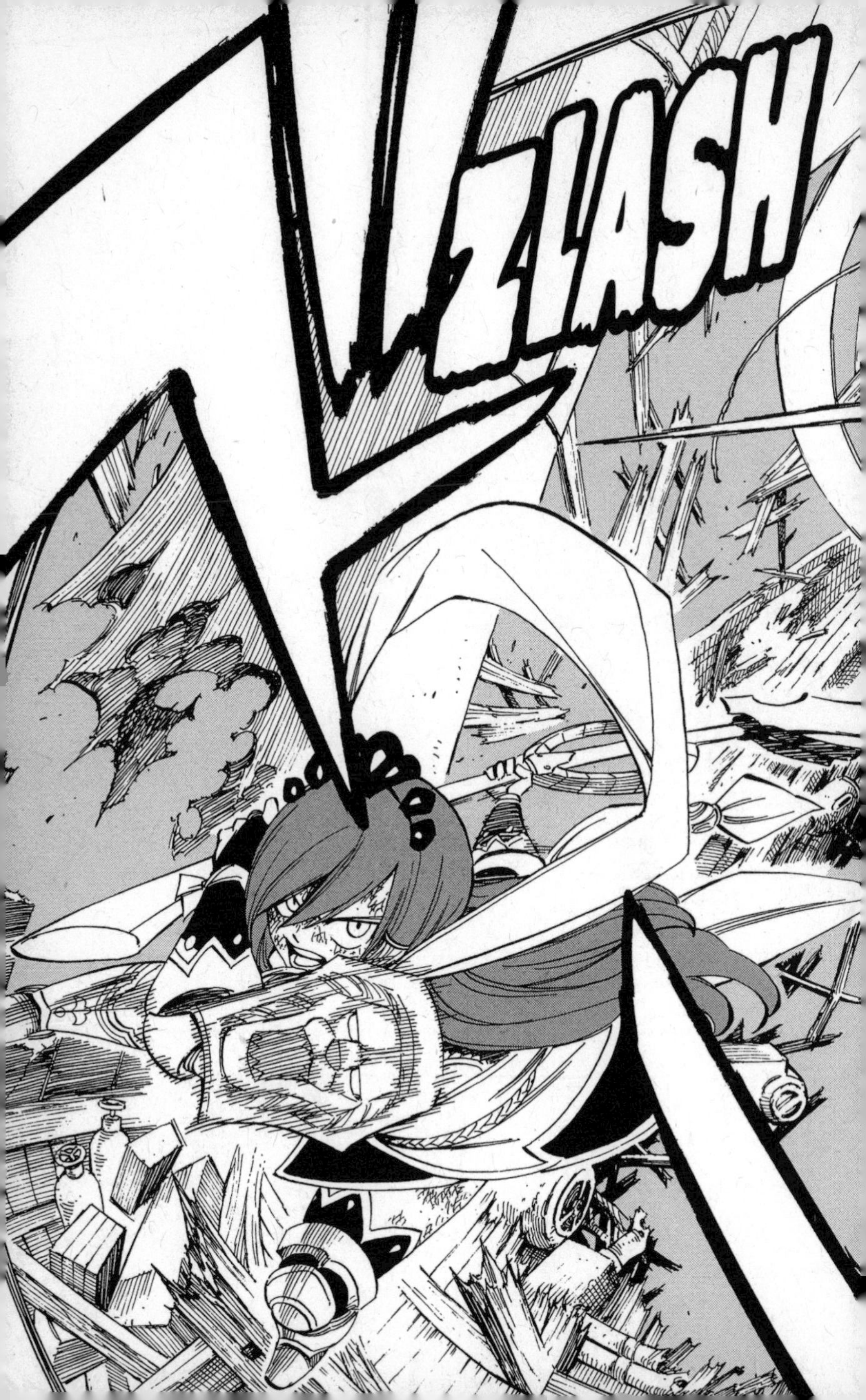
ZLASH

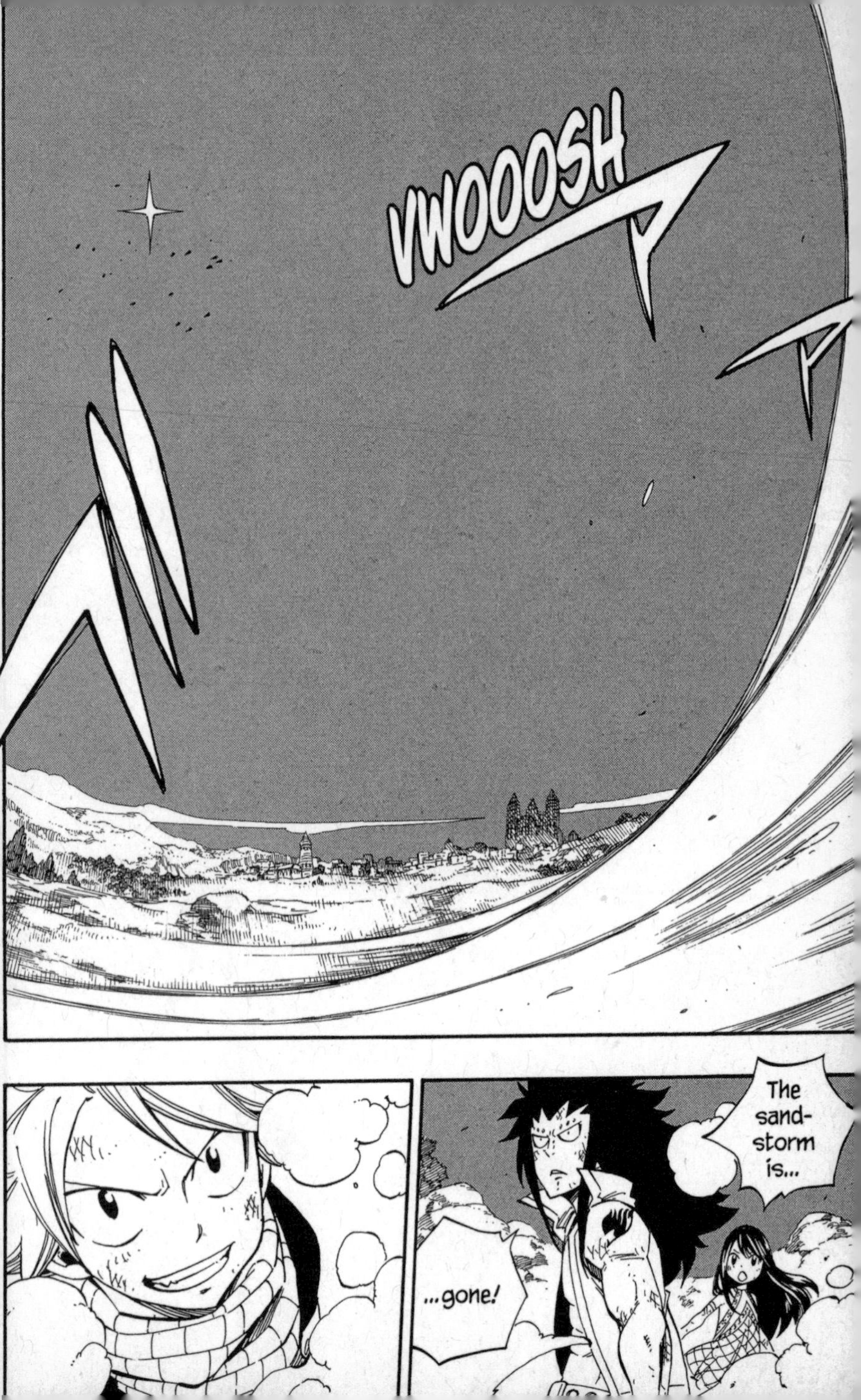
VWOOOSH
The sand-storm is...
...gone!

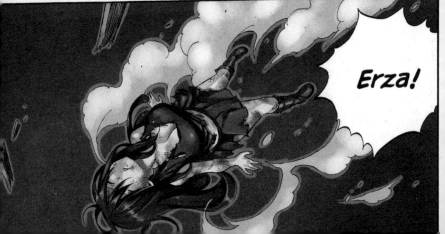

Erza!

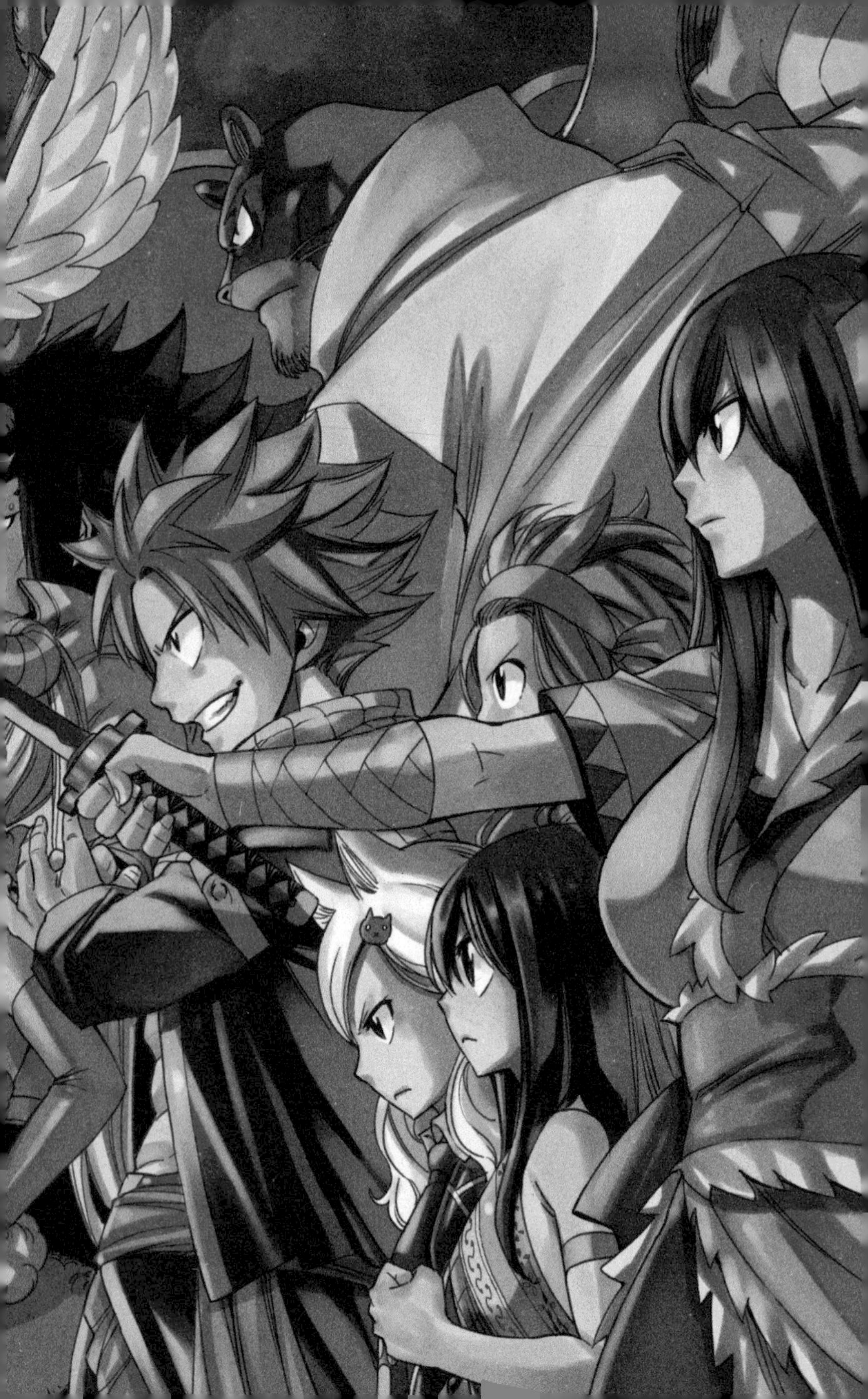

Chapter 459: Weakness

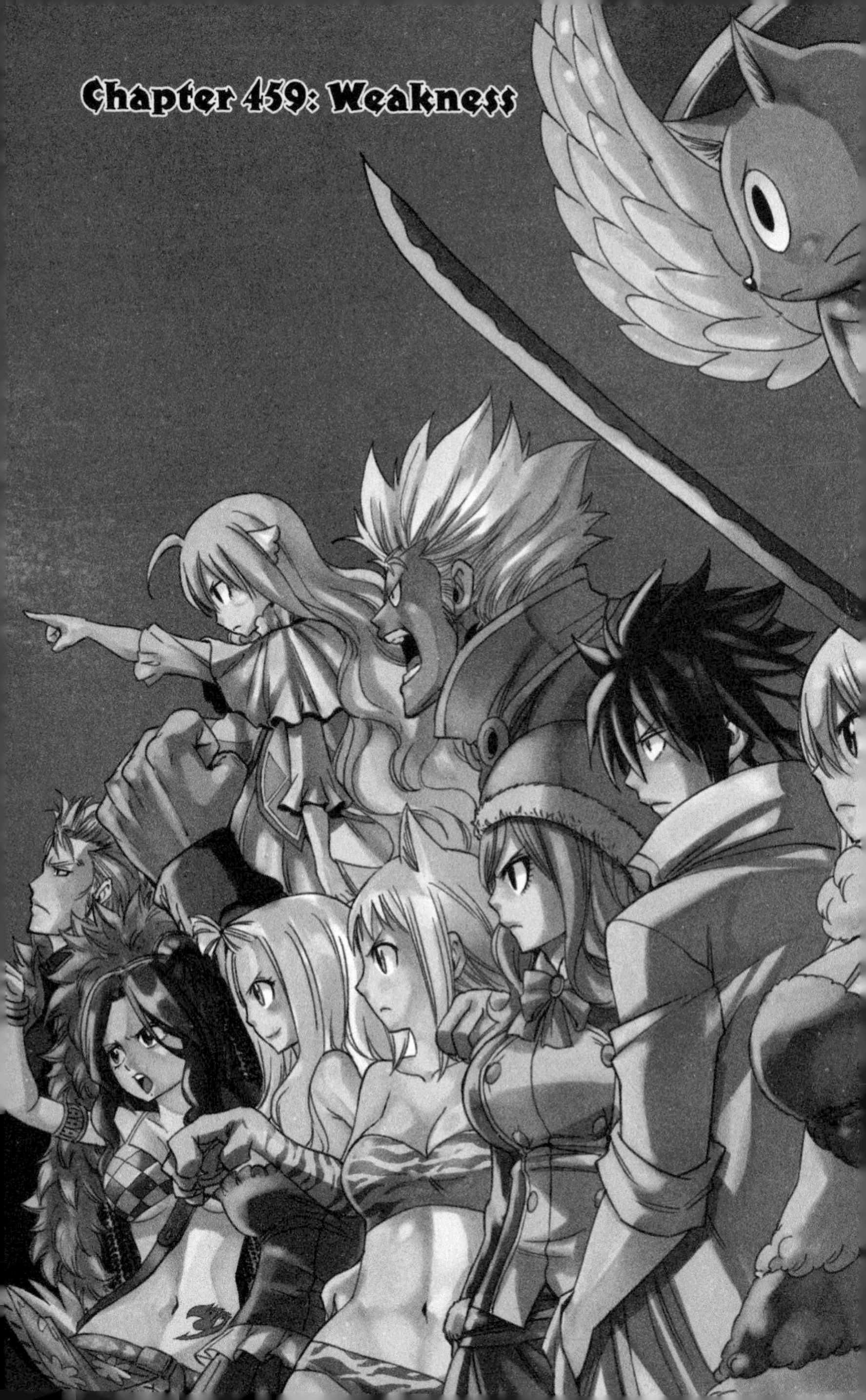

FAIRY TAIL
フェアリーテイル

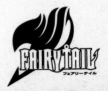

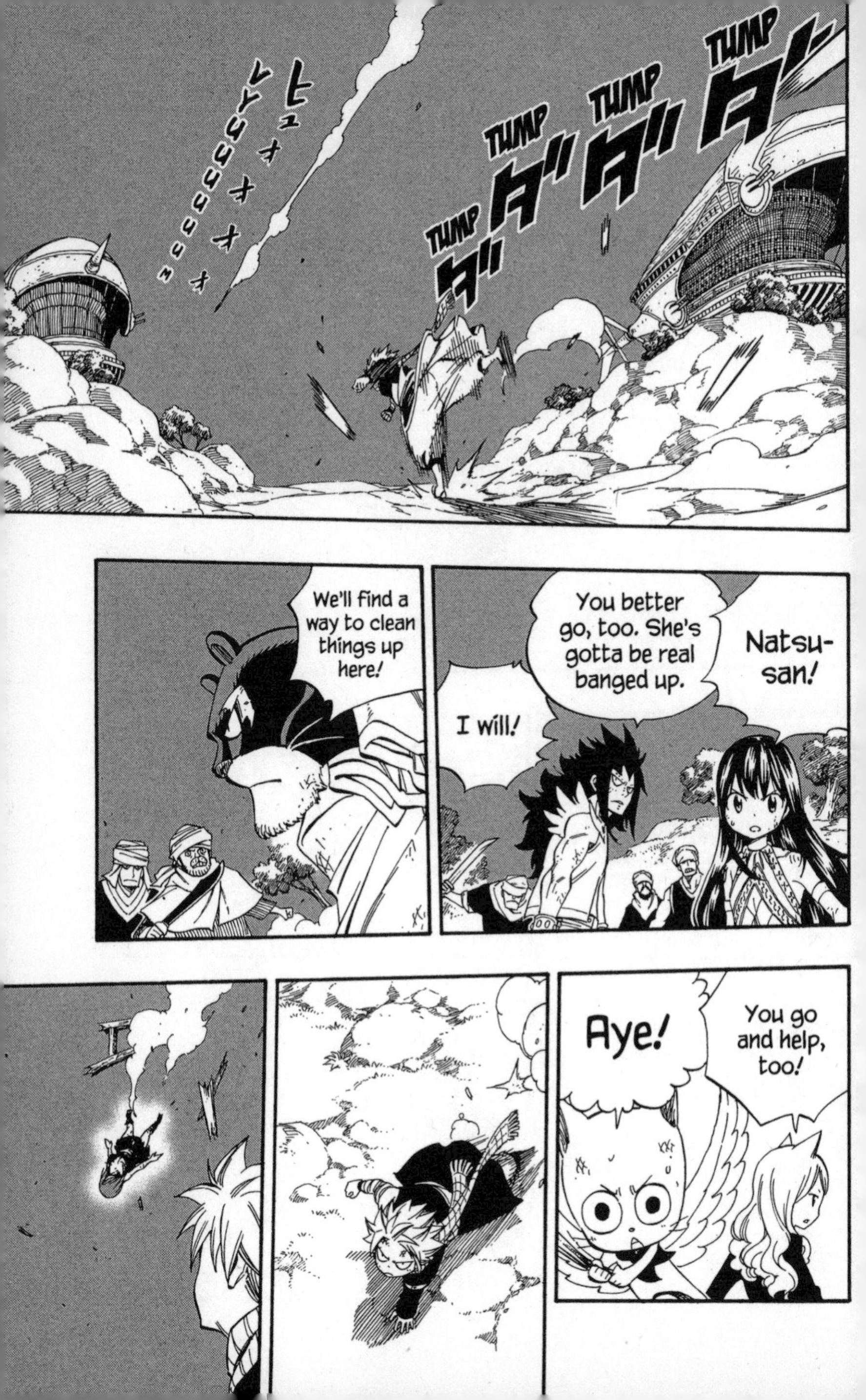
TUMP
ダッ
TUMP
ダッ
TUMP
ダッ
TUMP
ダッ
ヒュオオオオ
HYUUUUUUM
Natsu-san!
You better go, too. She's gotta be real banged up.
I will!
We'll find a way to clean things up here!
You go and help, too!
Aye!

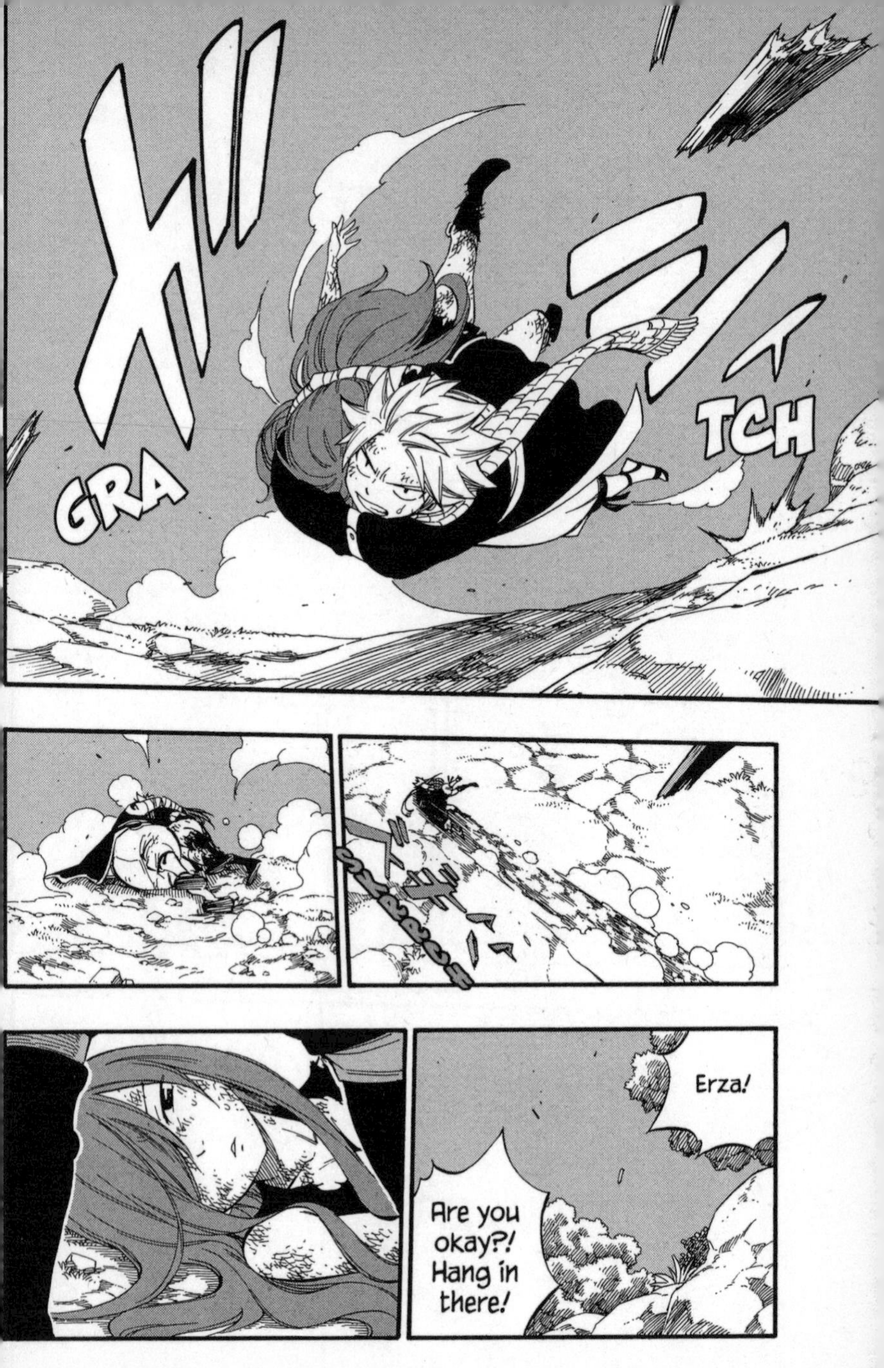
GRA
TCH
SKRRCH
Erza!
Are you okay?! Hang in there!

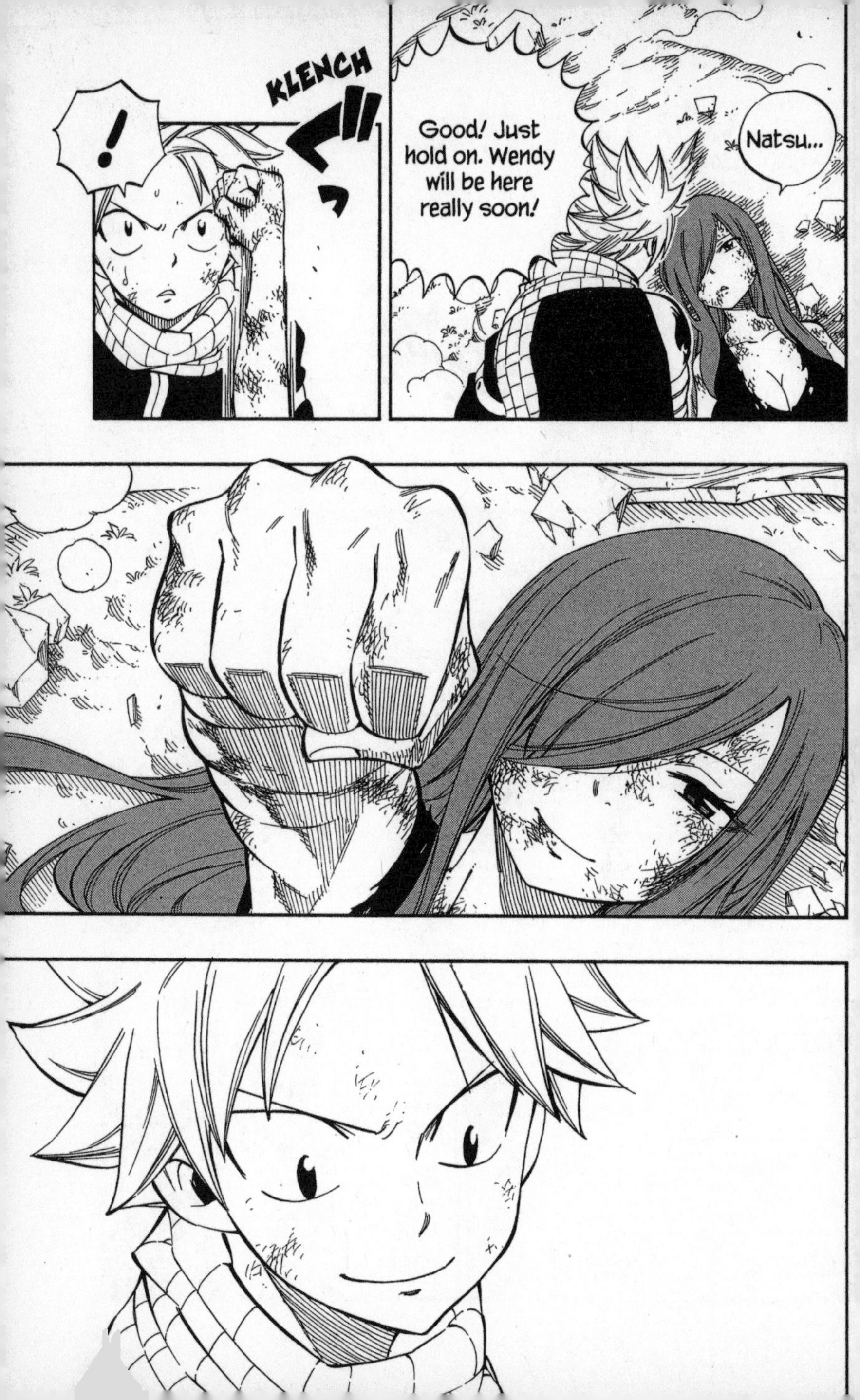
Natsu...
Good! Just hold on. Wendy will be here really soon!
!
KLENCH

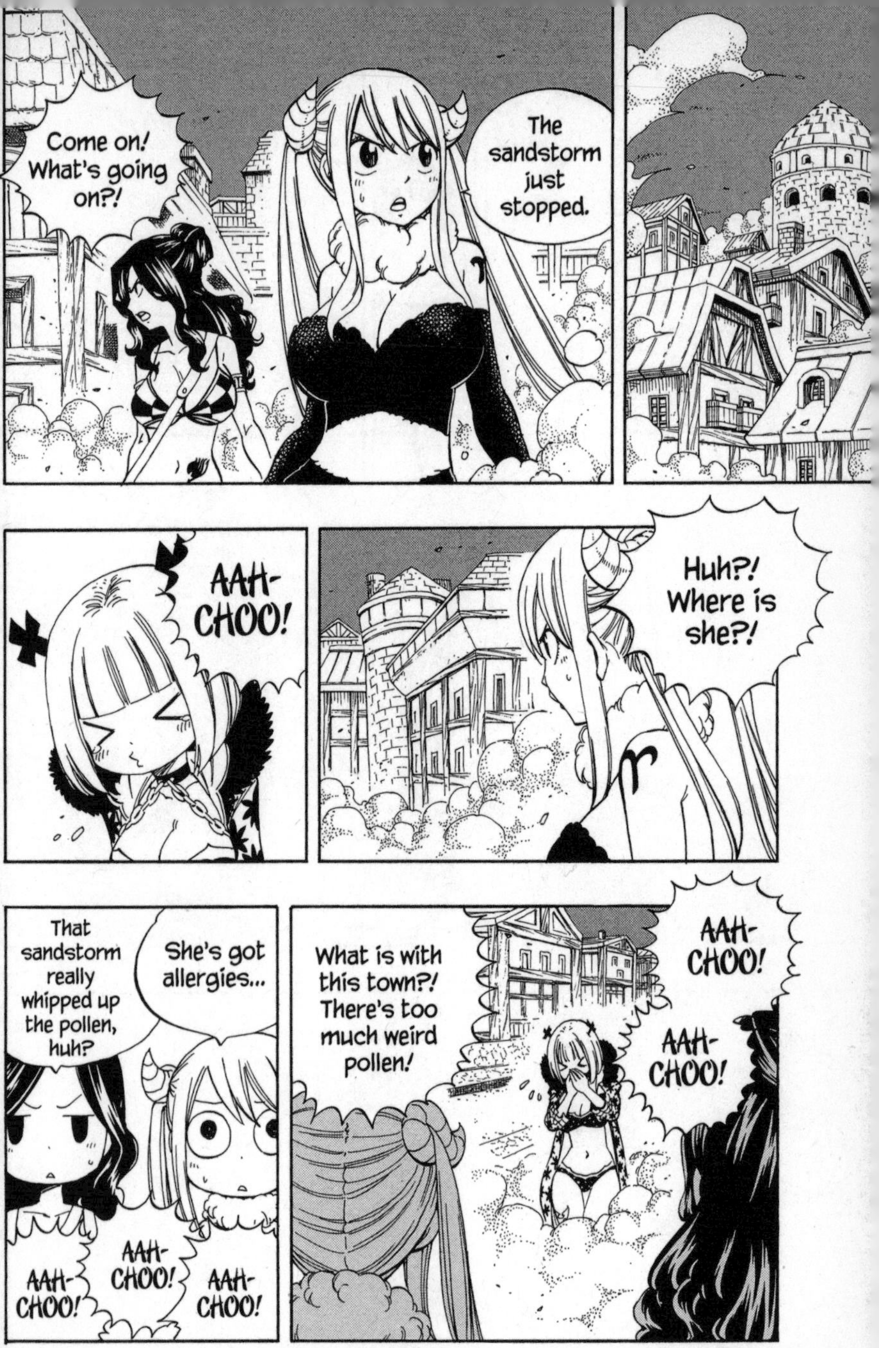
The sandstorm just stopped.
Come on! What's going on?!
Huh?! Where is she?!
AAH-CHOO!
AAH-CHOO!
AAH-CHOO!
What is with this town?! There's too much weird pollen!
She's got allergies...
That sandstorm really whipped up the pollen, huh?
AAH-CHOO!
AAH-CHOO!
AAH-CHOO!

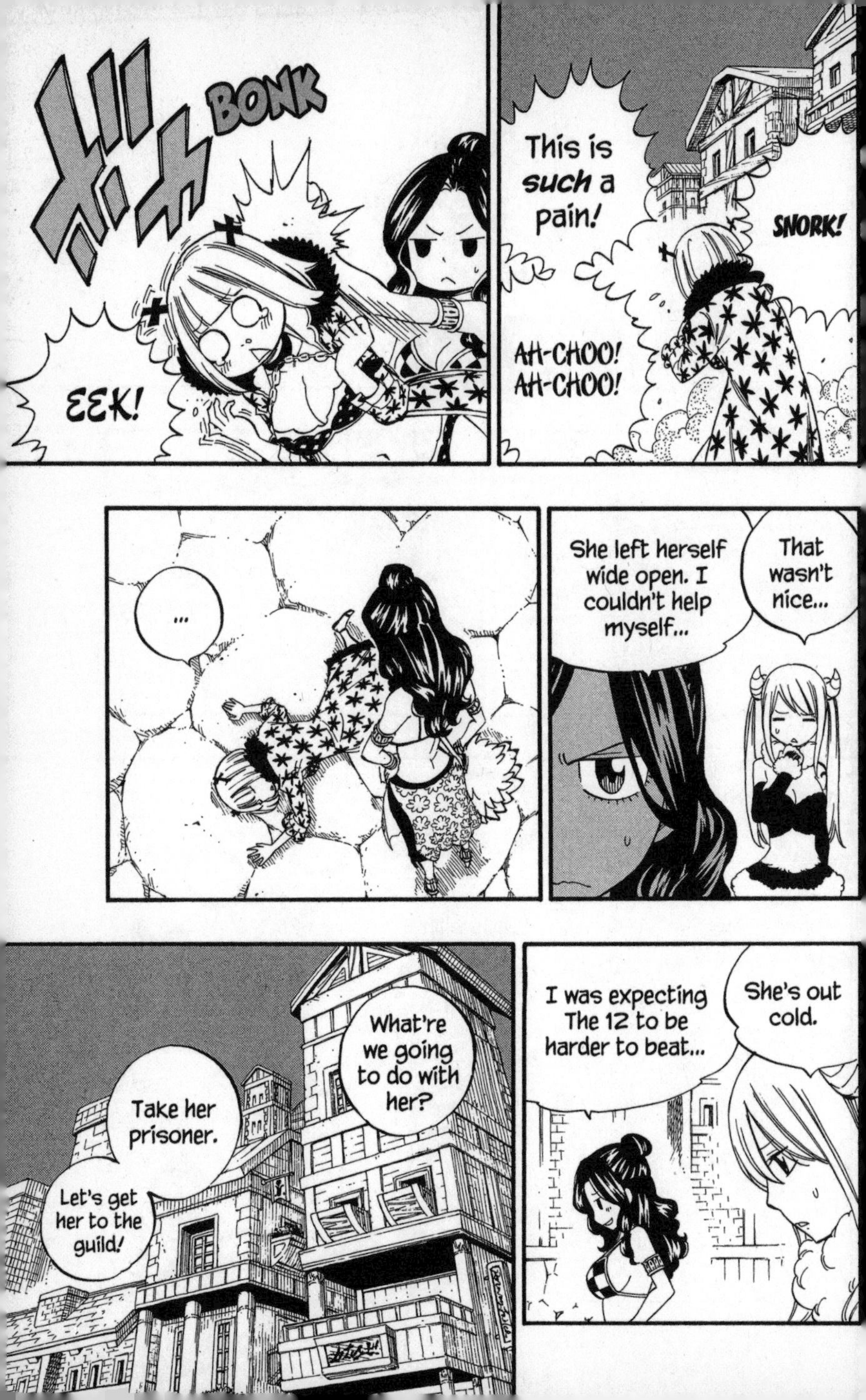
This is *such* a pain!
SNORK!
AH-CHOO! AH-CHOO!
BONK
EEK!
That wasn't nice...
She left herself wide open. I couldn't help myself...
...
She's out cold.
I was expecting The 12 to be harder to beat...
What're we going to do with her?
Take her prisoner.
Let's get her to the guild!

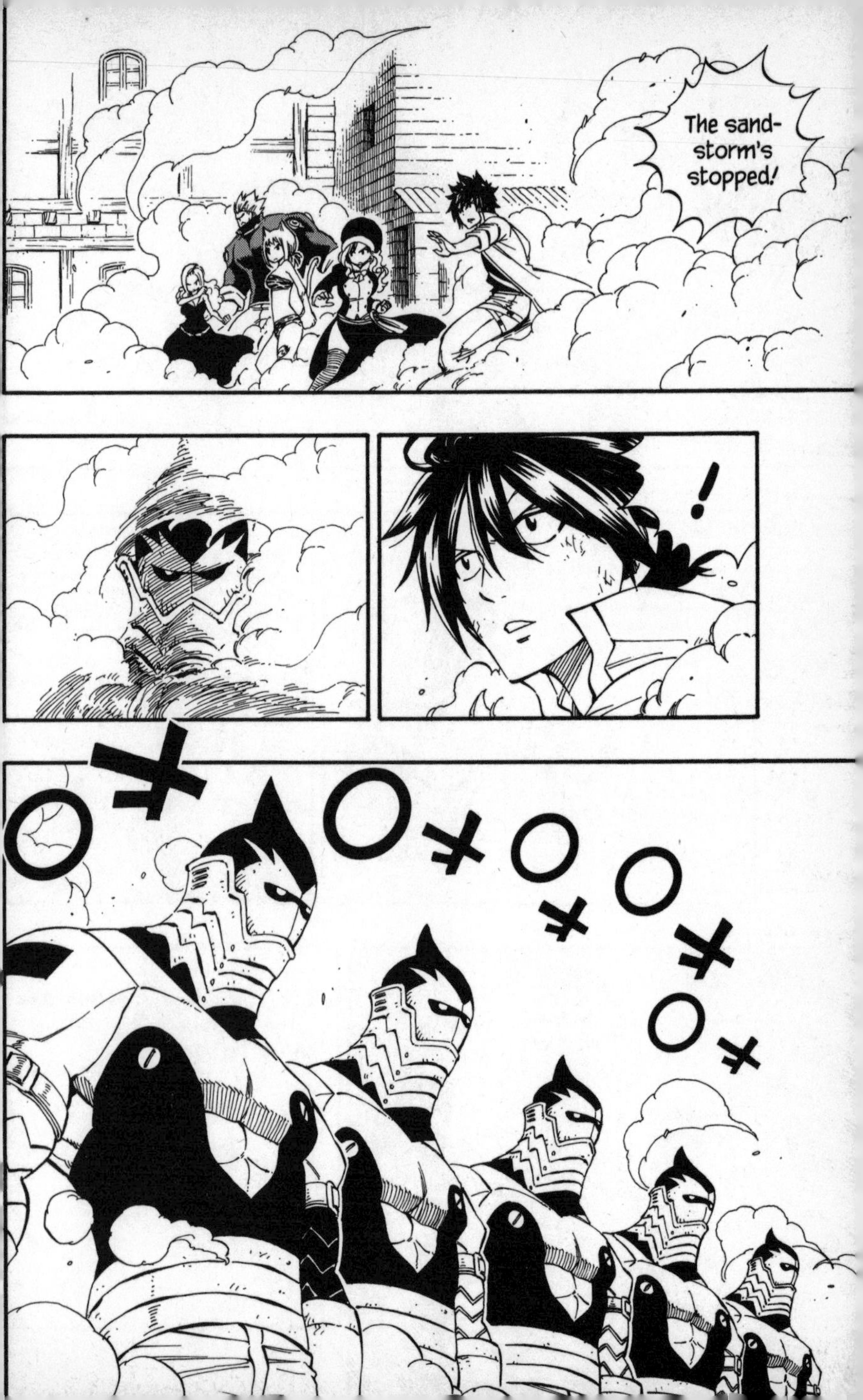
The sand-storm's stopped!
!

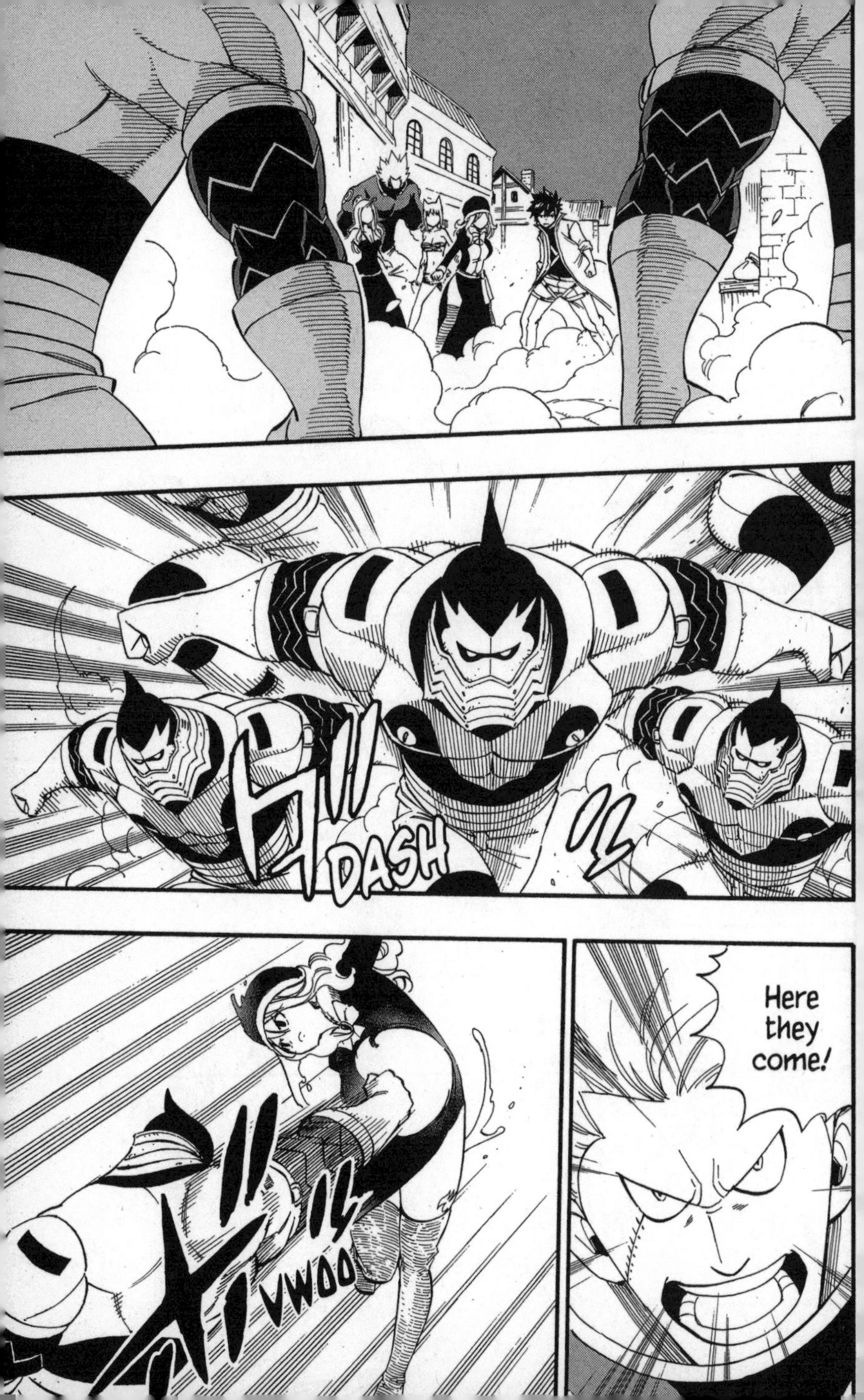
DASH
Here they come!
VWOO

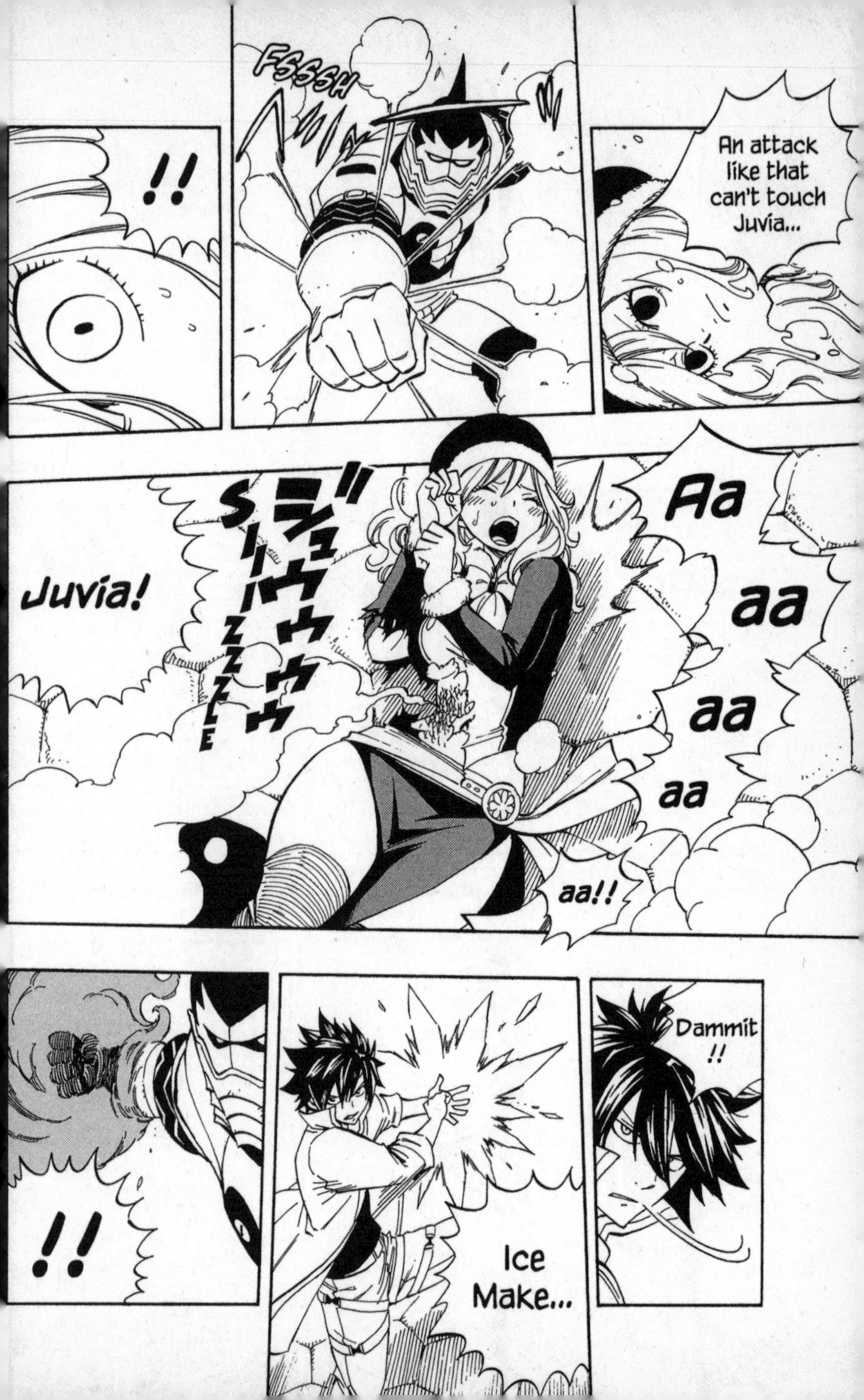

An attack like that can't touch Juvia...
FSSSH
!!
Aa aa aa aa aa!!
SIZZZZLE
Juvia!
Dammit !!
Ice Make...
!!

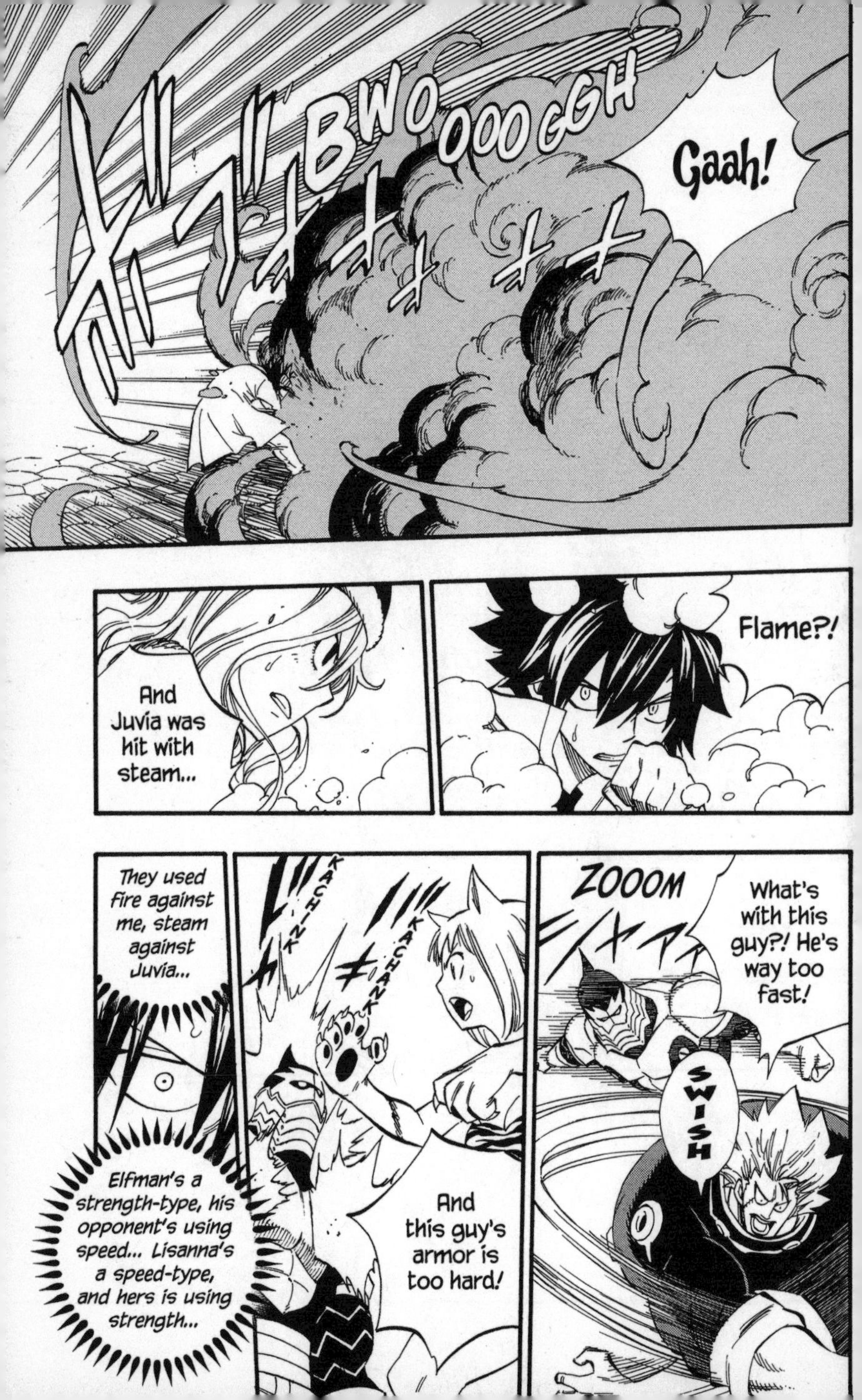
BWOOOOGGH
Gaah!
Flame?!
And Juvia was hit with steam...
ZOOOM
What's with this guy?! He's way too fast!
SWISH
KACHINK
KACHANK
And this guy's armor is too hard!
They used fire against me, steam against Juvia...
Elfman's a strength-type, his opponent's using speed... Lisanna's a speed-type, and hers is using strength...

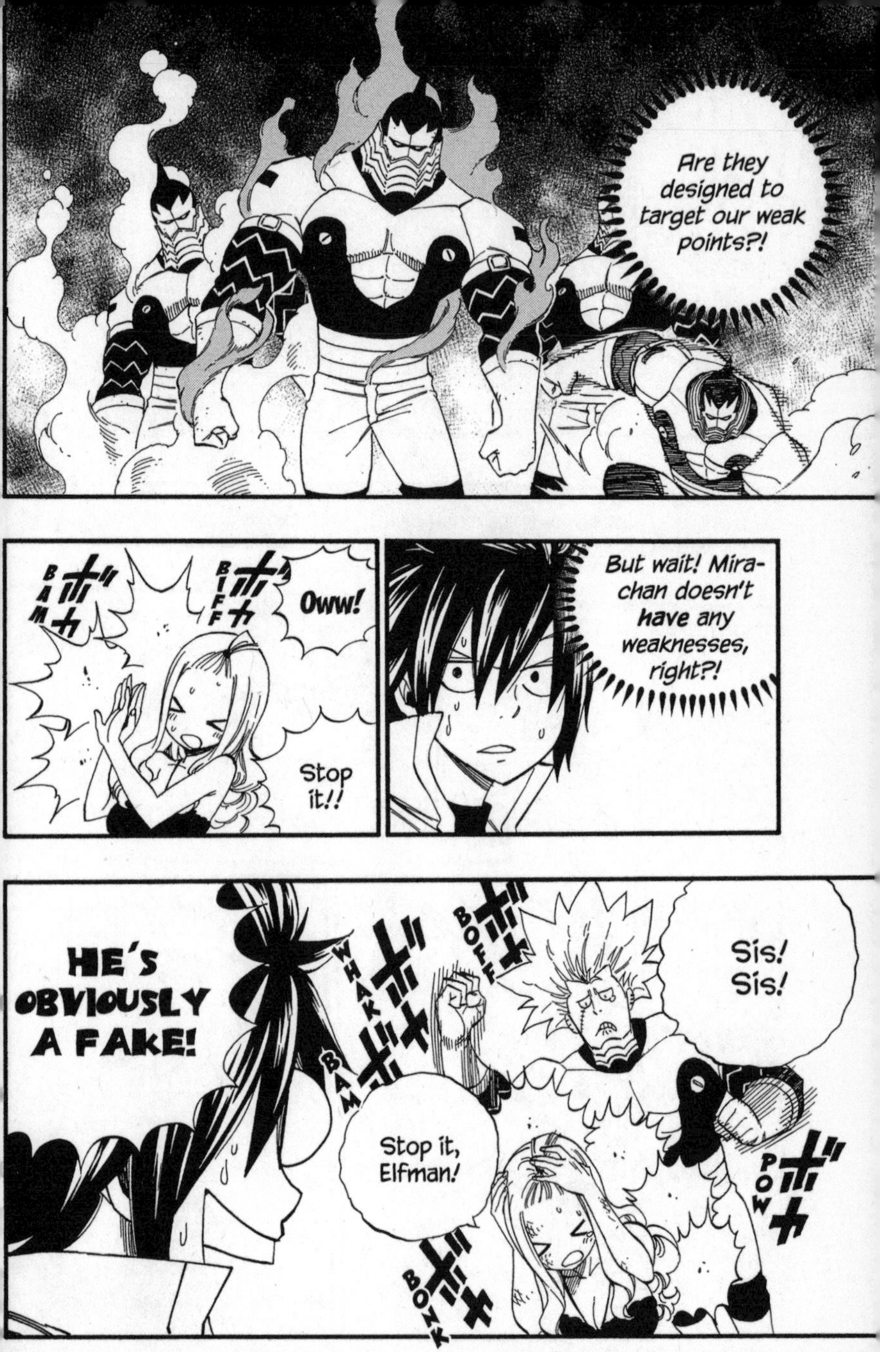
Are they designed to target our weak points?!
But wait! Mira-chan doesn't have any weaknesses, right?!
Oww!
BIFF
BAM
Stop it!!
Sis! Sis!
BOFF
WHAK
BAM
HE'S OBVIOUSLY A FAKE!
POW
Stop it, Elfman!
BONK

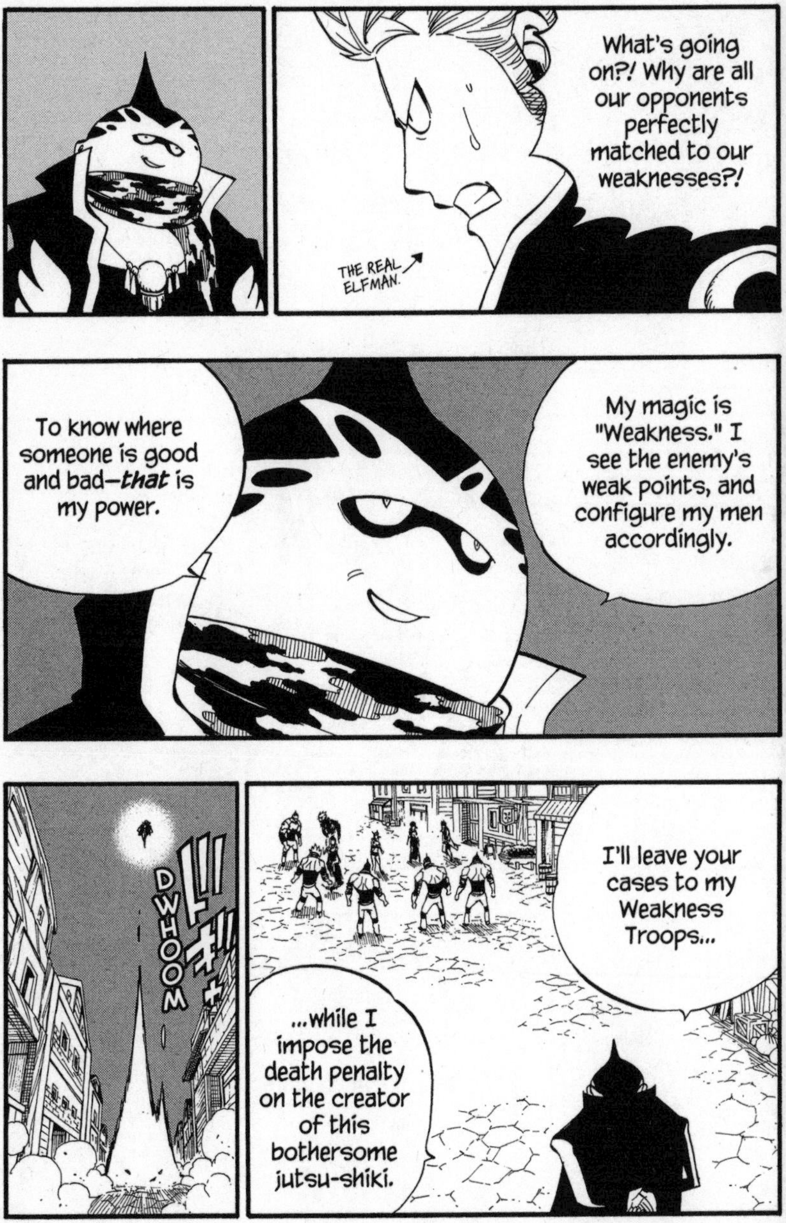
What's going on?! Why are all our opponents perfectly matched to our weaknesses?!
THE REAL ELFMAN.
My magic is "Weakness." I see the enemy's weak points, and configure my men accordingly.
To know where someone is good and bad—*that* is my power.
I'll leave your cases to my Weakness Troops...
...while I impose the death penalty on the creator of this bothersome jutsu-shiki.
DWHOOM

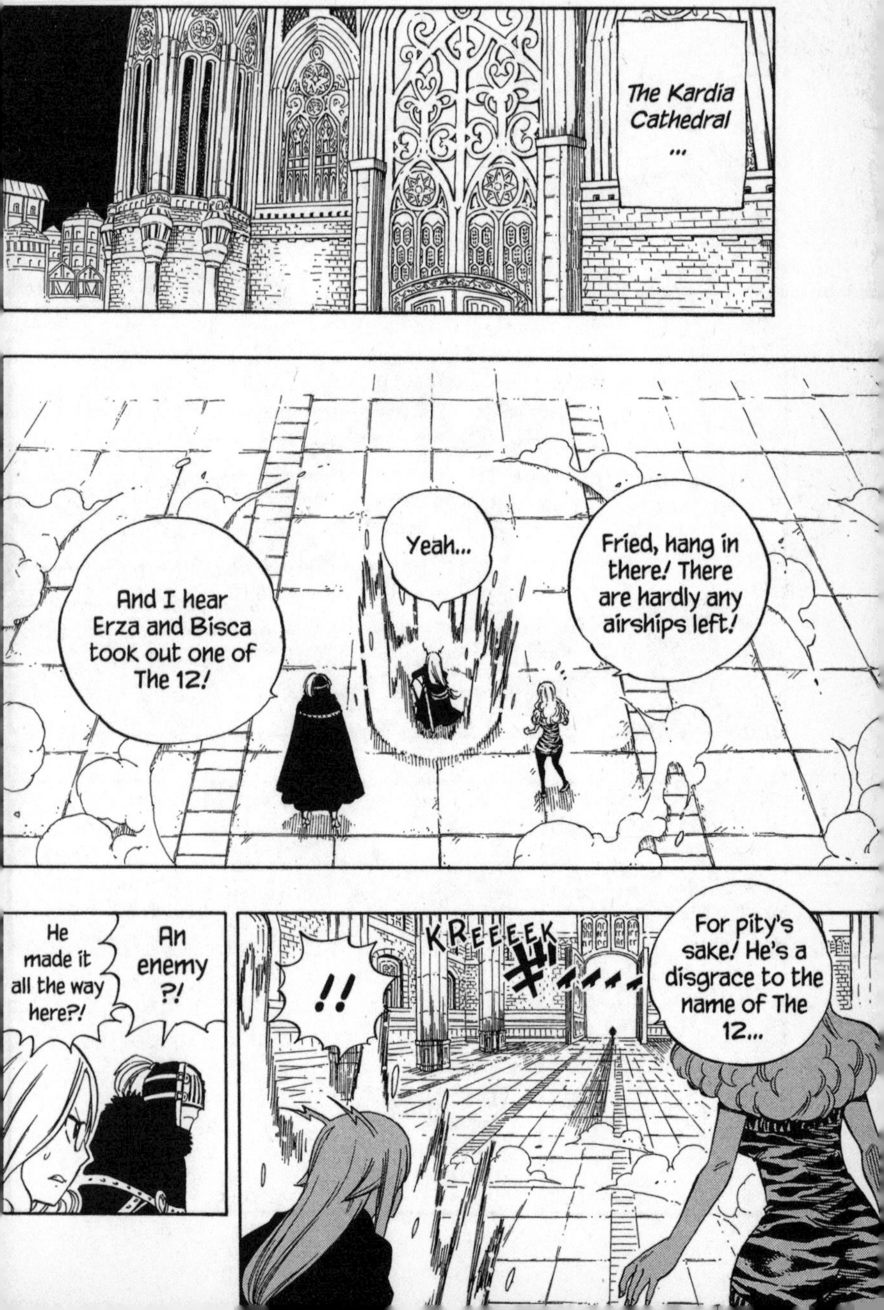
The Kardia Cathedral ...
Fried, hang in there! There are hardly any airships left!
Yeah...
And I hear Erza and Bisca took out one of The 12!
For pity's sake! He's a disgrace to the name of The 12...
KREEEEK
!!
An enemy?!
He made it all the way here?!

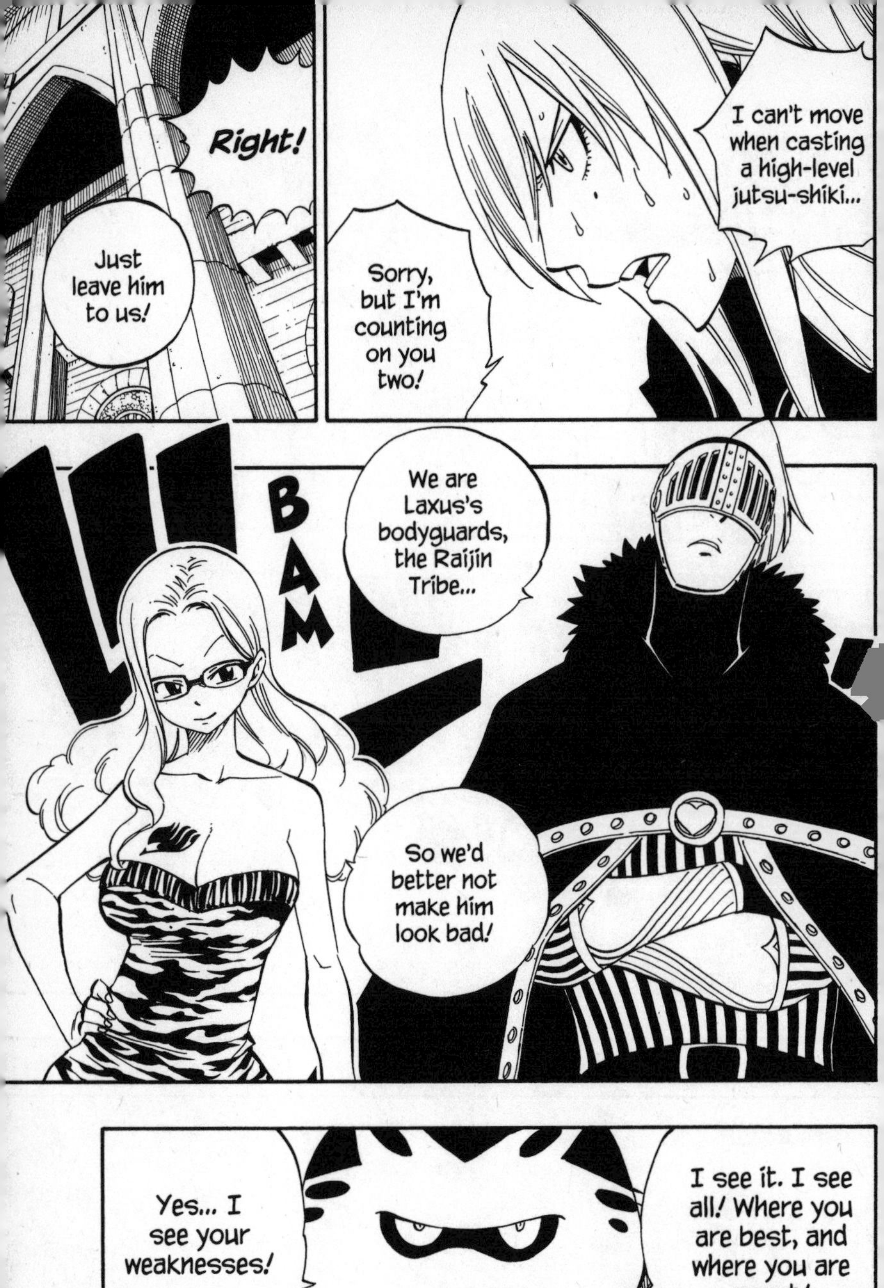
I can't move when casting a high-level jutsu-shiki...
Sorry, but I'm counting on you two!
Right!
Just leave him to us!
We are Laxus's bodyguards, the Raijin Tribe...
BAM
So we'd better not make him look bad!
I see it. I see all! Where you are best, and where you are worst!
Yes... I see your weaknesses!

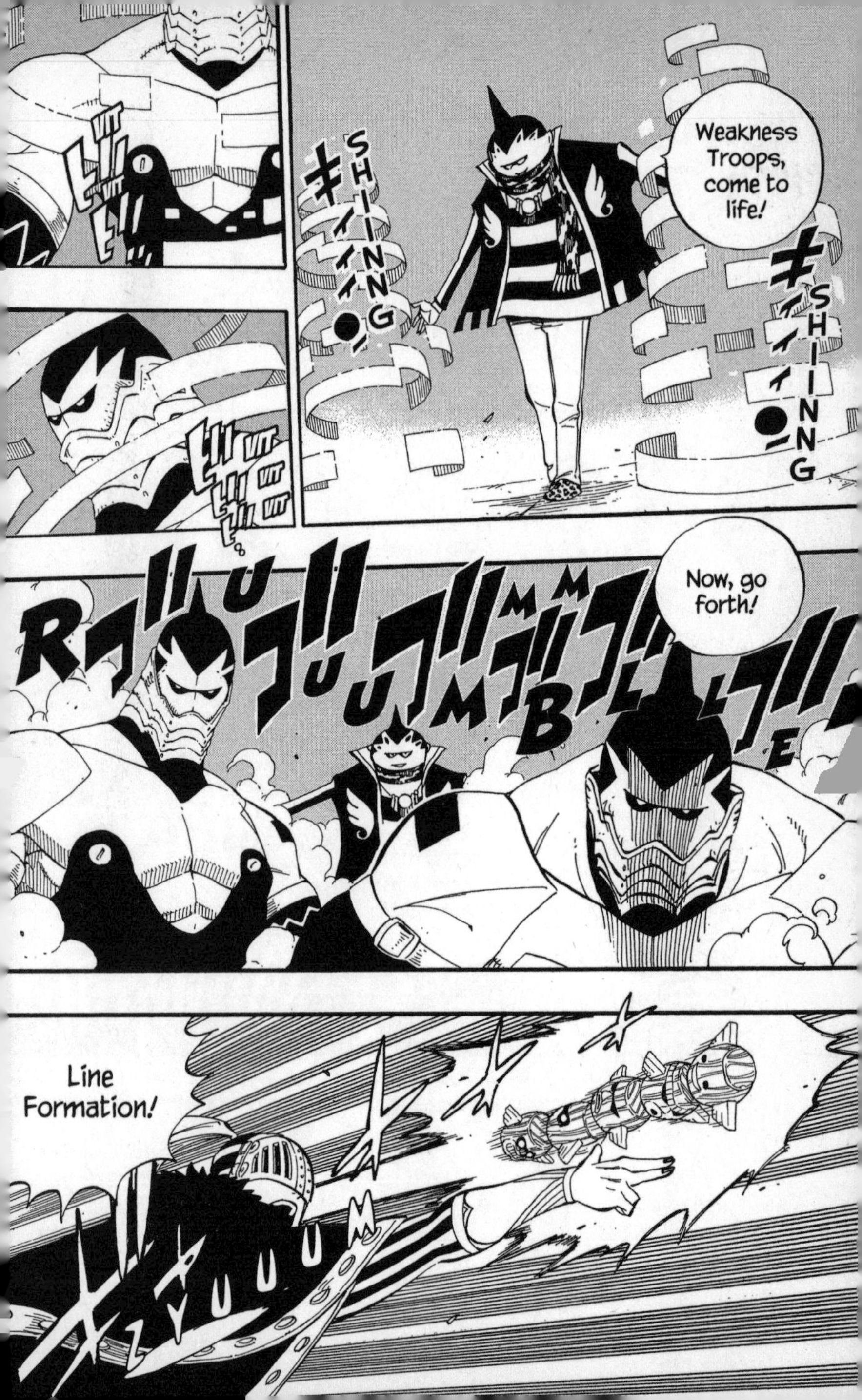
Weakness Troops, come to life!
SHIIING
SHIIING
VIT
VIT
Now, go forth!
Line Formation!
ZYUUUUM

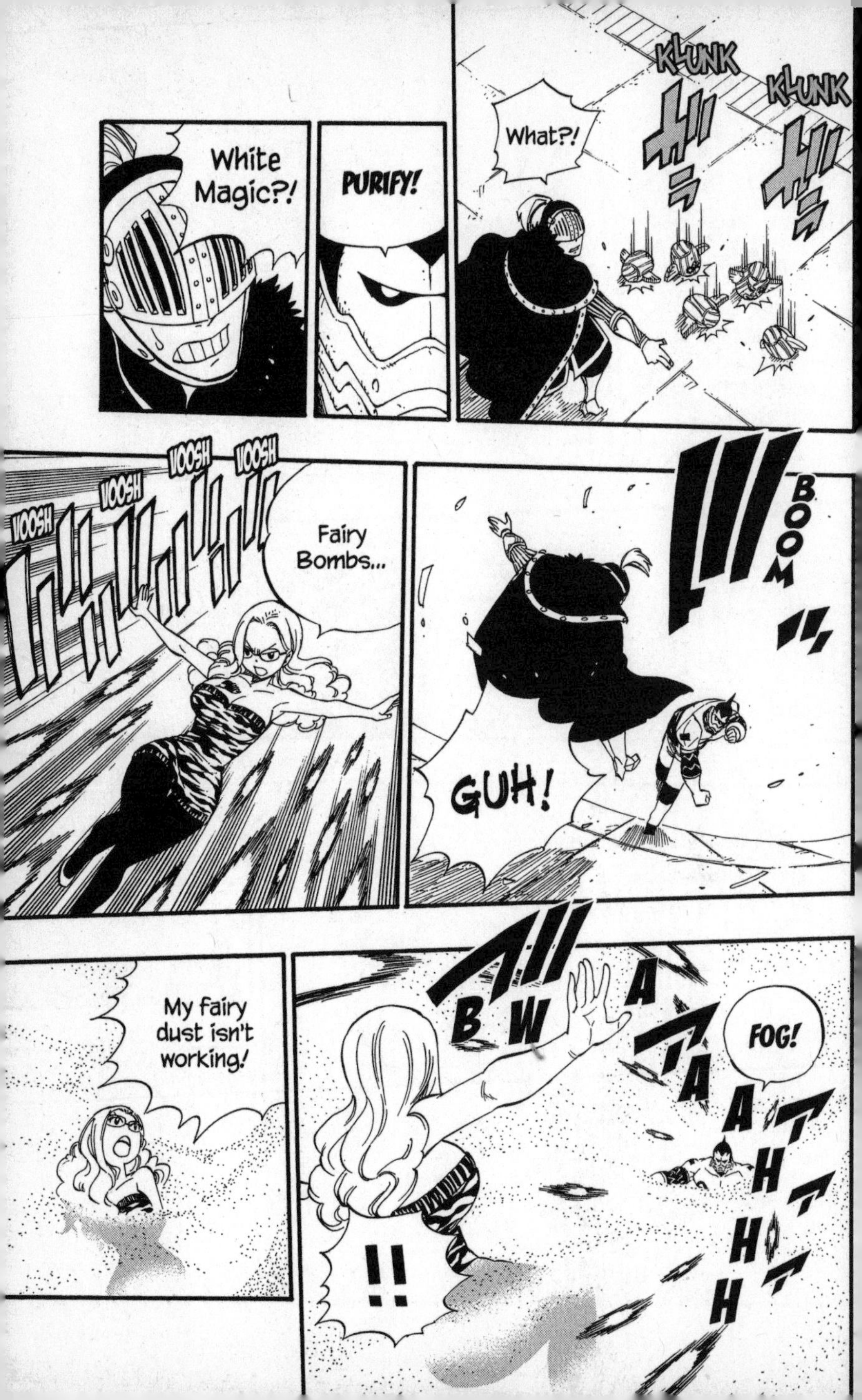
KLUNK
KLUNK
What?!
PURIFY!
White Magic?!
BOOM
GUH!
VOOSH
VOOSH
VOOSH
VOOSH
Fairy Bombs...
FOG!
BWAAAHHH
!!
My fairy dust isn't working!

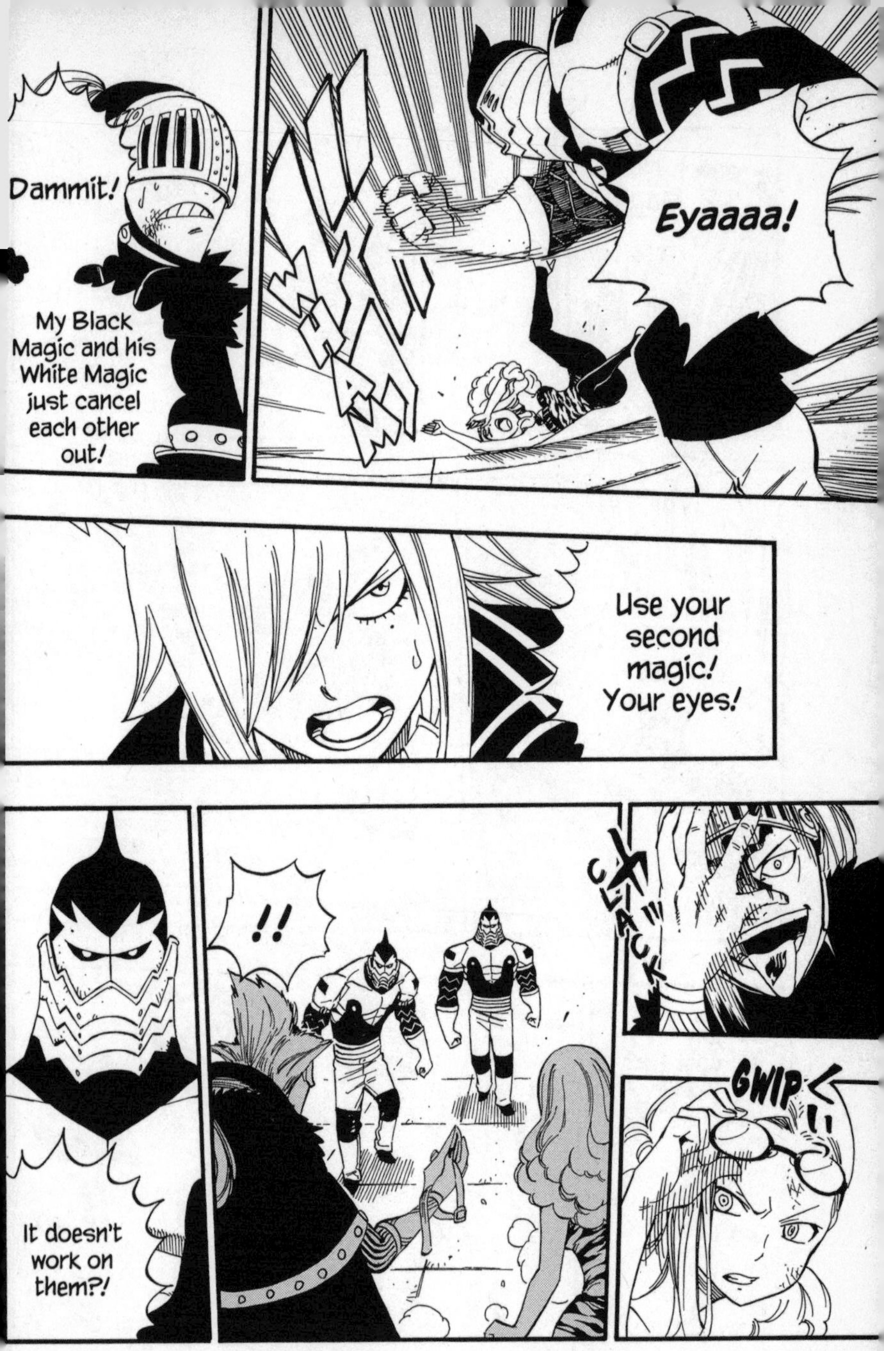

Eyaaaa!
Dammit!
My Black Magic and his White Magic just cancel each other out!
Use your second magic! Your eyes!
CLACK
GWIP
!!
It doesn't work on them?!

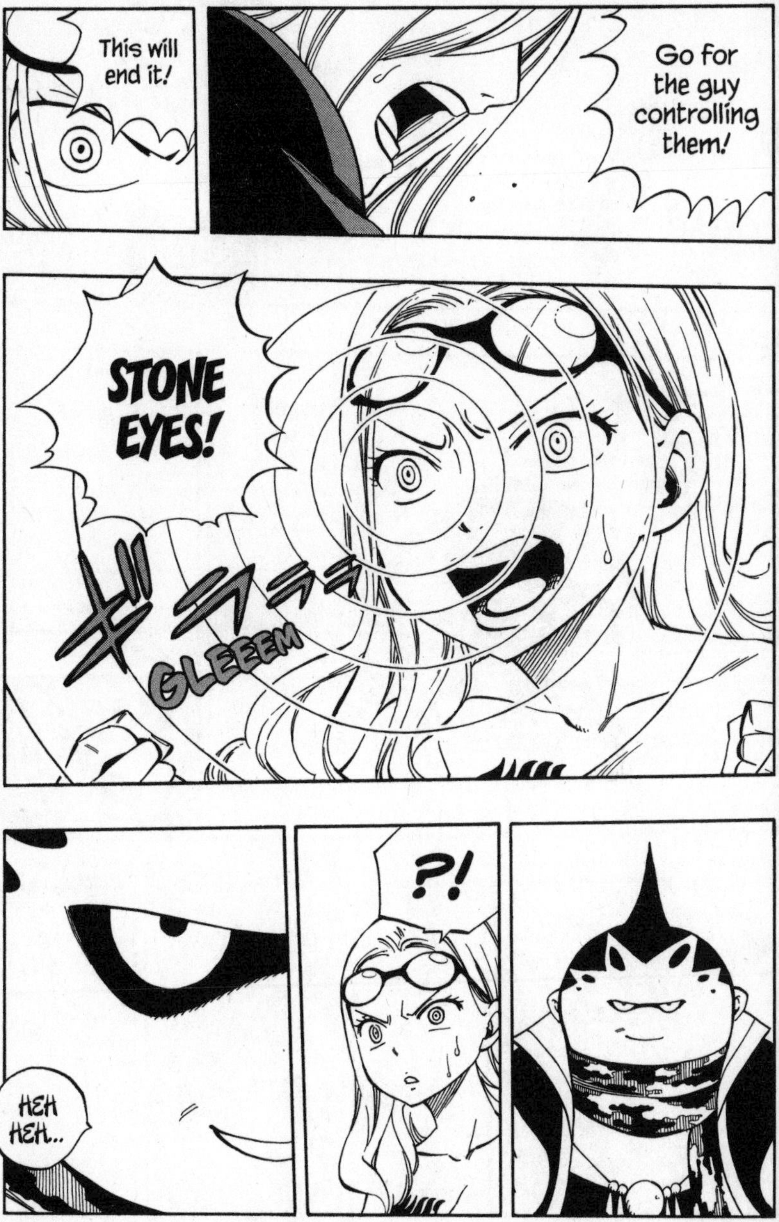
Go for the guy controlling them!
This will end it!
STONE EYES!
GLEEEM
?!
HEH HEH...

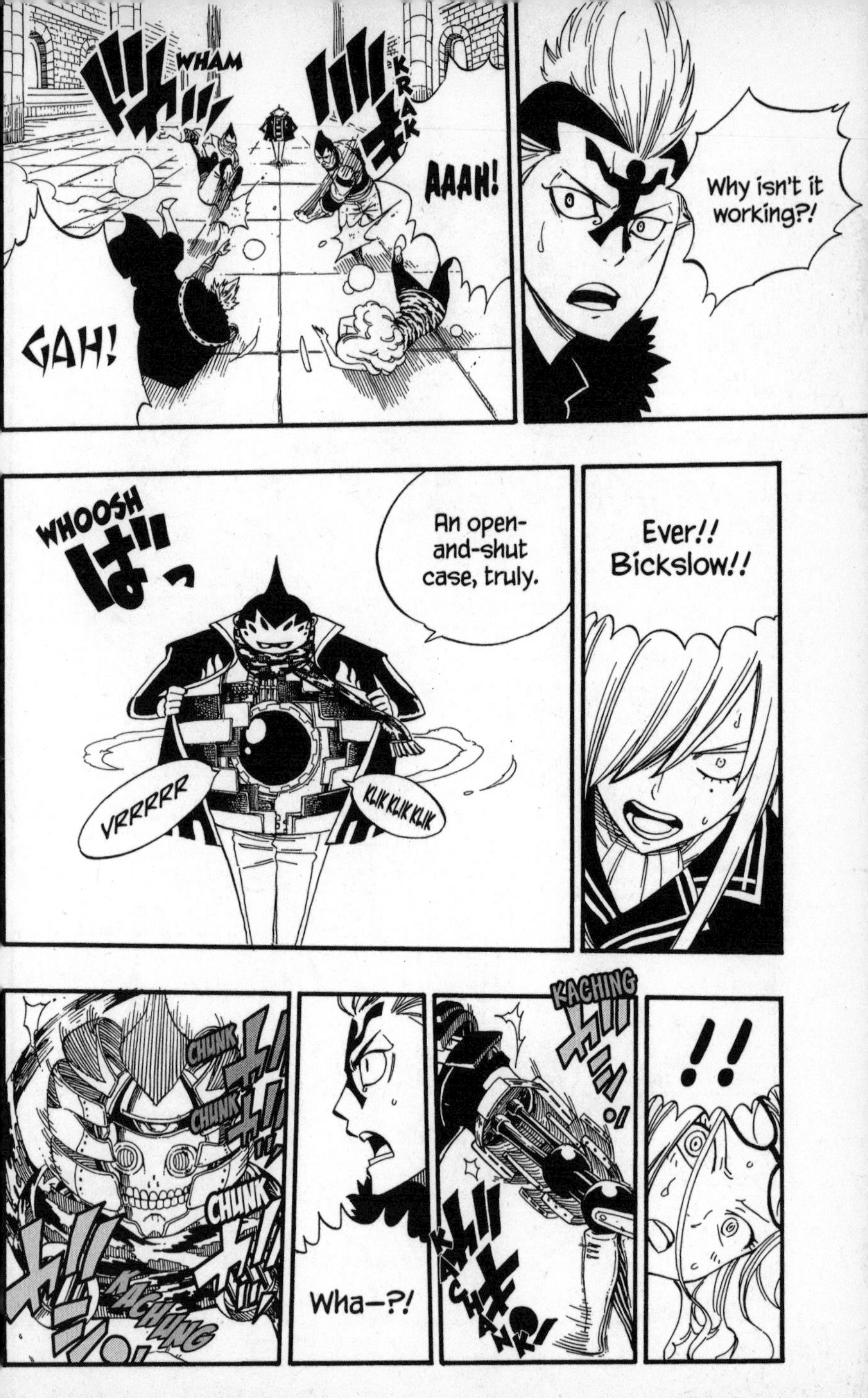
Why isn't it working?!
KRAK
WHAM
AAAH!
GAH!
Ever!! Bickslow!!
An open-and-shut case, truly.
WHOOSH
ばっ
KLIK KLIK KLIK
VRRRRR
!!
KACHING
KACHANK!
Wha—?!
CHUNK
CHUNK
CHUNK
KACHUNG

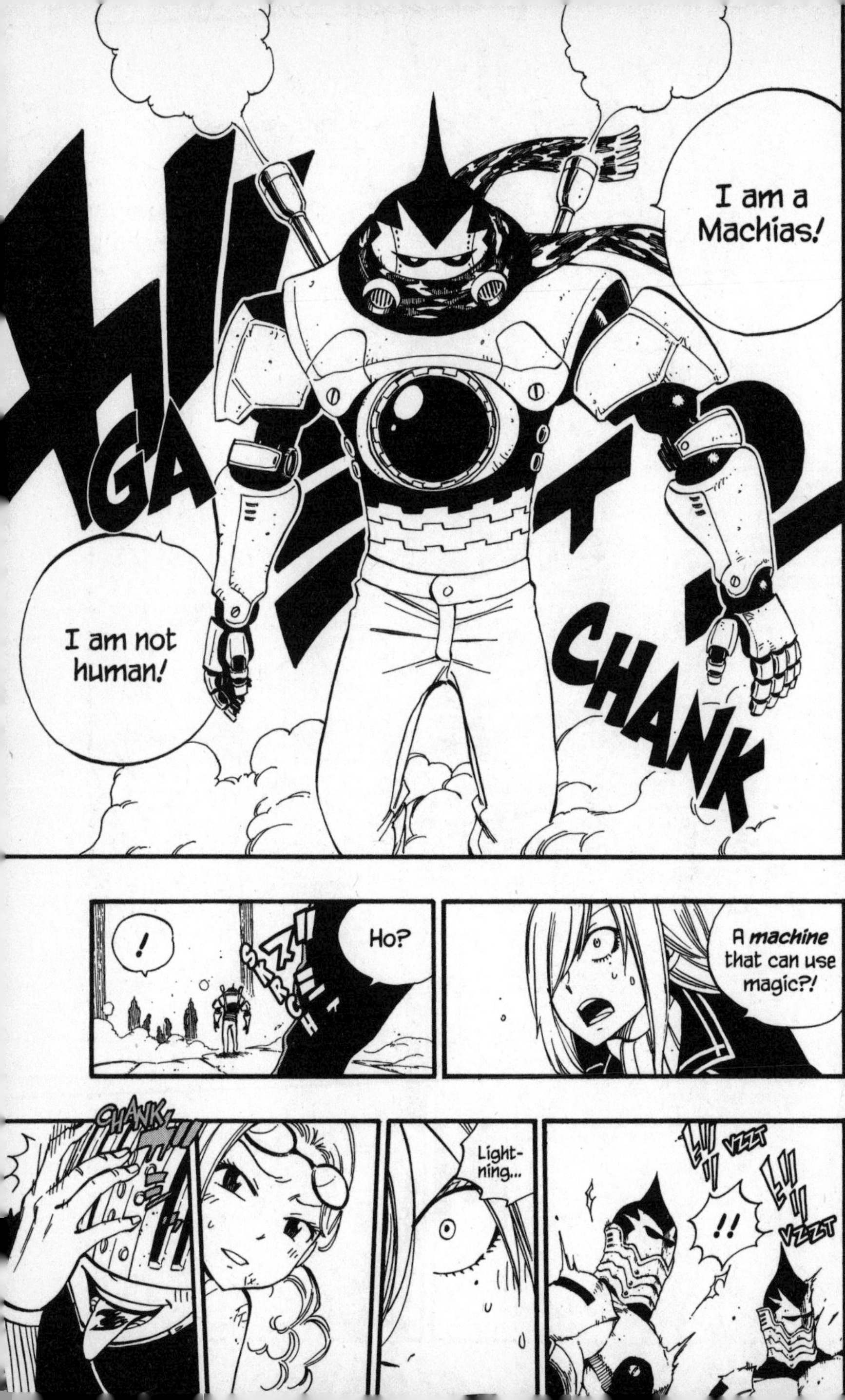

I am a Machias!
GA
CHANK
I am not human!
A *machine* that can use magic?!
Ho?
SKRCH
!
VZZT
!!
VZZT
Light-ning...
CHANK

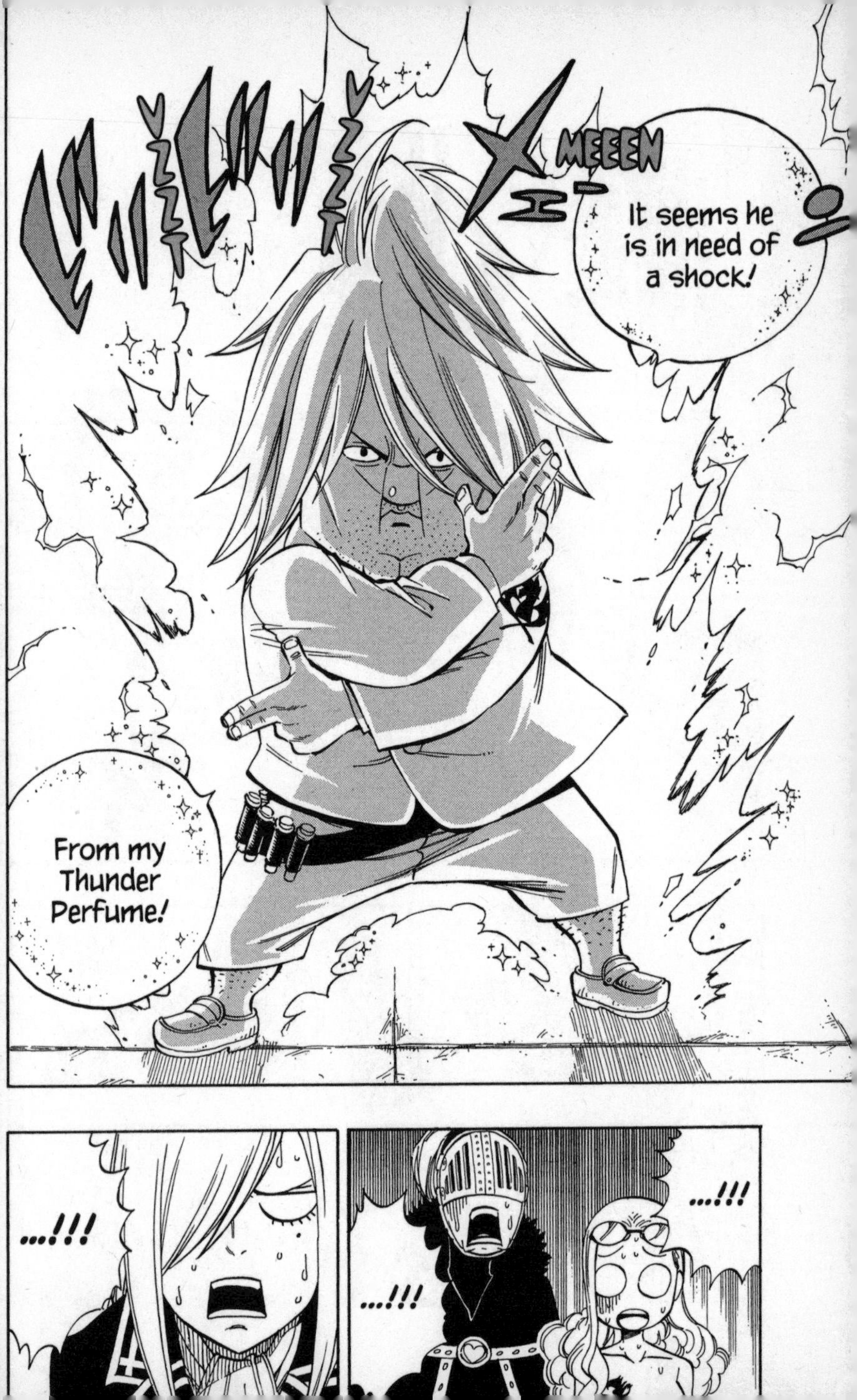
MEEEN
VZZZT
VZZZT
It seems he is in need of a shock!
From my Thunder Perfume!
...!!!
...!!!
...!!!

FAIRY TAIL
フェアリーテイル

Chapter 460: The Pegasus That Came to Earth

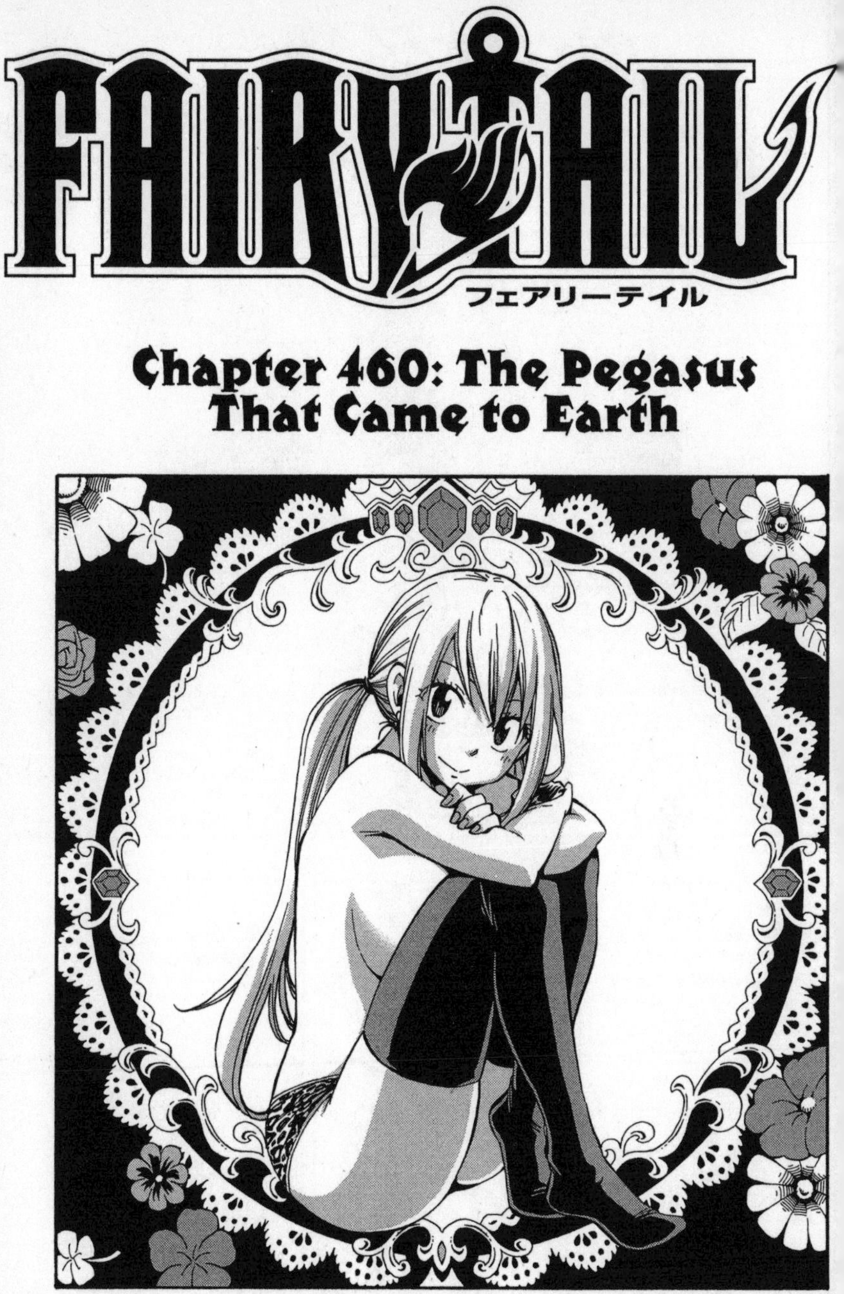

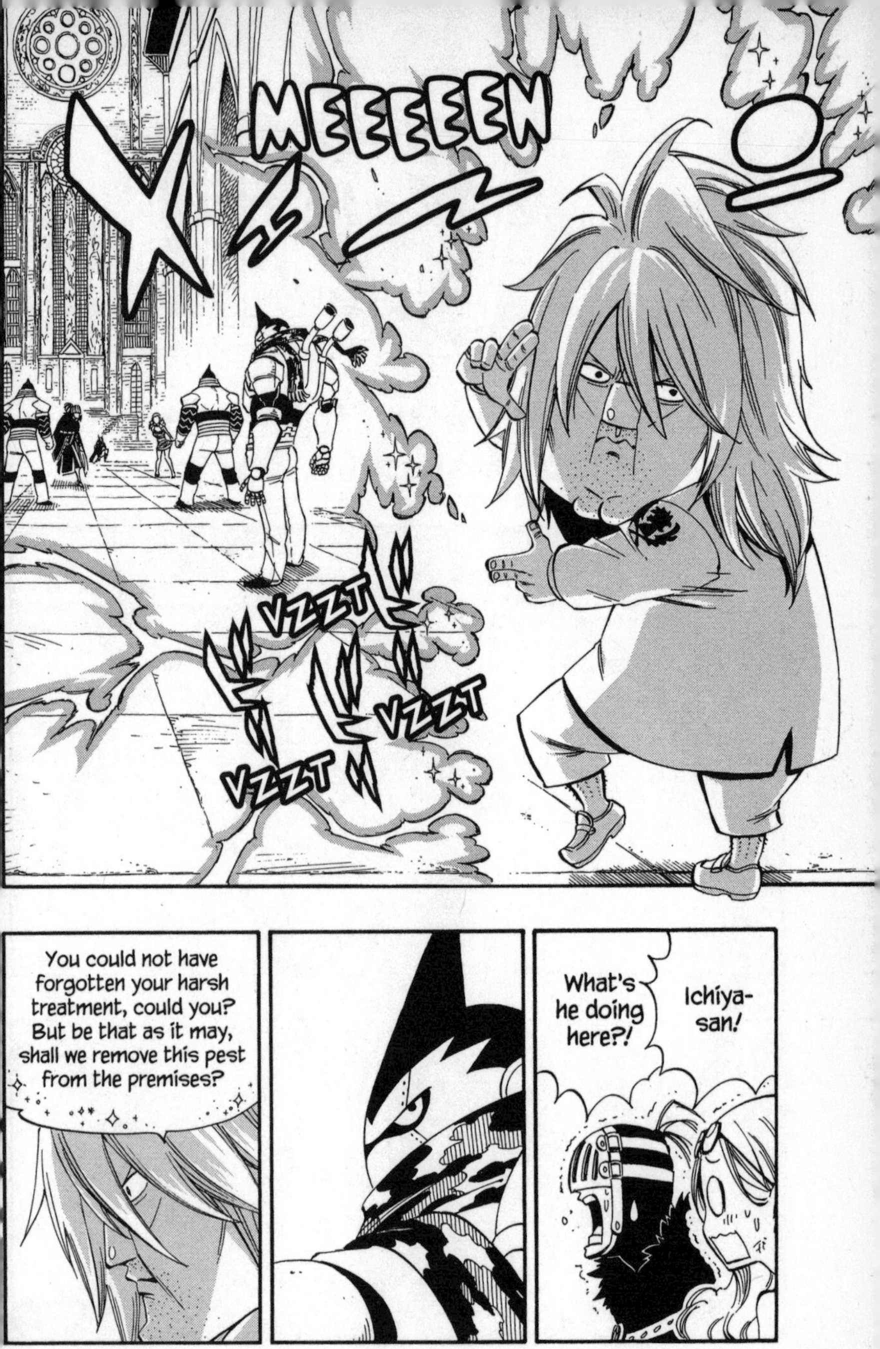
MEEEEEN
VZZT
VZZT
VZZT
Ichiya-san!
What's he doing here?!
You could not have forgotten your harsh treatment, could you? But be that as it may, shall we remove this pest from the premises?

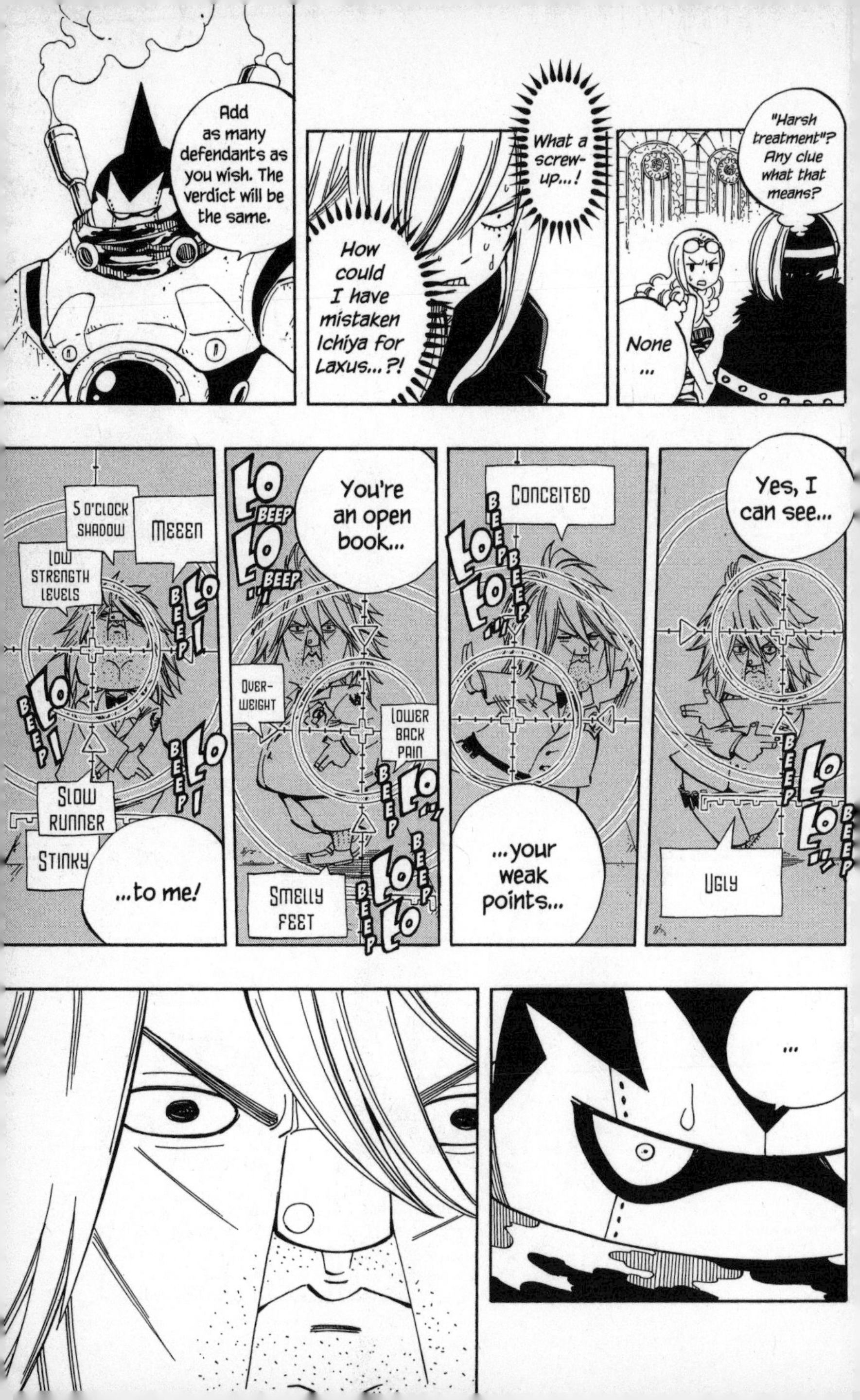
"Harsh treatment"? Any clue what that means?
None...
What a screw-up...!
How could I have mistaken Ichiya for Laxus...?!
Add as many defendants as you wish. The verdict will be the same.
Yes, I can see...
BEEP
BEEP
Ugly
Conceited
BEEP
BEEP
...your weak points...
You're an open book...
BEEP
BEEP
Overweight
Lower back pain
BEEP
BEEP
BEEP
Smelly feet
5 o'clock shadow
Meeen
Low strength levels
BEEP
BEEP
BEEP
Slow runner
Stinky
...to me!
...

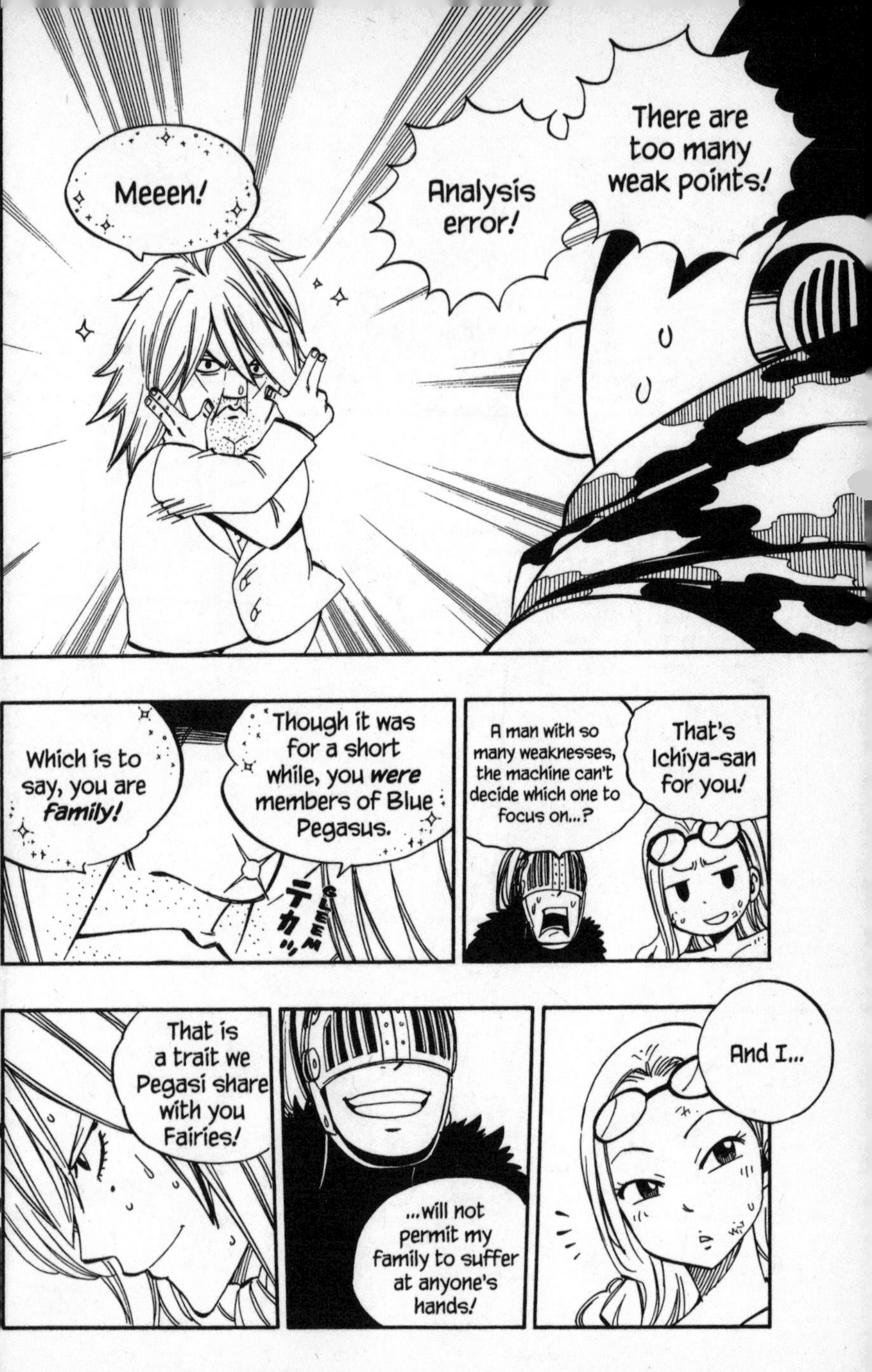
There are too many weak points!
Analysis error!
Meeen!
That's Ichiya-san for you!
A man with so many weaknesses, the machine can't decide which one to focus on...?
Though it was for a short while, you *were* members of Blue Pegasus.
Which is to say, you are *family!*
GLEEM
And I...
...will not permit my family to suffer at anyone's hands!
That is a trait we Pegasi share with you Fairies!

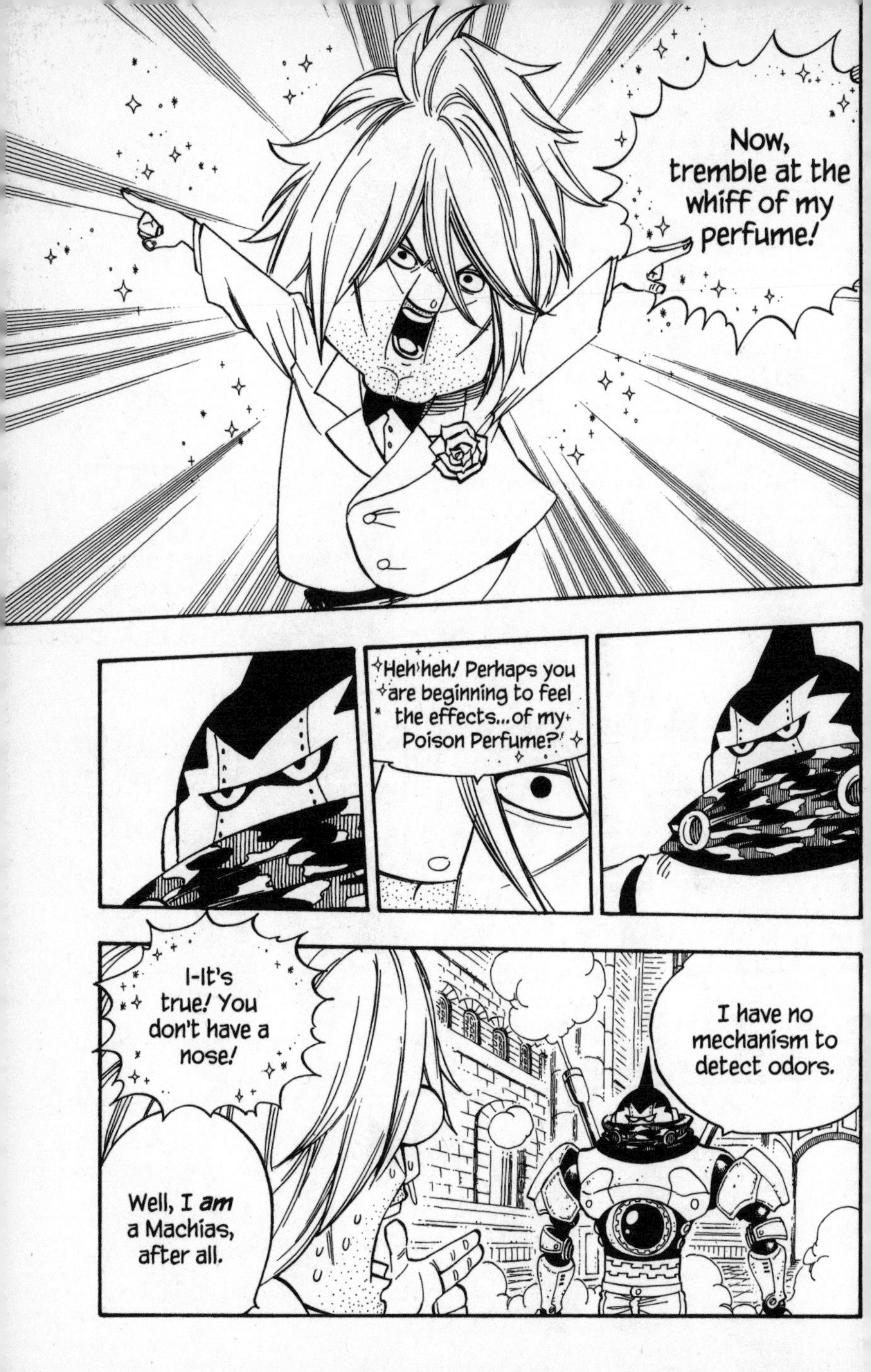
Now, tremble at the whiff of my perfume!
Heh heh! Perhaps you are beginning to feel the effects...of my Poison Perfume?
I have no mechanism to detect odors.
I-It's true! You don't have a nose!
Well, I *am* a Machias, after all.

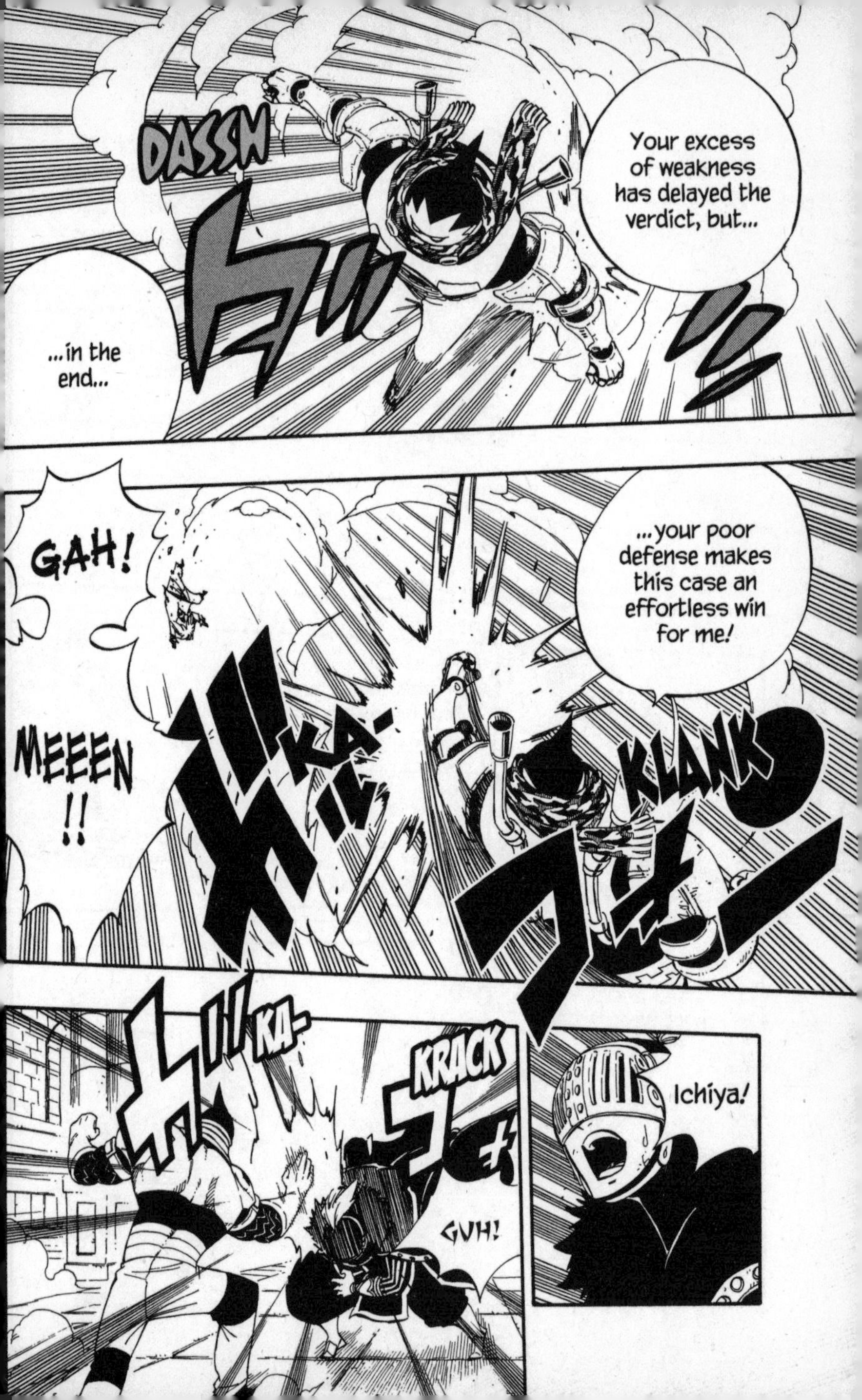
Your excess of weakness has delayed the verdict, but...
DASSH
...in the end...
...your poor defense makes this case an effortless win for me!
KLANK
KA-
GAH!
MEEEN!!
Ichiya!
KA-
KRACK
GUH!

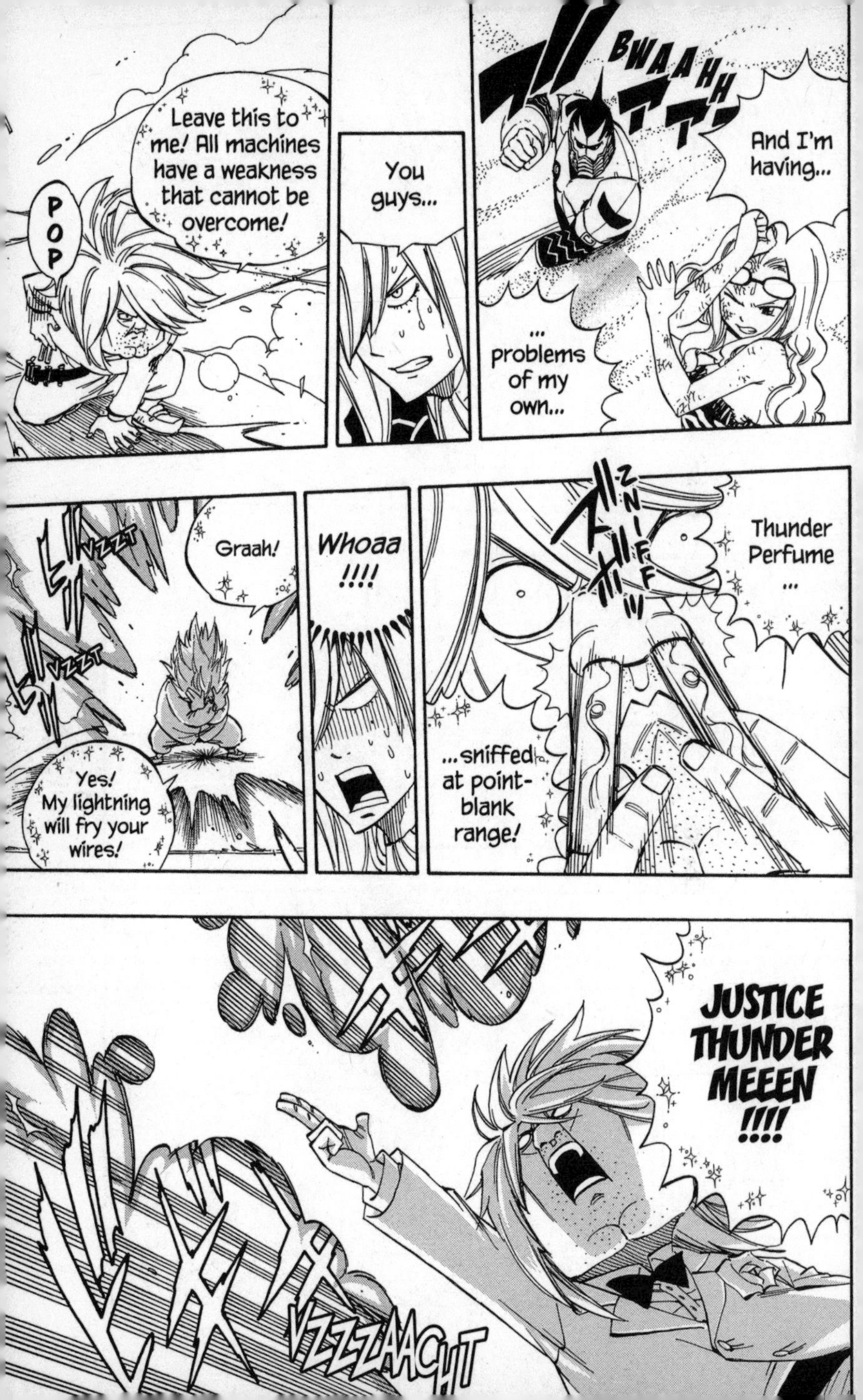
BWAAHH
And I'm having...
... problems of my own...
You guys...
Leave this to me! All machines have a weakness that cannot be overcome!
POP
ZNIFF
Thunder Perfume ...
...sniffed at point-blank range!
Whoaa !!!!
Graah!
VZZZT
VZZZT
Yes! My lightning will fry your wires!
JUSTICE THUNDER MEEEN !!!!
VZZZAACHT

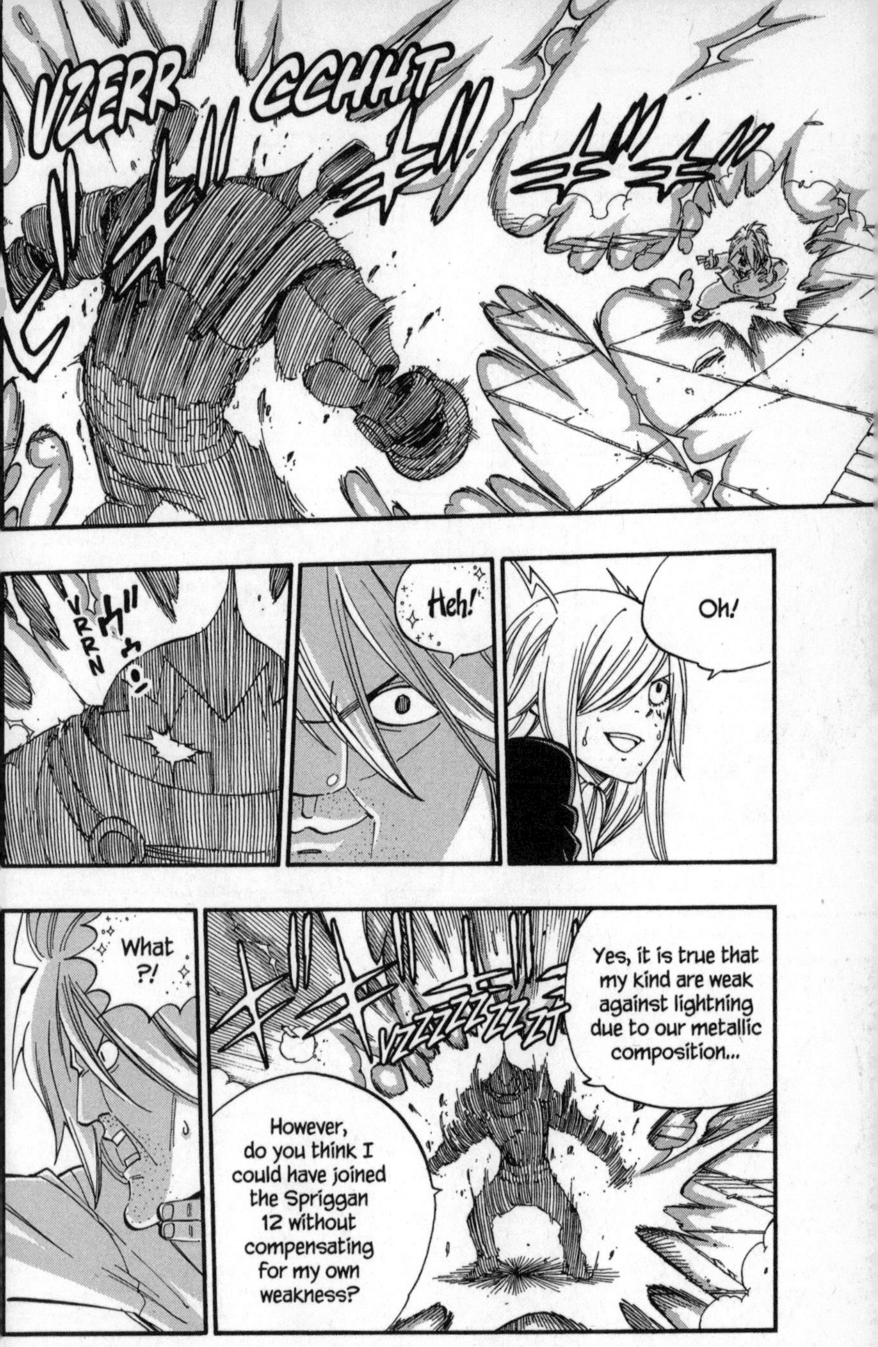
GCHHT
VZERR
Oh!
Heh!
VRRN
Yes, it is true that my kind are weak against lightning due to our metallic composition...
VZZZZZZZT
However, do you think I could have joined the Spriggan 12 without compensating for my own weakness?
What?!

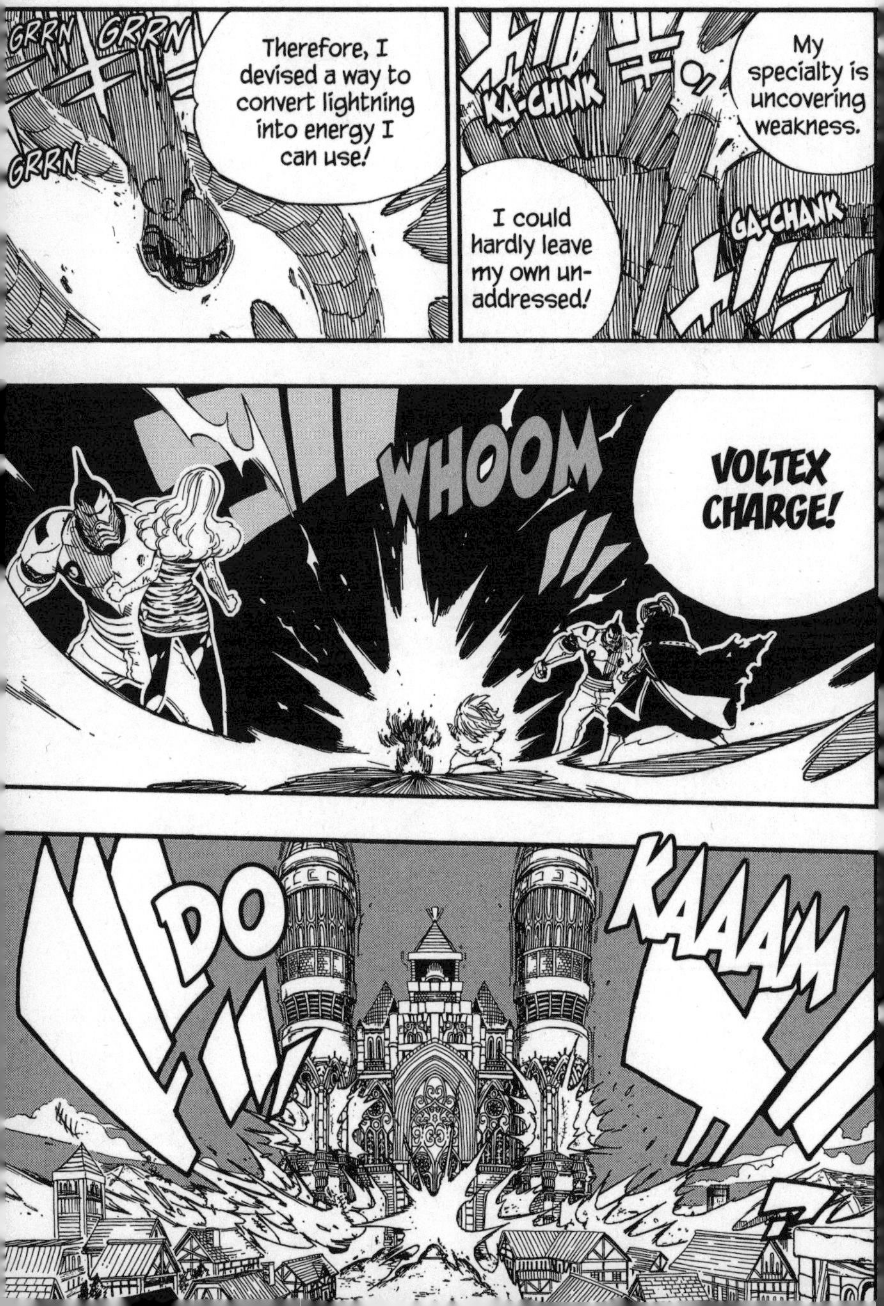
My specialty is uncovering weakness.
KA-CHINK
GA-CHANK
I could hardly leave my own un-addressed!
GRRN GRRN
GRRN
Therefore, I devised a way to convert lightning into energy I can use!
VOLTEX CHARGE!
WHOOM
KAAAM
DO

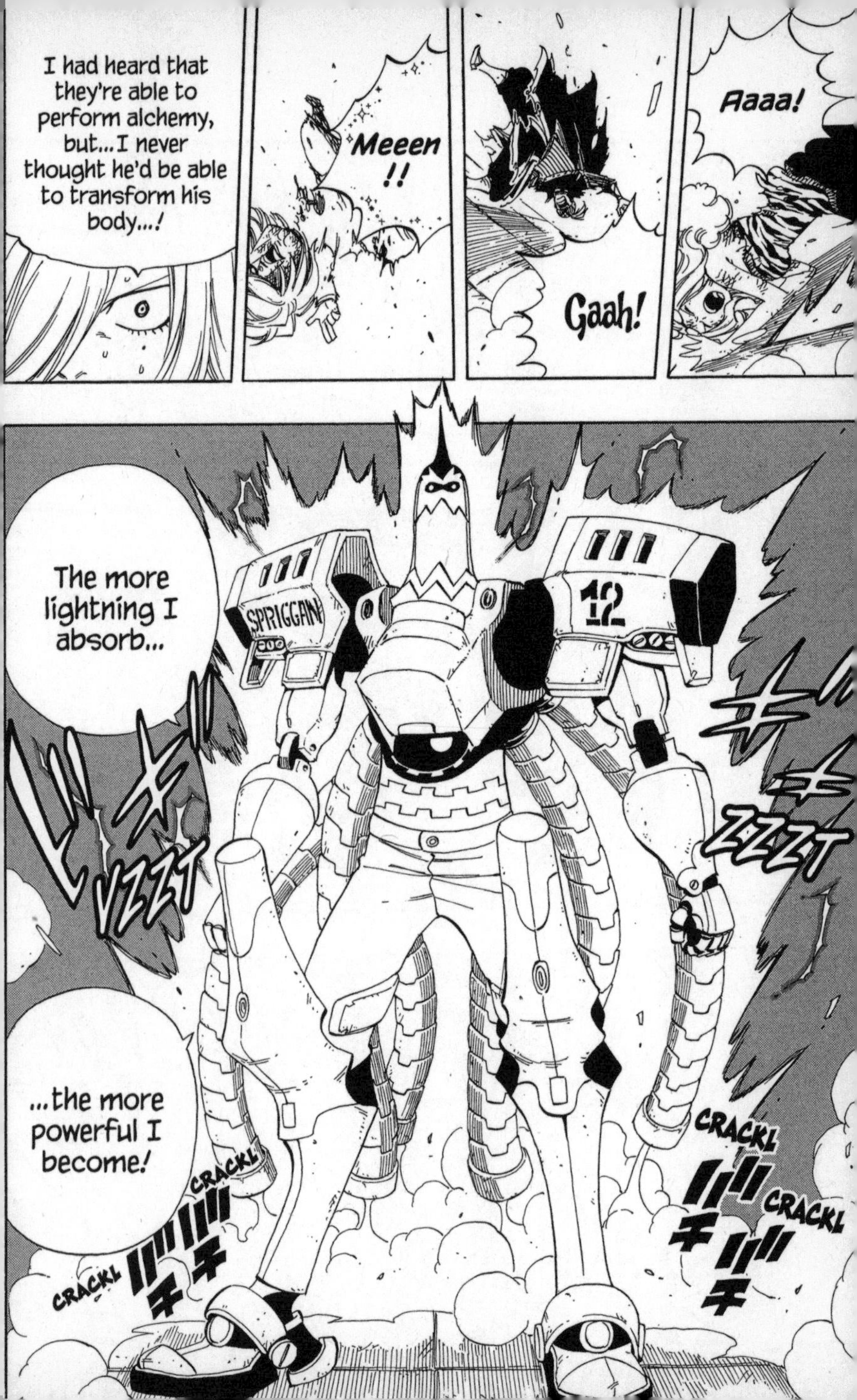
Aaaa!
Gaah!
Meeen !!
I had heard that they're able to perform alchemy, but...I never thought he'd be able to transform his body...!
SPRIGGAN
12
ZZZT
CRACKL
CRACKL
The more lightning I absorb...
VZZT
...the more powerful I become!
CRACKL
CRACKL

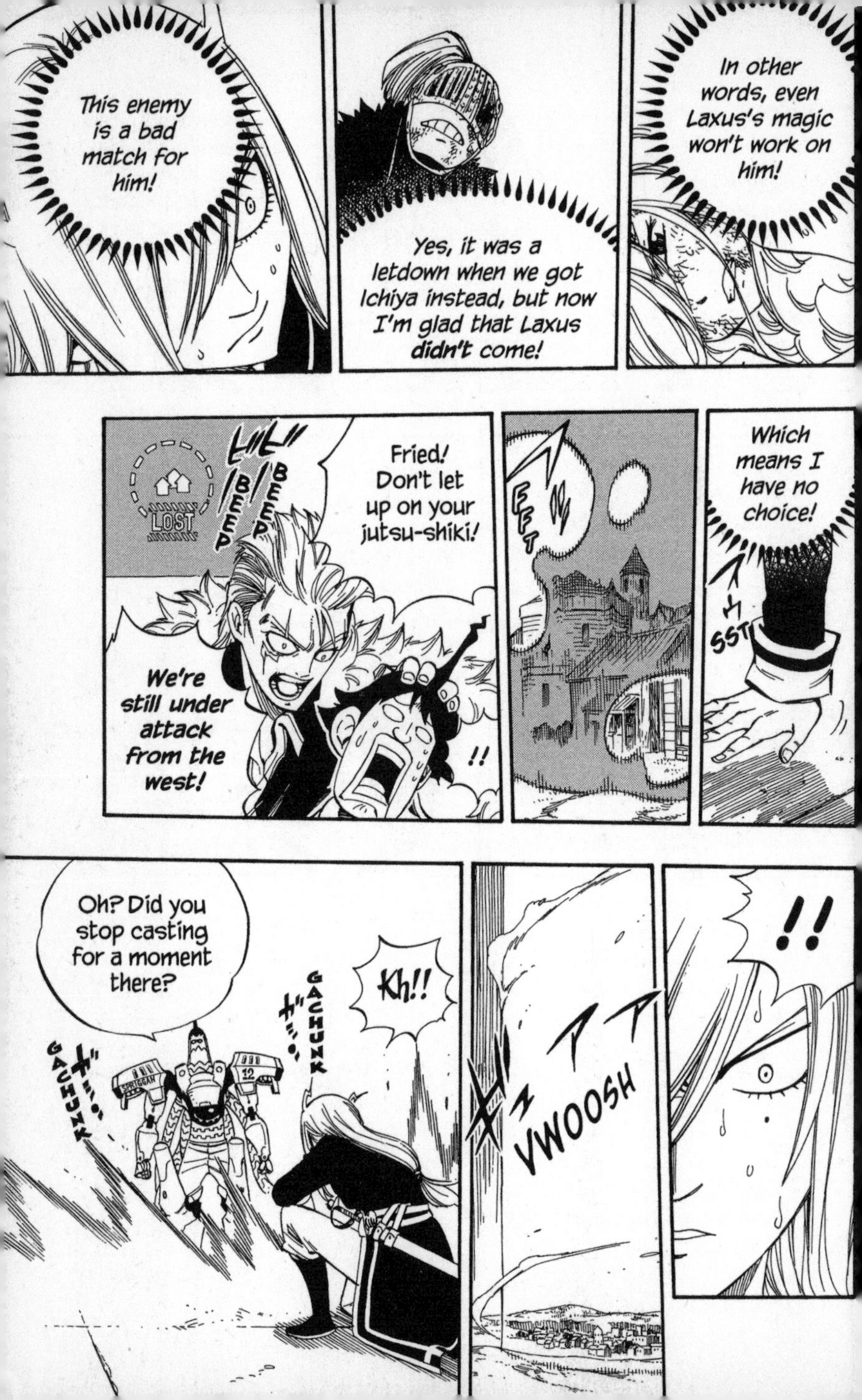

In other words, even Laxus's magic won't work on him!
Yes, it was a letdown when we got Ichiya instead, but now I'm glad that Laxus didn't come!
This enemy is a bad match for him!
Which means I have no choice!
SST
FFT
!!
Fried! Don't let up on your jutsu-shiki!
BEEP
BEEP
LOST
We're still under attack from the west!
!!
VWOOSH
Oh? Did you stop casting for a moment there?
Kh!!
GACHUNK
GACHUNK

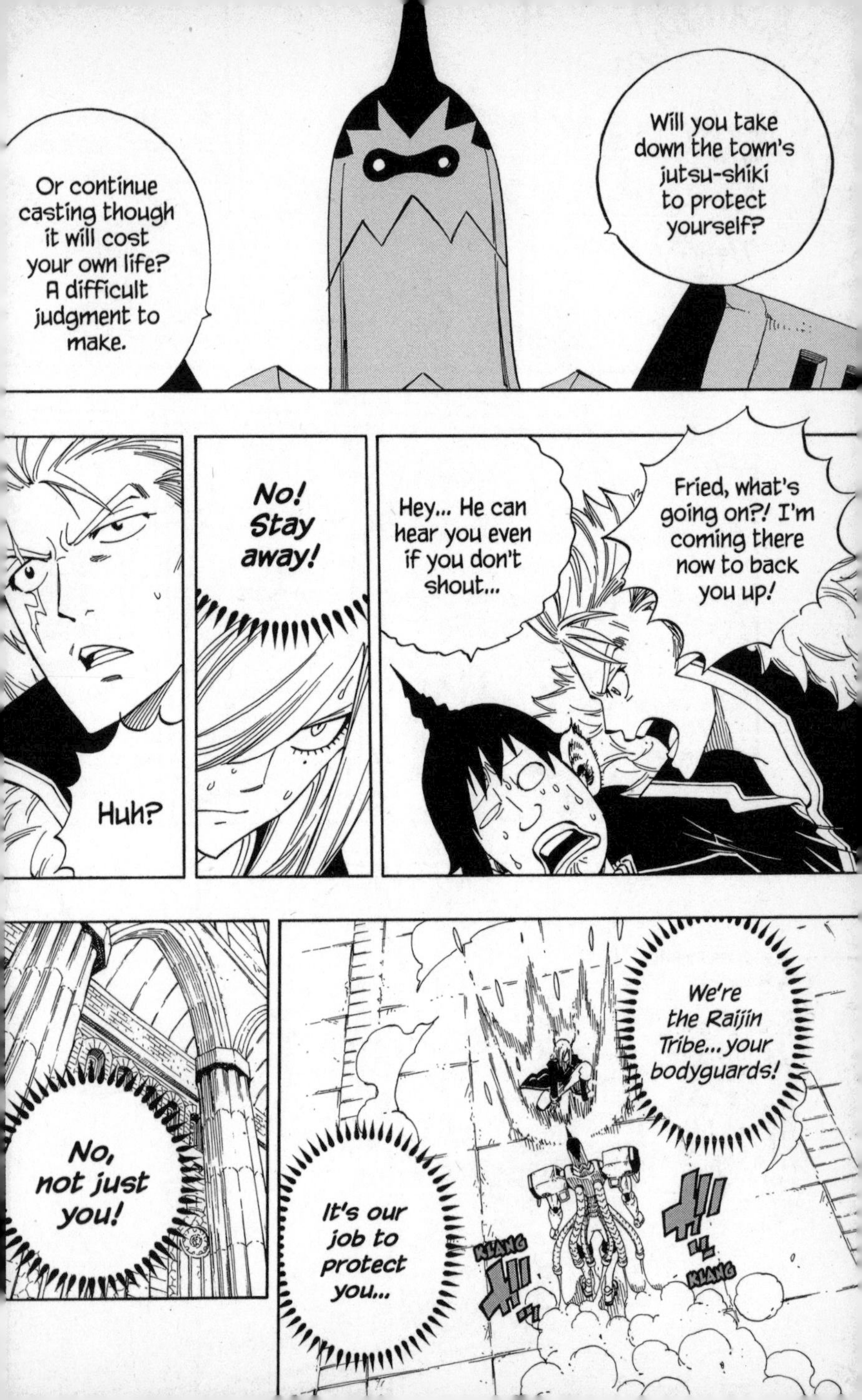
Will you take down the town's jutsu-shiki to protect yourself?
Or continue casting though it will cost your own life? A difficult judgment to make.
Fried, what's going on?! I'm coming there now to back you up!
Hey... He can hear you even if you don't shout...
No! Stay away!
Huh?
We're the Raijin Tribe... your bodyguards!
It's our job to protect you...
KLANG
KLANG
No, not just you!

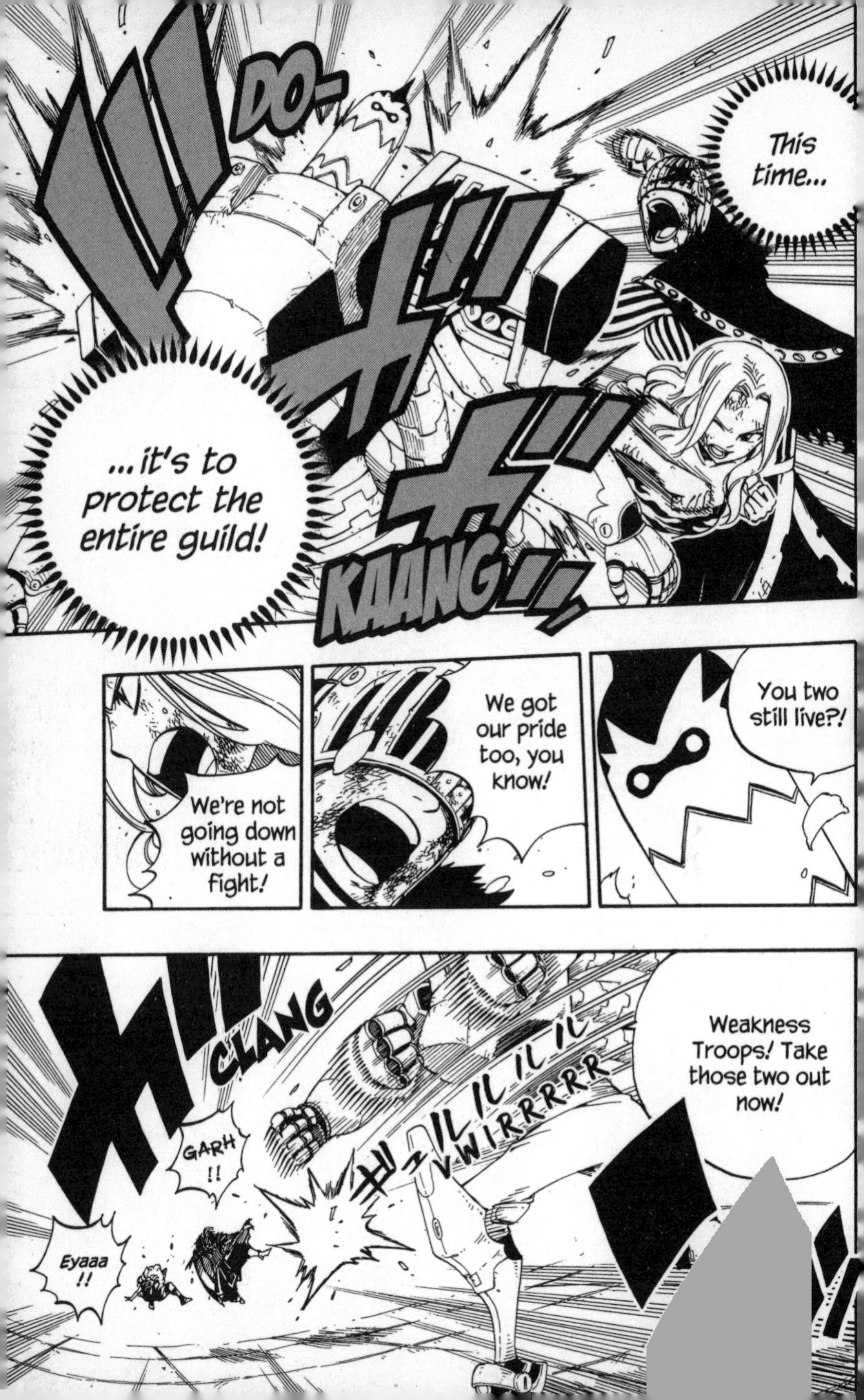
This time...
DO-
...it's to protect the entire guild!
KAANG
You two still live?!
We got our pride too, you know!
We're not going down without a fight!
Weakness Troops! Take those two out now!
VWIRRRRR
CLANG
GARH !!
Eyaaa !!

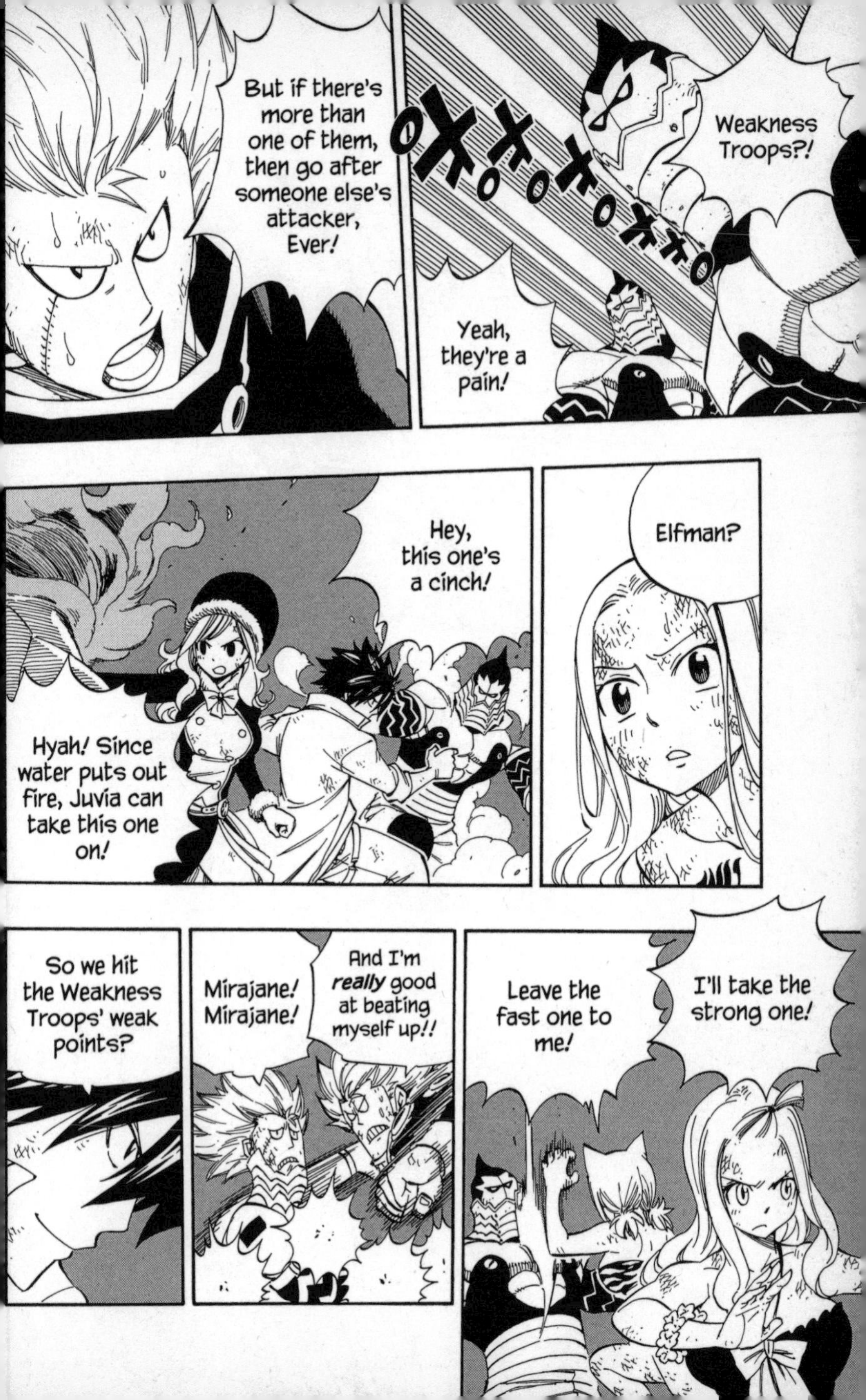
Weakness Troops?!
Yeah, they're a pain!
But if there's more than one of them, then go after someone else's attacker, Ever!
Elfman?
Hey, this one's a cinch!
Hyah! Since water puts out fire, Juvia can take this one on!
I'll take the strong one!
Leave the fast one to me!
And I'm *really* good at beating myself up!!
Mirajane! Mirajane!
So we hit the Weakness Troops' weak points?

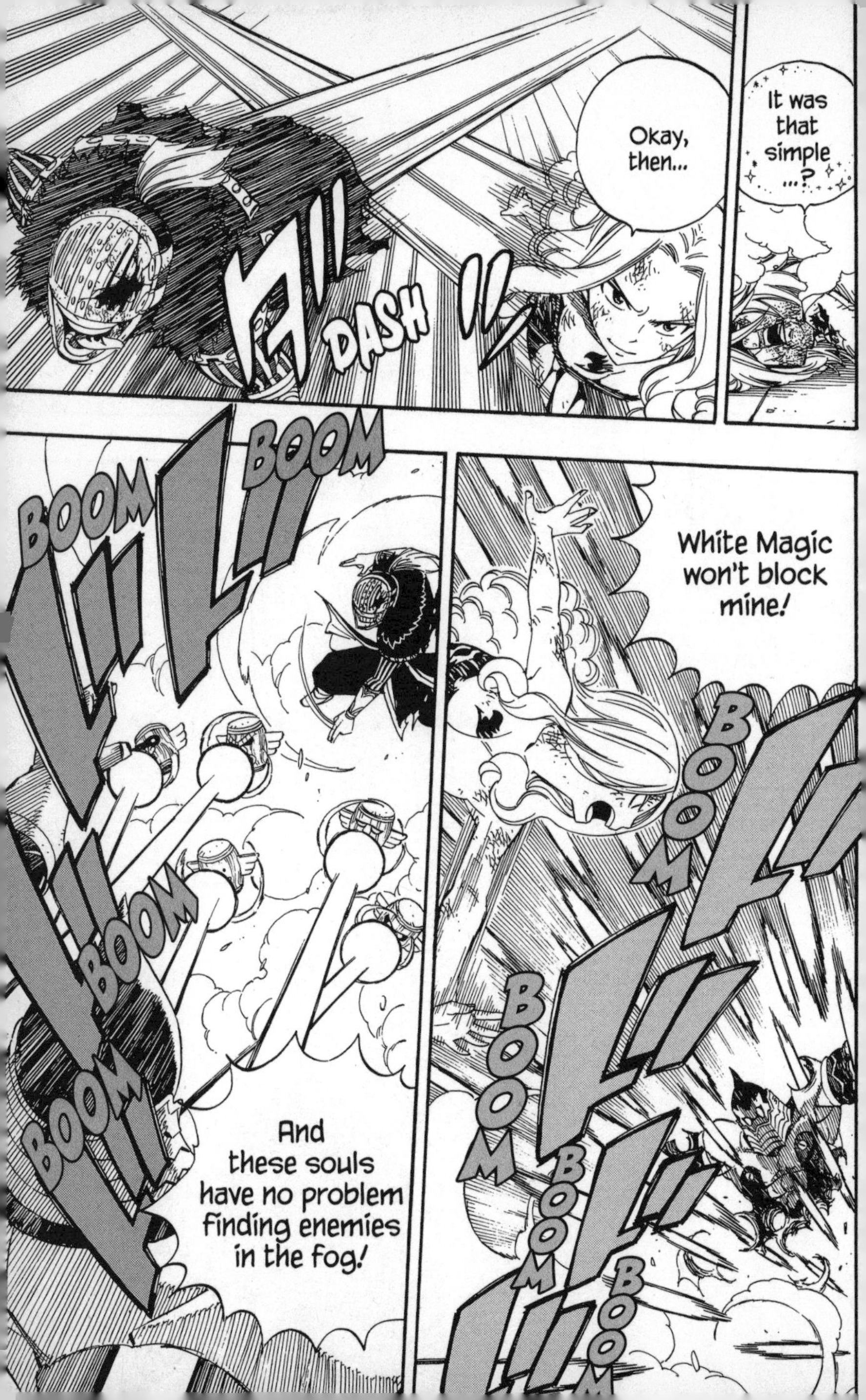
It was that simple...?
Okay, then...
DASH
White Magic won't block mine!
BOOM
BOOM
BOOM
BOOM
BOOM
BOOM
BOOM
And these souls have no problem finding enemies in the fog!
BOOM
BOOM
BOOM
BOOM

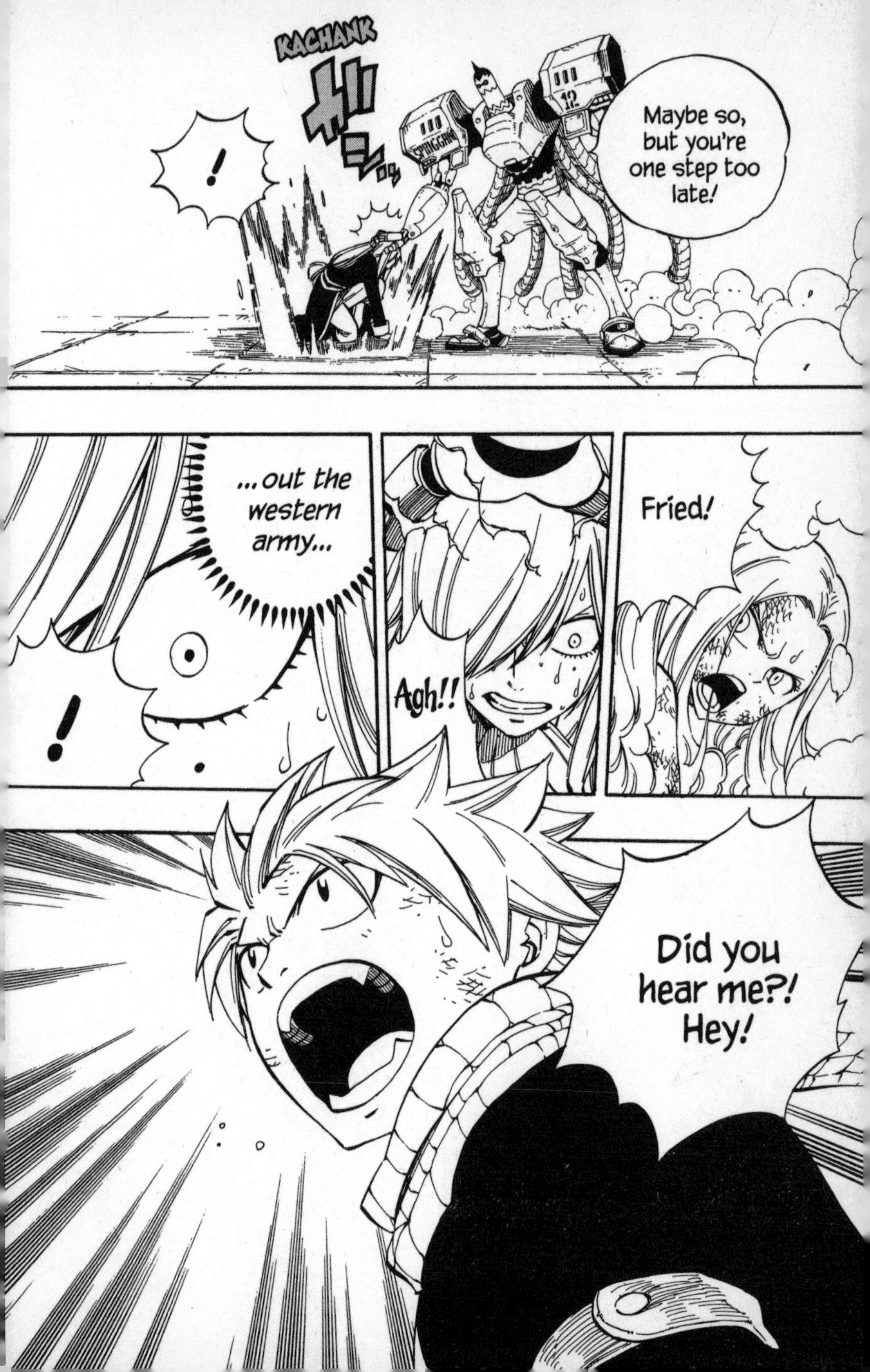
Maybe so, but you're one step too late!
KACHANK
!
Fried!
Agh!!
...out the western army...
!
Did you hear me?! Hey!

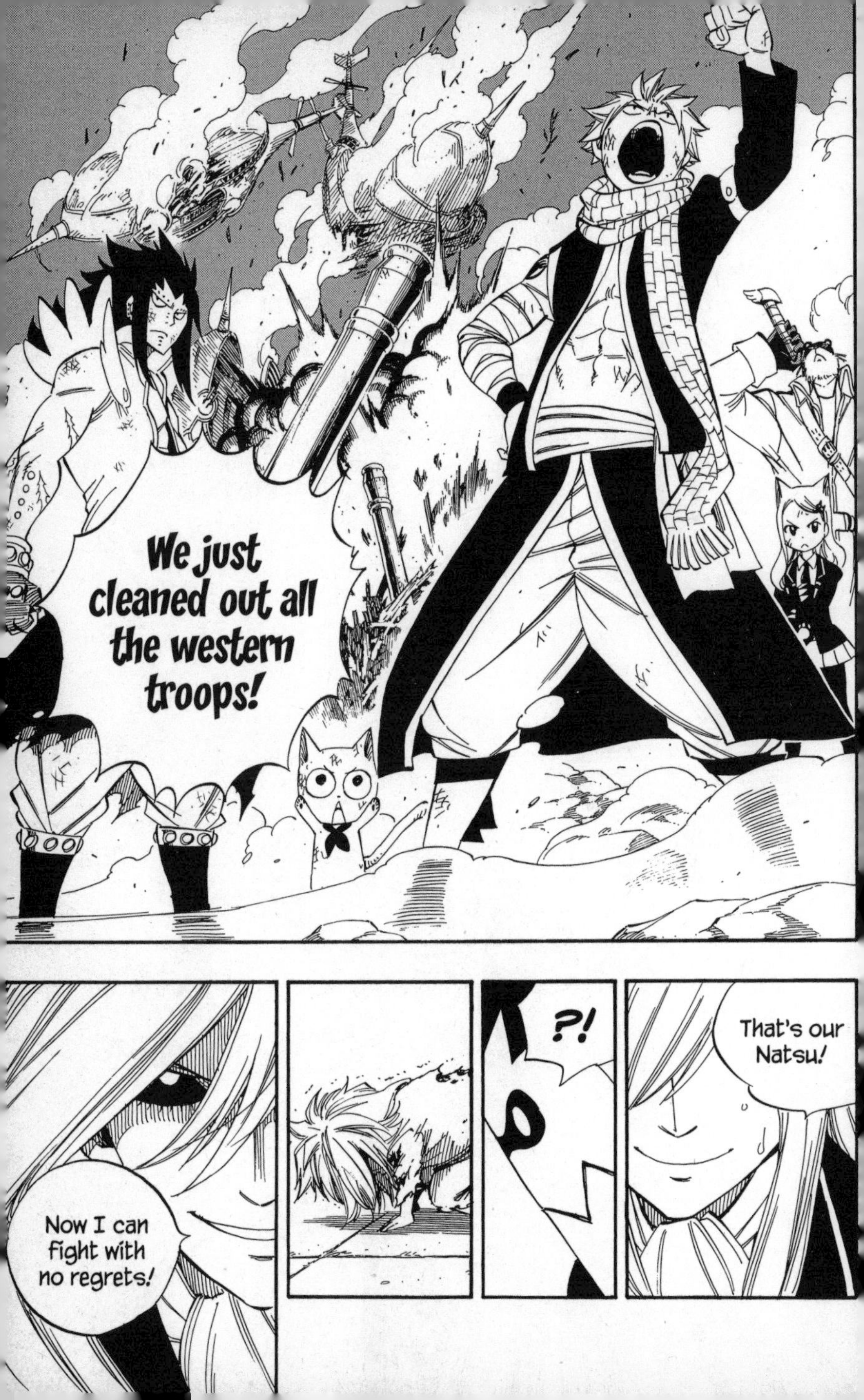
We just cleaned out all the western troops!
That's our Natsu!
?!
Now I can fight with no regrets!

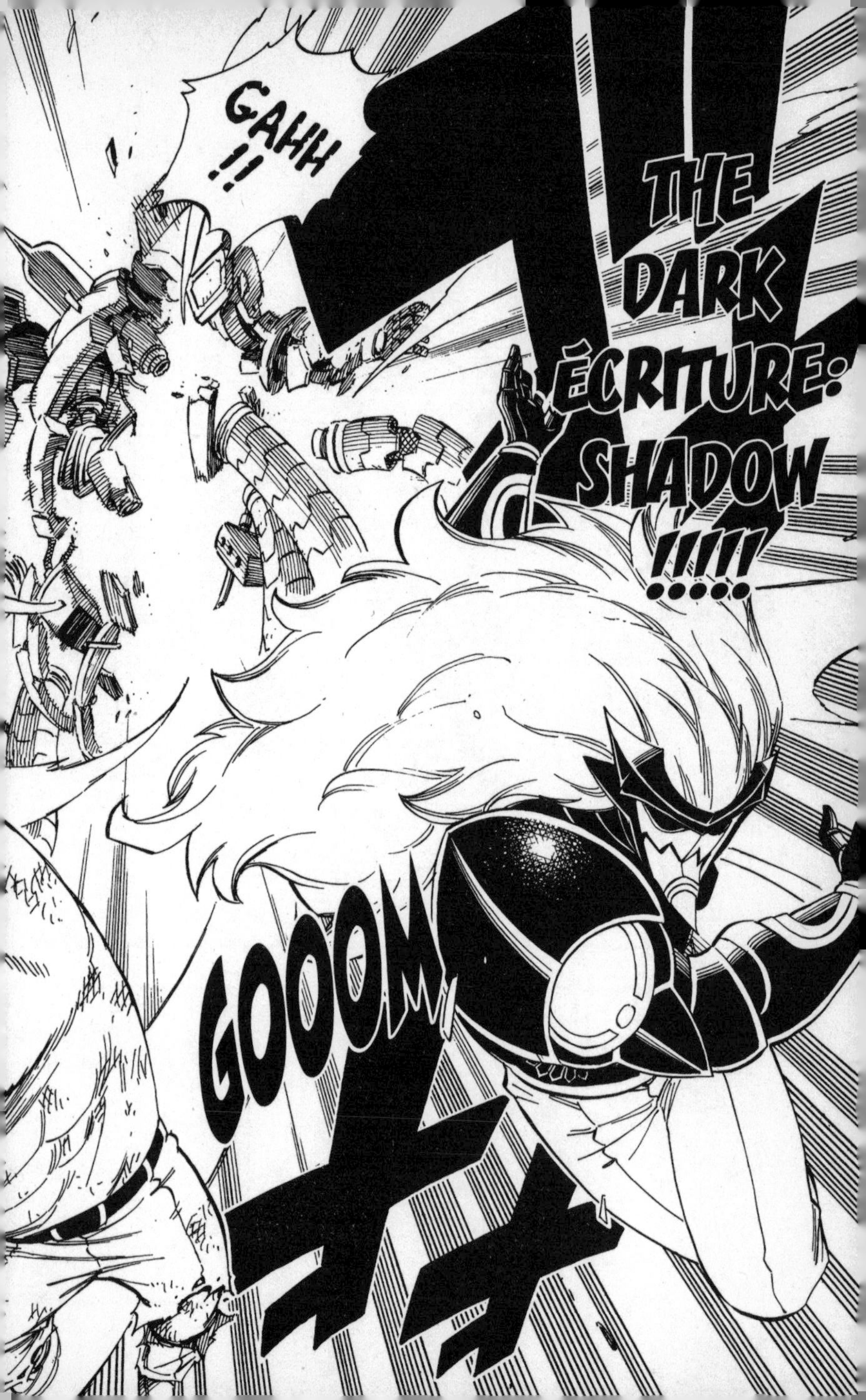
THE DARK ÉCRITURE: SHADOW!!!!!
GAHH!!!
GOOOM

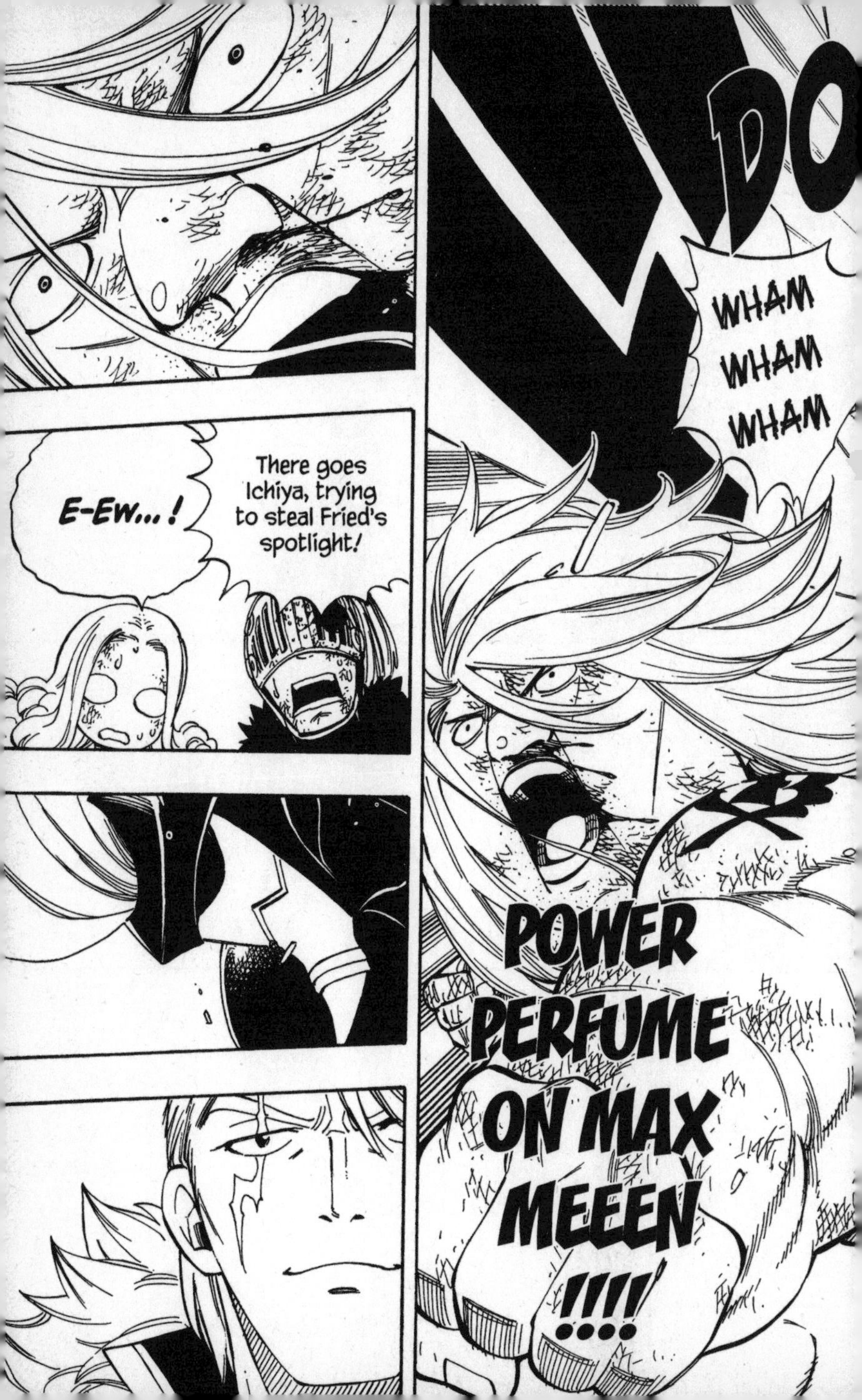
DO
WHAM WHAM WHAM
POWER PERFUME ON MAX MEEEN!!!!
There goes Ichiya, trying to steal Fried's spotlight!
E-Ew...!

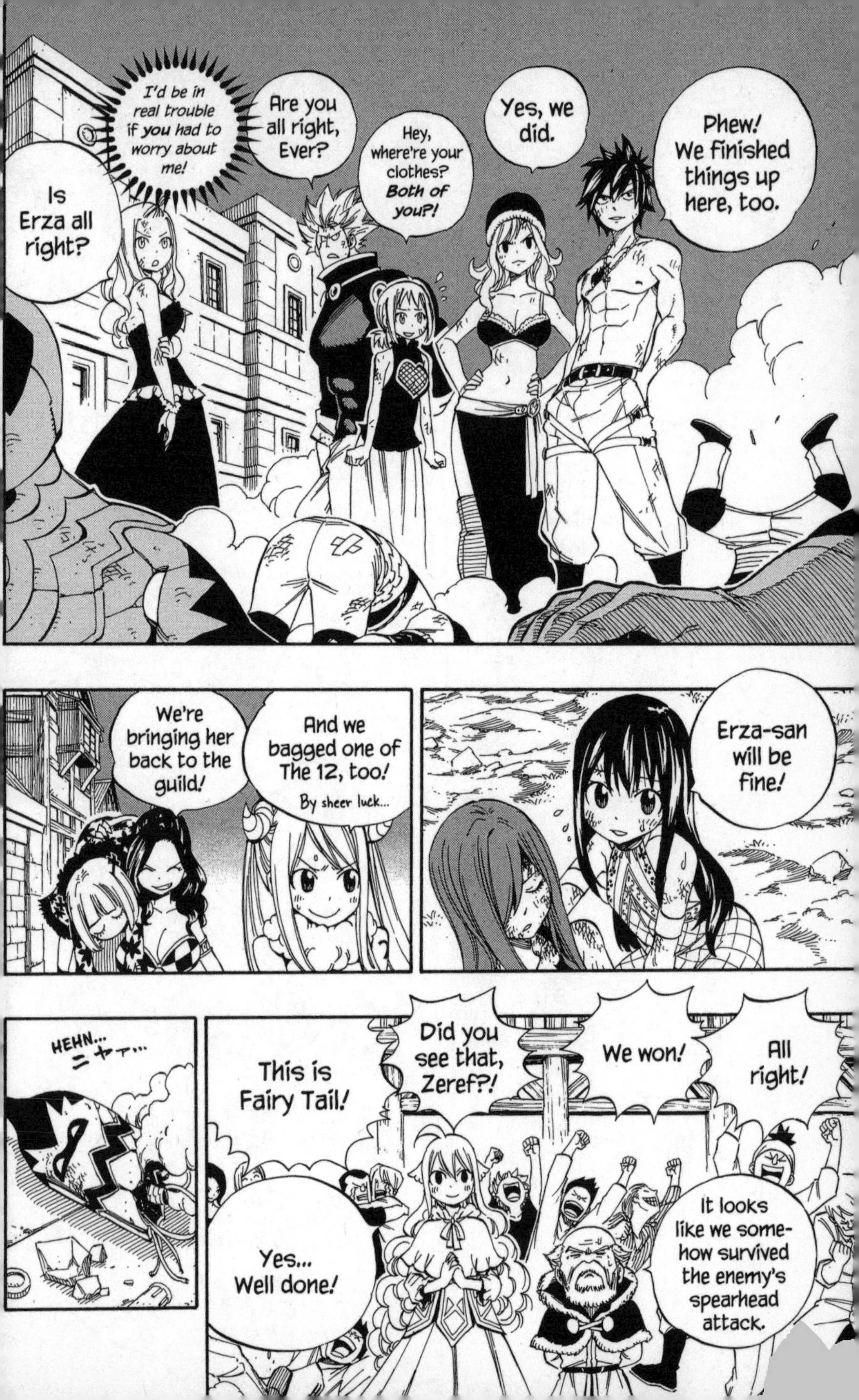

Phew! We finished things up here, too.
Yes, we did.
Hey, where're your clothes? Both of you?!
Are you all right, Ever?
I'd be in real trouble if you had to worry about me!
Is Erza all right?
Erza-san will be fine!
And we bagged one of The 12, too!
By sheer luck...
We're bringing her back to the guild!
All right!
We won!
Did you see that, Zeref?!
This is Fairy Tail!
It looks like we somehow survived the enemy's spearhead attack.
Yes... Well done!
HEHN...
ニャァ...

FAIRY TAIL

フェアリーテイル

Chapter 461: This Perfume Goes To...

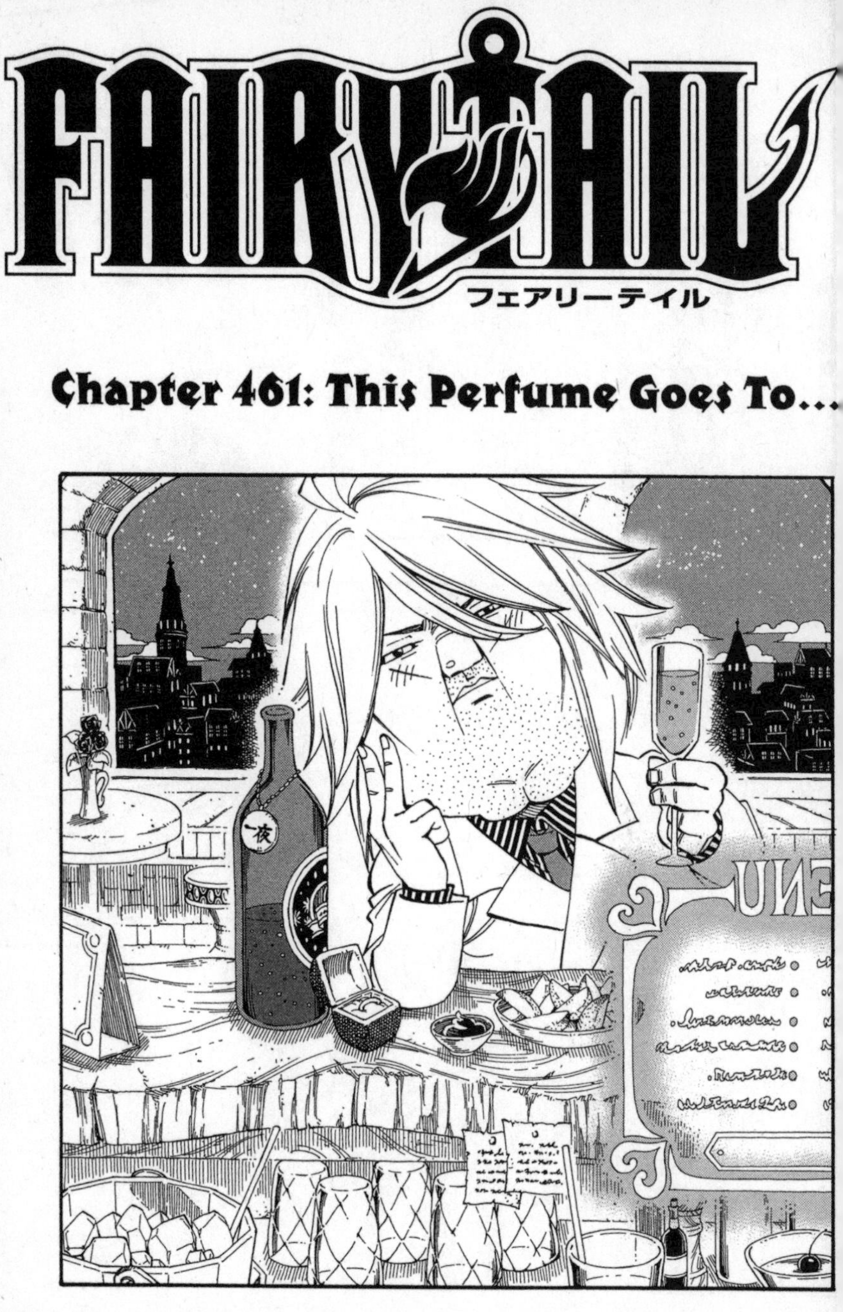
一夜

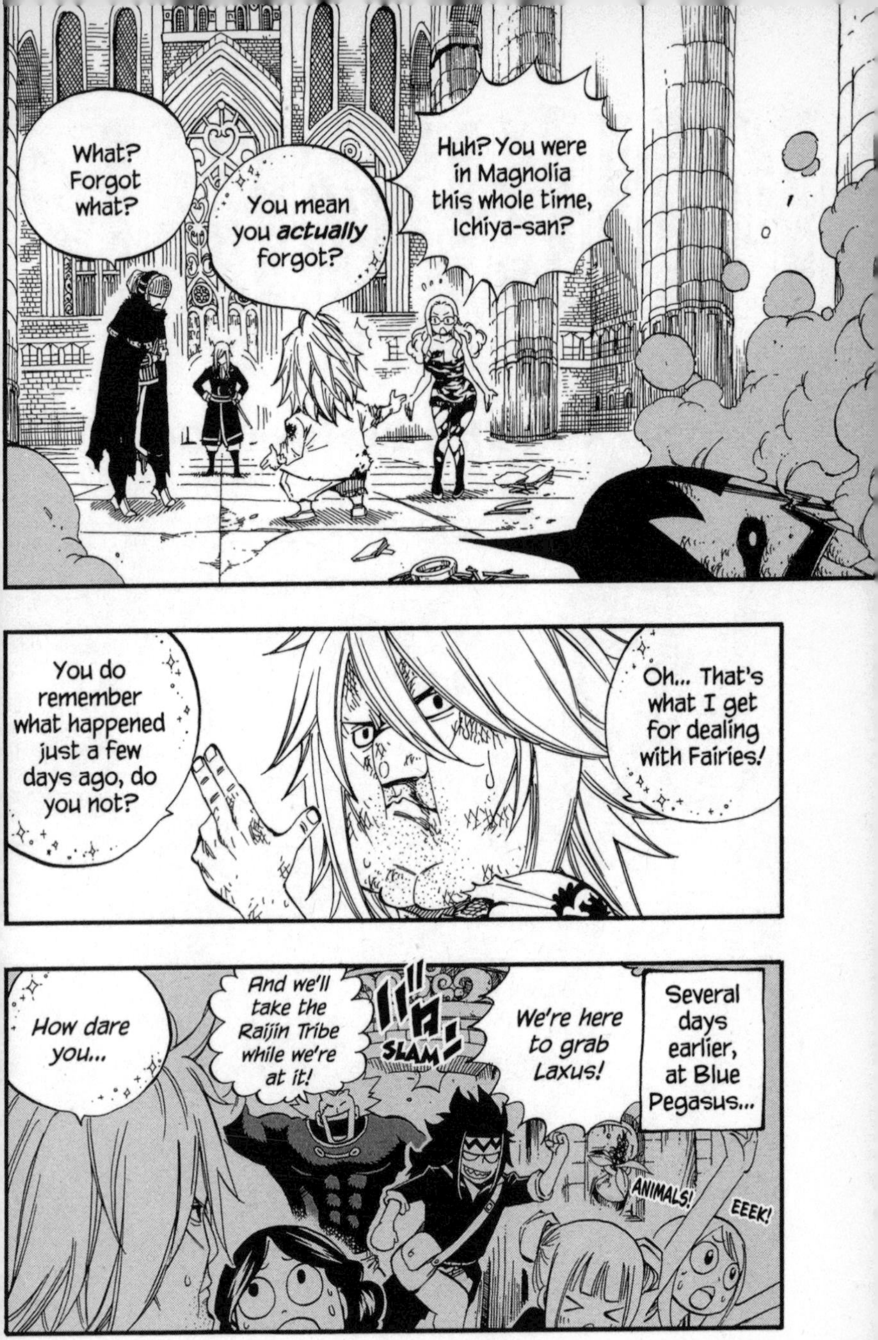
Huh? You were in Magnolia this whole time, Ichiya-san?
You mean you *actually* forgot?
What? Forgot what?
Oh... That's what I get for dealing with Fairies!
You do remember what happened just a few days ago, do you not?
Several days earlier, at Blue Pegasus...
We're here to grab Laxus!
SLAM
And we'll take the Raijin Tribe while we're at it!
How dare you...
EEEK!
ANIMALS!

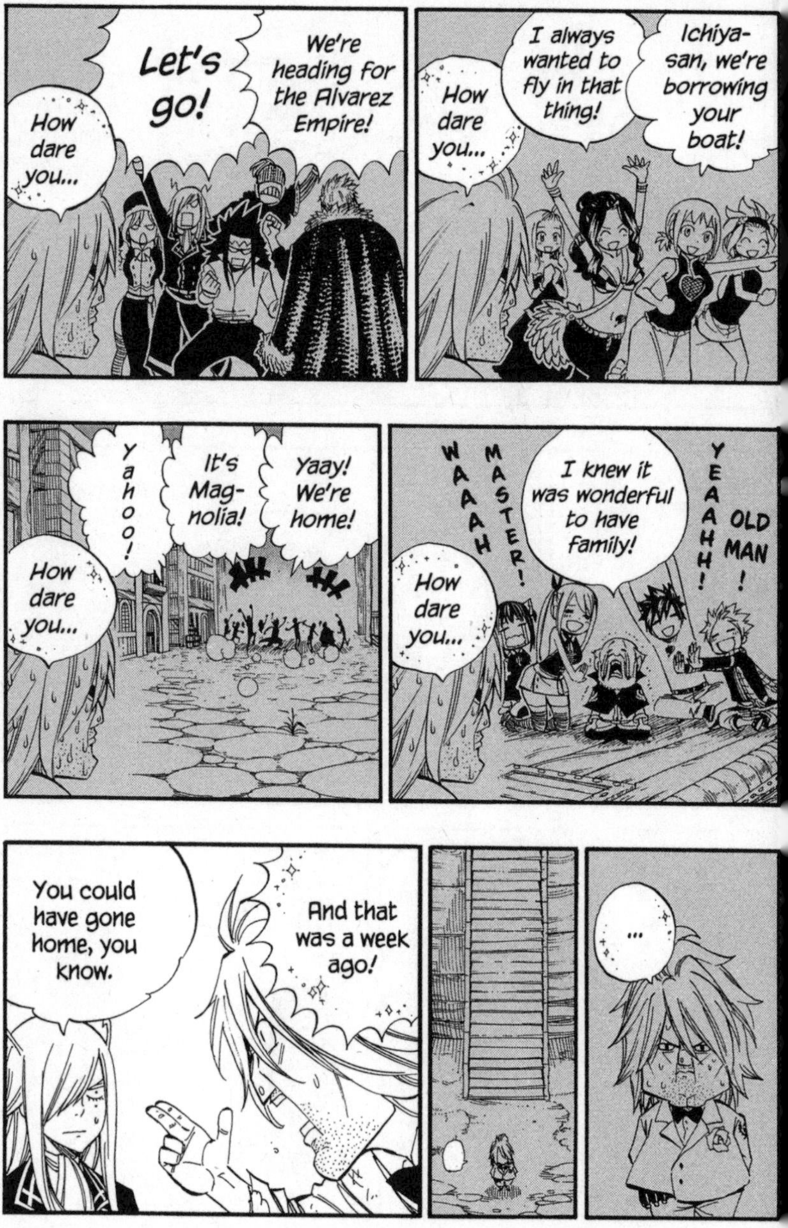
Ichiya-san, we're borrowing your boat!
I always wanted to fly in that thing!
How dare you...
We're heading for the Alvarez Empire!
Let's go!
How dare you...
OLD MAN!
YEAAHH!
I knew it was wonderful to have family!
MASTER!
WAAAAH
How dare you...
Yaay! We're home!
It's Magnolia!
Yahoo!
How dare you...
...
And that was a week ago!
You could have gone home, you know.

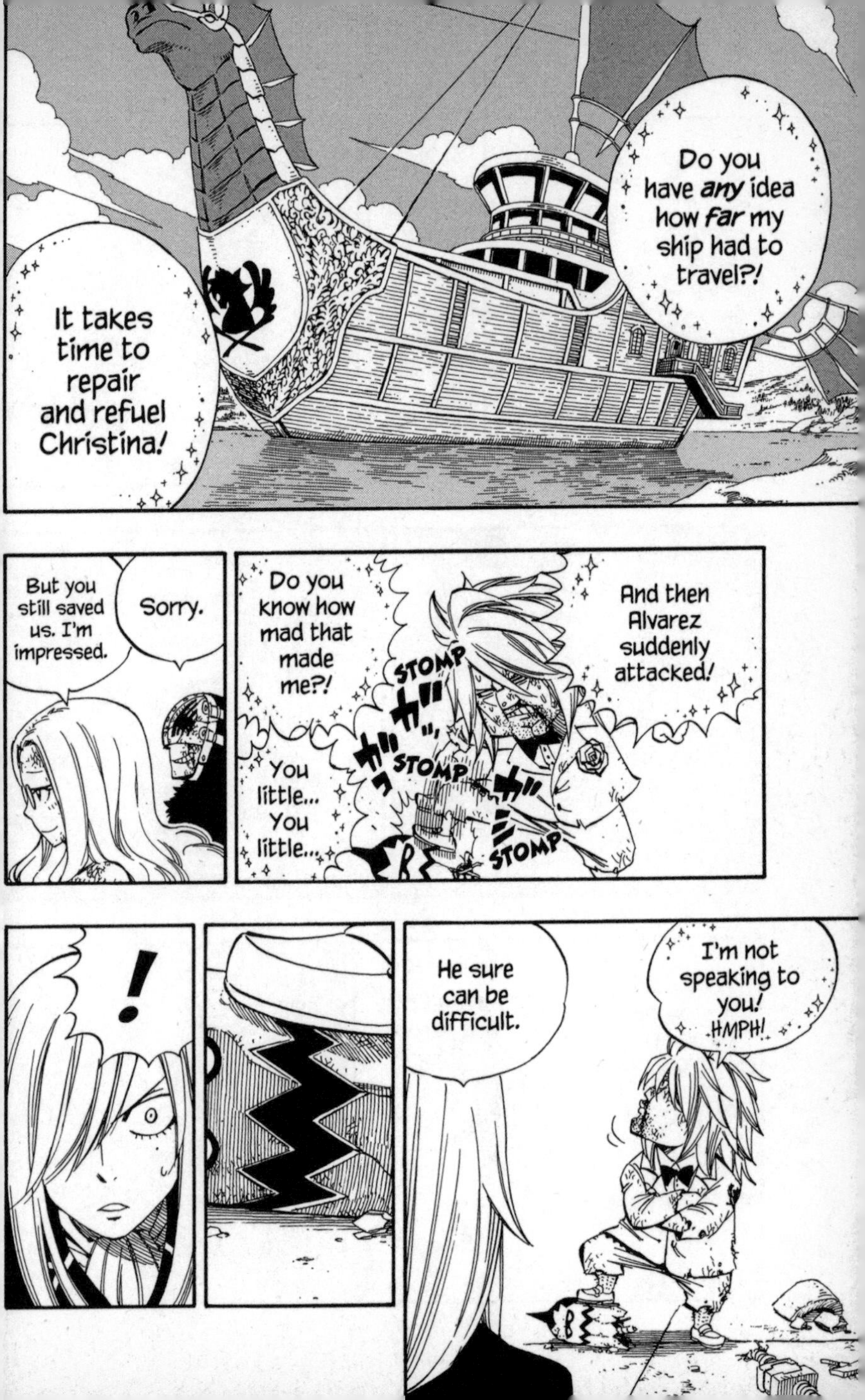
Do you have *any* idea how *far* my ship had to travel?!
It takes time to repair and refuel Christina!
And then Alvarez suddenly attacked!
Do you know how mad that made me?!
STOMP
STOMP
STOMP
You little... You little...
Sorry.
But you still saved us. I'm impressed.
I'm not speaking to you! HMPH!
He sure can be difficult.
!

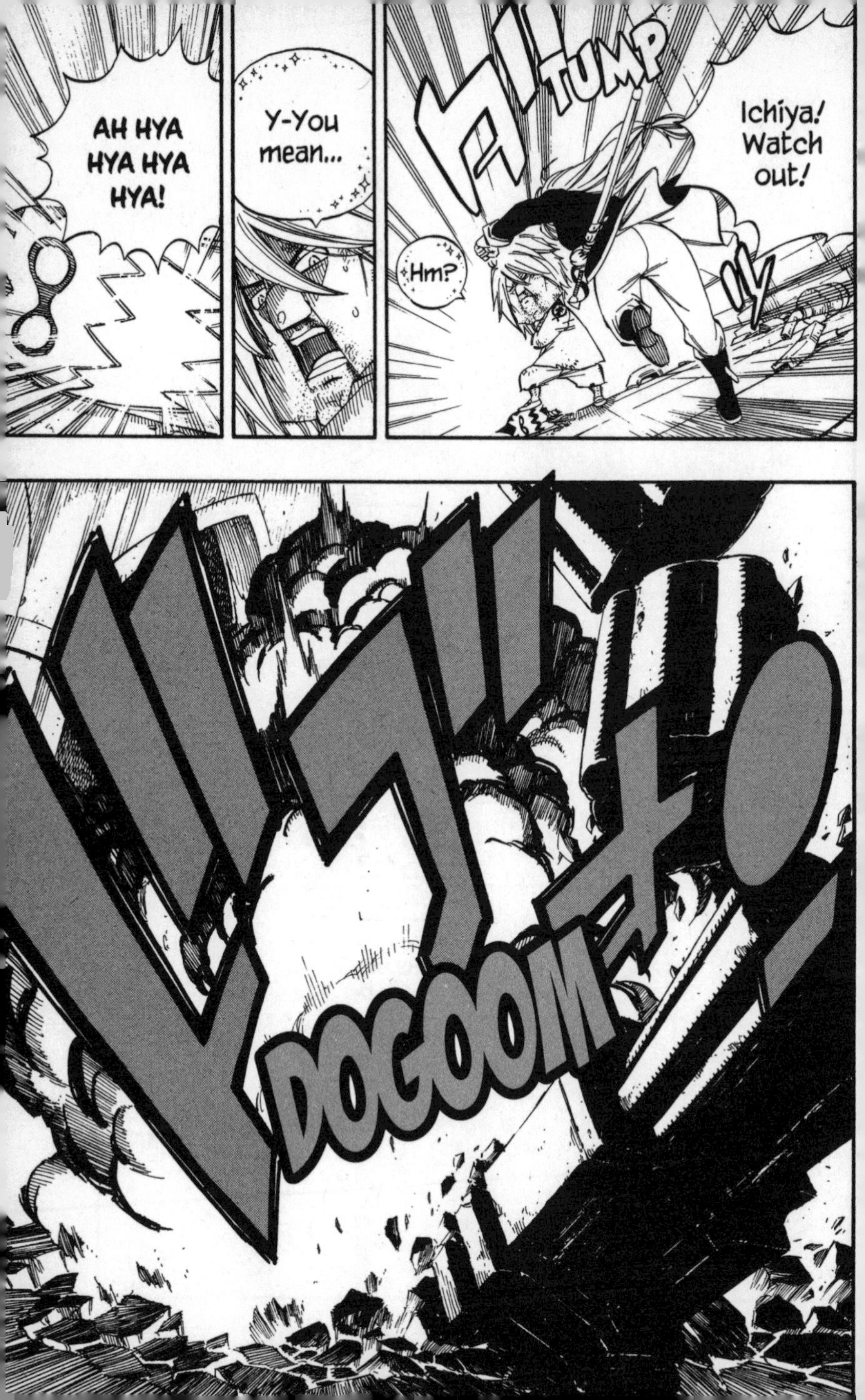

Ichiya! Watch out!
TUMP
Hm?
Y-You mean...
AH HYA HYA HYA HYA!
DOGOOM

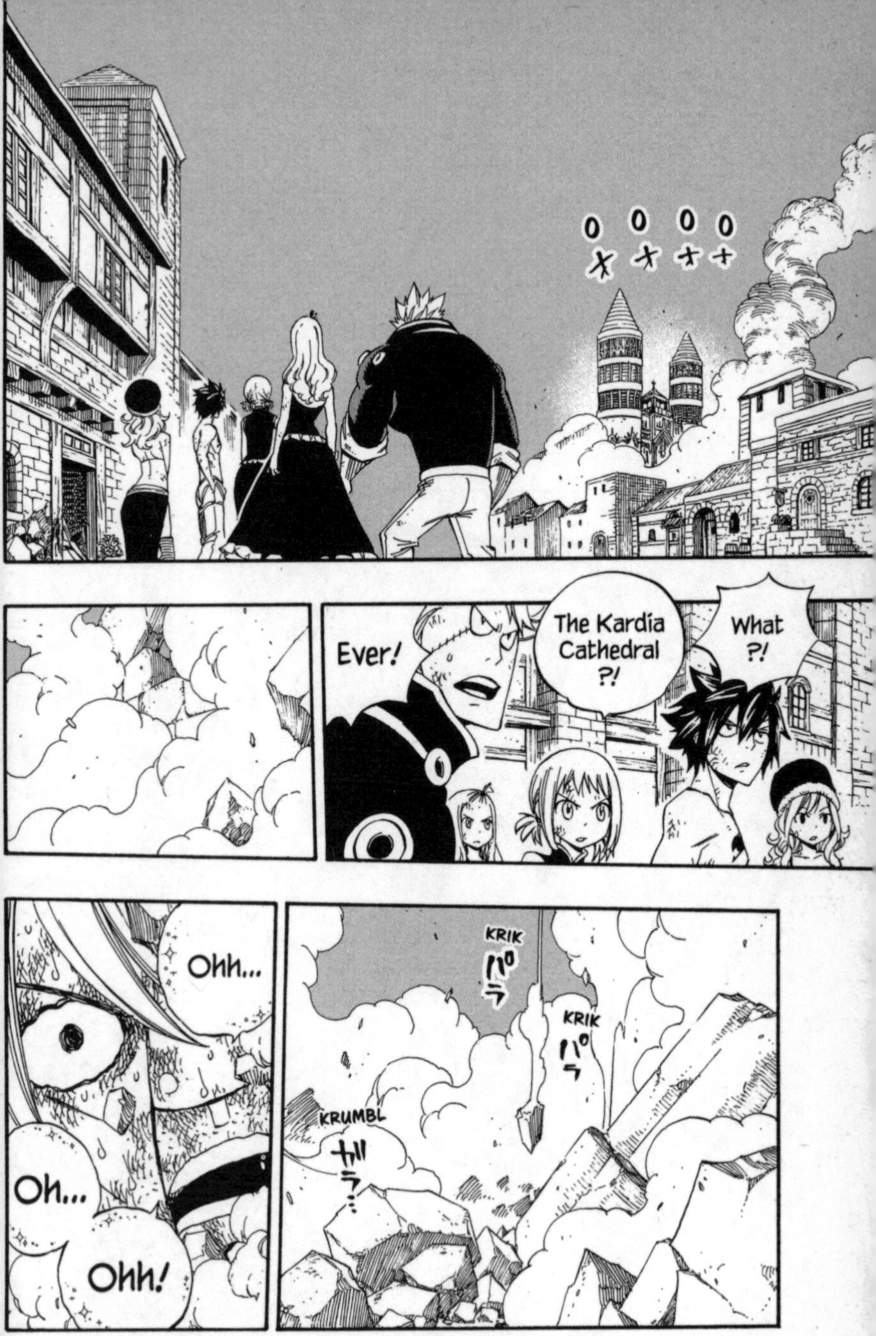
OOOO
What ?!
The Kardia Cathedral ?!
Ever!
KRIK
KRIK
KRUMBL
Ohh...
Oh...
Ohh!

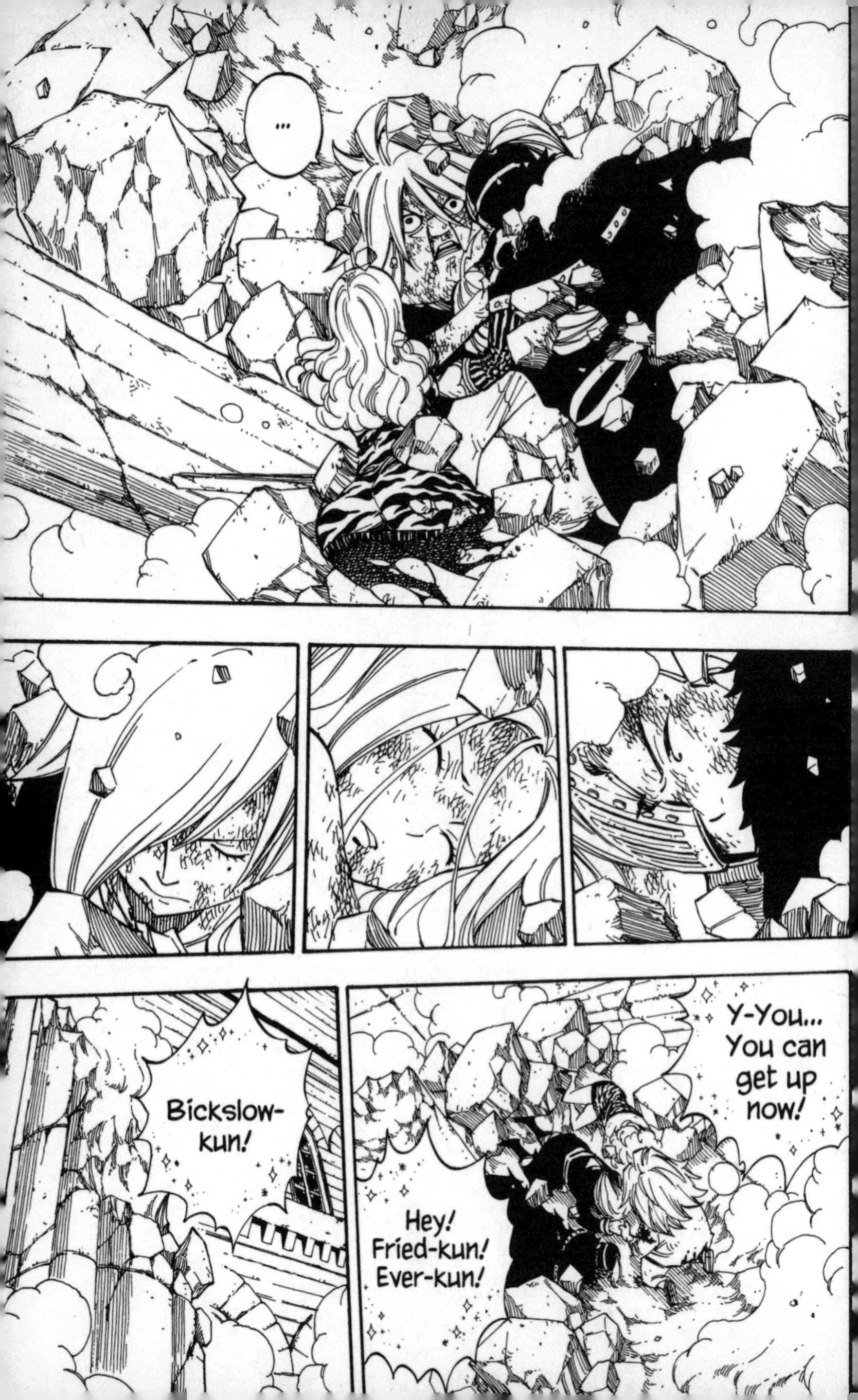
...
Y-You... You can get up now!
Hey! Fried-kun! Ever-kun!
Bickslow-kun!

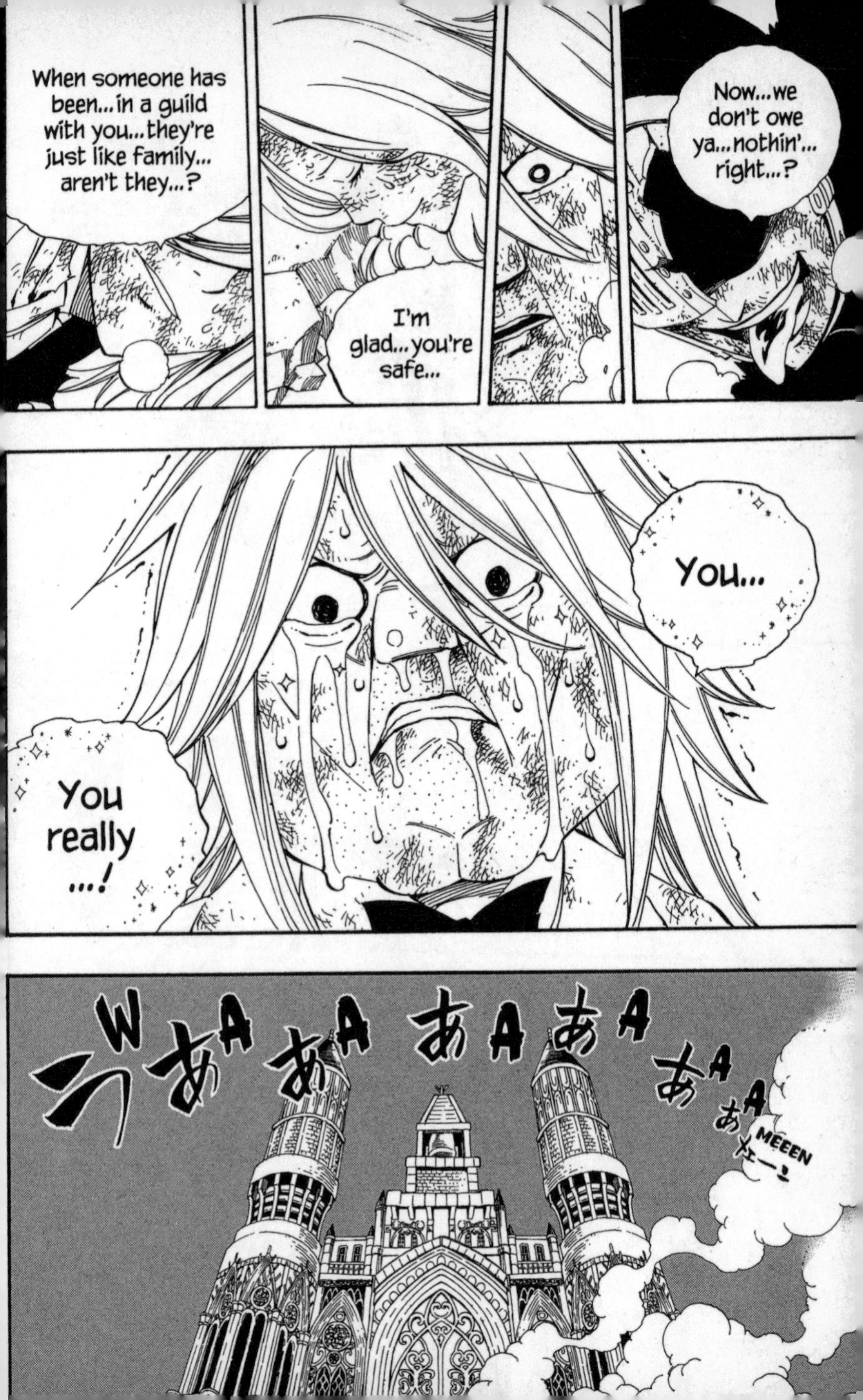
Now...we don't owe ya...nothin'... right...?
I'm glad...you're safe...
When someone has been...in a guild with you...they're just like family... aren't they...?
You...
You really ...!
うWあAあAあAあAあAあA
MEEEN

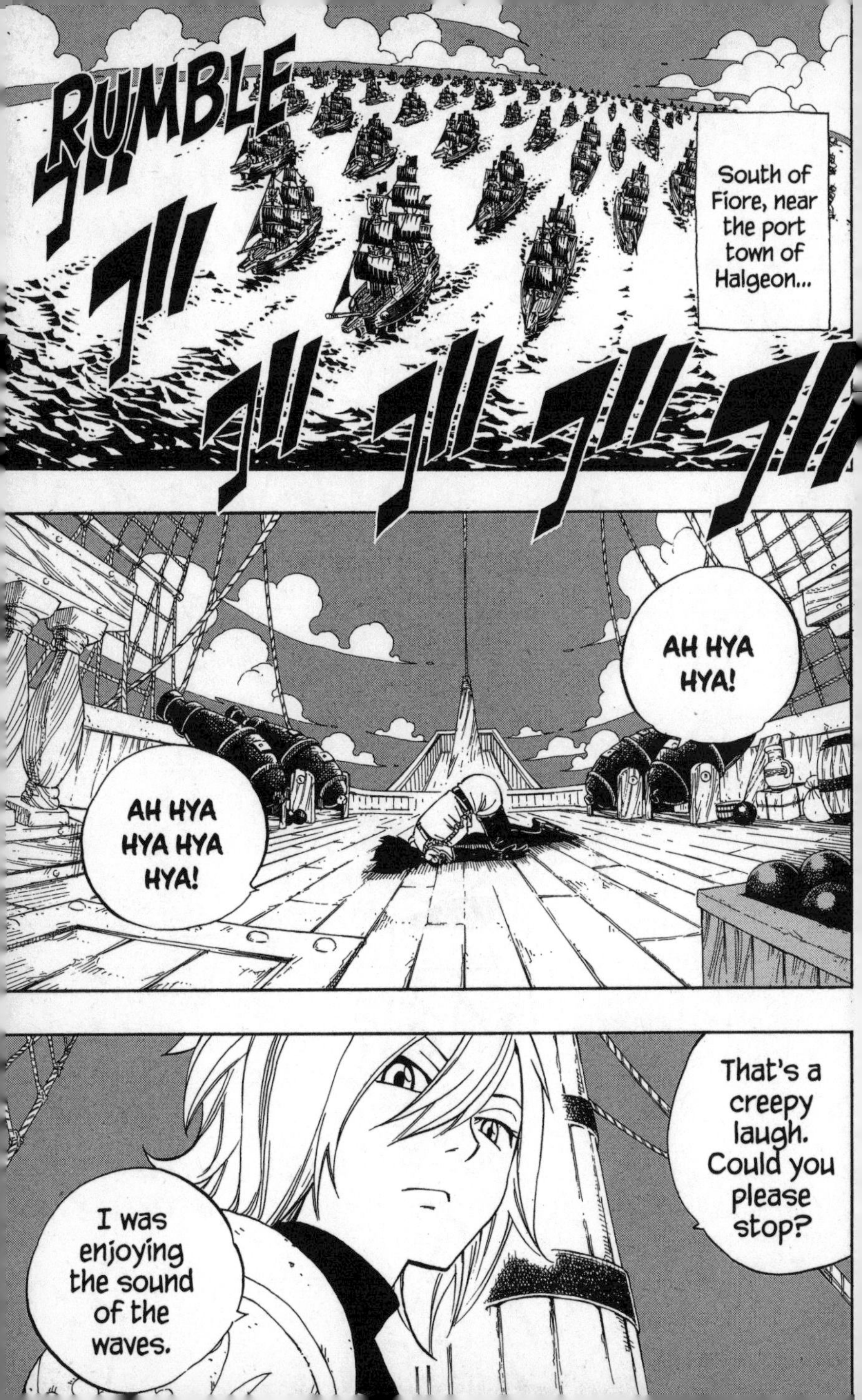
South of Fiore, near the port town of Halgeon...
RUMBLE
AH HYA HYA!
AH HYA HYA HYA HYA!
That's a creepy laugh. Could you please stop?
I was enjoying the sound of the waves.

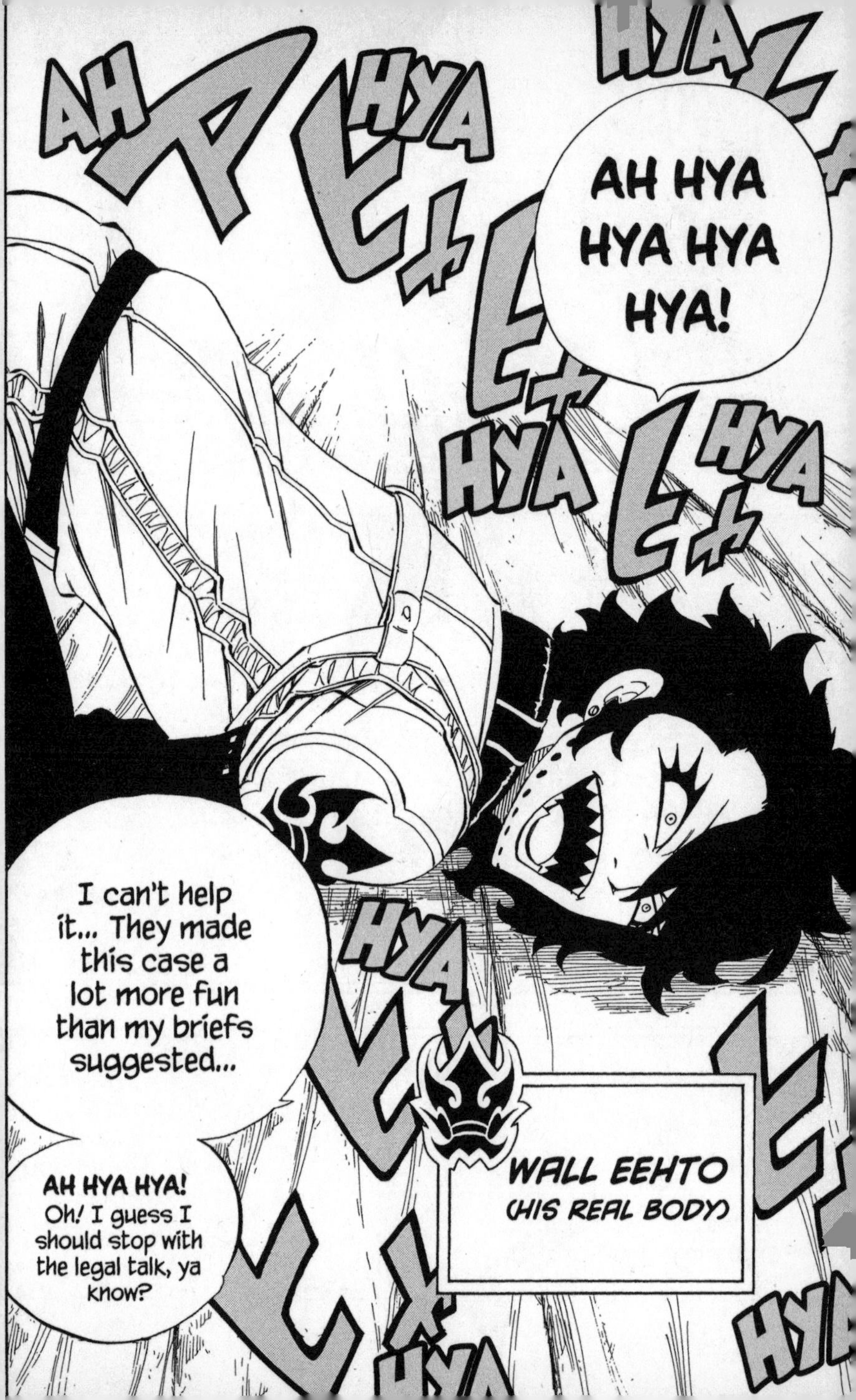
HYA
AH HYA HYA HYA HYA!
AH
HYA
HYA
HYA
WALL EEHTO (HIS REAL BODY)
HYA
HYA
I can't help it... They made this case a lot more fun than my briefs suggested...
AH HYA HYA! Oh! I guess I should stop with the legal talk, ya know?

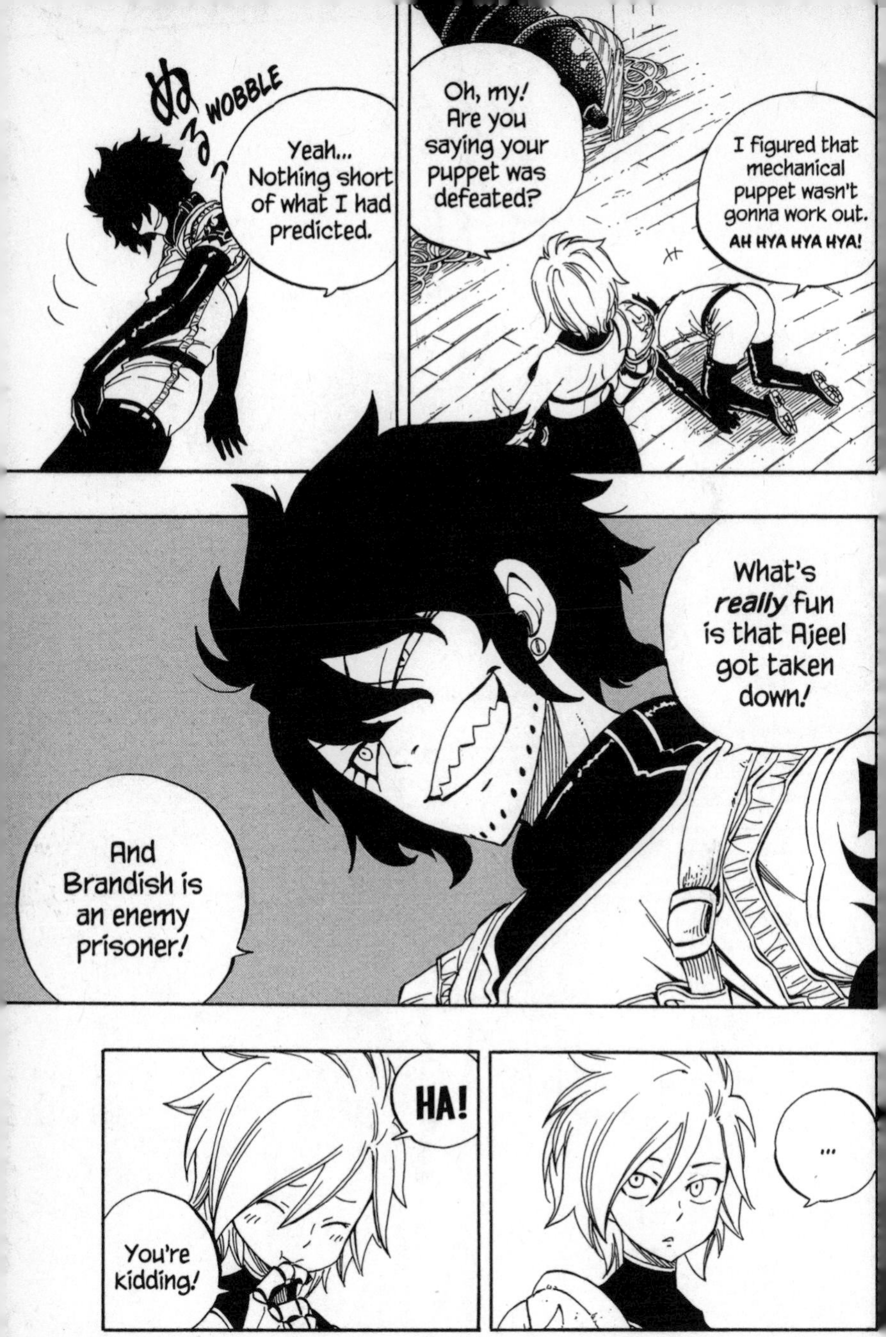
Oh, my! Are you saying your puppet was defeated?
I figured that mechanical puppet wasn't gonna work out.
AH HYA HYA HYA!
ぬる
WOBBLE
Yeah... Nothing short of what I had predicted.
What's *really* fun is that Ajeel got taken down!
And Brandish is an enemy prisoner!
...
HA!
You're kidding!

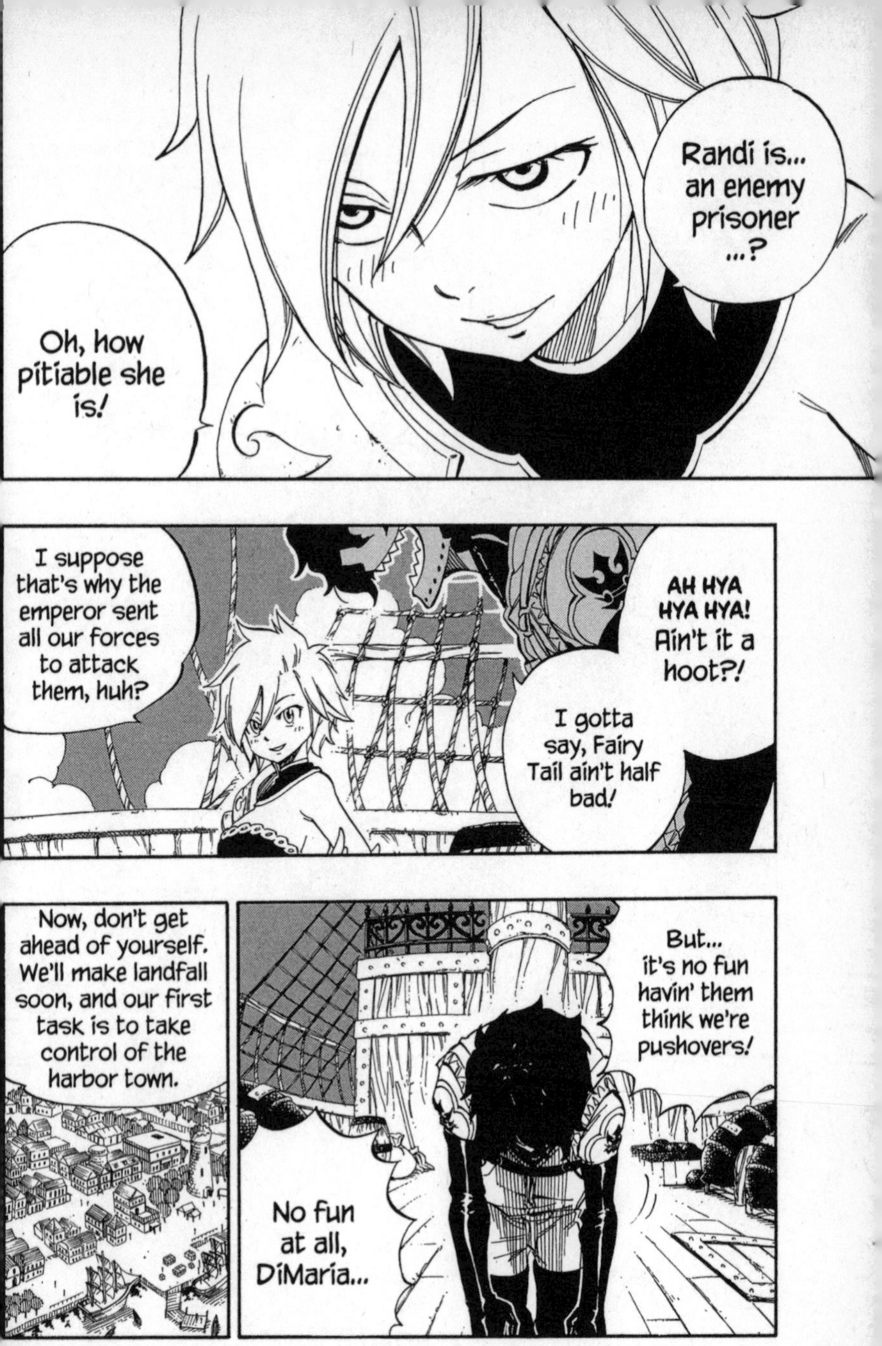
Randi is... an enemy prisoner ...?
Oh, how pitiable she is!
AH HYA HYA HYA! Ain't it a hoot?!
I gotta say, Fairy Tail ain't half bad!
I suppose that's why the emperor sent all our forces to attack them, huh?
But... it's no fun havin' them think we're pushovers!
No fun at all, DiMaria...
Now, don't get ahead of yourself. We'll make landfall soon, and our first task is to take control of the harbor town.

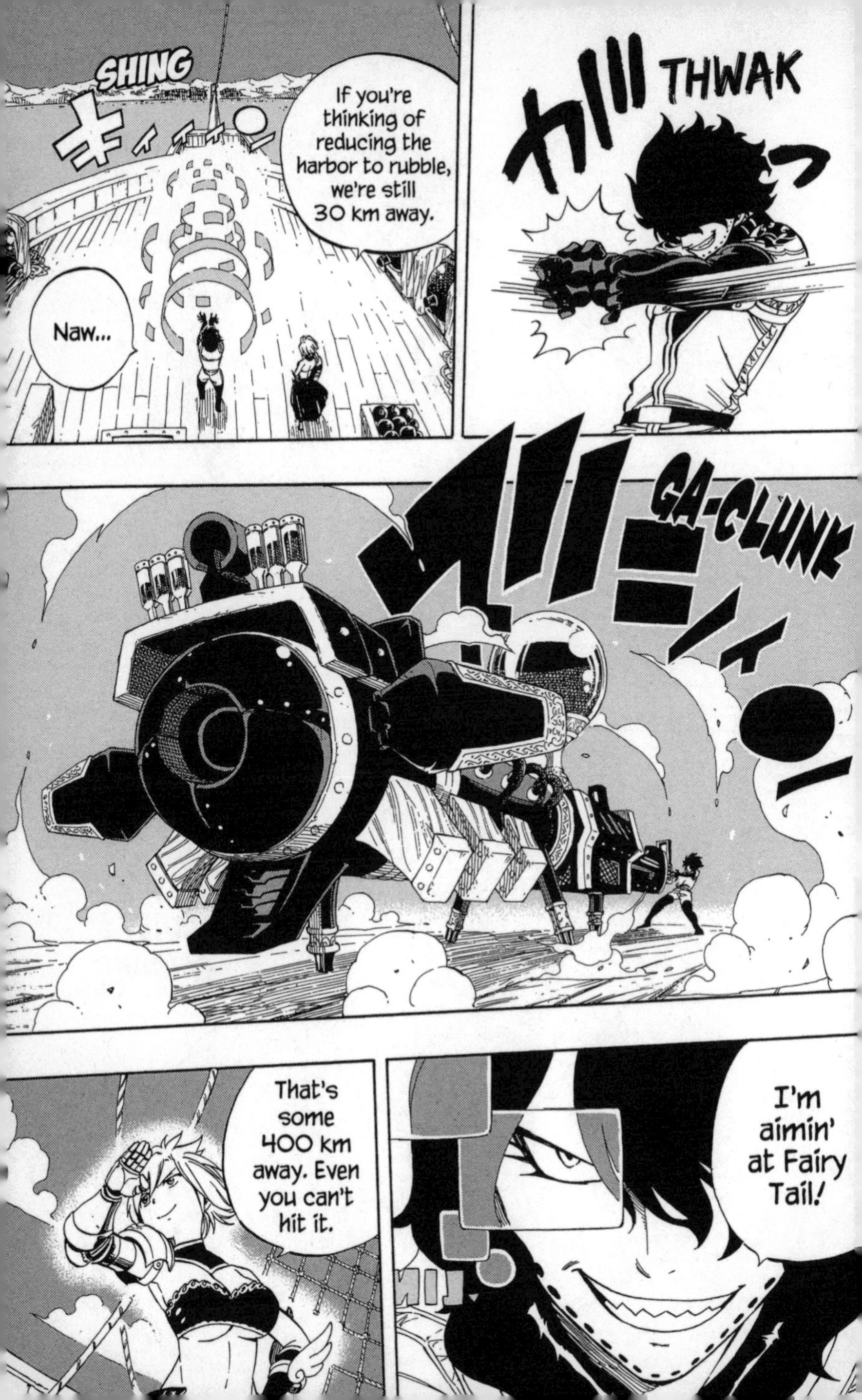
THWAK
If you're thinking of reducing the harbor to rubble, we're still 30 km away.
SHING
Naw...
GA-CLUNK
I'm aimin' at Fairy Tail!
That's some 400 km away. Even you can't hit it.

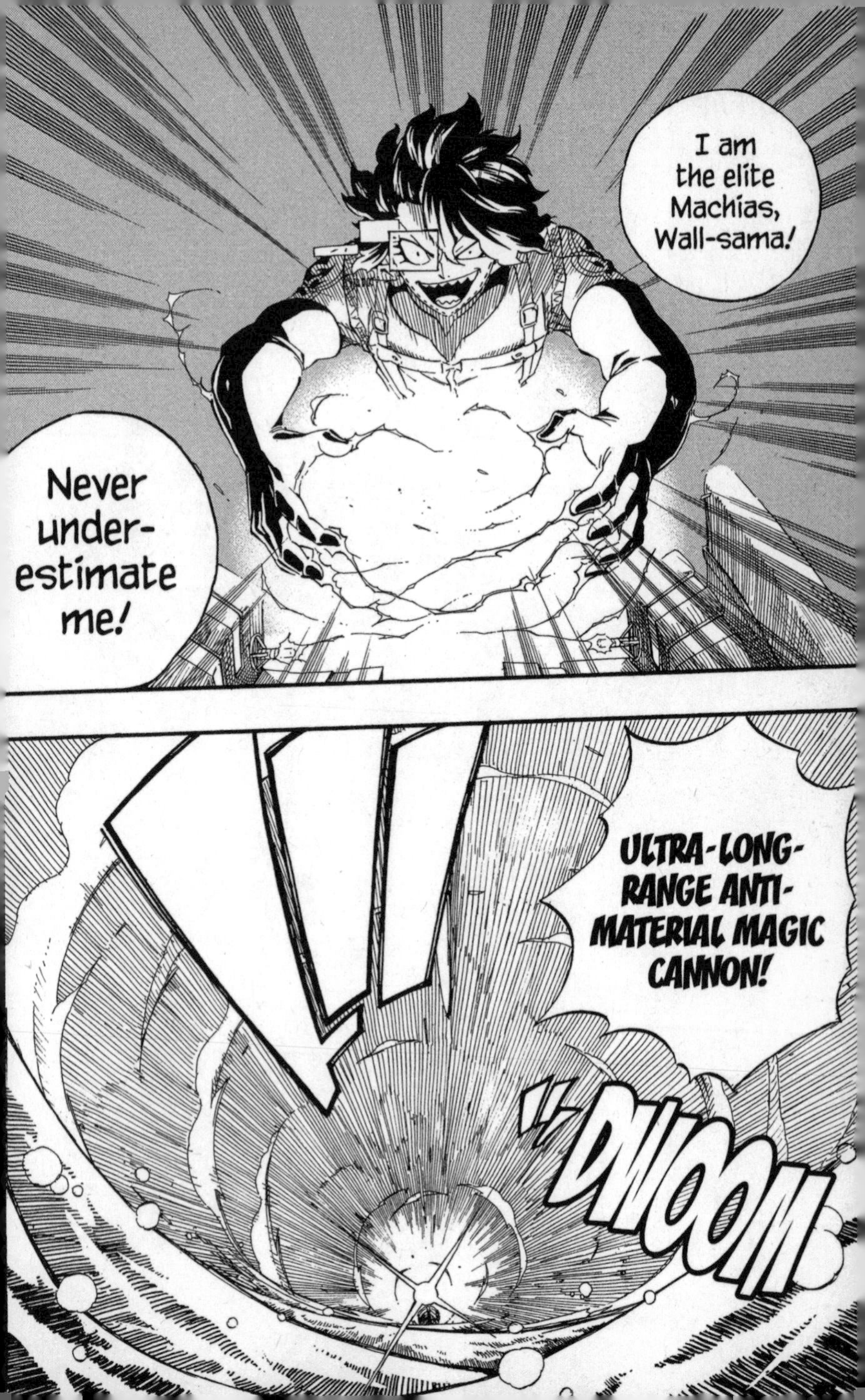
I am the elite Machias, Wall-sama!
Never under-estimate me!
ULTRA-LONG-RANGE ANTI-MATERIAL MAGIC CANNON!
DWOOM

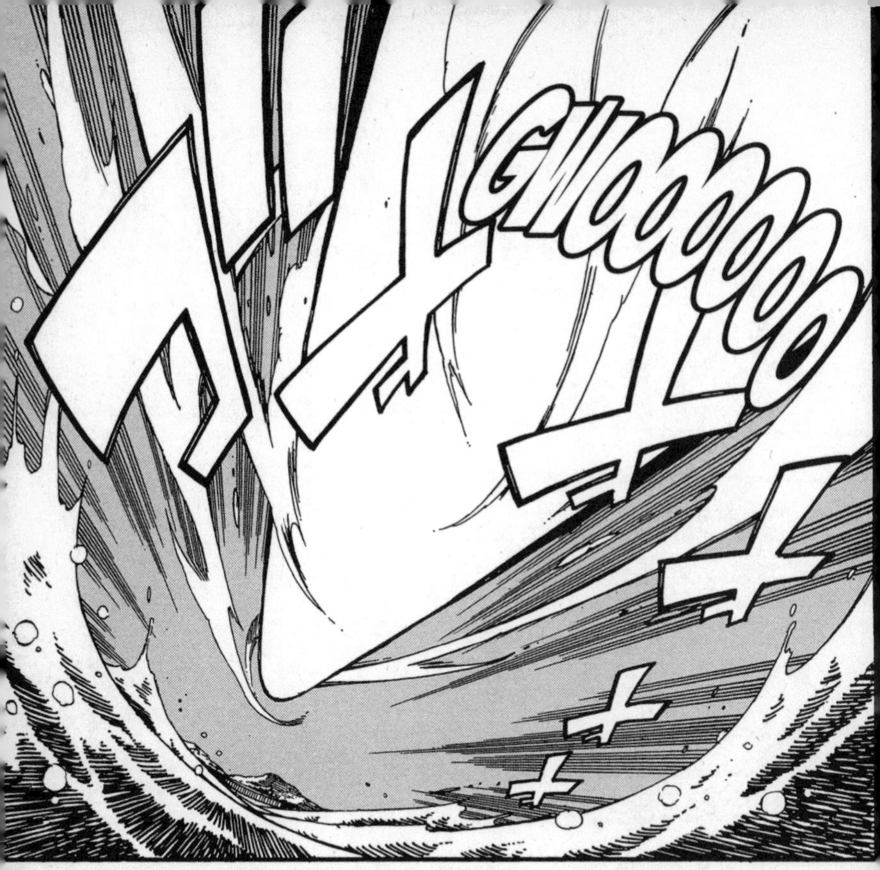
GUOOOOOO
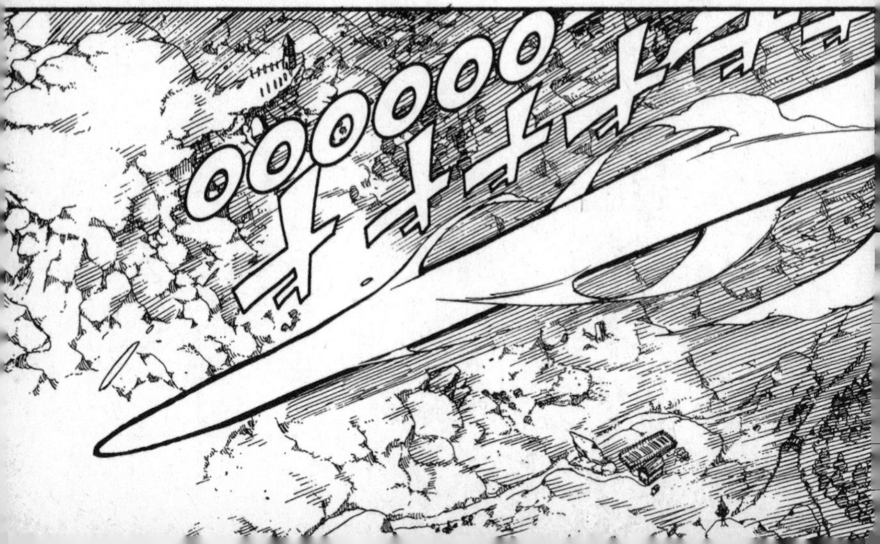
OOOOOOO

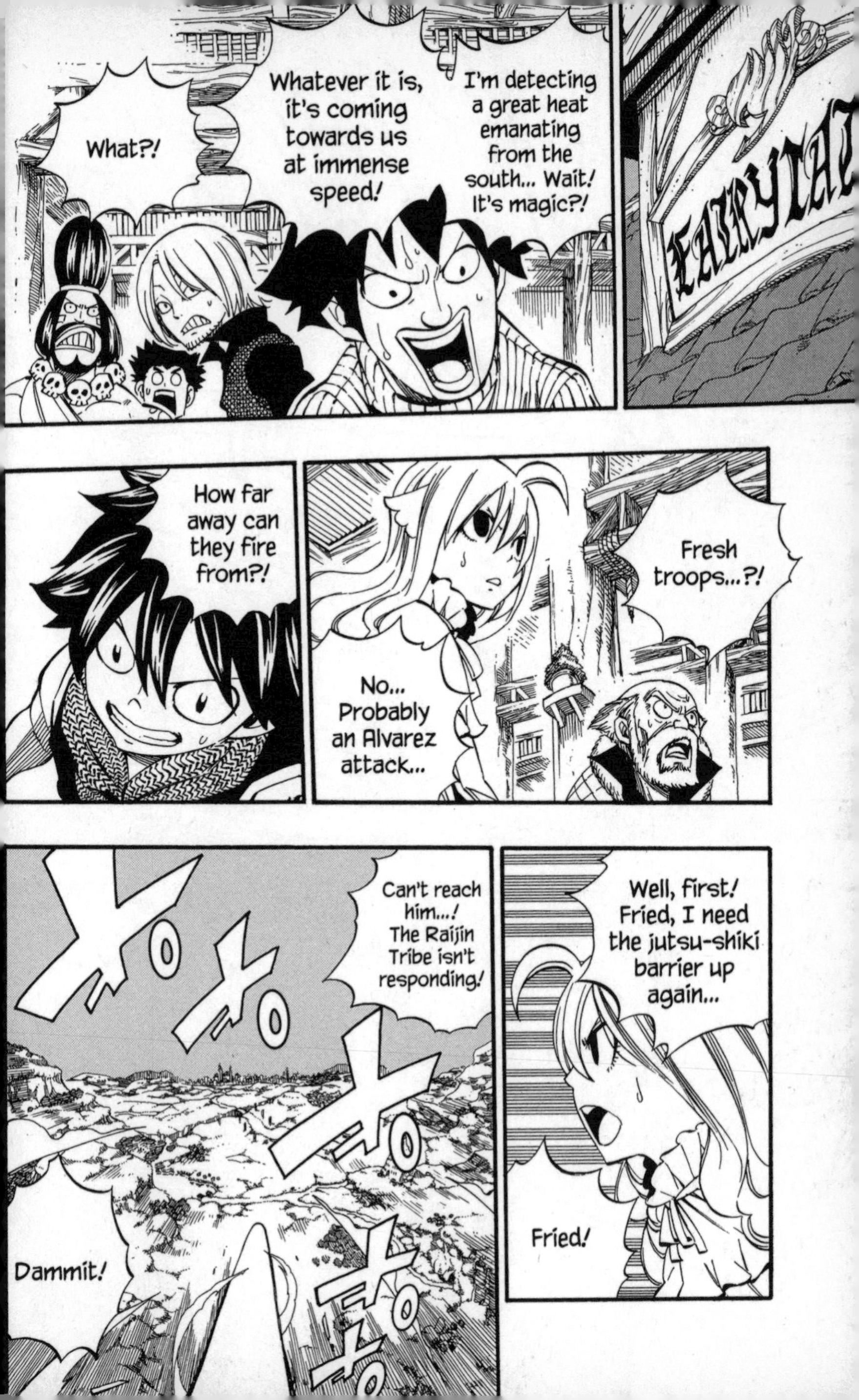
I'm detecting a great heat emanating from the south... Wait! It's magic?!
Whatever it is, it's coming towards us at immense speed!
What?!
Fresh troops...?!
No... Probably an Alvarez attack...
How far away can they fire from?!
Well, first! Fried, I need the jutsu-shiki barrier up again...
Fried!
Can't reach him...! The Raijin Tribe isn't responding!
Dammit!

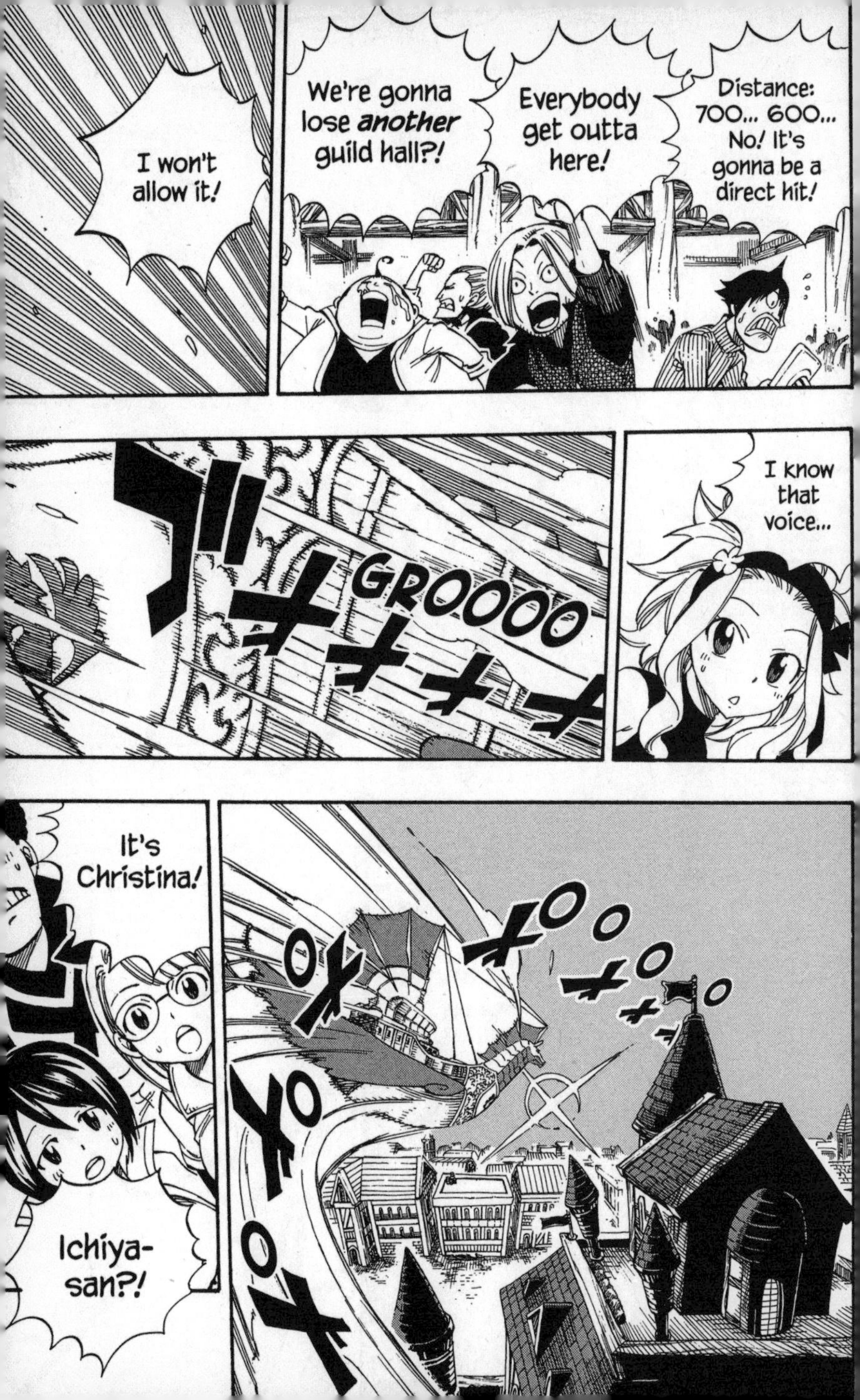
Distance: 700... 600... No! It's gonna be a direct hit!
Everybody get outta here!
We're gonna lose *another* guild hall?!
I won't allow it!
I know that voice...
GROOOOO
It's Christina!
Ichiya-san?!

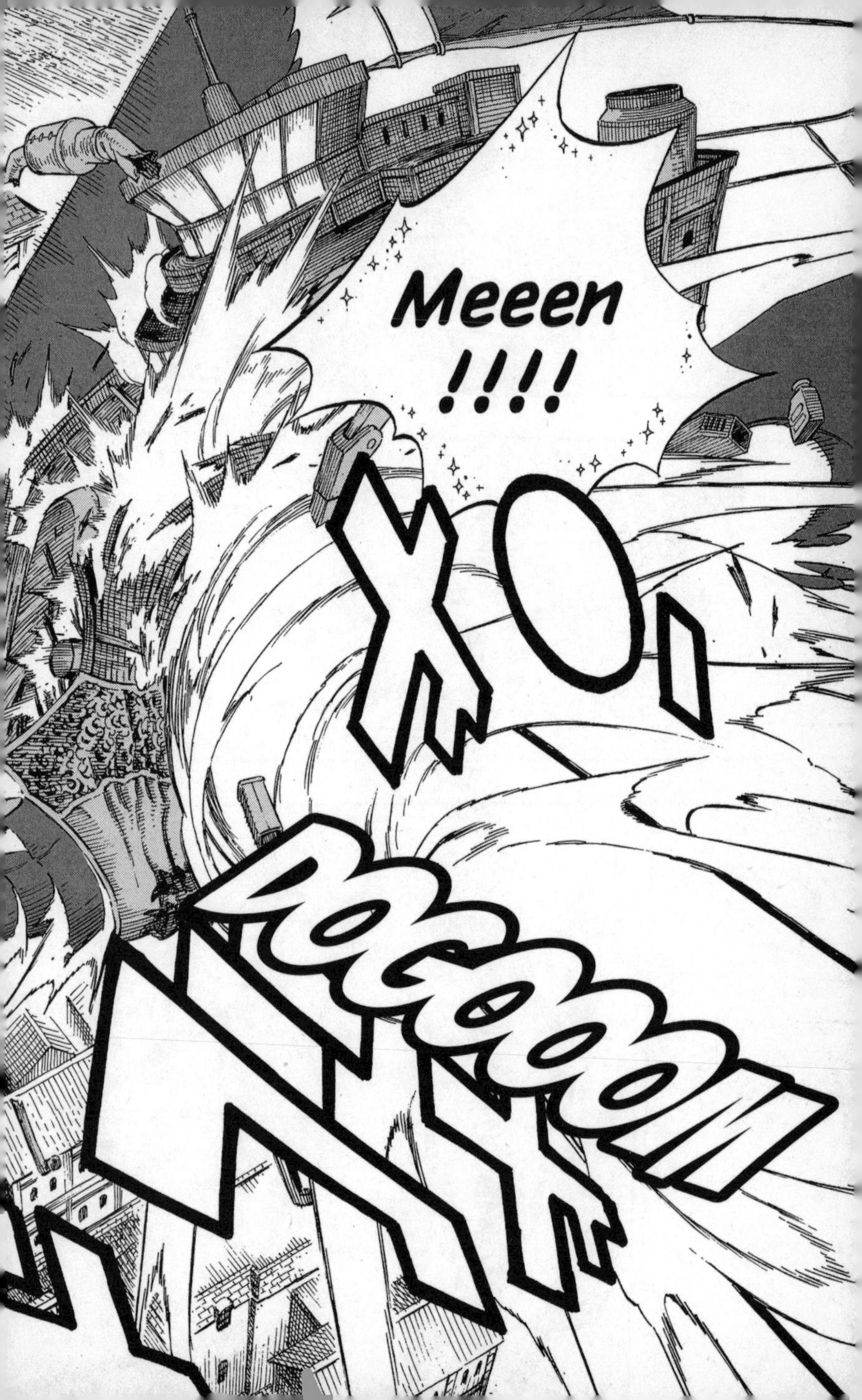
Meeen !!!!

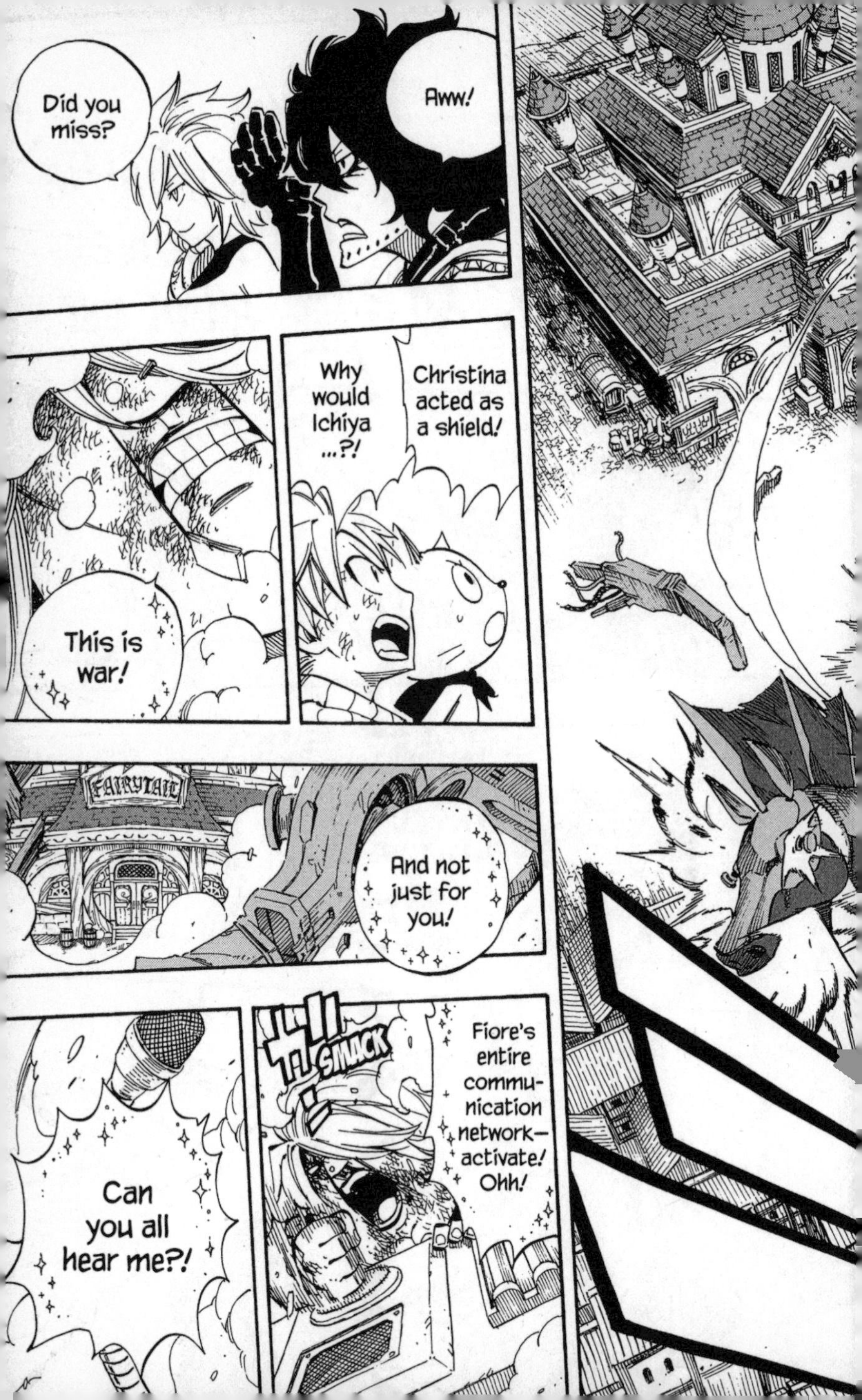
Aww!
Did you miss?
Christina acted as a shield!
Why would Ichiya ...?!
This is war!
And not just for you!
SMACK
Fiore's entire communication network—activate! Ohh!
Can you all hear me?!

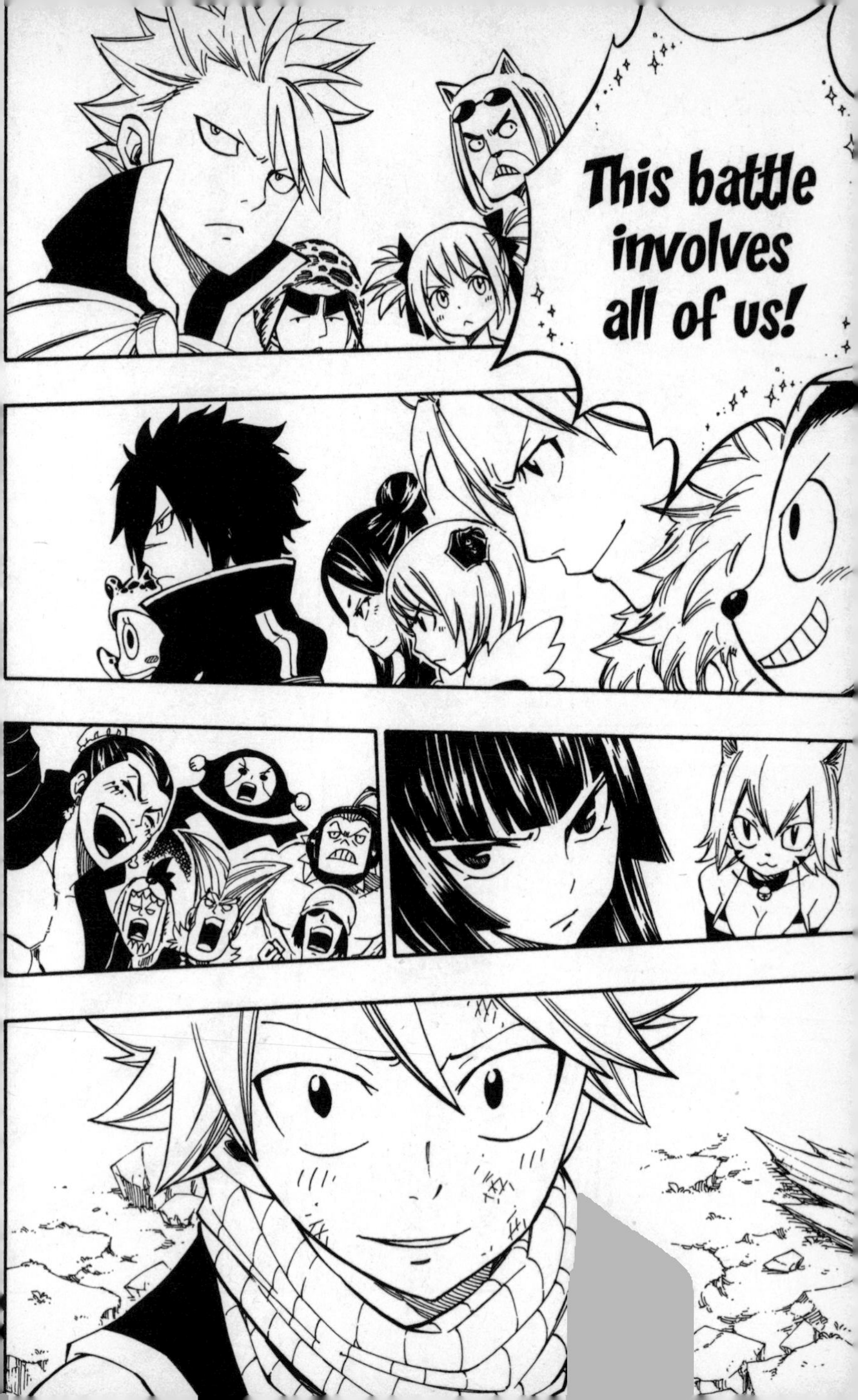
This battle involves all of us!

FAIRY TAIL

フェアリーテイル

Chapter 462: Battlefield

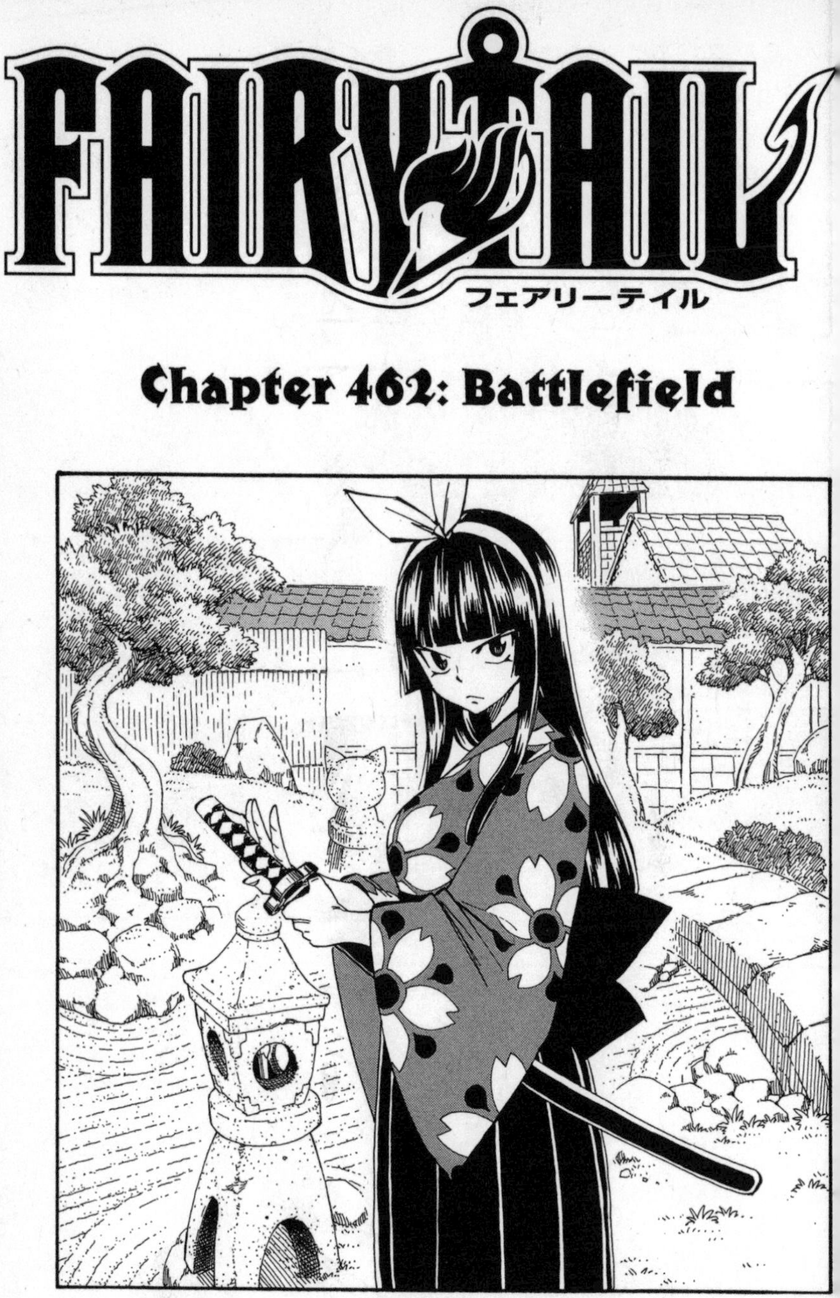

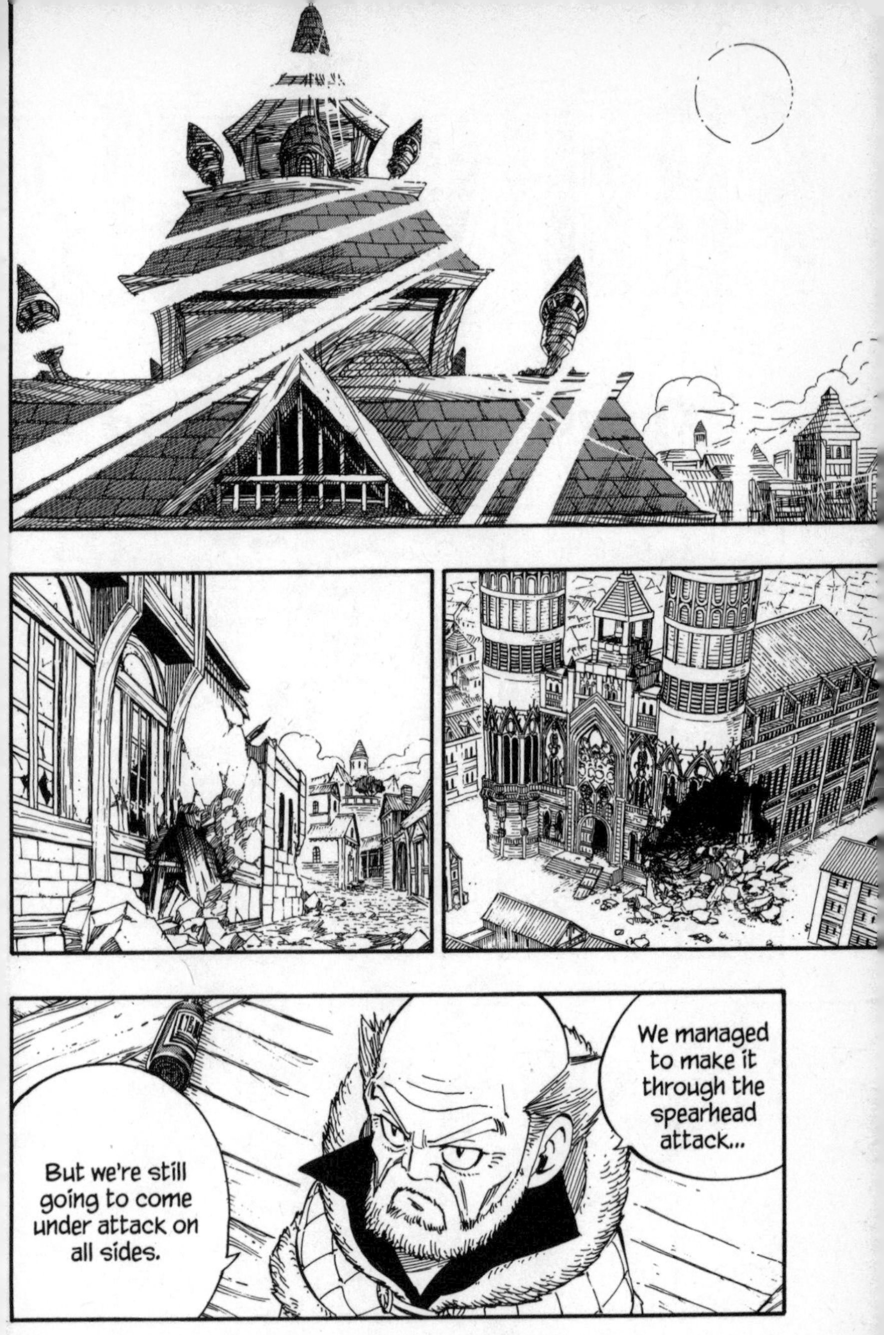
We managed to make it through the spearhead attack...
But we're still going to come under attack on all sides.

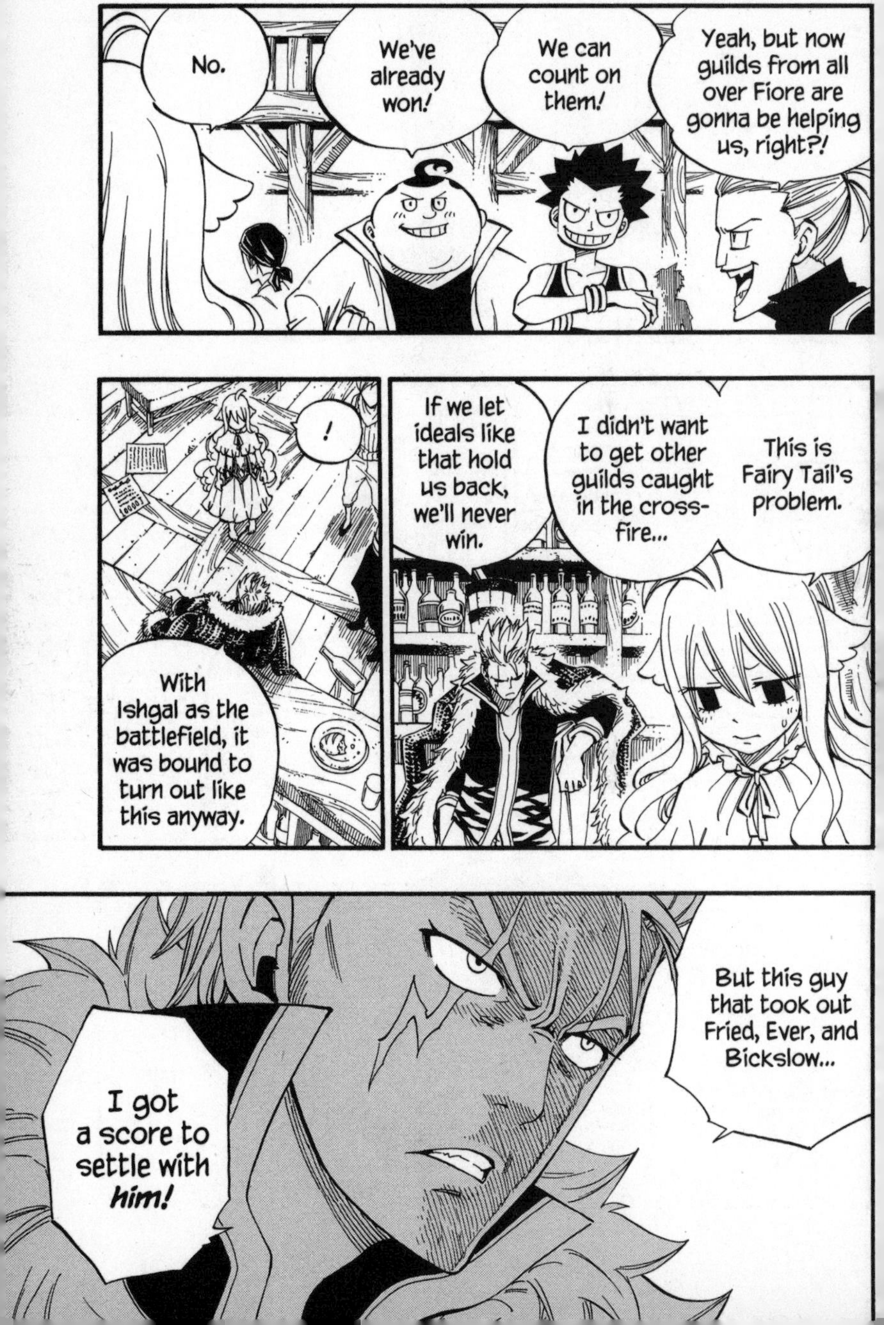
Yeah, but now guilds from all over Fiore are gonna be helping us, right?!
We can count on them!
We've already won!
No.
This is Fairy Tail's problem.
I didn't want to get other guilds caught in the cross-fire...
If we let ideals like that hold us back, we'll never win.
!
With Ishgal as the battlefield, it was bound to turn out like this anyway.
But this guy that took out Fried, Ever, and Bickslow...
I got a score to settle with *him!*

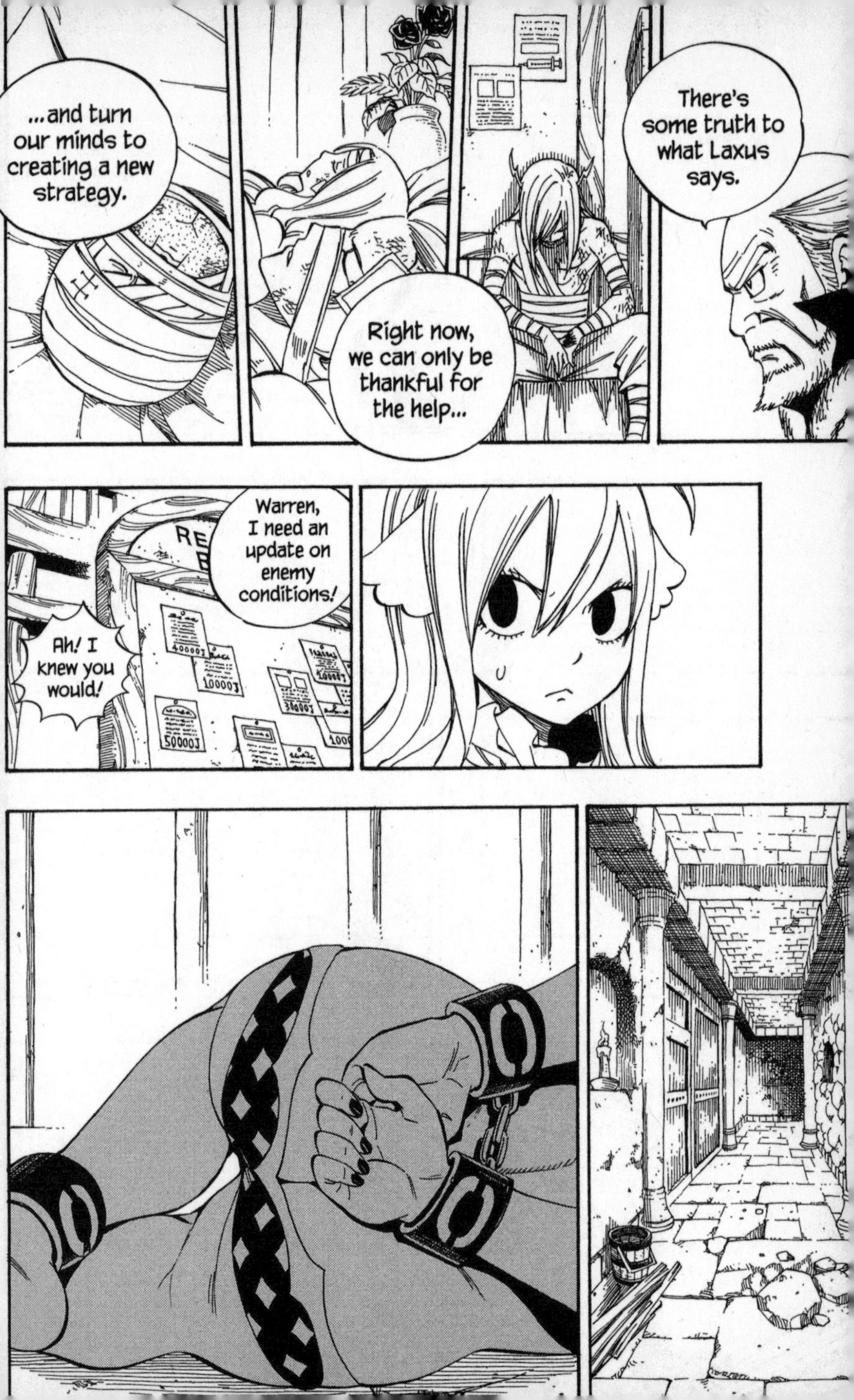
There's some truth to what Laxus says.
Right now, we can only be thankful for the help...
...and turn our minds to creating a new strategy.
Warren, I need an update on enemy conditions!
Ah! I knew you would!

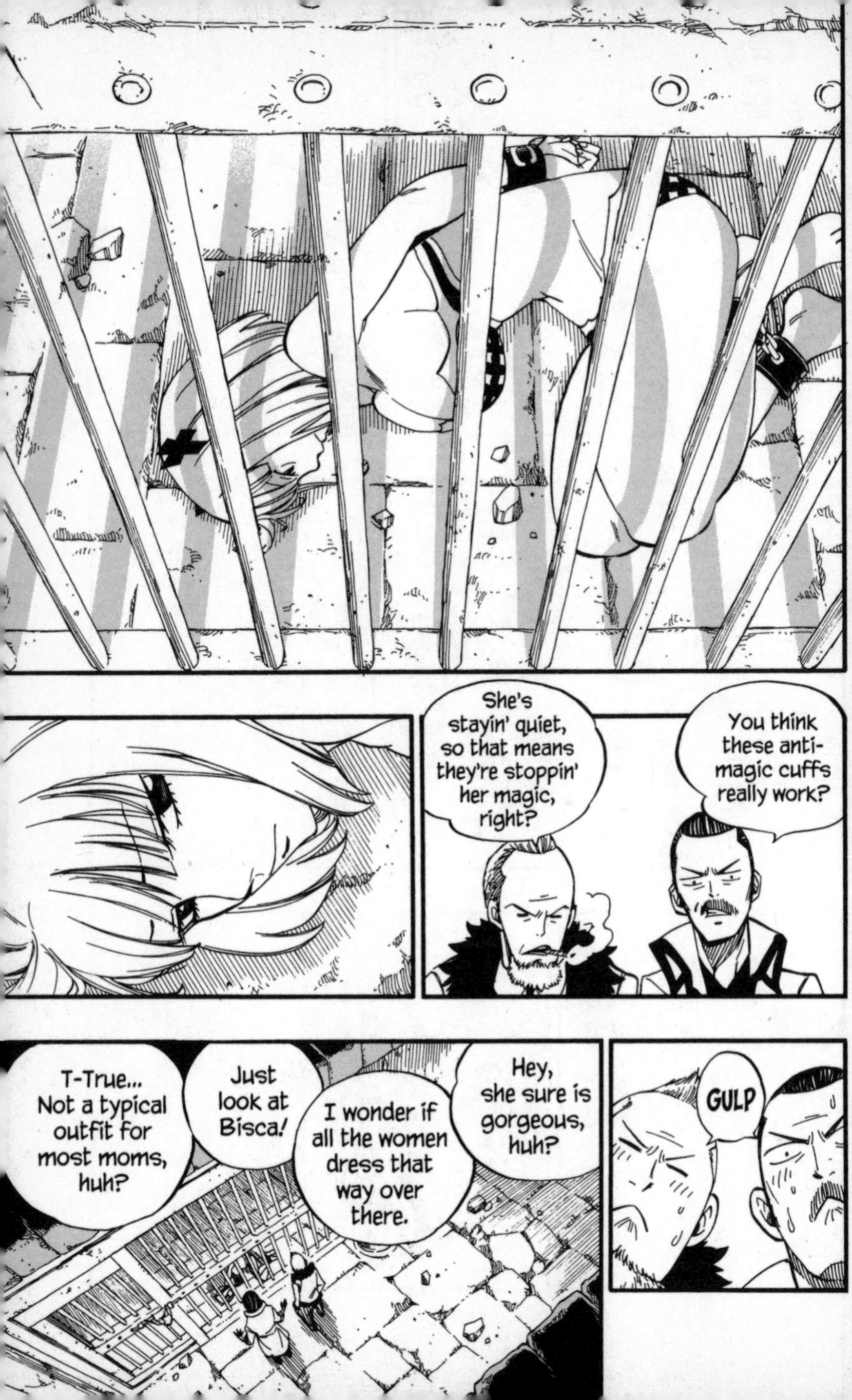
You think these anti-magic cuffs really work?
She's stayin' quiet, so that means they're stoppin' her magic, right?
GULP
Hey, she sure is gorgeous, huh?
I wonder if all the women dress that way over there.
Just look at Bisca!
T-True... Not a typical outfit for most moms, huh?

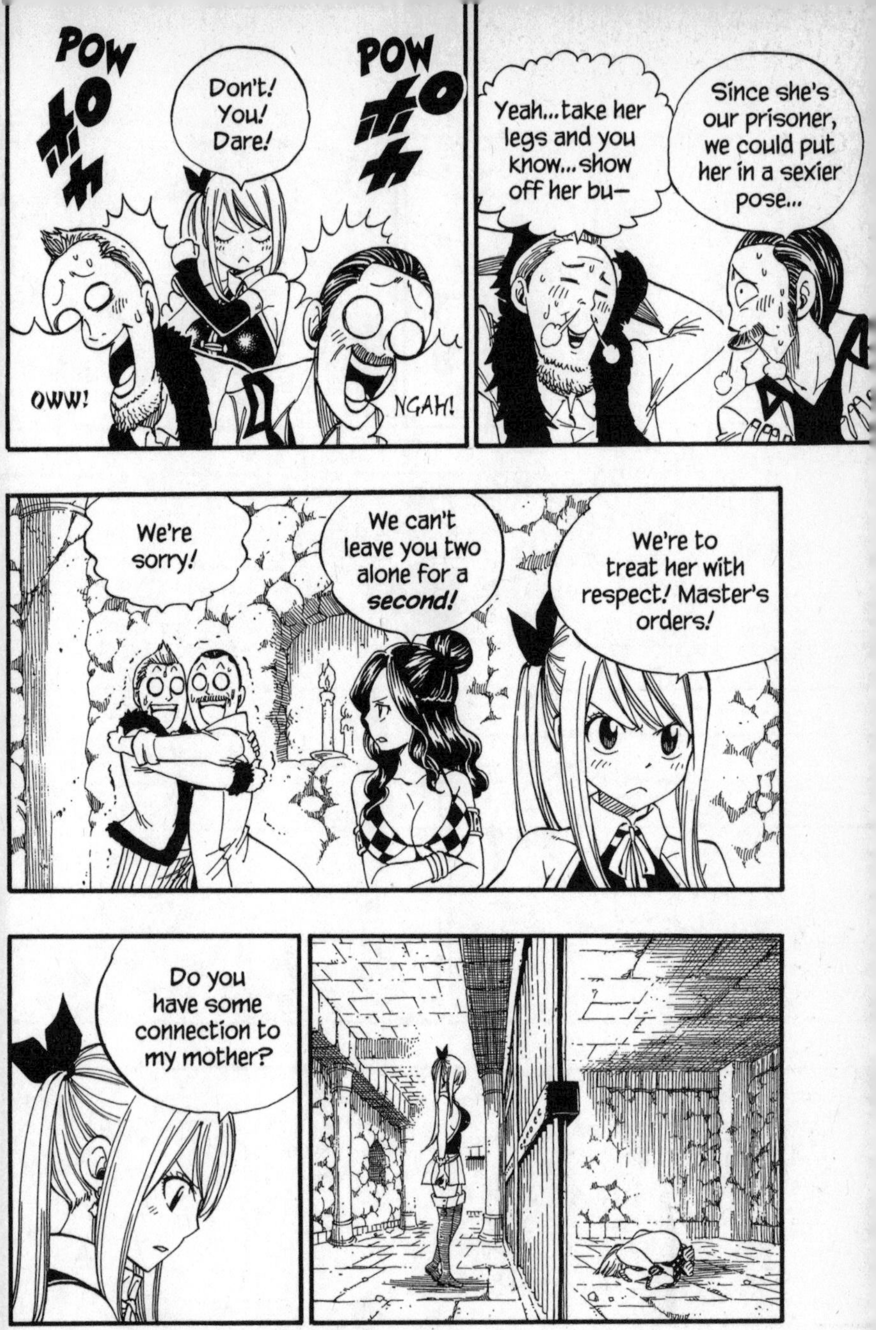
Since she's our prisoner, we could put her in a sexier pose...
Yeah...take her legs and you know...show off her bu–
POW
Don't! You! Dare!
POW
NGAH!
OWW!
We're to treat her with respect! Master's orders!
We can't leave you two alone for a *second!*
We're sorry!
Do you have some connection to my mother?

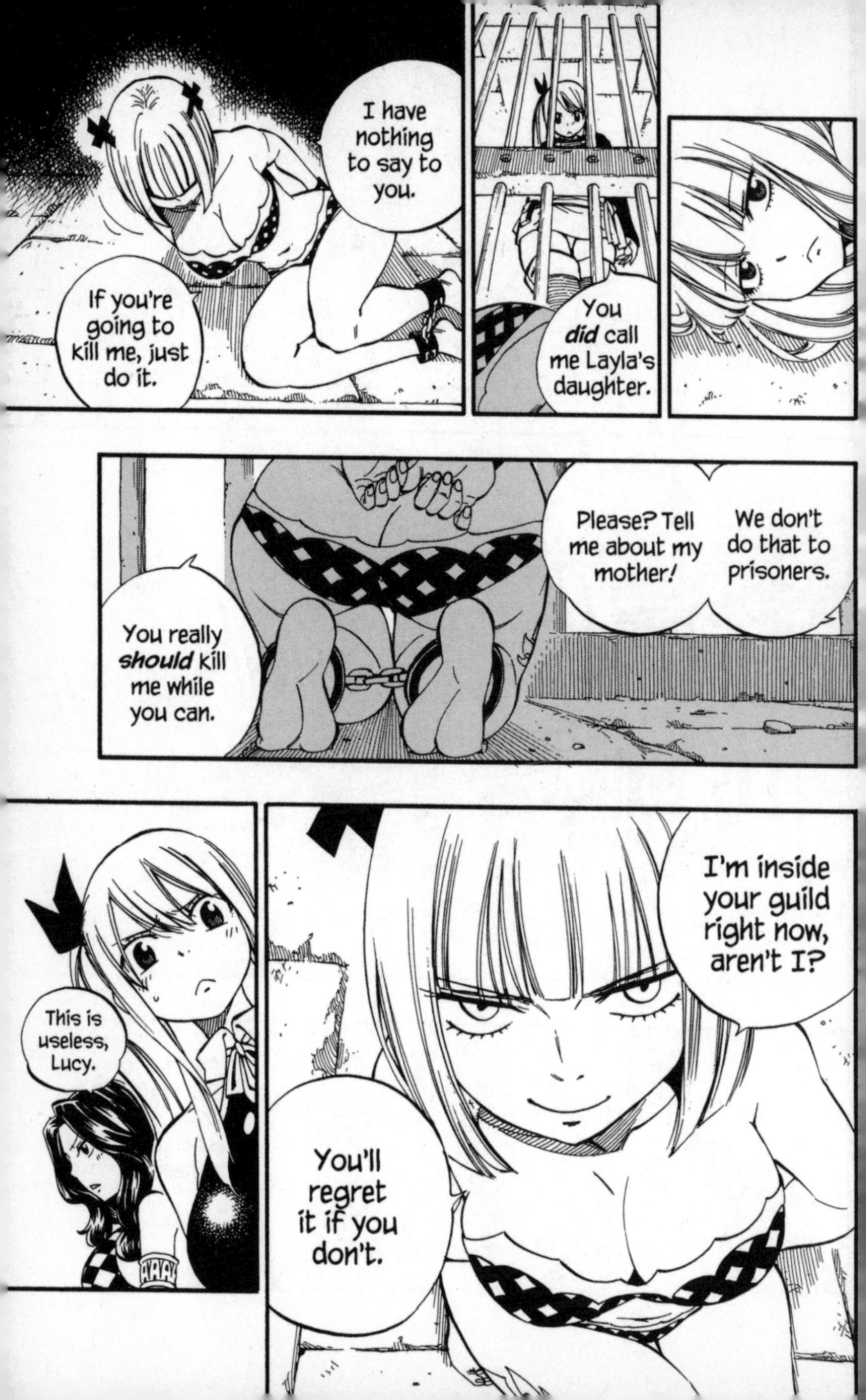
You *did* call me Layla's daughter.
I have nothing to say to you.
If you're going to kill me, just do it.
We don't do that to prisoners.
Please? Tell me about my mother!
You really *should* kill me while you can.
I'm inside your guild right now, aren't I?
You'll regret it if you don't.
This is useless, Lucy.

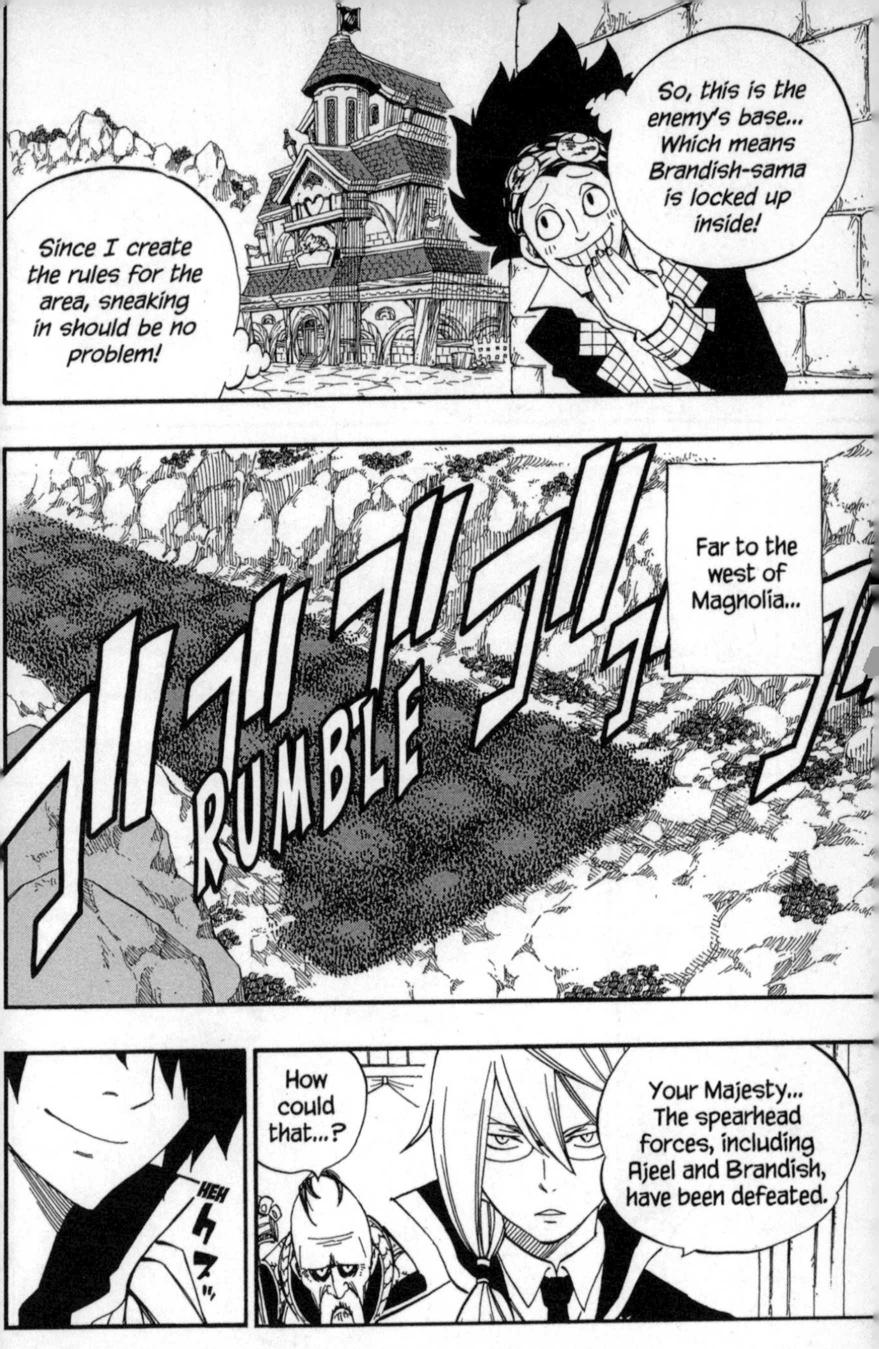
So, this is the enemy's base... Which means Brandish-sama is locked up inside!
Since I create the rules for the area, sneaking in should be no problem!
Far to the west of Magnolia...
RUMBLE
Your Majesty... The spearhead forces, including Ajeel and Brandish, have been defeated.
How could that...?
HEH

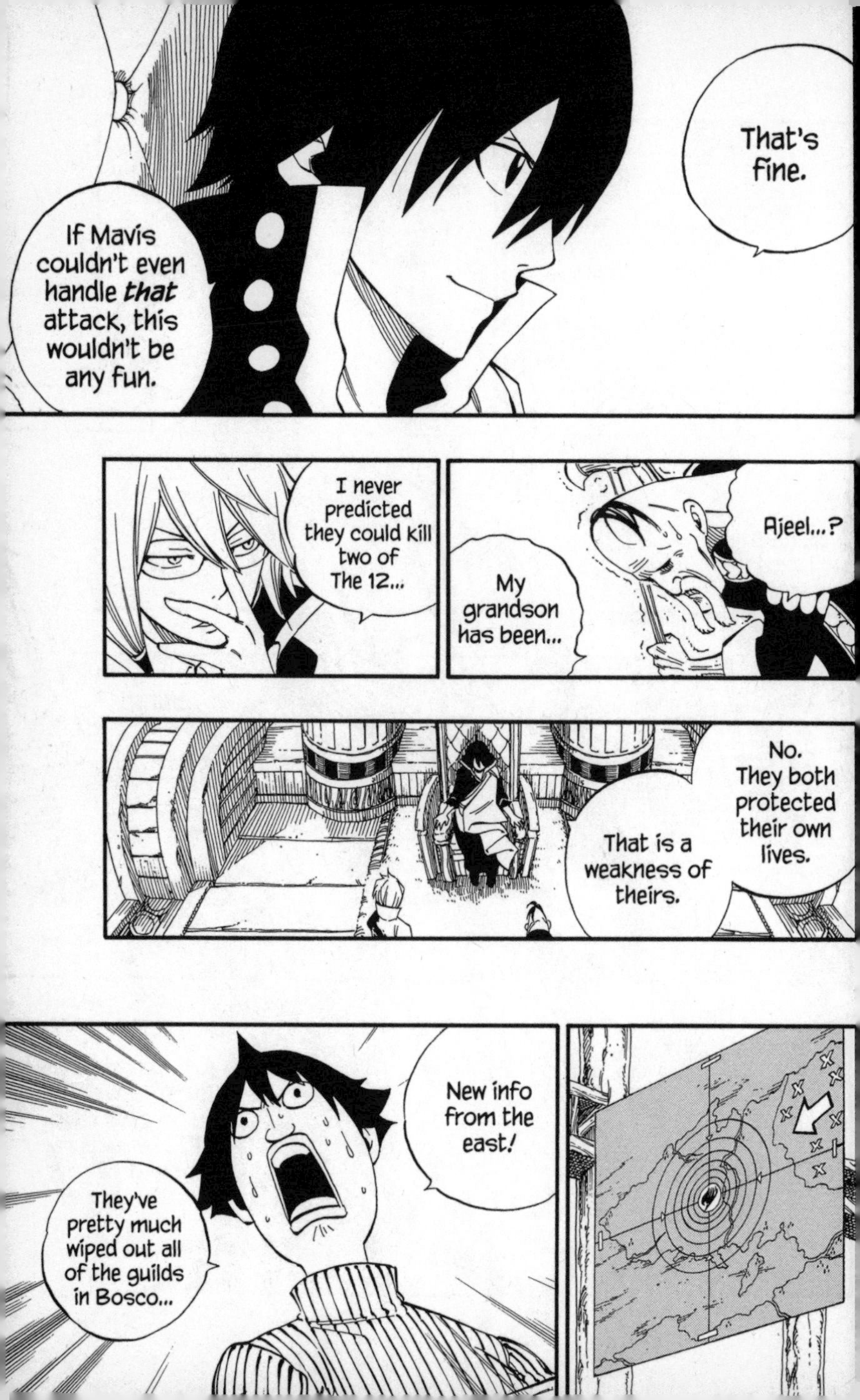
That's fine.
If Mavis couldn't even handle *that* attack, this wouldn't be any fun.
Ajeel...?
My grandson has been...
I never predicted they could kill two of The 12...
No. They both protected their own lives.
That is a weakness of theirs.
New info from the east!
They've pretty much wiped out all of the guilds in Bosco...

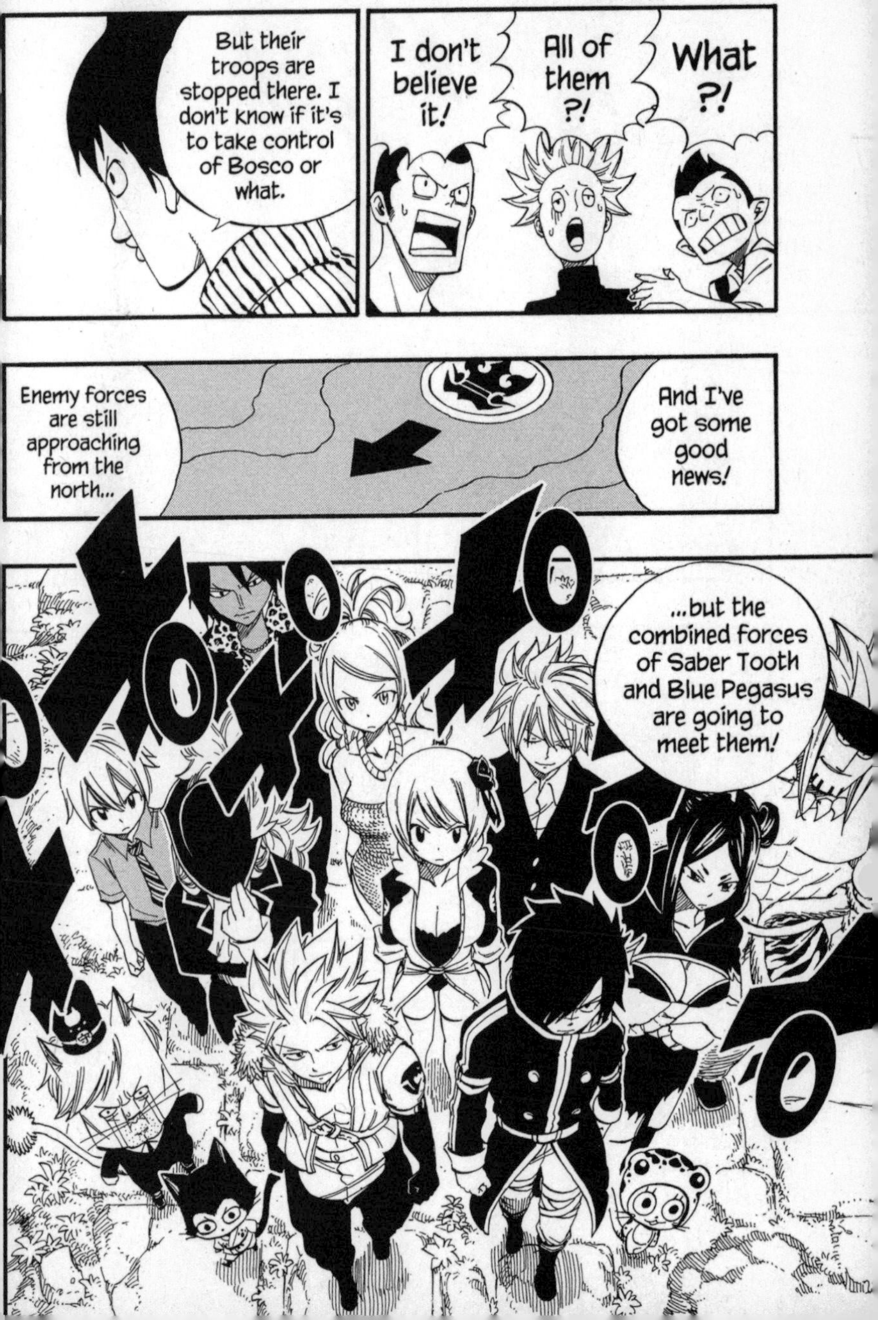
What ?!
All of them ?!
I don't believe it!
But their troops are stopped there. I don't know if it's to take control of Bosco or what.
And I've got some good news!
Enemy forces are still approaching from the north...
...but the combined forces of Saber Tooth and Blue Pegasus are going to meet them!

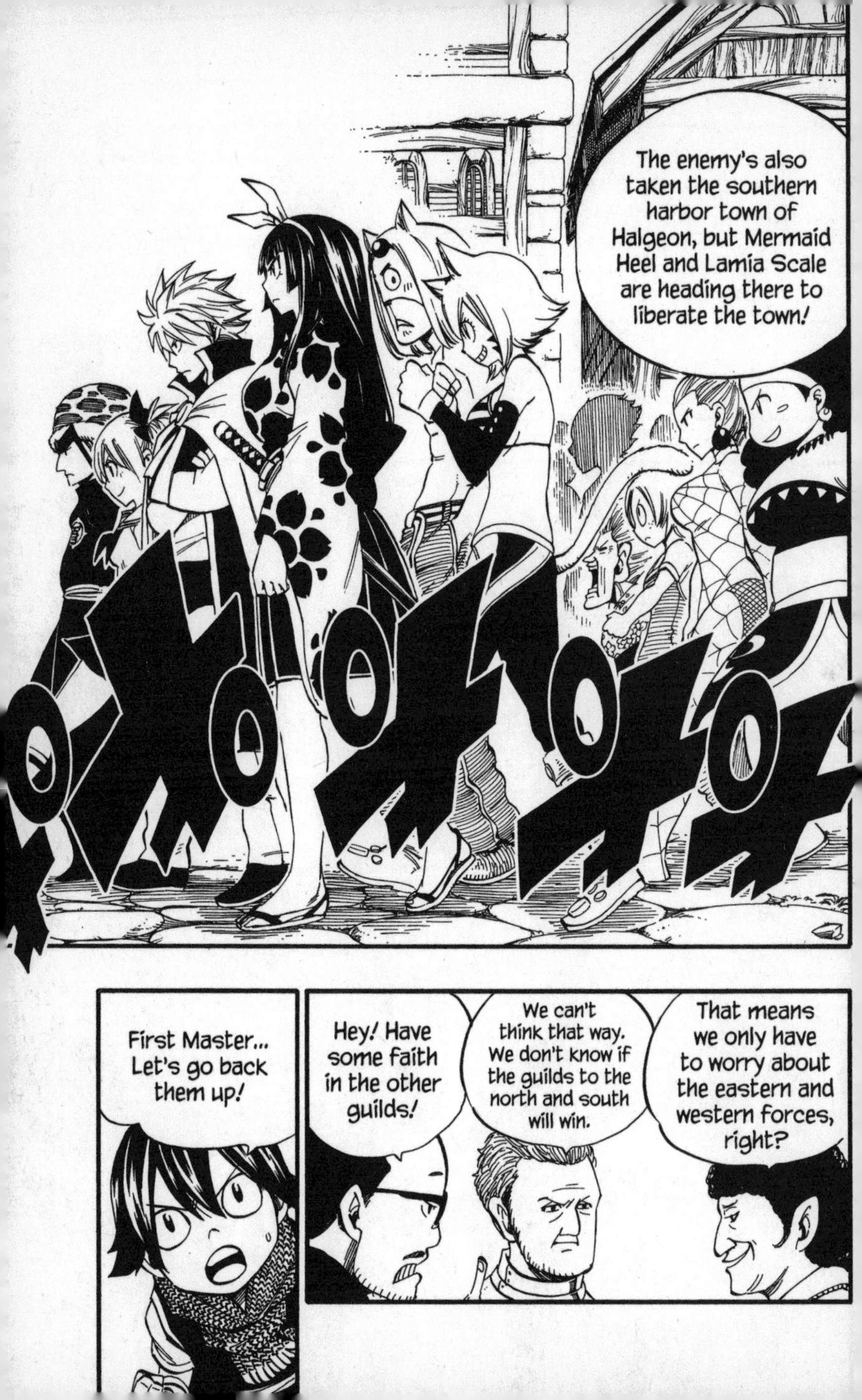
The enemy's also taken the southern harbor town of Halgeon, but Mermaid Heel and Lamia Scale are heading there to liberate the town!
That means we only have to worry about the eastern and western forces, right?
We can't think that way. We don't know if the guilds to the north and south will win.
Hey! Have some faith in the other guilds!
First Master... Let's go back them up!

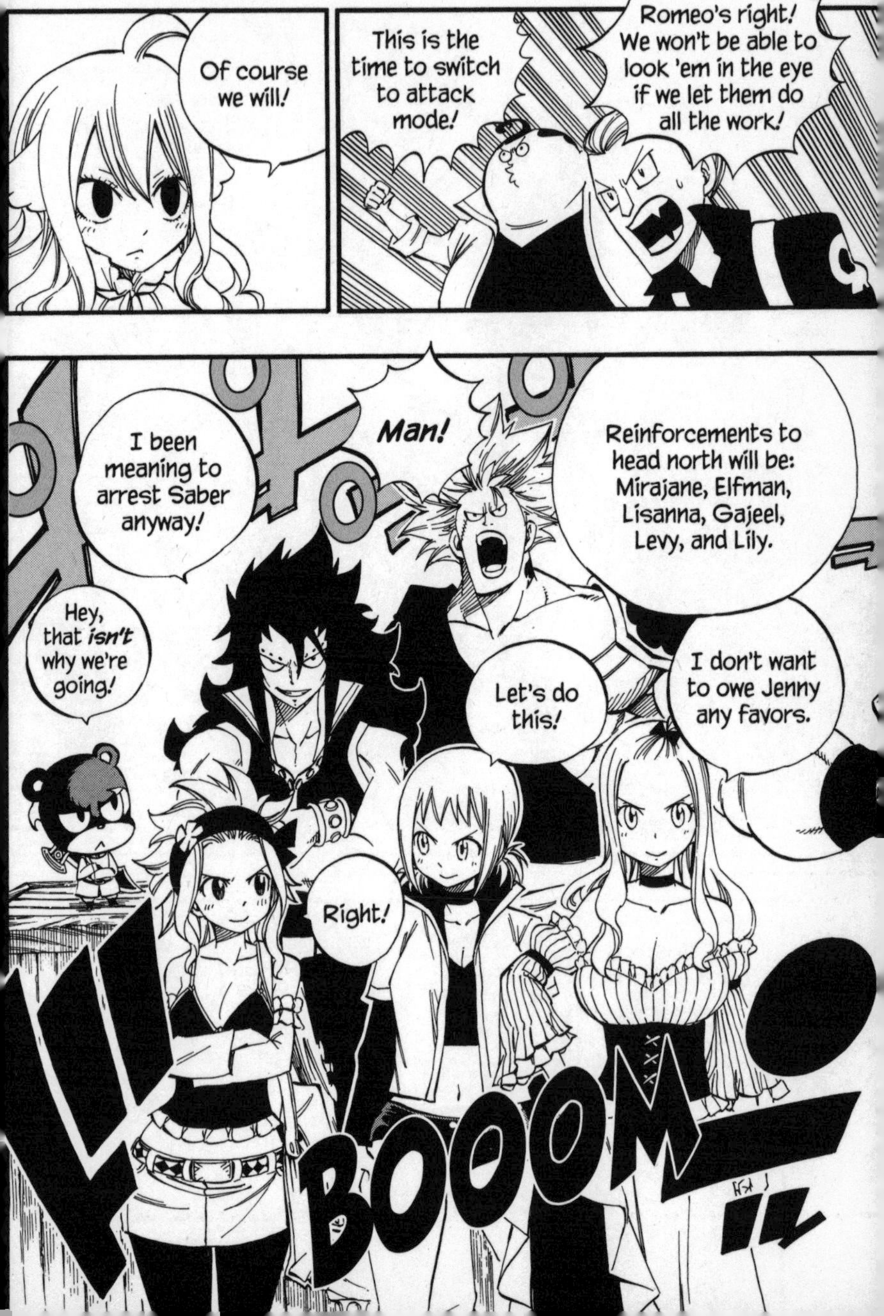
Romeo's right! We won't be able to look 'em in the eye if we let them do all the work!
This is the time to switch to attack mode!
Of course we will!
Reinforcements to head north will be: Mirajane, Elfman, Lisanna, Gajeel, Levy, and Lily.
Man!
I been meaning to arrest Saber anyway!
I don't want to owe Jenny any favors.
Let's do this!
Hey, that *isn't* why we're going!
Right!
BOOOM!!

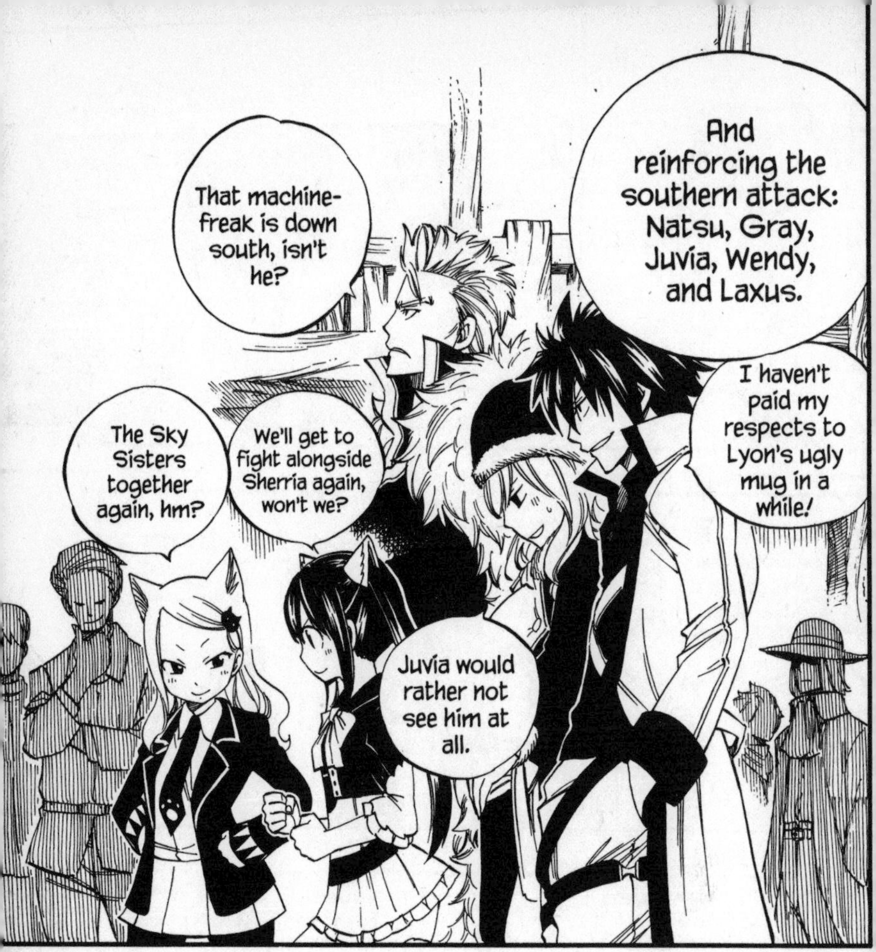
And reinforcing the southern attack: Natsu, Gray, Juvia, Wendy, and Laxus.
That machine-freak is down south, isn't he?
I haven't paid my respects to Lyon's ugly mug in a while!
We'll get to fight alongside Sherria again, won't we?
The Sky Sisters together again, hm?
Juvia would rather not see him at all.

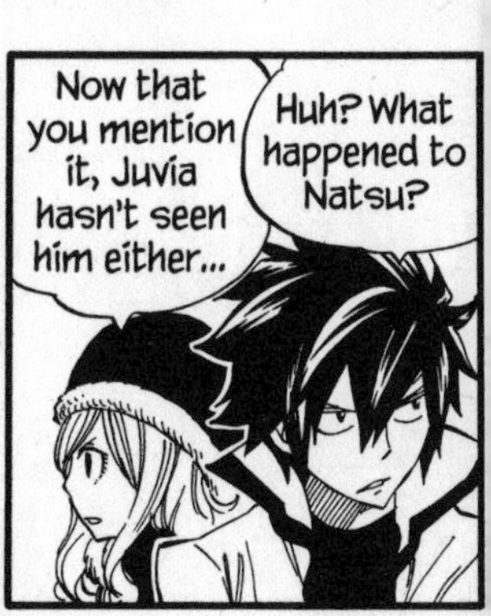
Huh? What happened to Natsu?
Now that you mention it, Juvia hasn't seen him either...

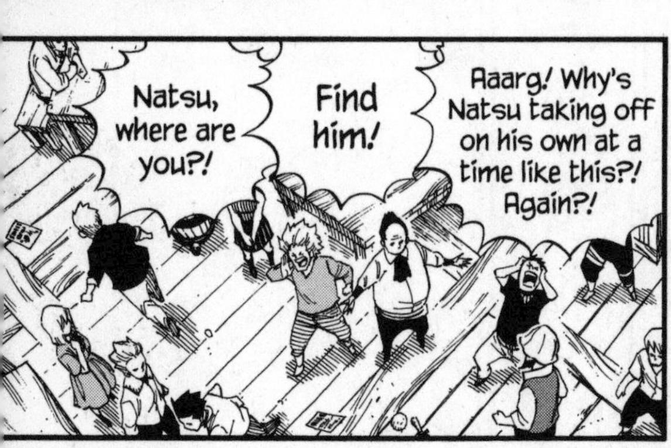
Aaarg! Why's Natsu taking off on his own at a time like this?! Again?!
Find him!
Natsu, where are you?!

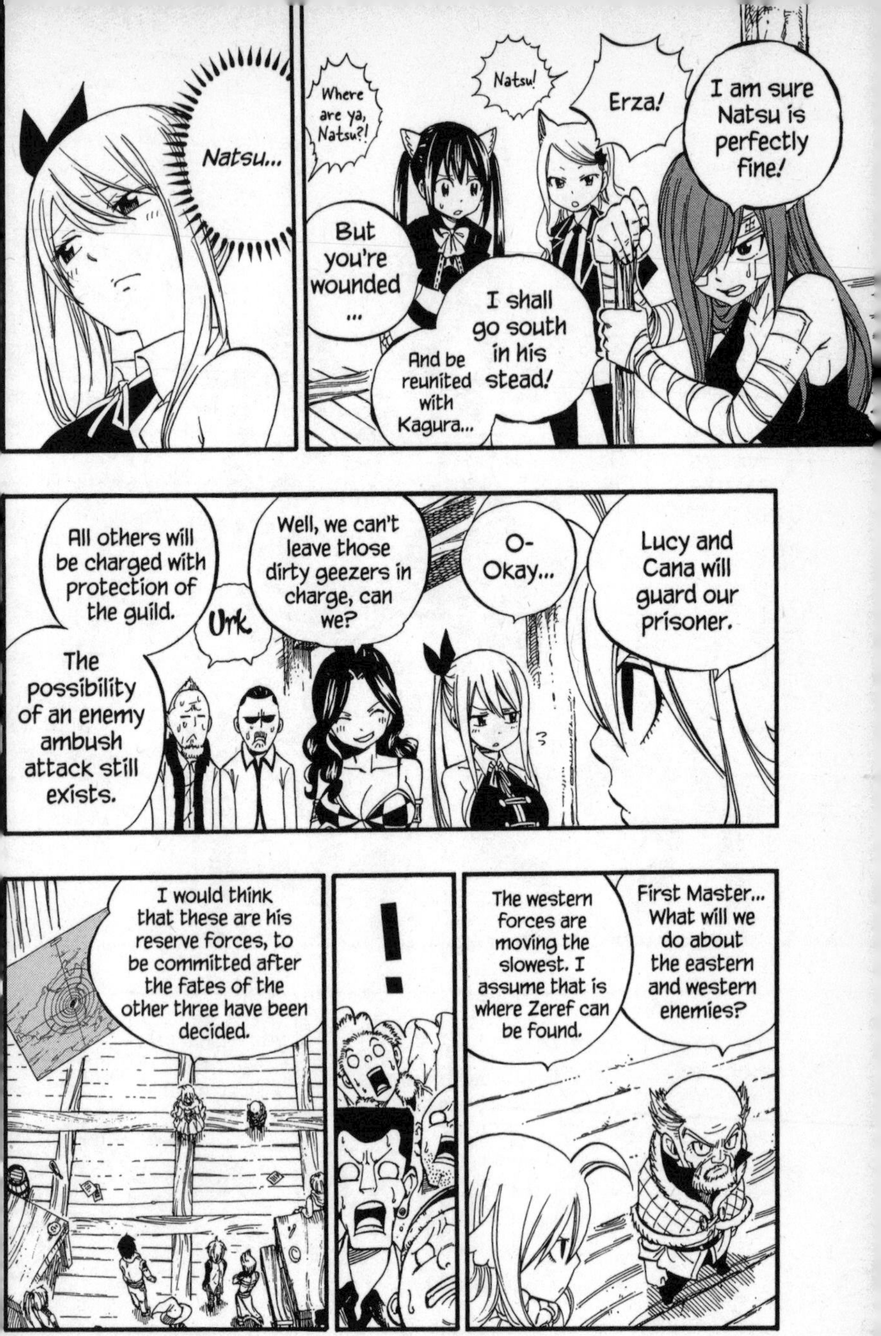
I am sure Natsu is perfectly fine!
Erza!
Natsu!
Where are ya, Natsu?!
I shall go south in his stead!
But you're wounded ...
And be reunited with Kagura...
Natsu...
Lucy and Cana will guard our prisoner.
O- Okay...
Well, we can't leave those dirty geezers in charge, can we?
Urk.
All others will be charged with protection of the guild.
The possibility of an enemy ambush attack still exists.
First Master... What will we do about the eastern and western enemies?
The western forces are moving the slowest. I assume that is where Zeref can be found.
!
I would think that these are his reserve forces, to be committed after the fates of the other three have been decided.

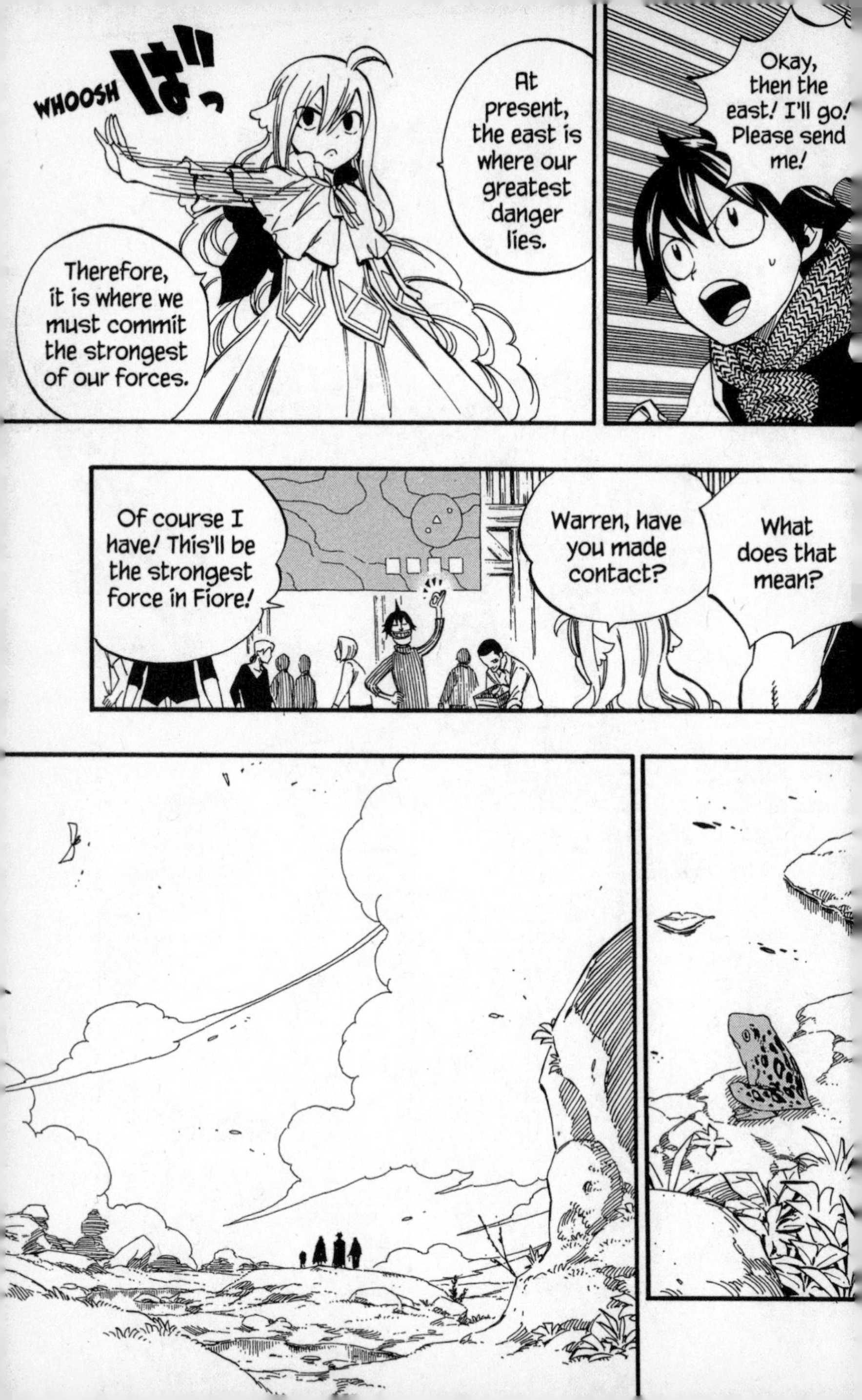
Okay, then the east! I'll go! Please send me!
At present, the east is where our greatest danger lies.
WHOOSH
ばっ
Therefore, it is where we must commit the strongest of our forces.
What does that mean?
Warren, have you made contact?
Of course I have! This'll be the strongest force in Fiore!

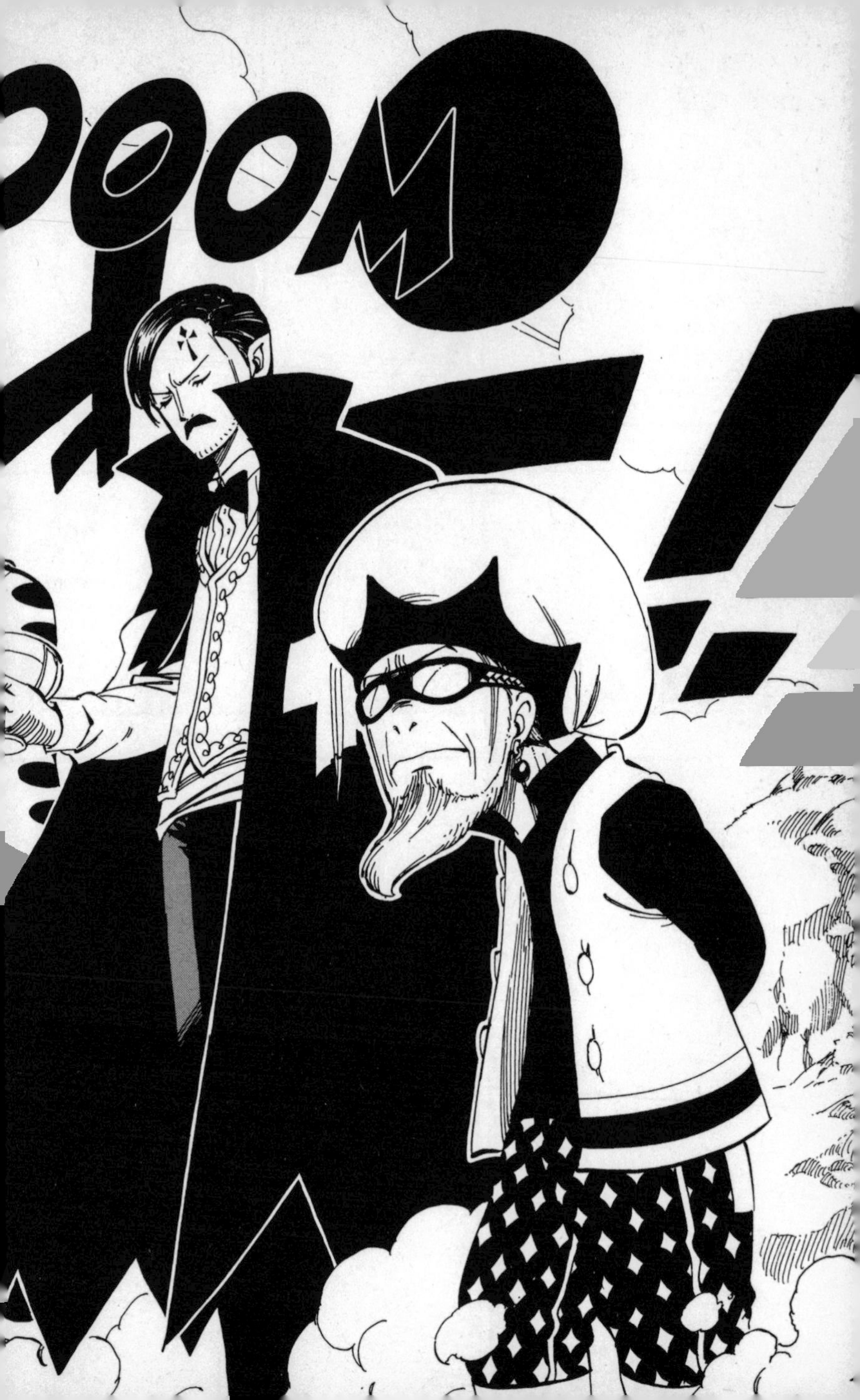

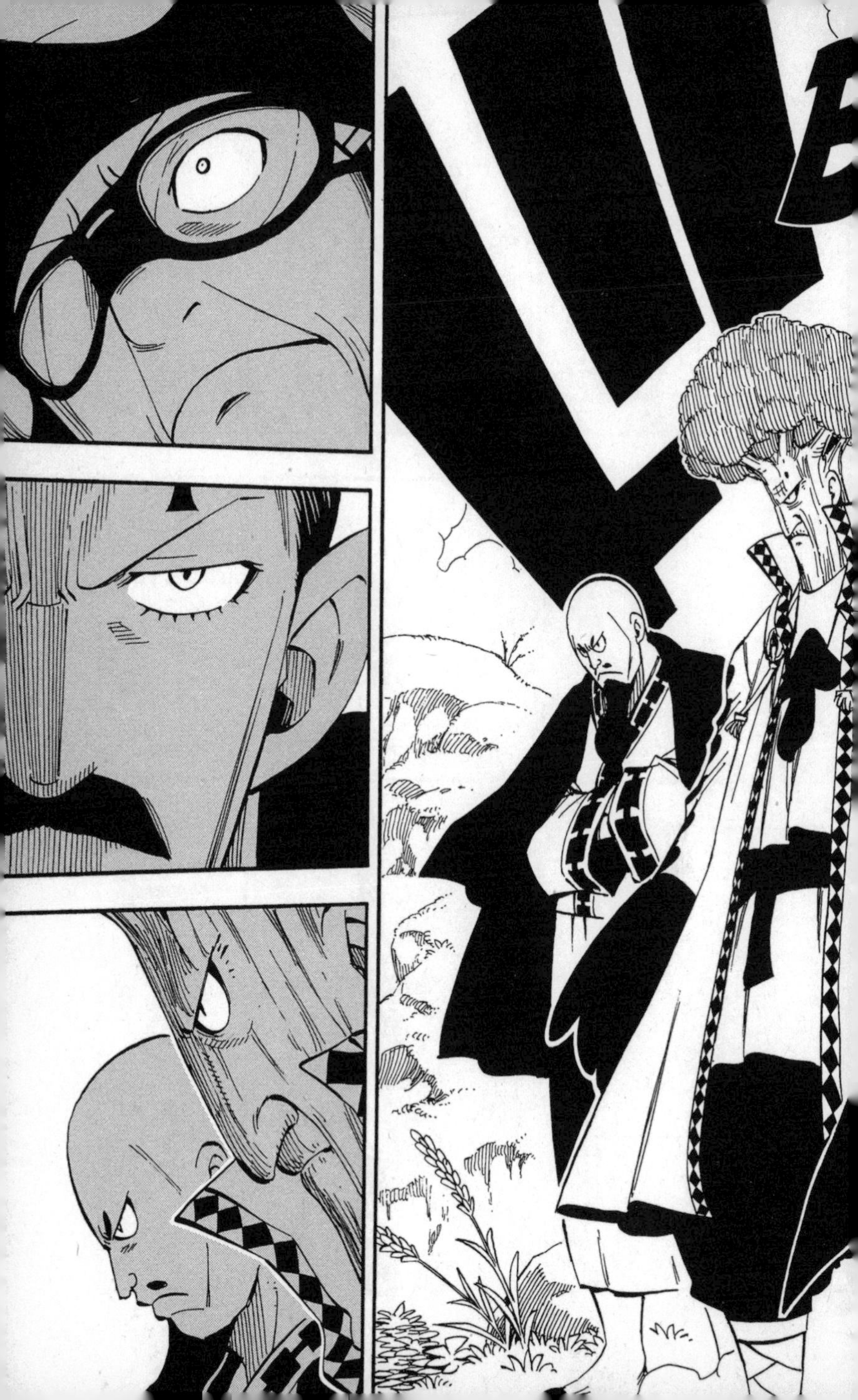

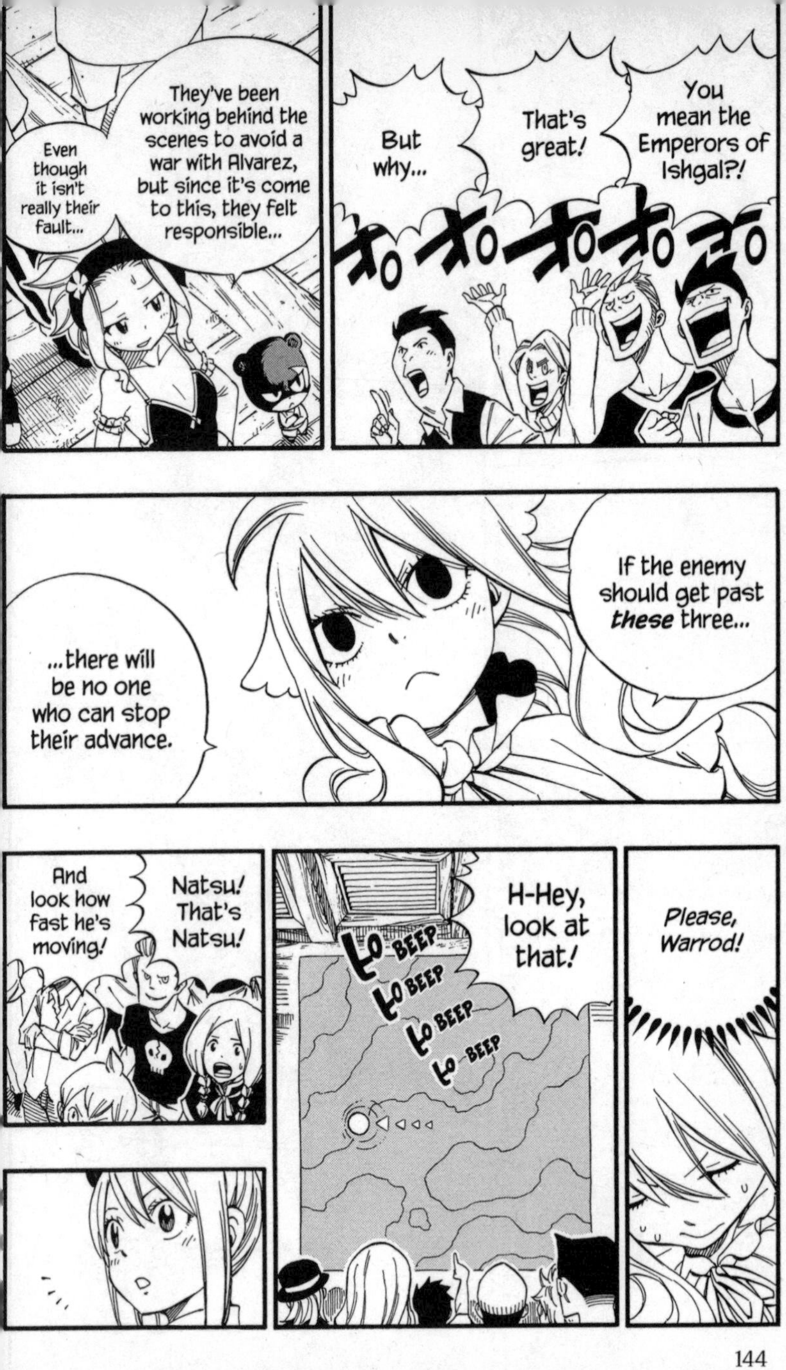
You mean the Emperors of Ishgal?!
That's great!
But why...
They've been working behind the scenes to avoid a war with Alvarez, but since it's come to this, they felt responsible...
Even though it isn't really their fault...
If the enemy should get past *these* three...
...there will be no one who can stop their advance.
Please, Warrod!
H-Hey, look at that!
BEEP
BEEP
BEEP
BEEP
Natsu! That's Natsu!
And look how fast he's moving!
...

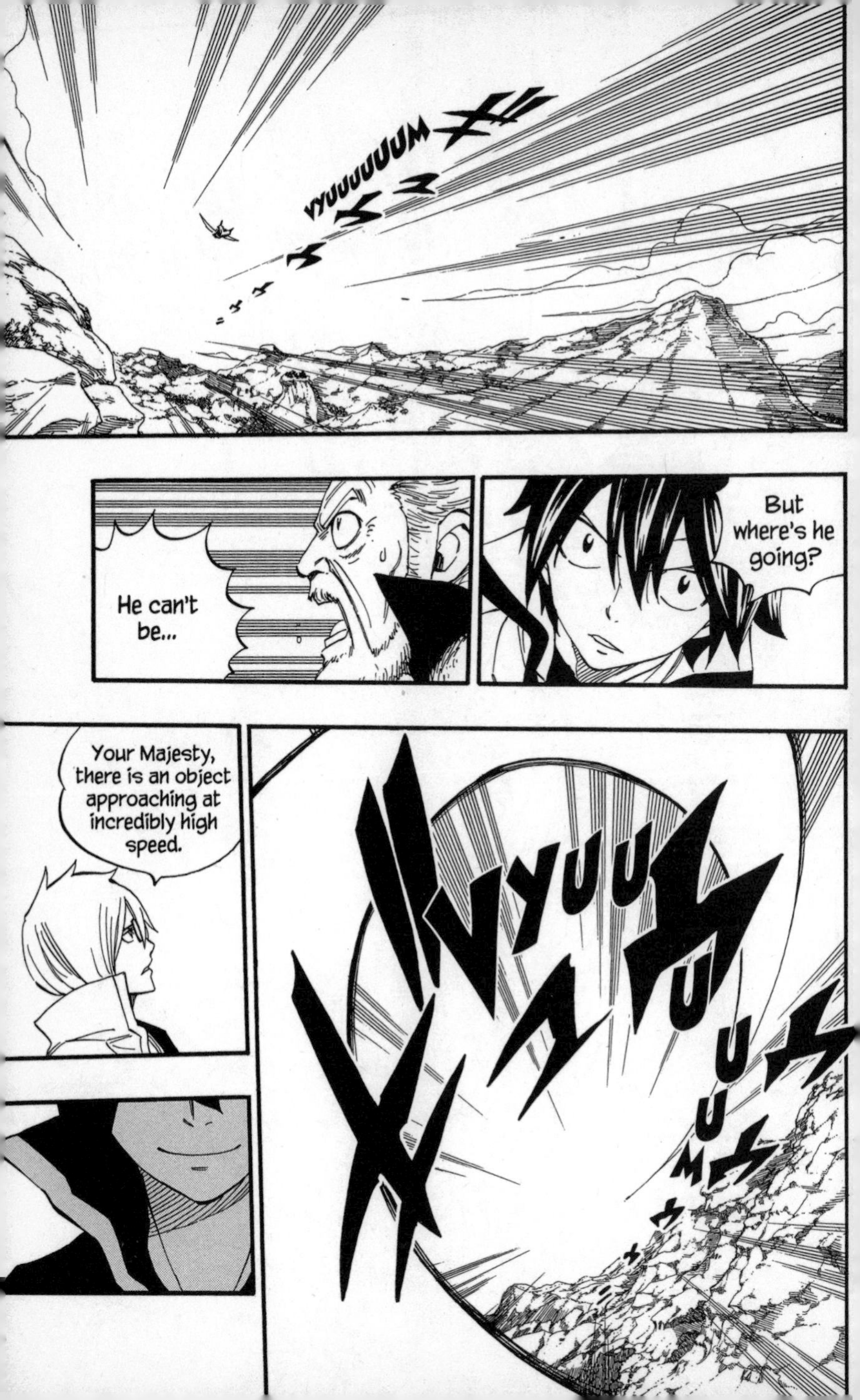
VYUUUUUUUM
But where's he going?
He can't be...
VYUUUUUUUM
Your Majesty, there is an object approaching at incredibly high speed.

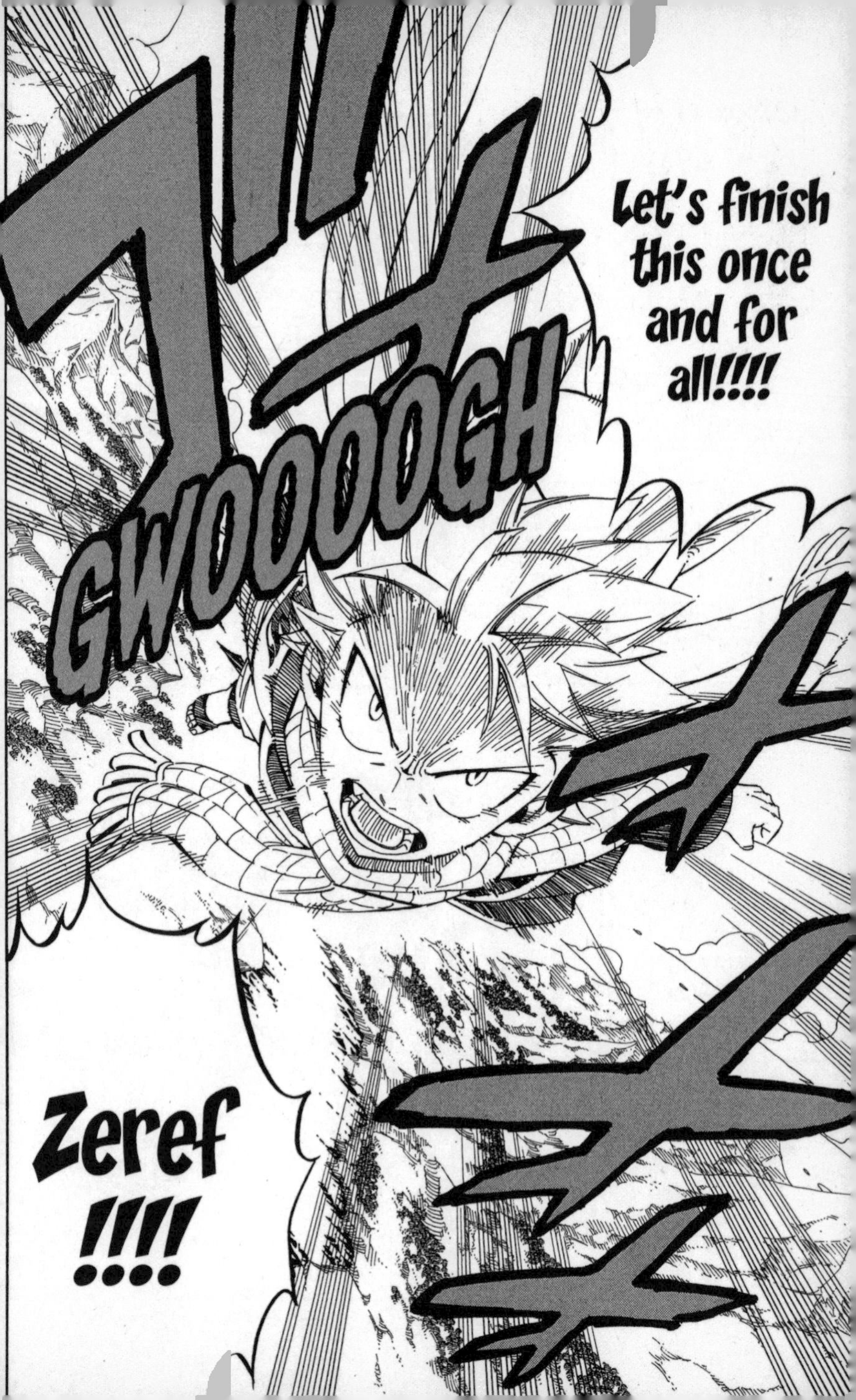
Let's finish this once and for all!!!!
GWOOOOGH
Zeref!!!!

FAIRY TAIL
フェアリーテイル

Chapter 463: Black Carpet

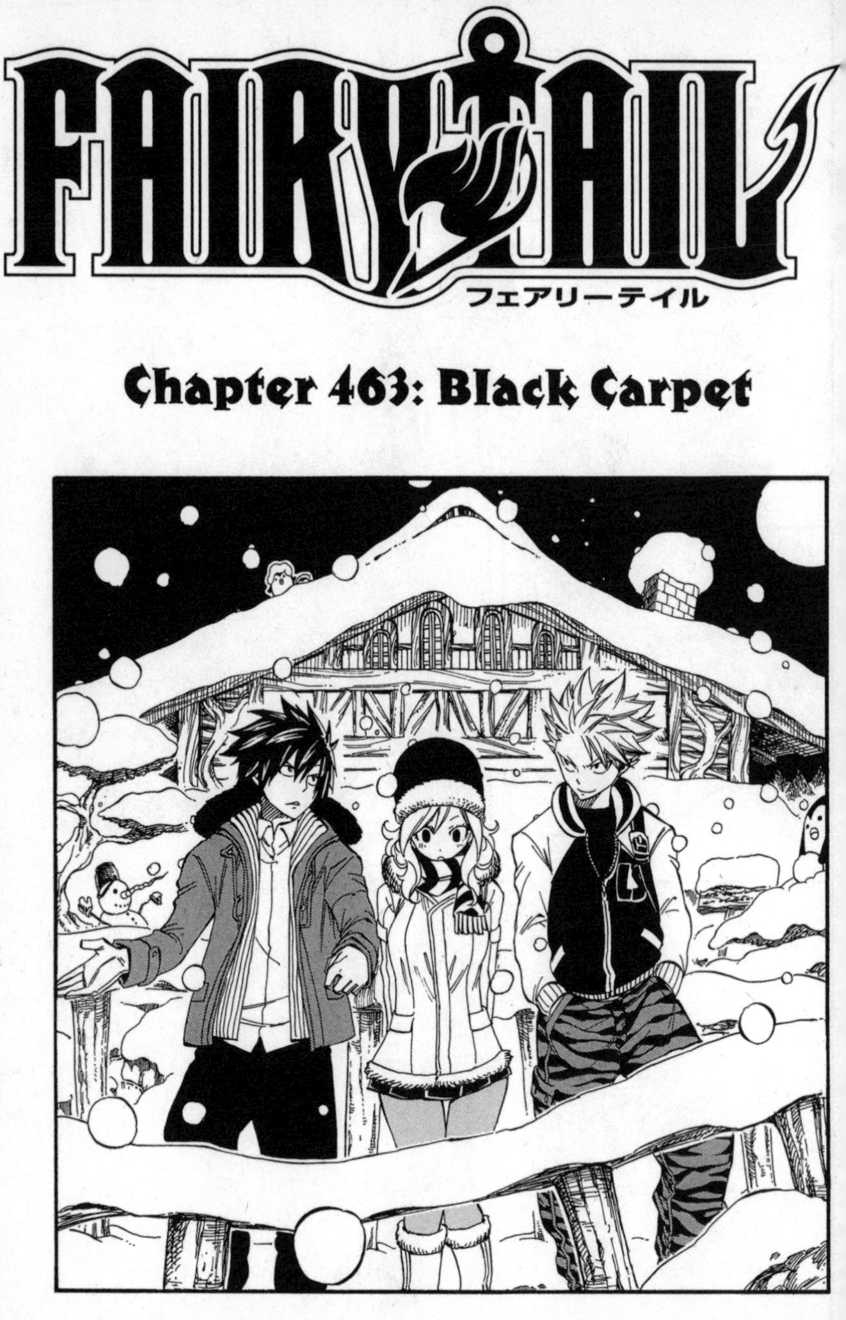

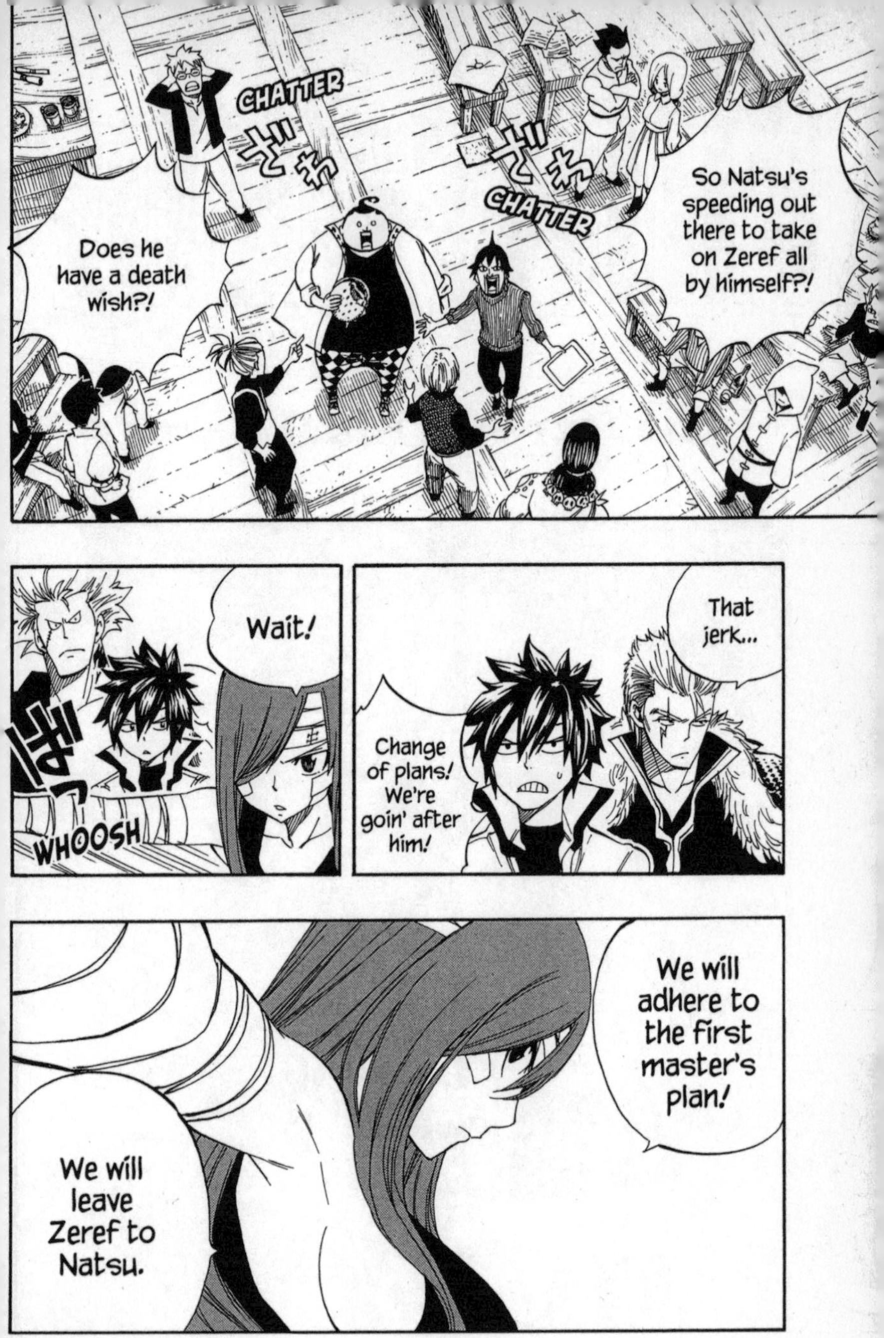
So Natsu's speeding out there to take on Zeref all by himself?!
CHATTER
ざわ
ざわ
CHATTER
Does he have a death wish?!
That jerk...
Change of plans! We're goin' after him!
Wait!
WHOOSH
We will adhere to the first master's plan!
We will leave Zeref to Natsu.

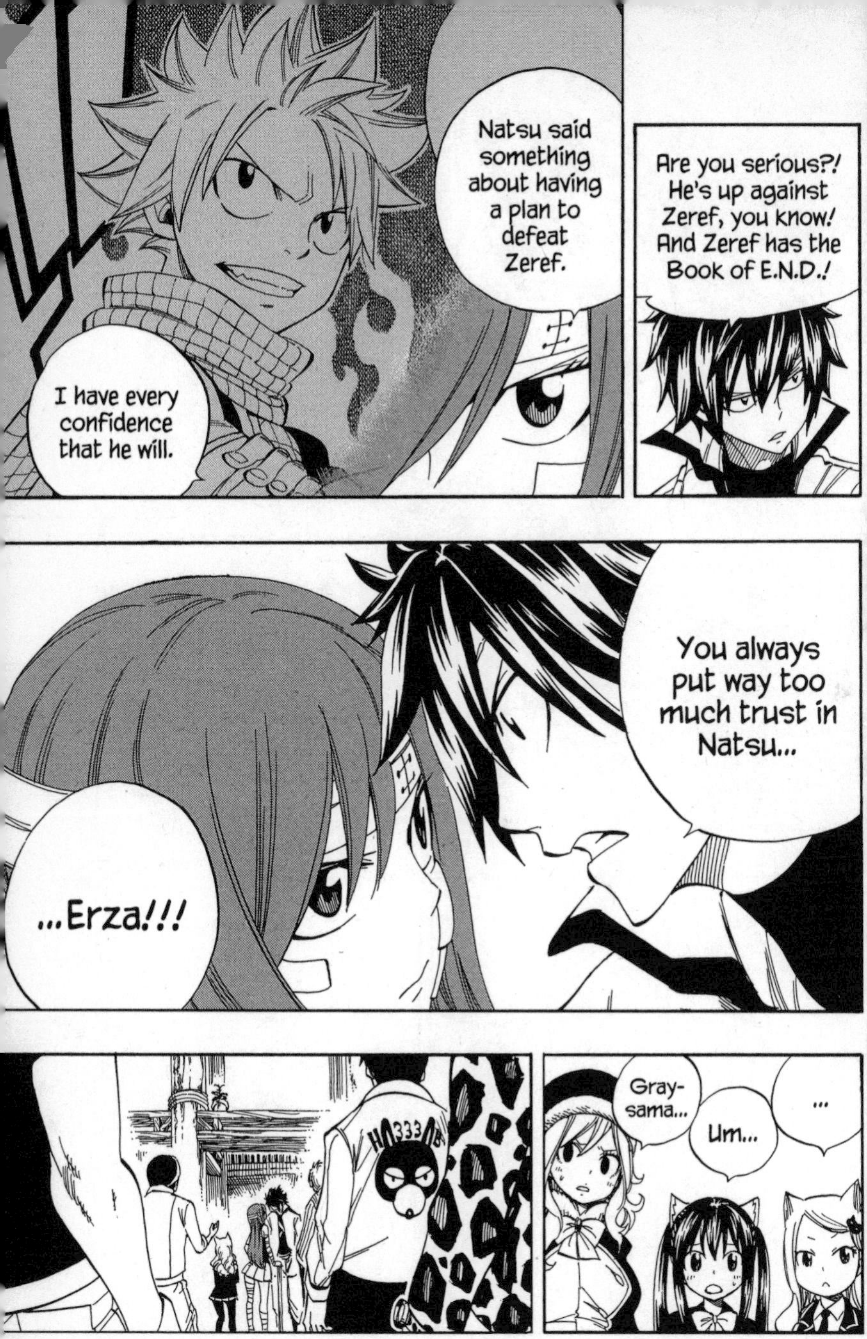
Are you serious?! He's up against Zeref, you know! And Zeref has the Book of E.N.D.!
Natsu said something about having a plan to defeat Zeref.
I have every confidence that he will.
You always put way too much trust in Natsu...
...Erza!!!
...
Gray-sama...
Um...

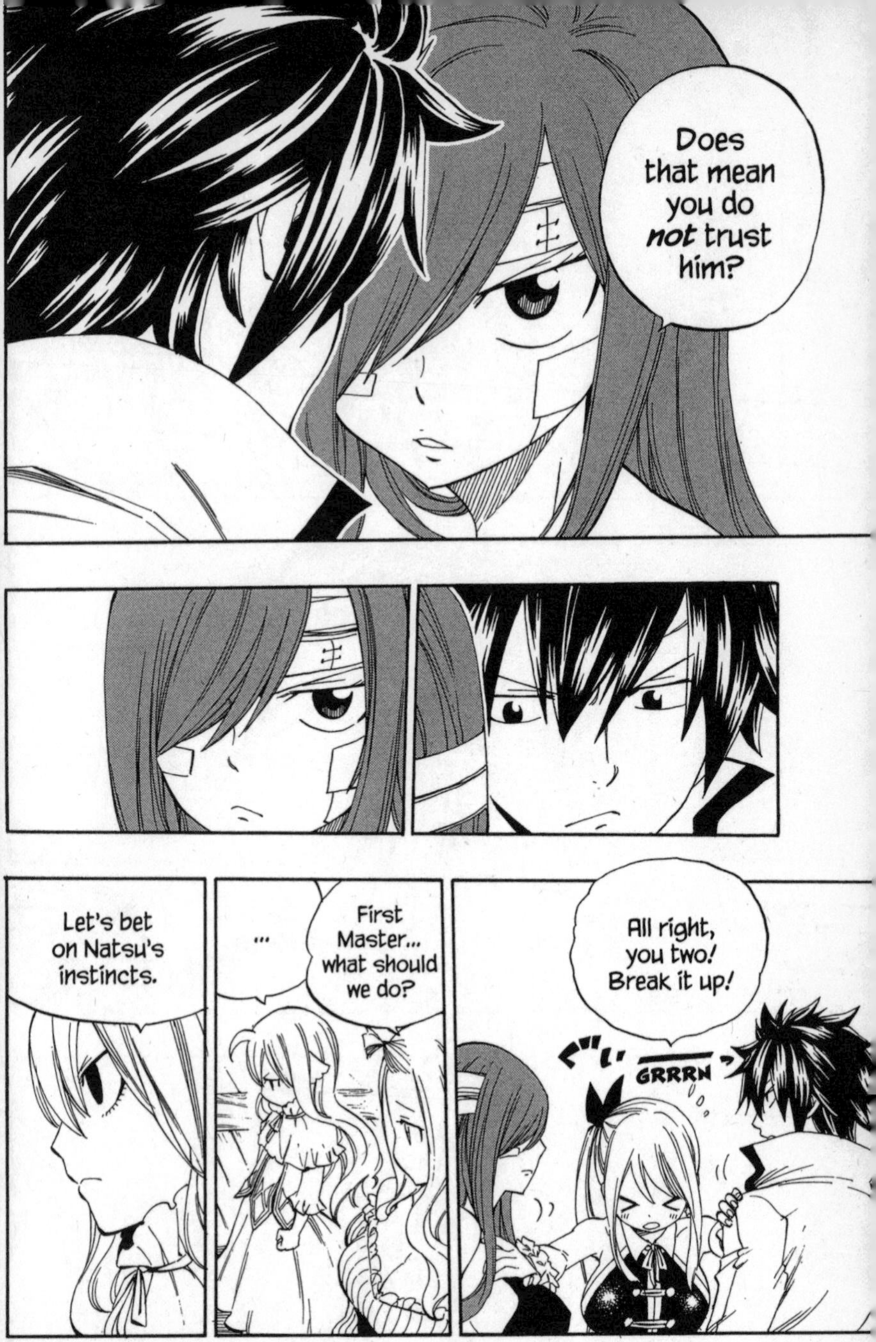
Does that mean you do *not* trust him?
All right, you two! Break it up!
GRRRN
First Master... what should we do?
...
Let's bet on Natsu's instincts.

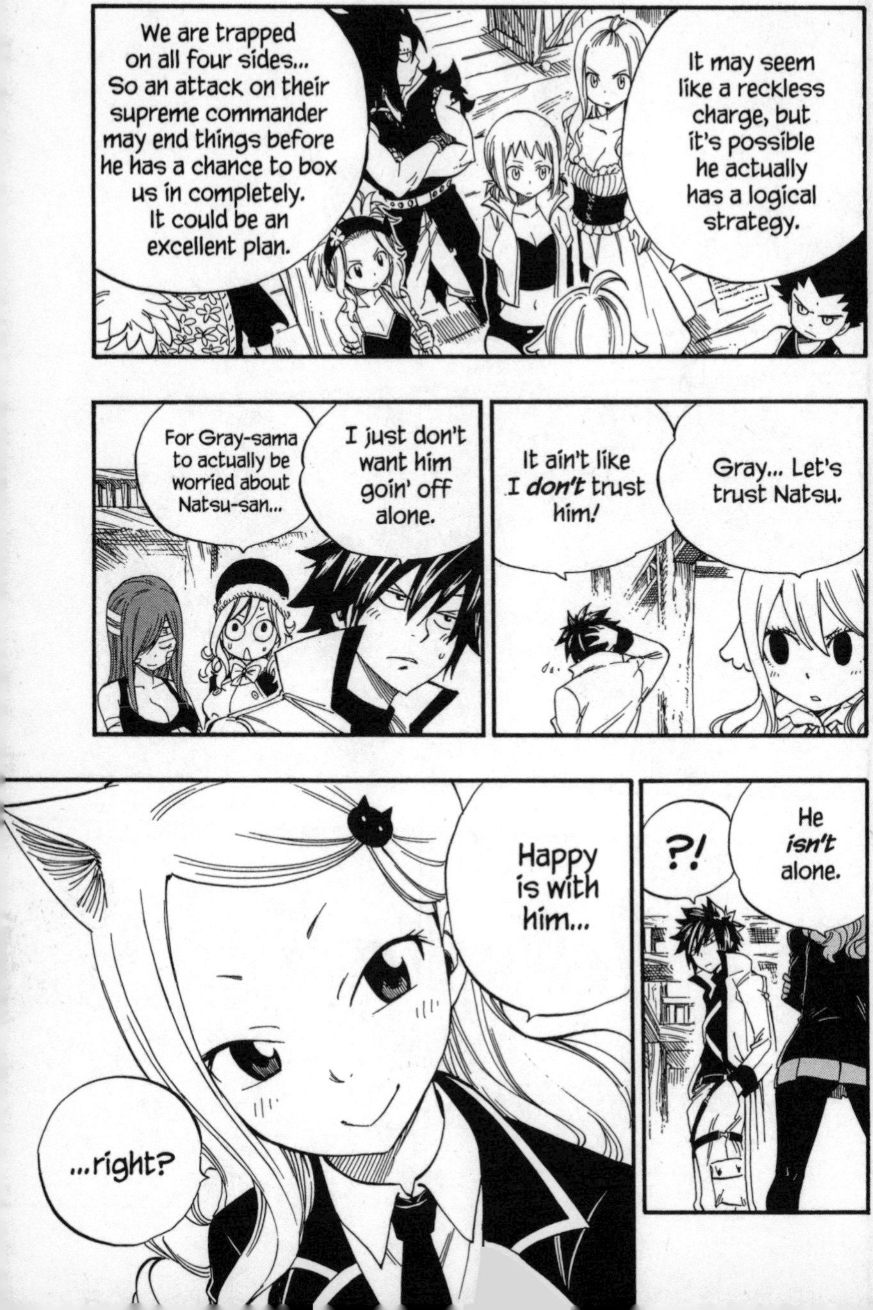
It may seem like a reckless charge, but it's possible he actually has a logical strategy.
We are trapped on all four sides... So an attack on their supreme commander may end things before he has a chance to box us in completely. It could be an excellent plan.
Gray... Let's trust Natsu.
It ain't like I *don't* trust him!
I just don't want him goin' off alone.
For Gray-sama to actually be worried about Natsu-san...
He *isn't* alone.
?!
Happy is with him...
...right?

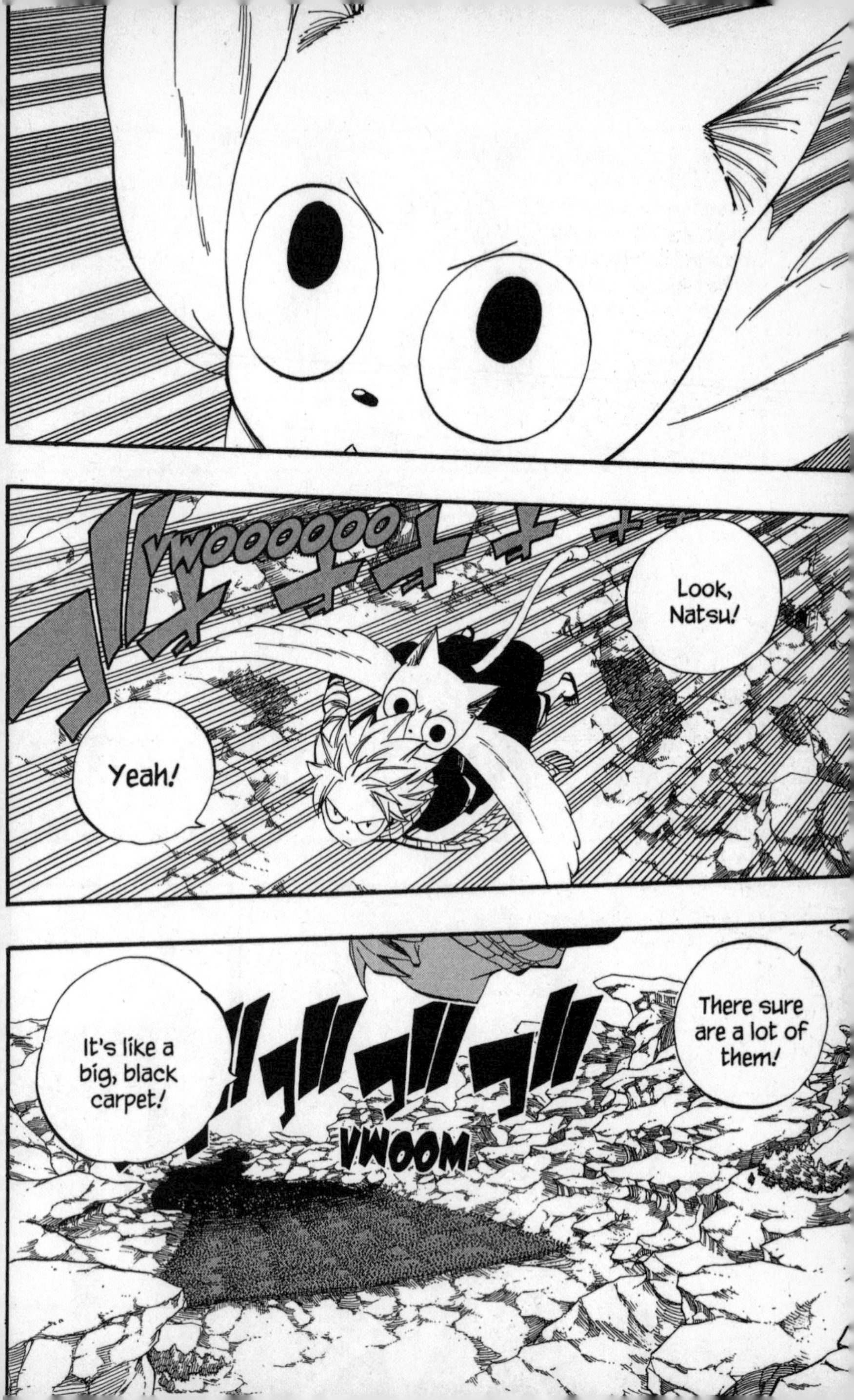
Look, Natsu!
VWOOOOOO
Yeah!
There sure are a lot of them!
It's like a big, black carpet!
VWOOM

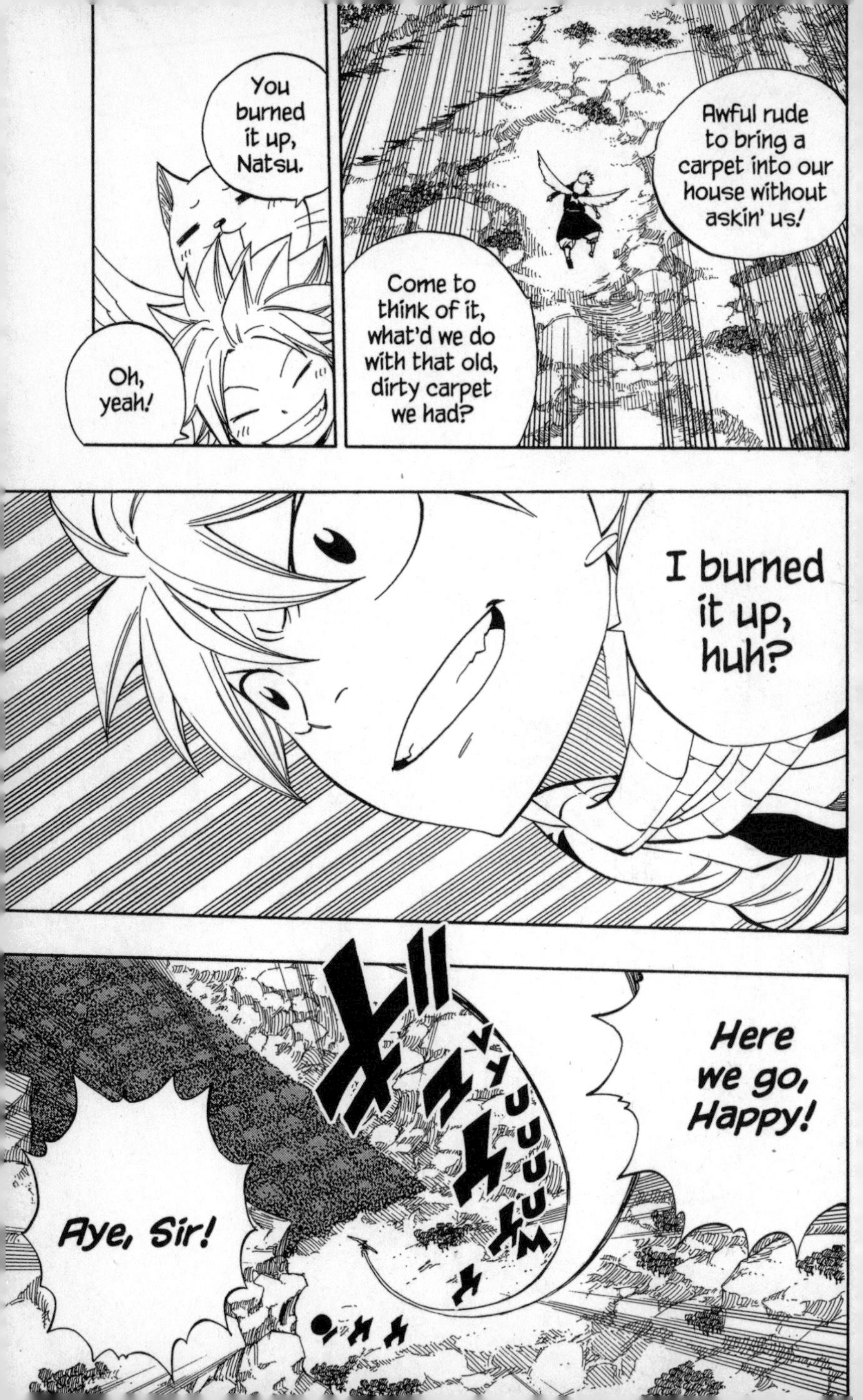

Awful rude to bring a carpet into our house without askin' us!
Come to think of it, what'd we do with that old, dirty carpet we had?
You burned it up, Natsu.
Oh, yeah!
I burned it up, huh?
Here we go, Happy!
Aye, Sir!
VYUUUUM

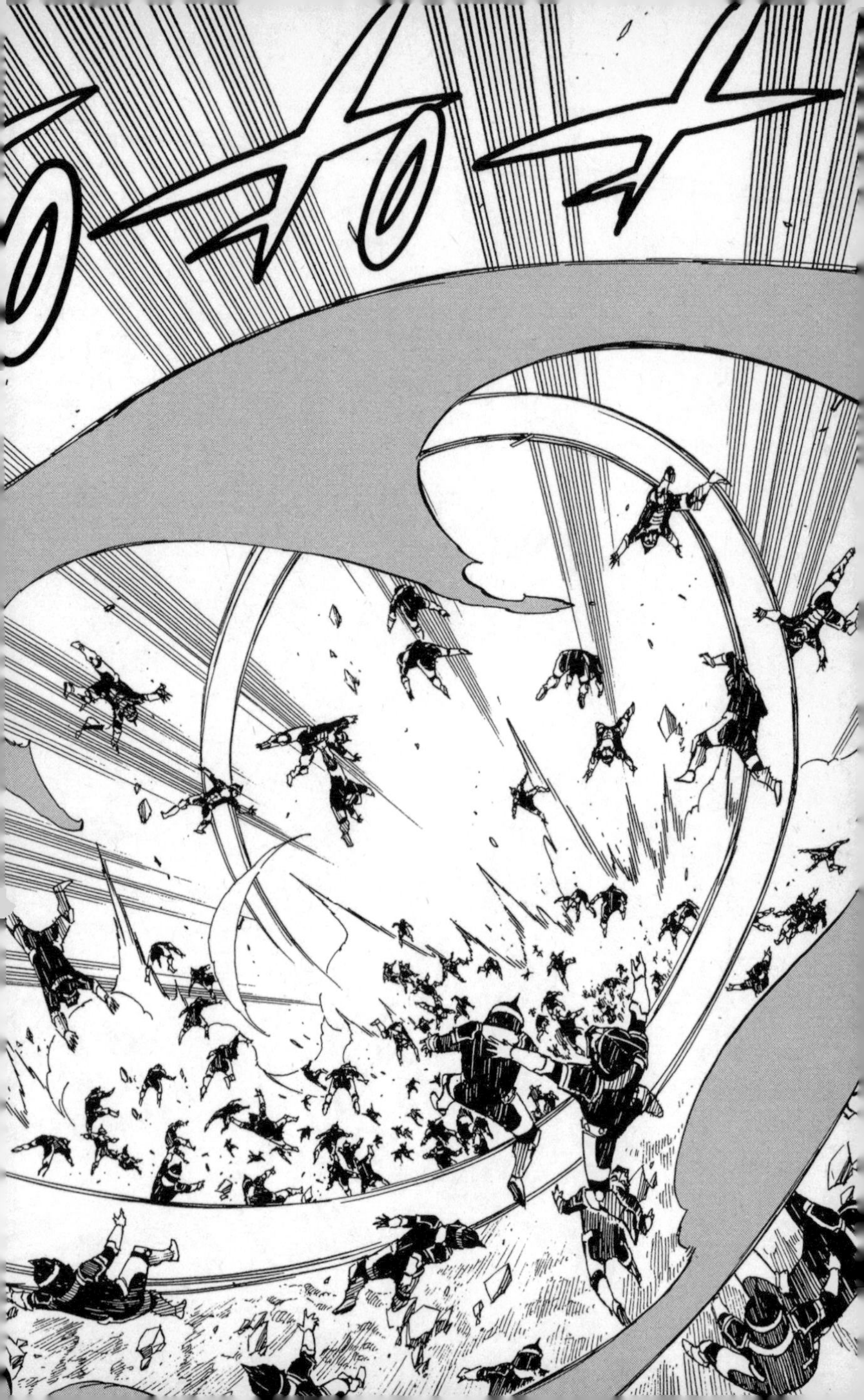

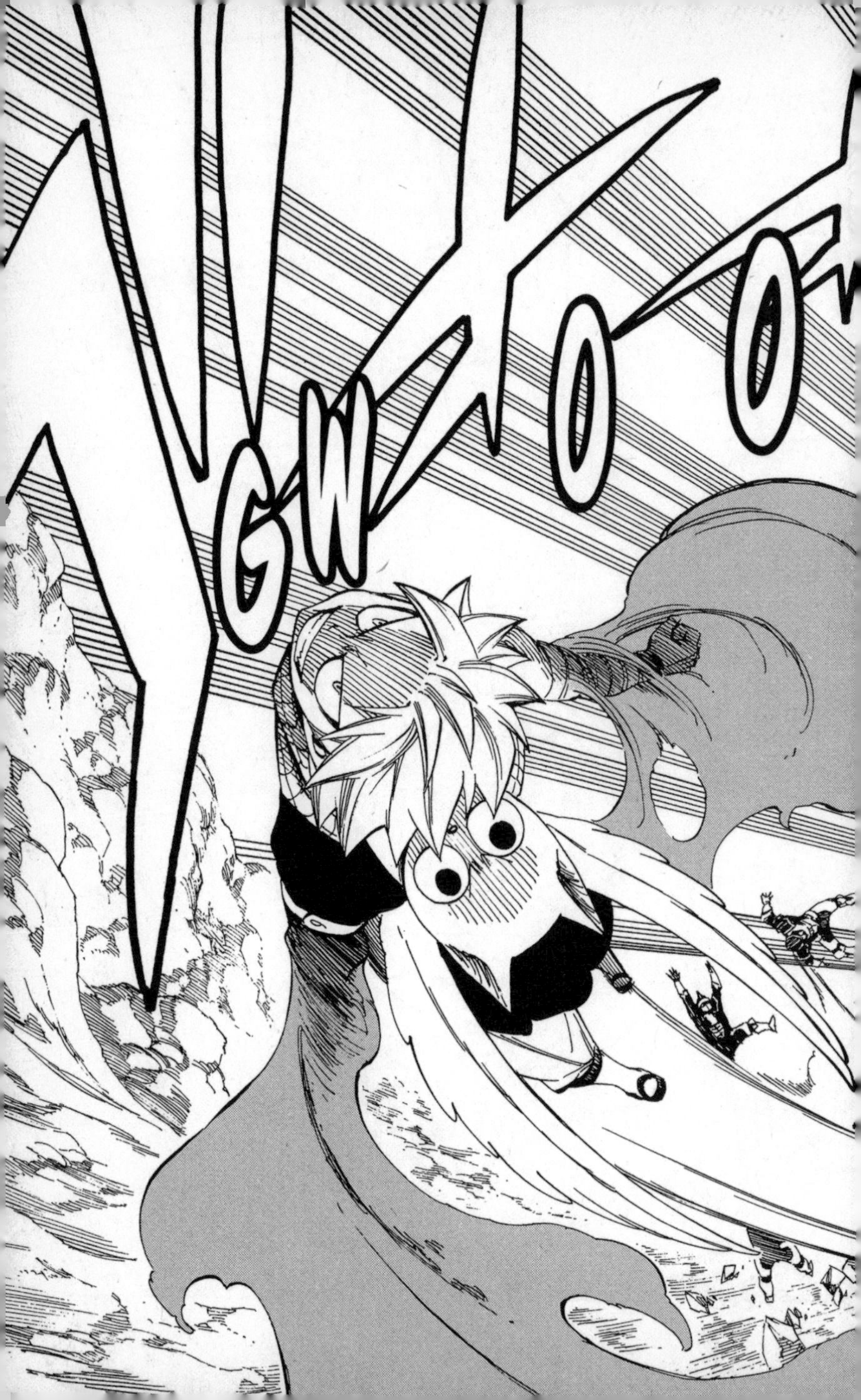
GWOOO

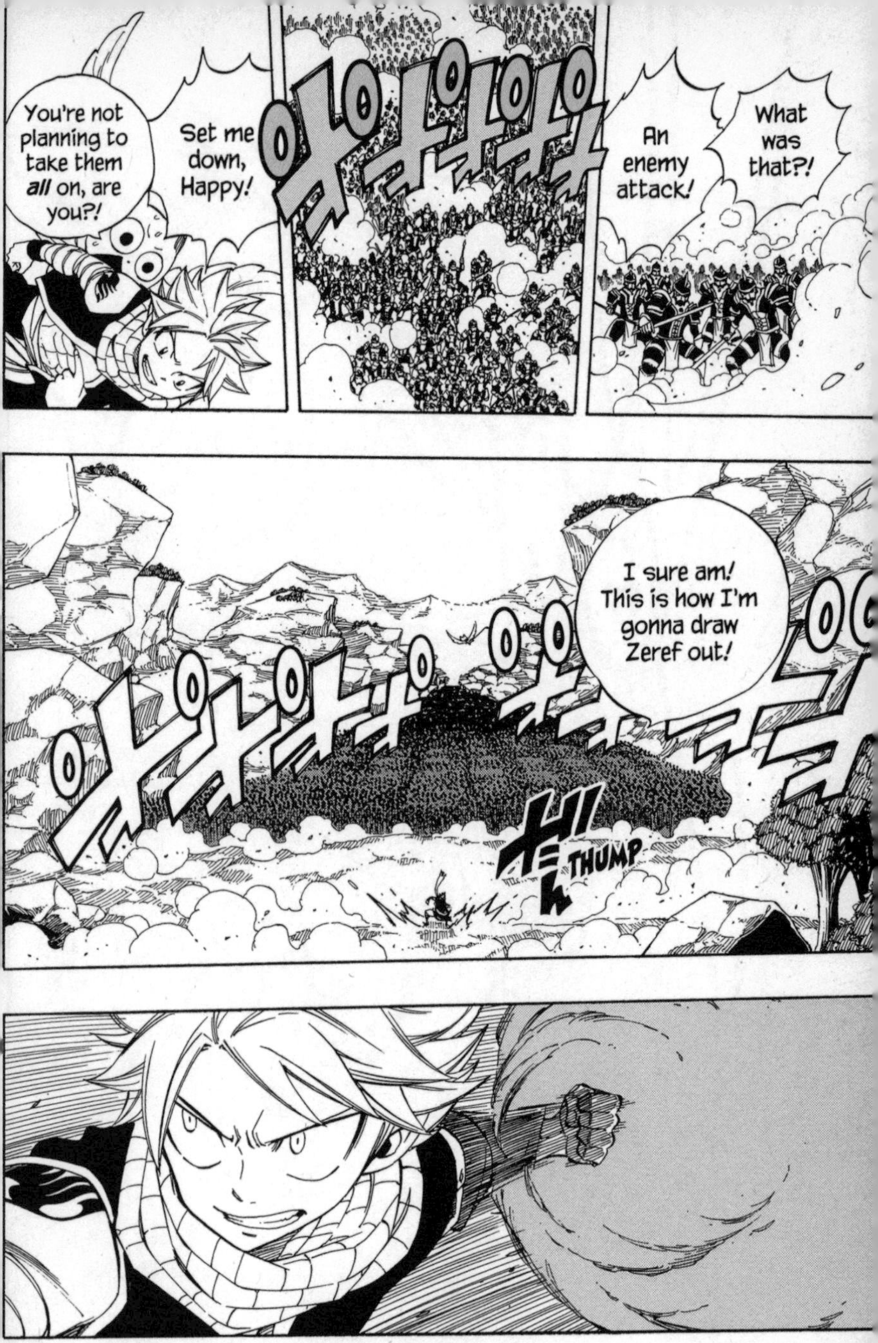
What was that?!
An enemy attack!
Set me down, Happy!
You're not planning to take them *all* on, are you?!
I sure am! This is how I'm gonna draw Zeref out!
THUMP

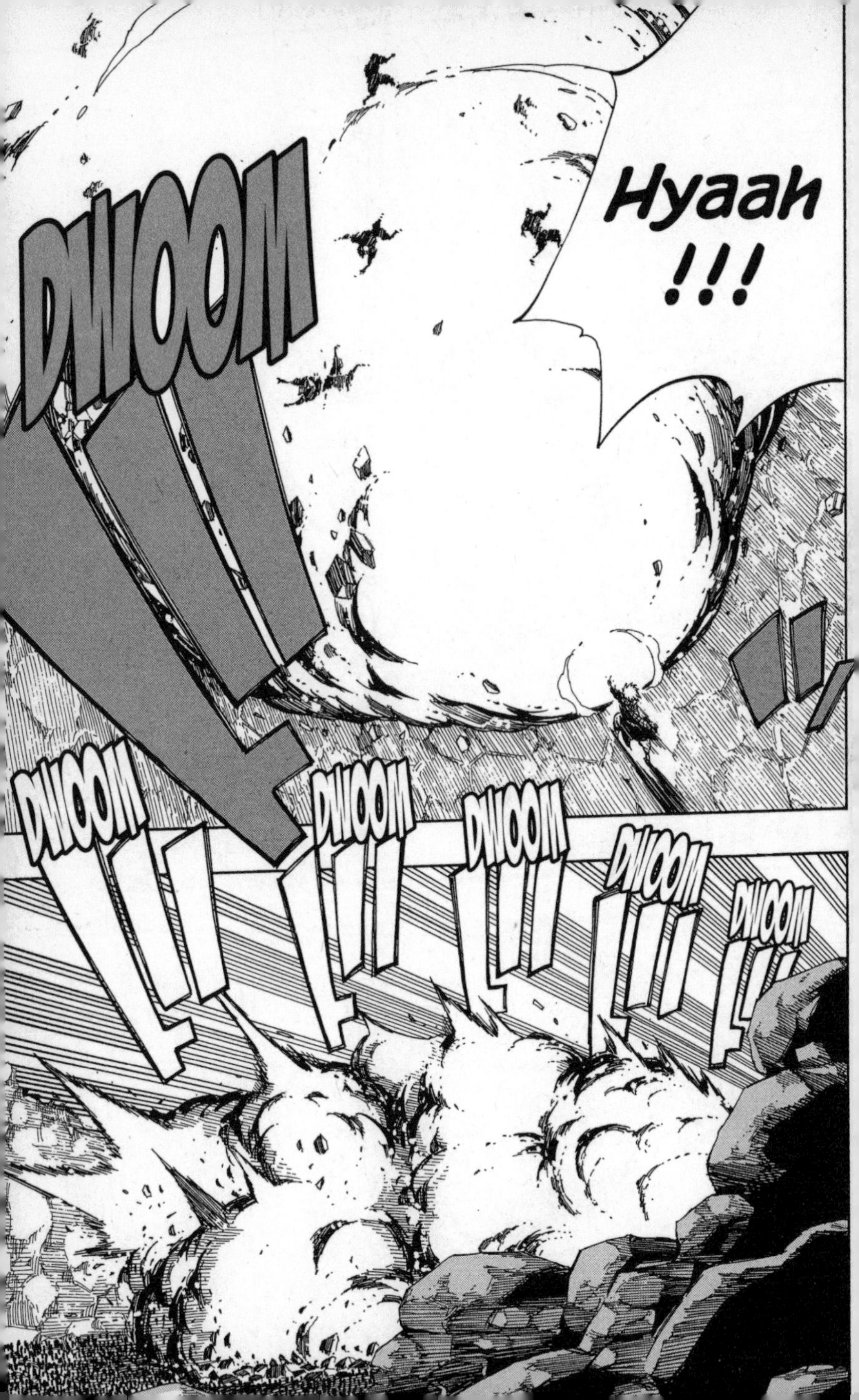
Hyaah!!!
DWOOM!!
DWOOM!!
DWOOM!!
DWOOM!!
DWOOM!!
DWOOM!!

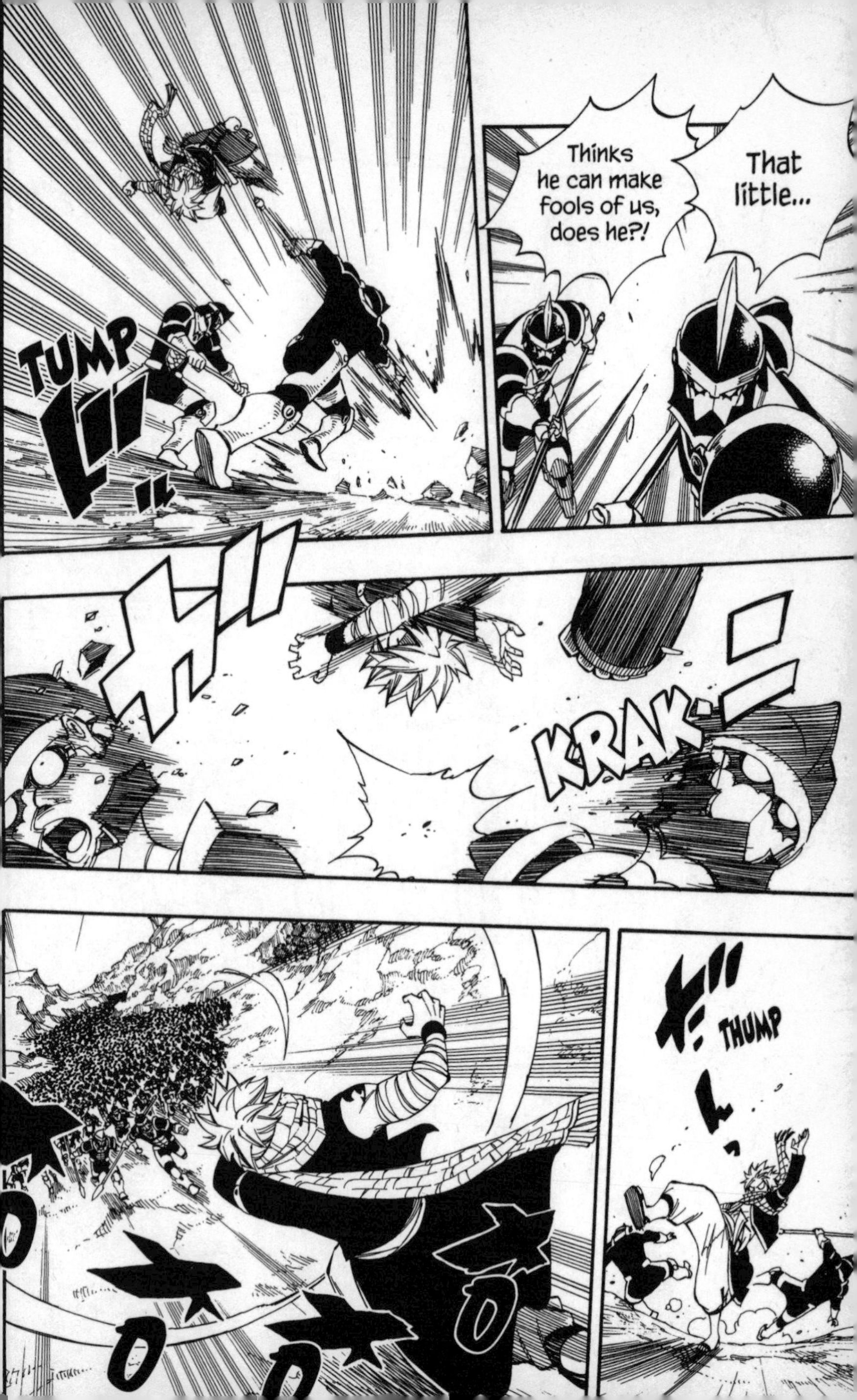

That little...
Thinks he can make fools of us, does he?!
TUMP
KRAK
THUMP

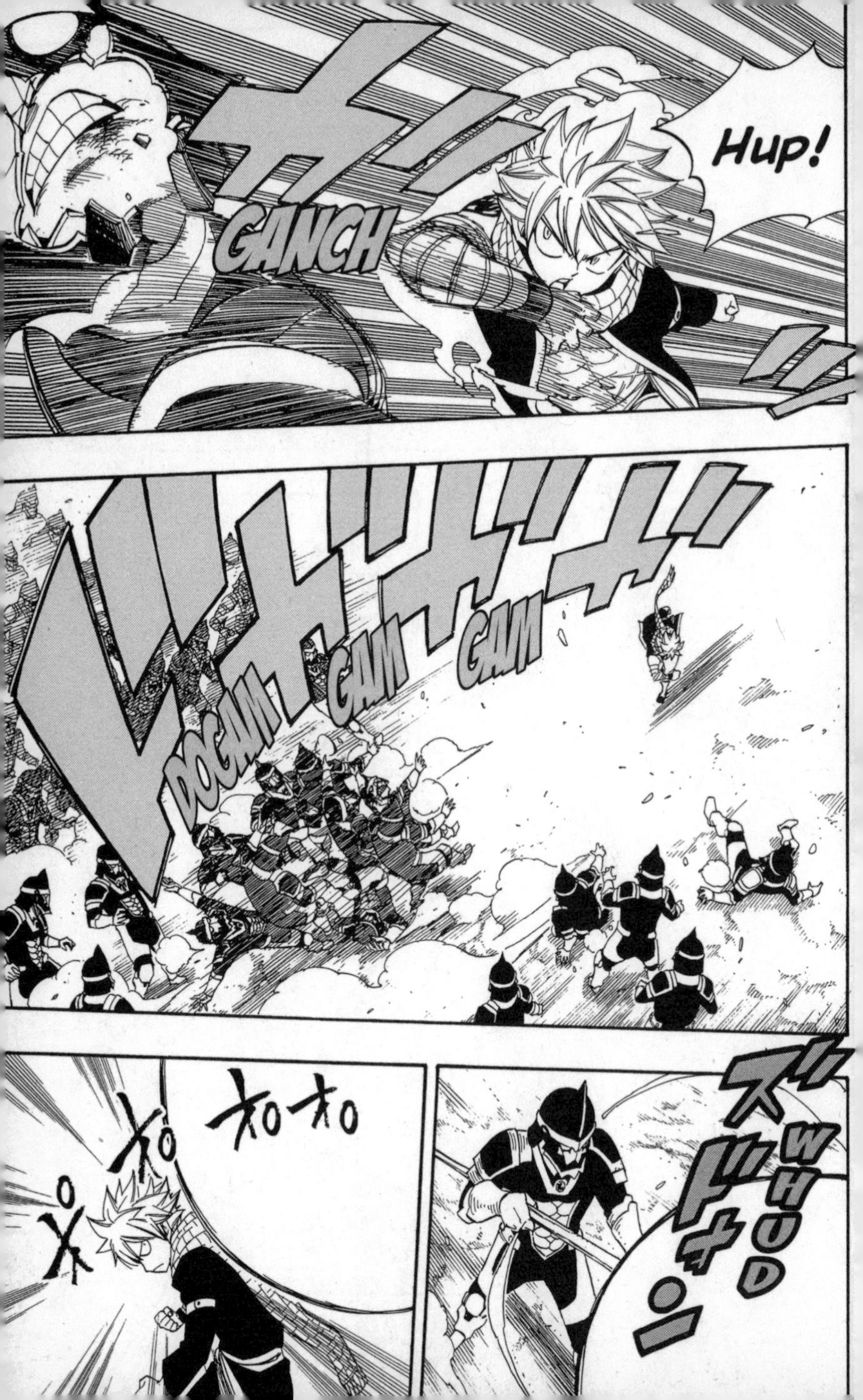
Hup!
GANCH
GAM
GAM
DOGAM
WHUD

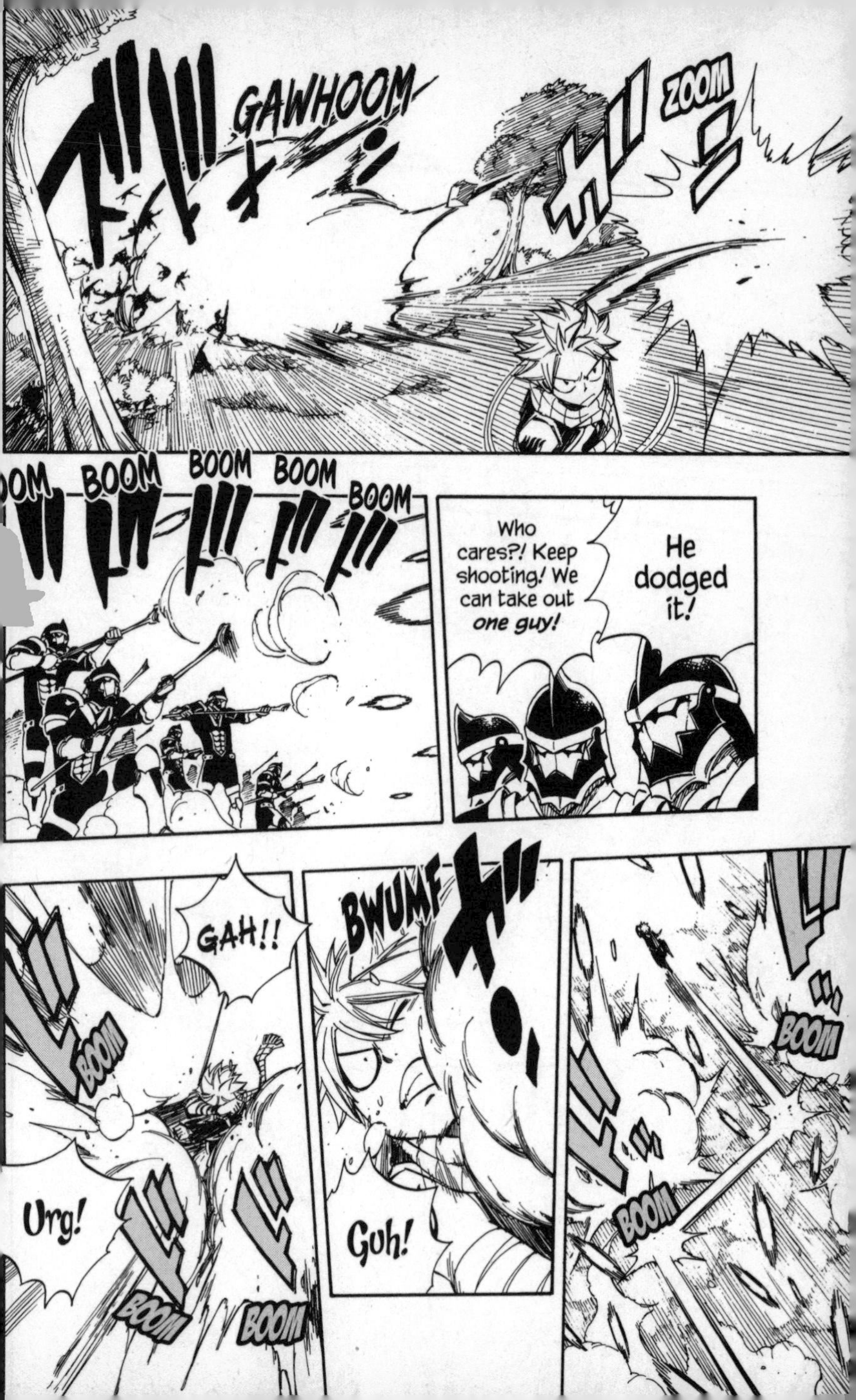
ZOOM
GAWHOOM
He dodged it!
Who cares?! Keep shooting! We can take out one guy!
BOOM
BOOM
BOOM
BOOM
OOM
BOOM
BOOM
BWUMF
Guh!
GAH!!
BOOM
Urg!
BOOM
BOOM

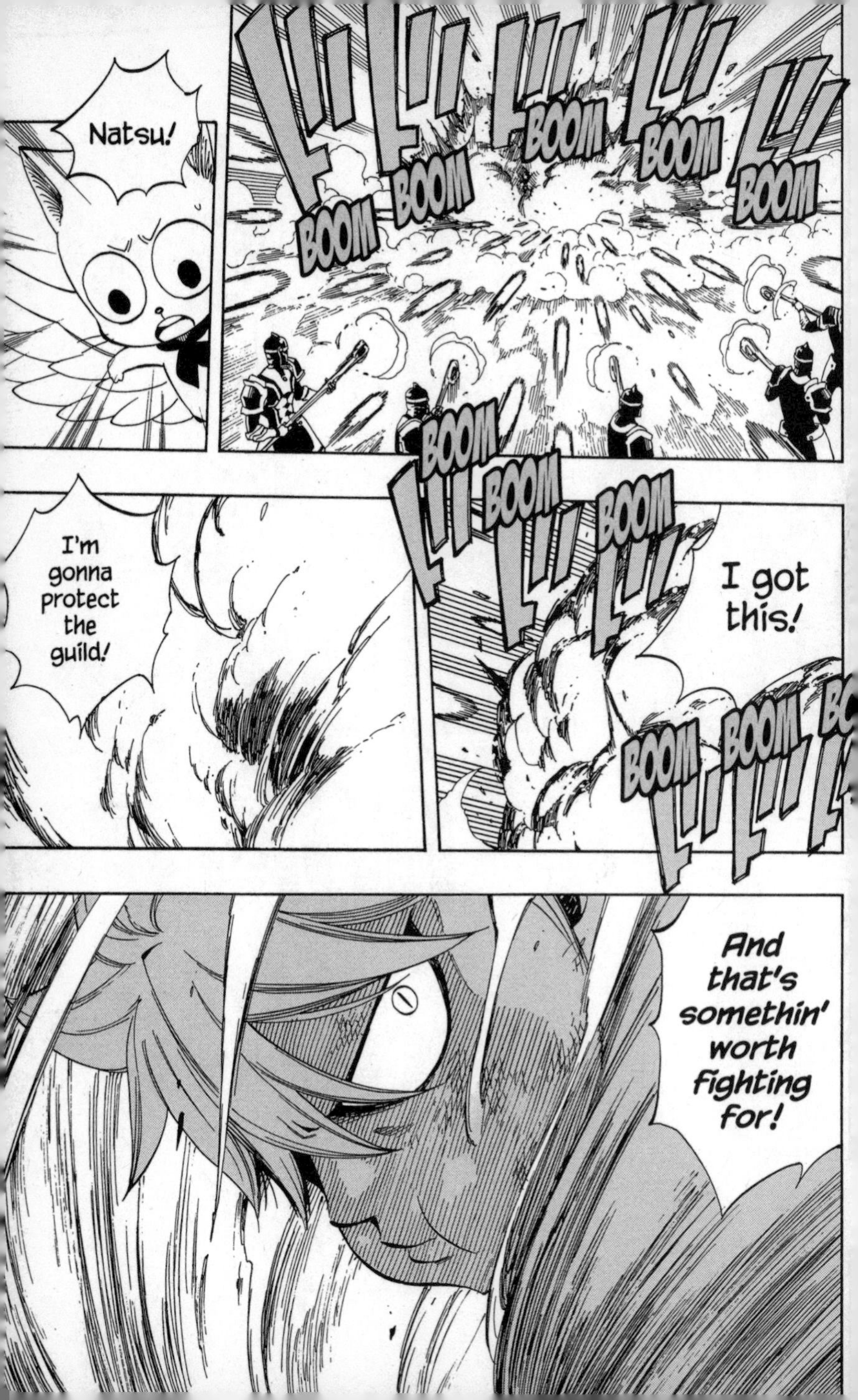
BOOM
BOOM
BOOM
BOOM
BOOM
Natsu!
BOOM
BOOM
BOOM
I got this!
BOOM
BOOM
I'm gonna protect the guild!
And that's somethin' worth fighting for!

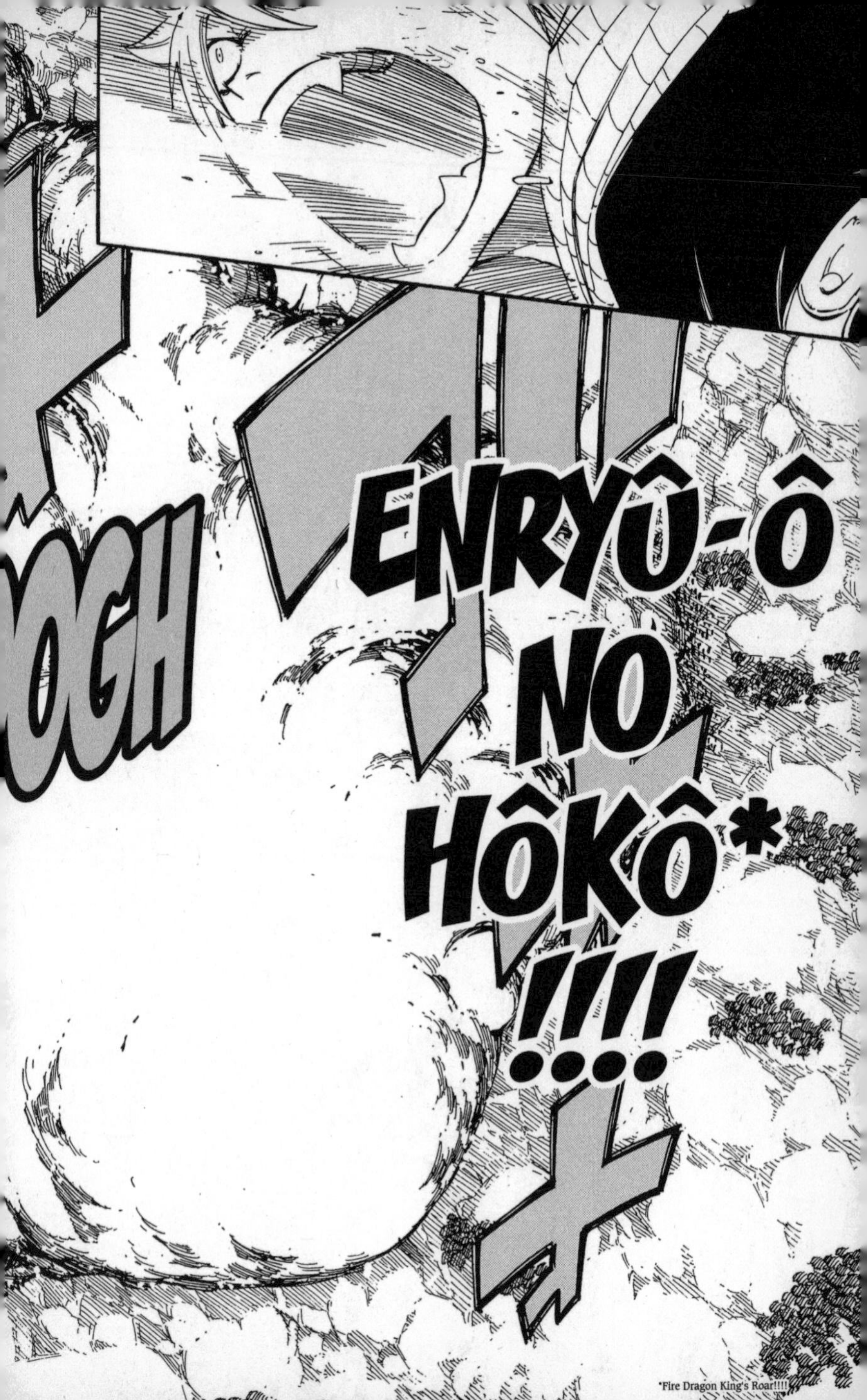
ENRYÛ-Ô NO HÔKÔ* !!!!
OGH
*Fire Dragon King's Roar!!!!

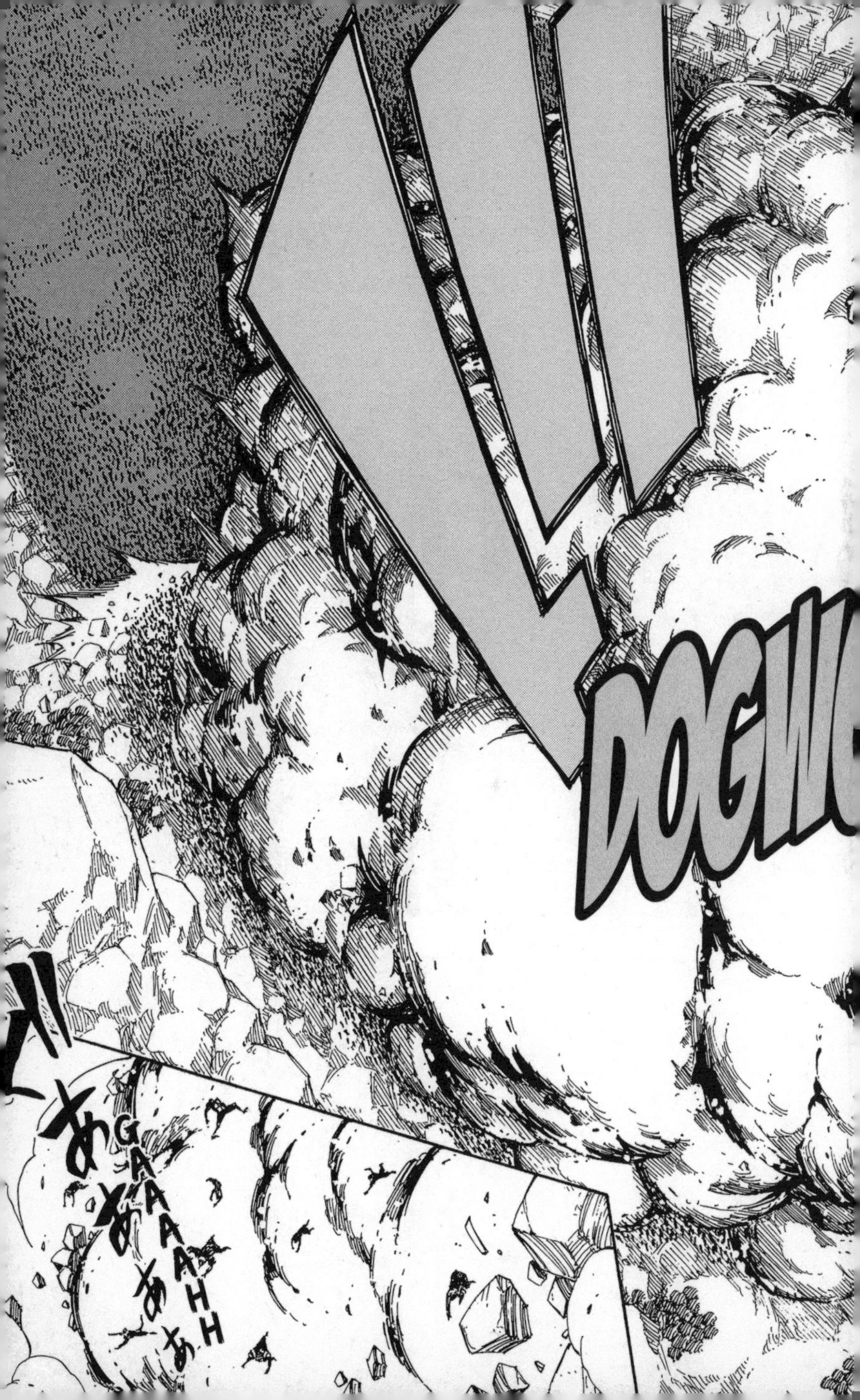
DOGW
GAAAAAHH

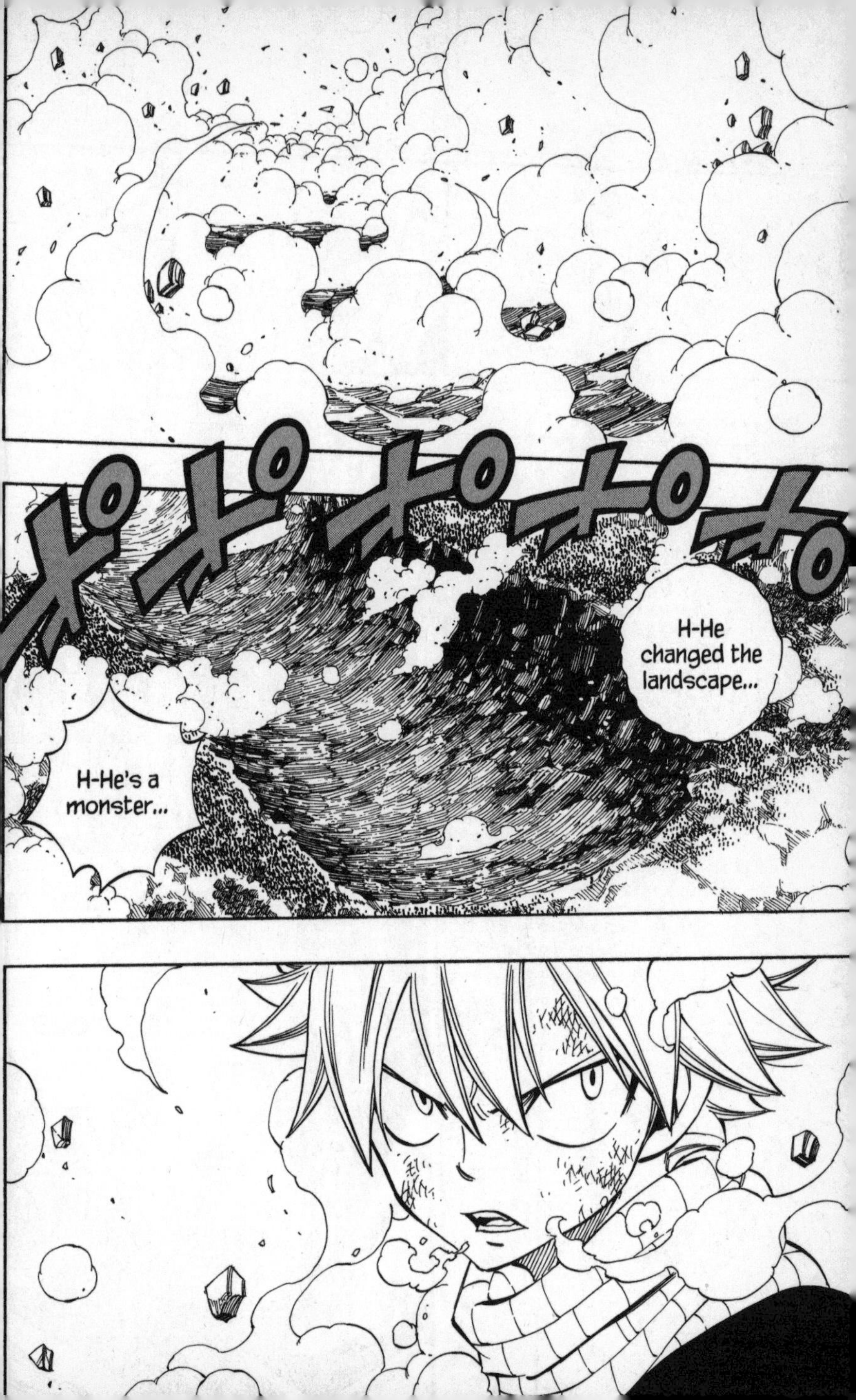
H-He changed the landscape...
H-He's a monster...

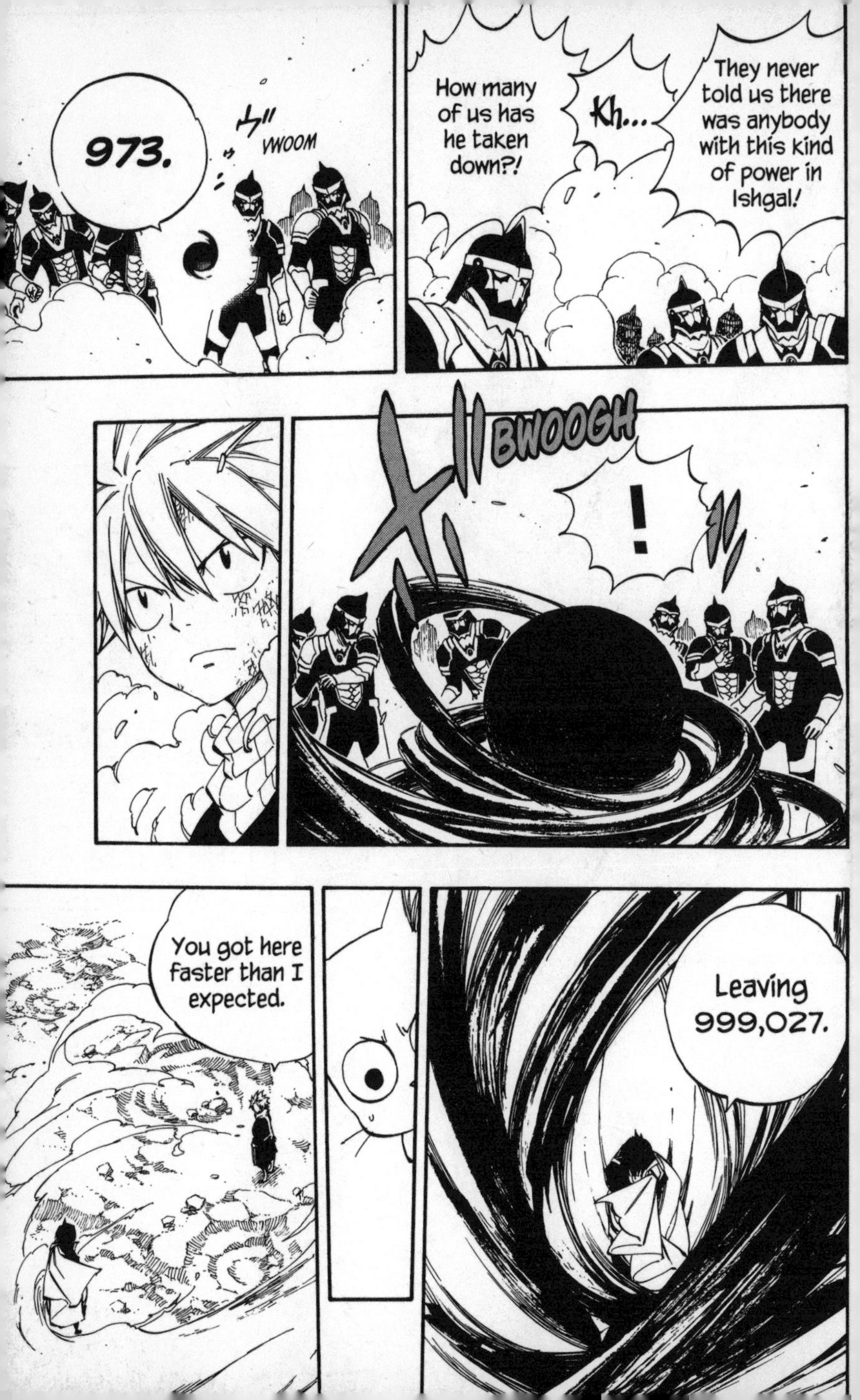
They never told us there was anybody with this kind of power in Ishgal!
Kh...
How many of us has he taken down?!
VWOOM
973.
BWOOGH
!
Leaving 999,027.
You got here faster than I expected.

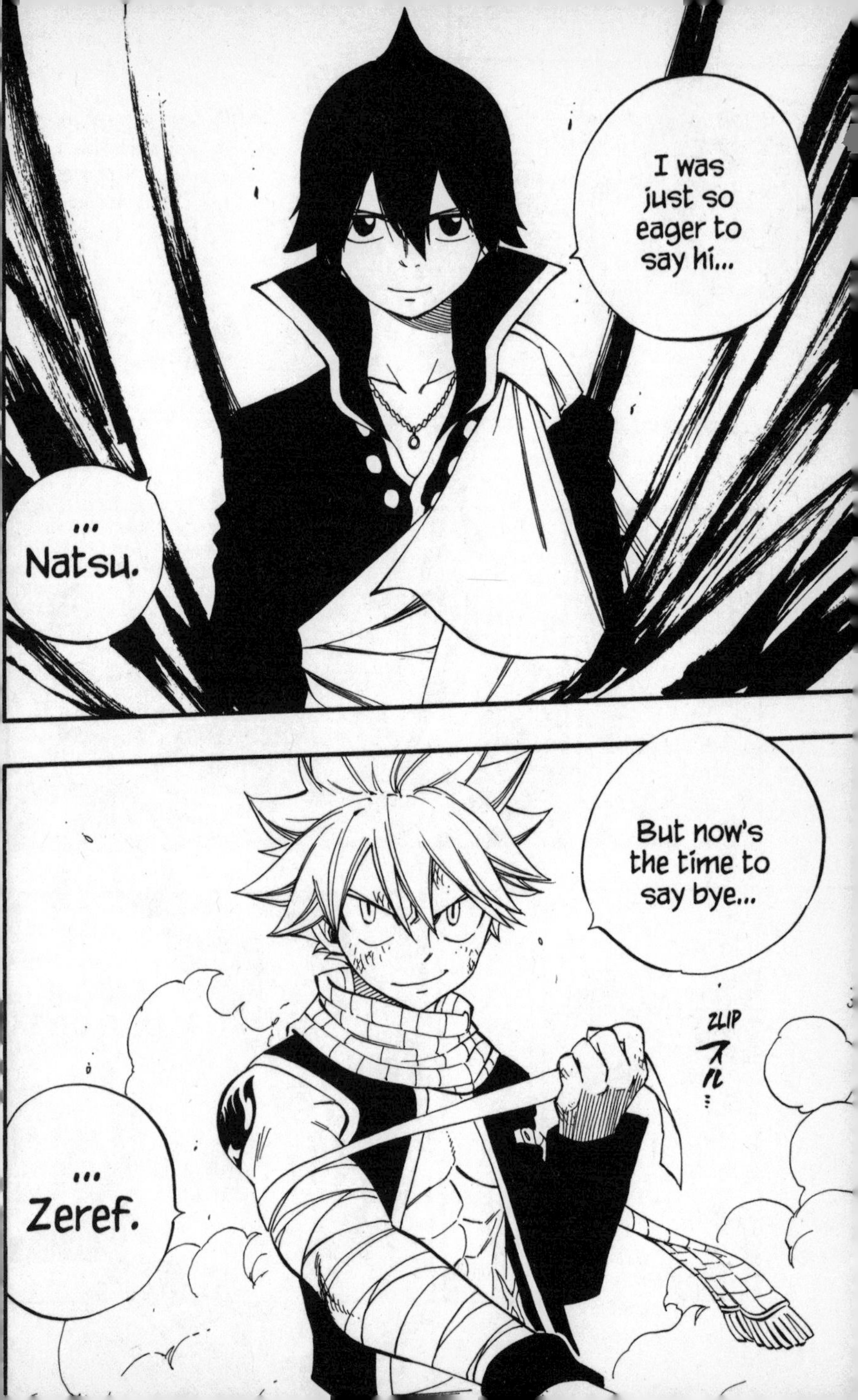
I was just so eager to say hi...
... Natsu.
But now's the time to say bye...
ZLIP
スル…
... Zeref.

FAIRY TAIL

フェアリーテイル

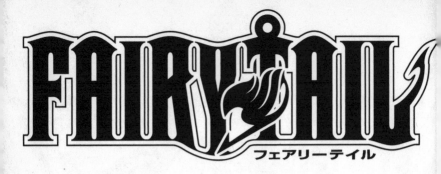

Chapter 464: Natsu vs. Zeref

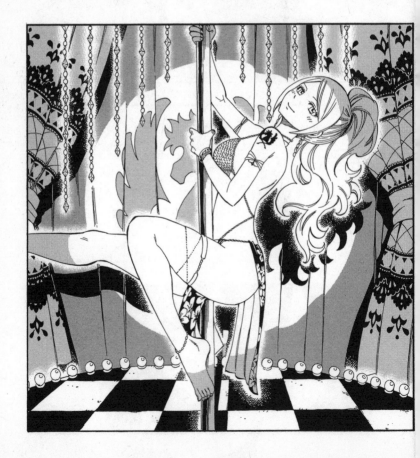

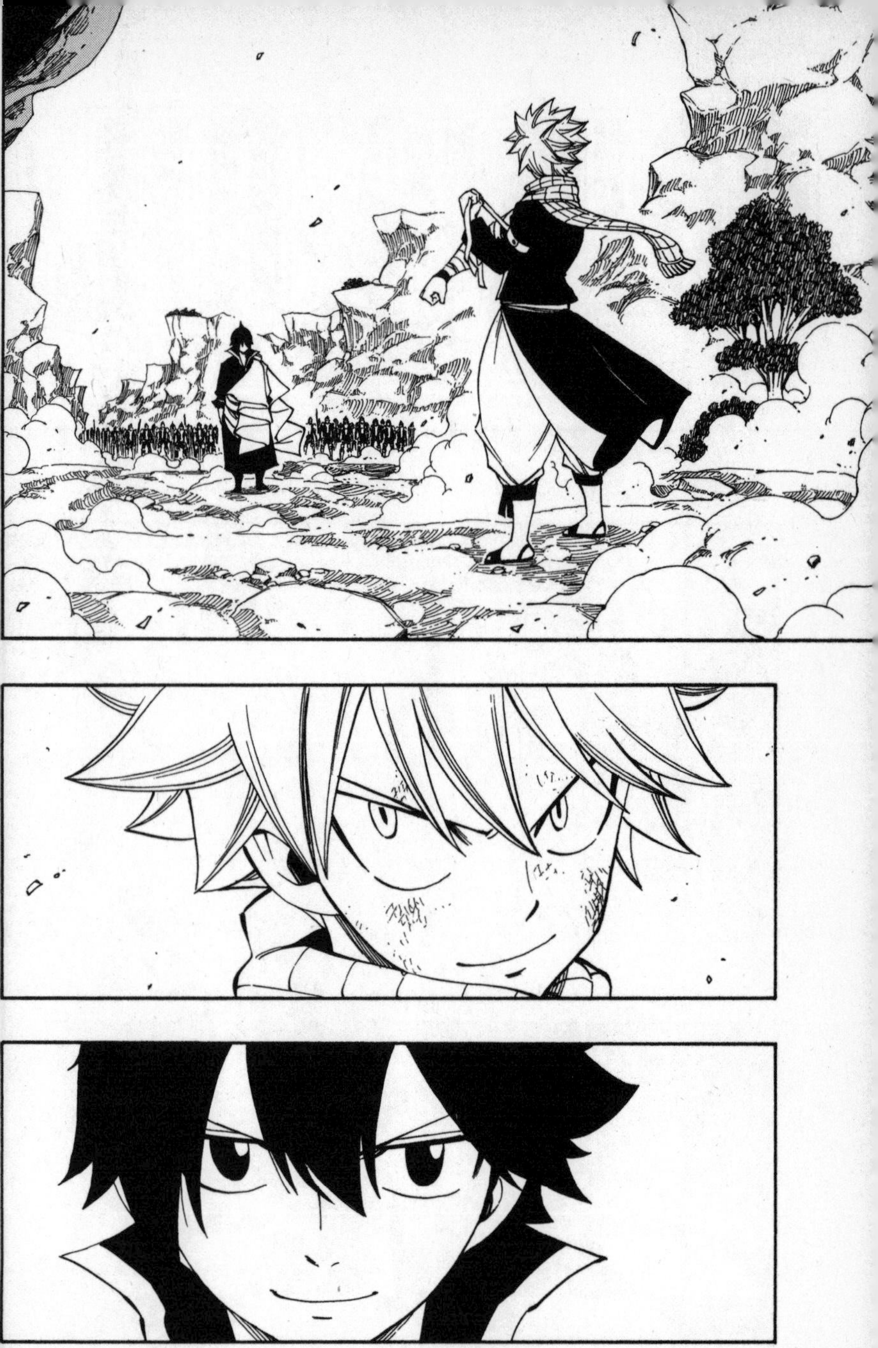

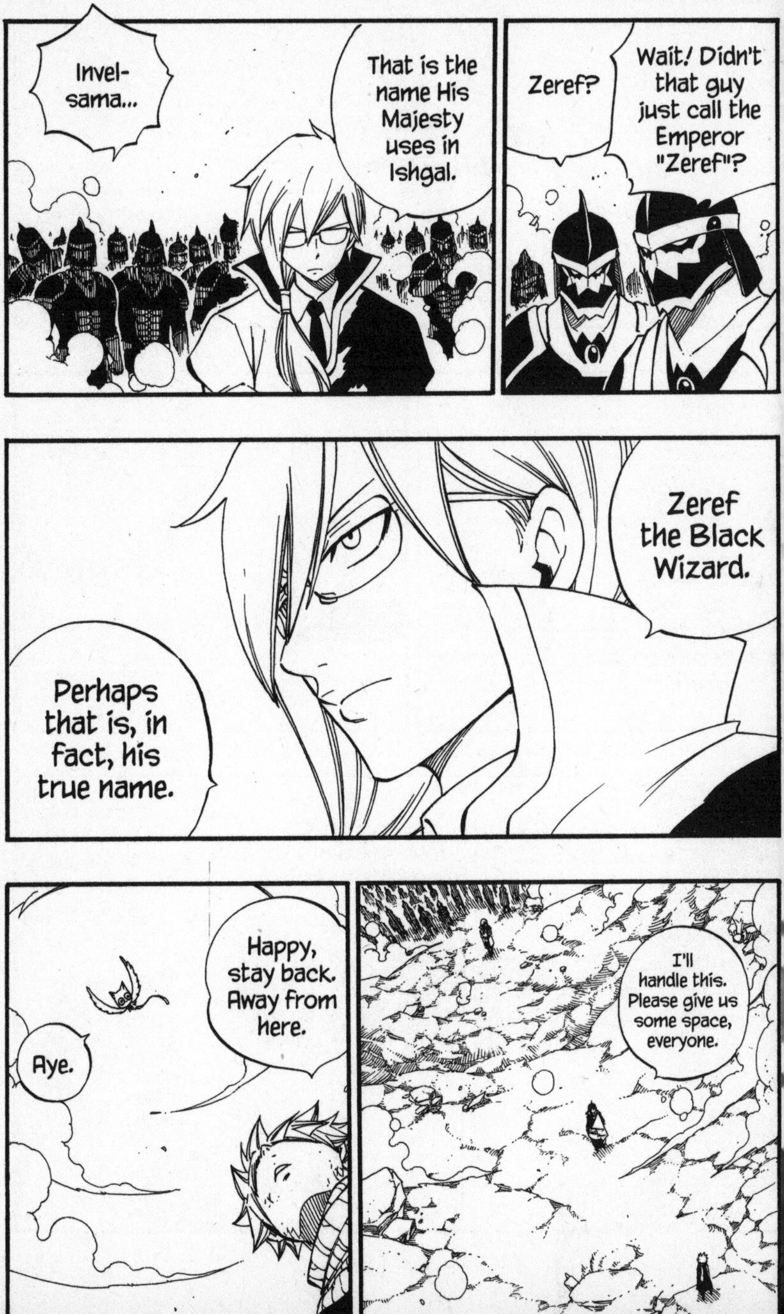
Wait! Didn't that guy just call the Emperor "Zeref"?
Zeref?
That is the name His Majesty uses in Ishgal.
Invel-sama...
Zeref the Black Wizard.
Perhaps that is, in fact, his true name.
I'll handle this. Please give us some space, everyone.
Happy, stay back. Away from here.
Aye.

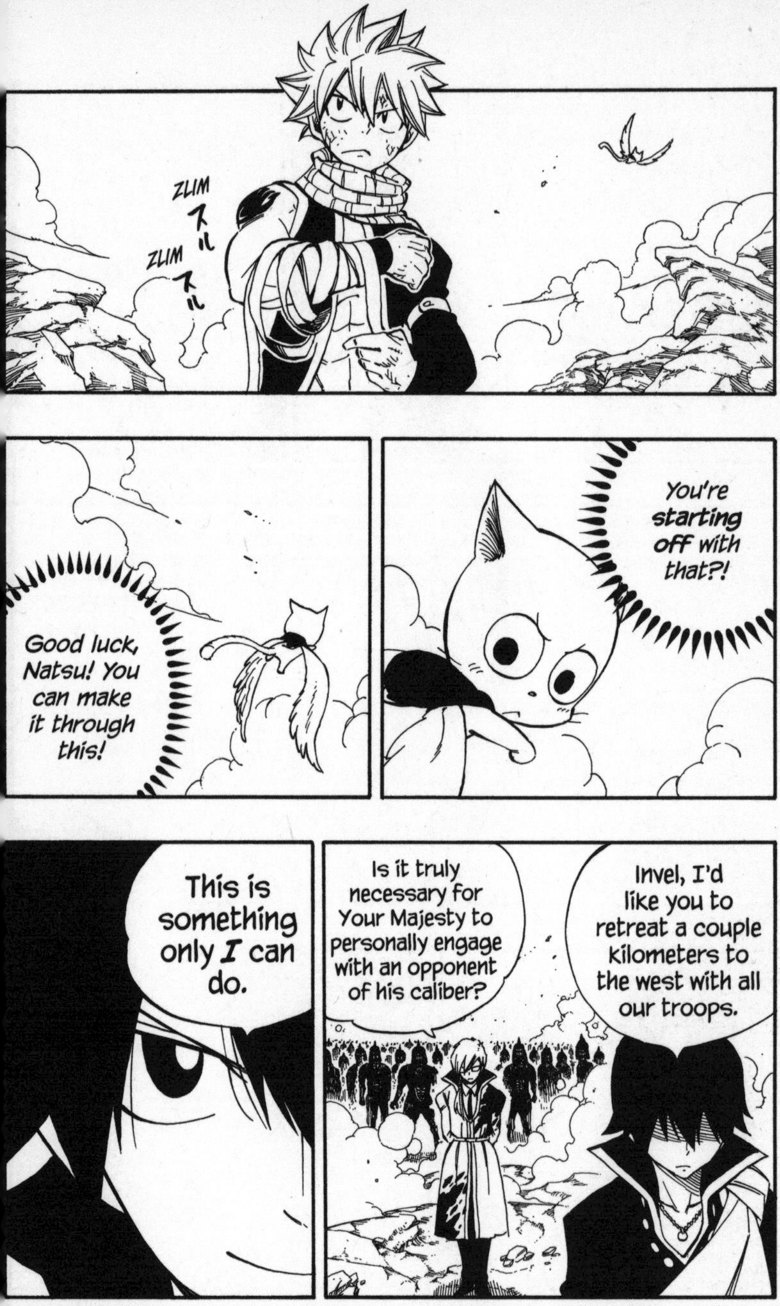
ZLIM スル
ZLIM スル
You're starting off with that?!
Good luck, Natsu! You can make it through this!
Invel, I'd like you to retreat a couple kilometers to the west with all our troops.
Is it truly necessary for Your Majesty to personally engage with an opponent of his caliber?
This is something only I can do.

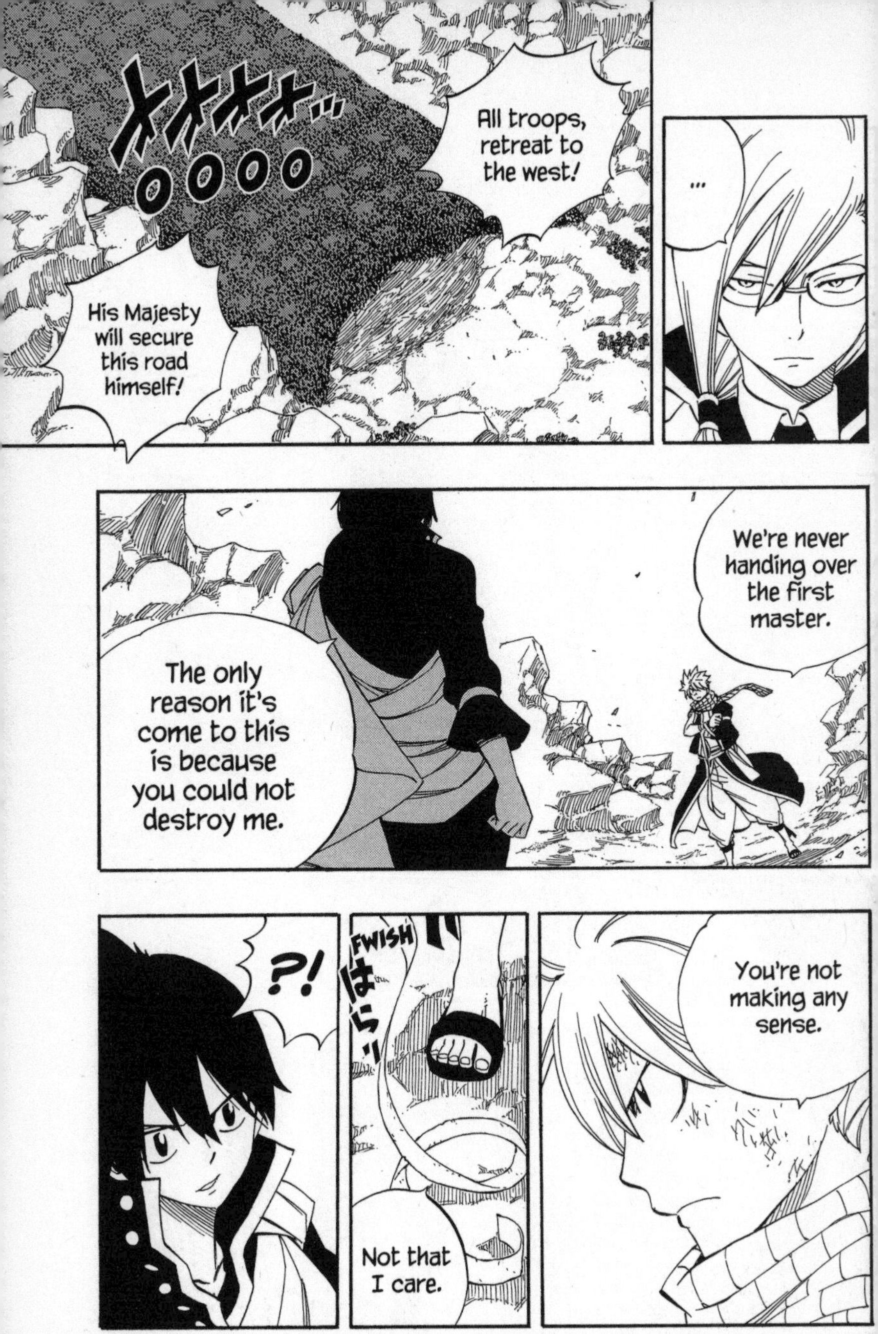
...
All troops, retreat to the west!
オオオォ OOOO
His Majesty will secure this road himself!
We're never handing over the first master.
The only reason it's come to this is because you could not destroy me.
You're not making any sense.
FWISH はらり
Not that I care.
?!

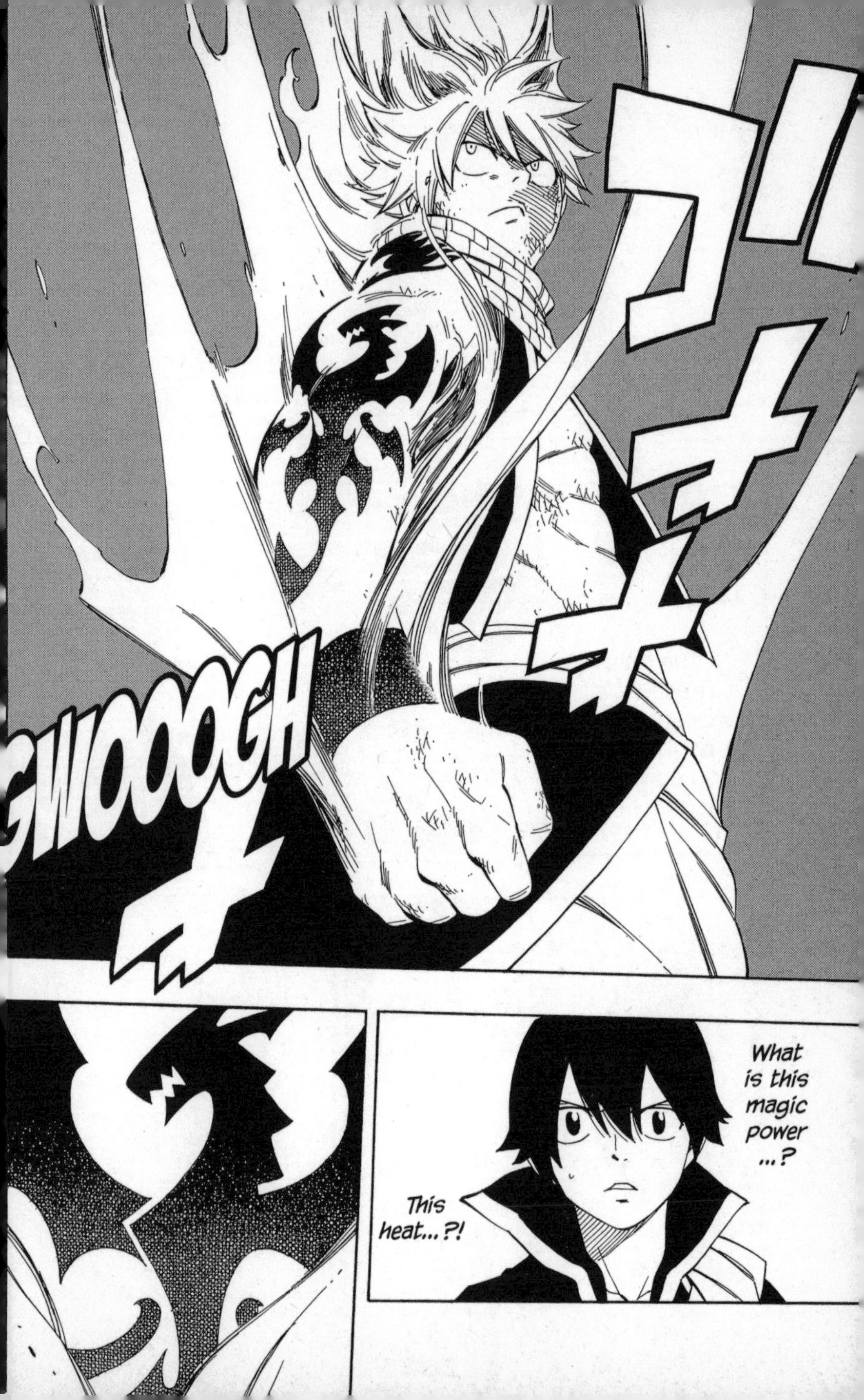
GWOOOGH
What is this magic power ...?
This heat...?!

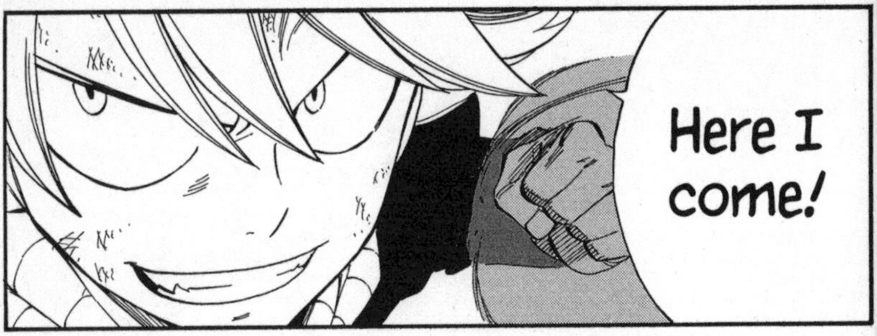
Here I come!

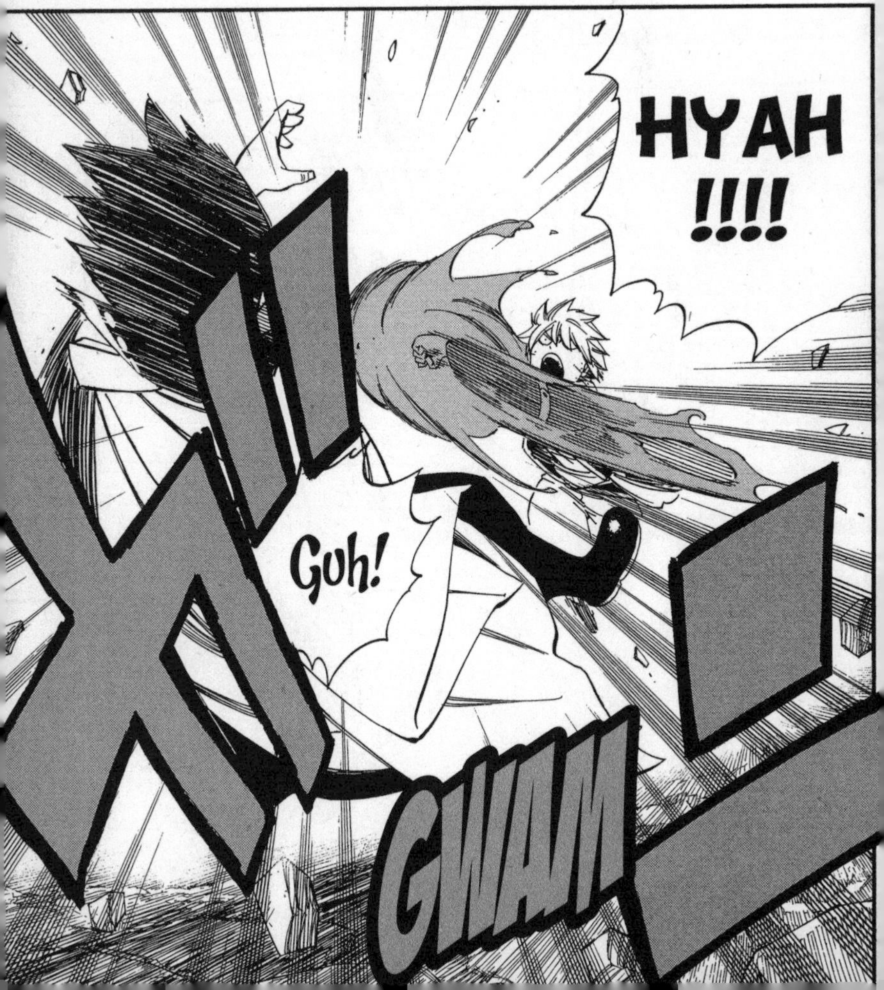
HYAH !!!!
Guh!
GWAM

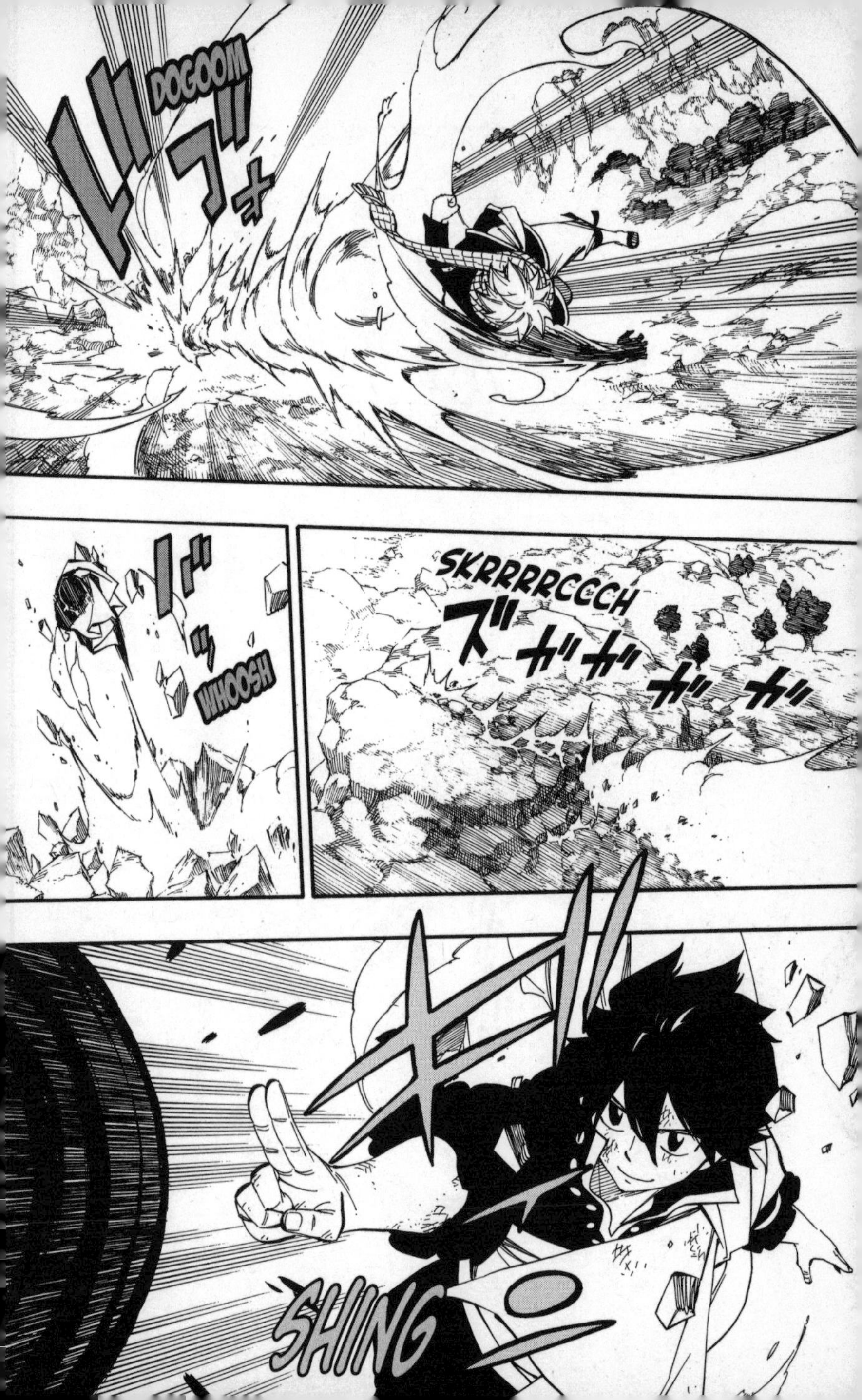

ドゴォ
DOGOOM
SKRRRRCCCH
ズガガガガ
WHOOSH
SHING

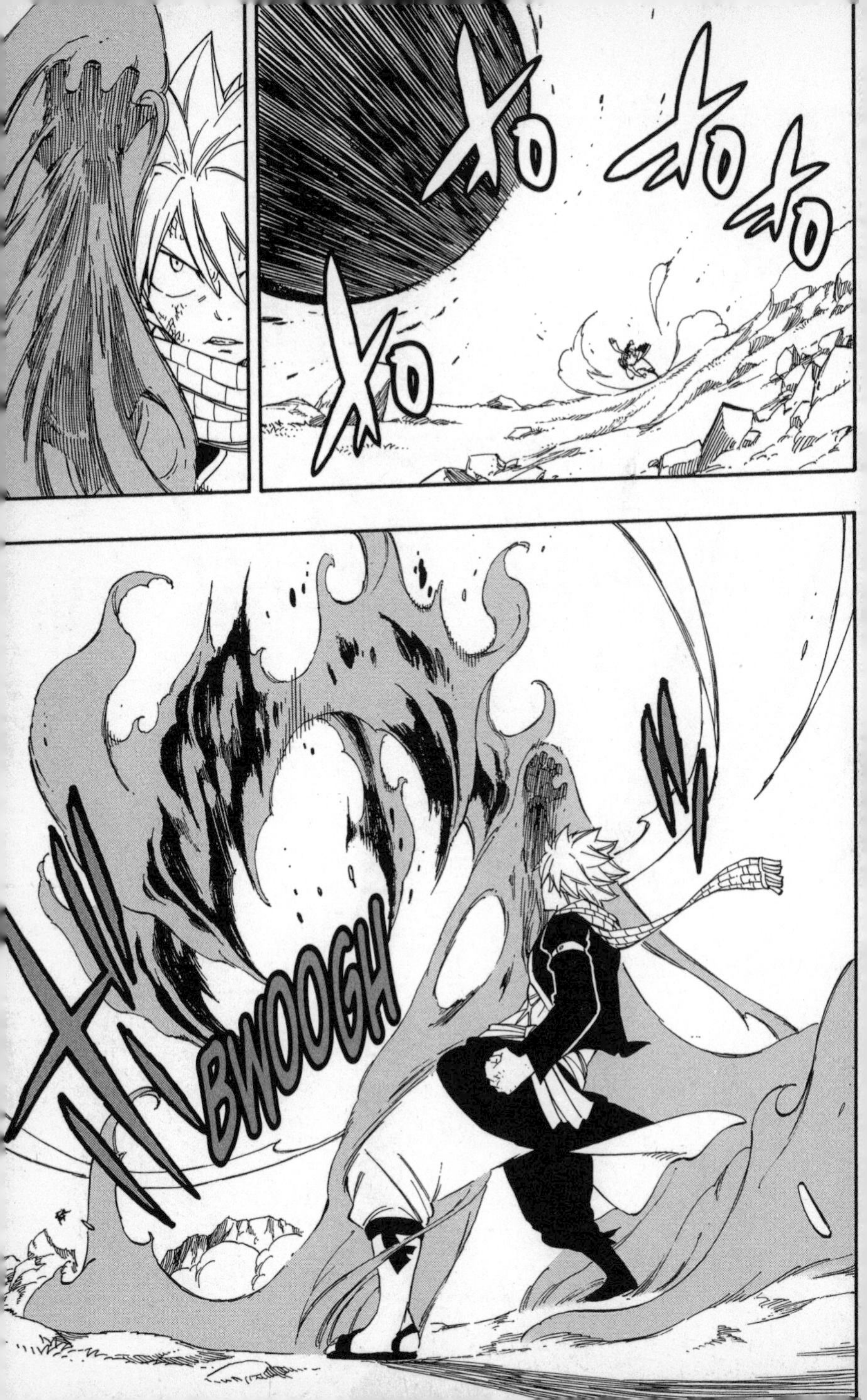
BWOOGH

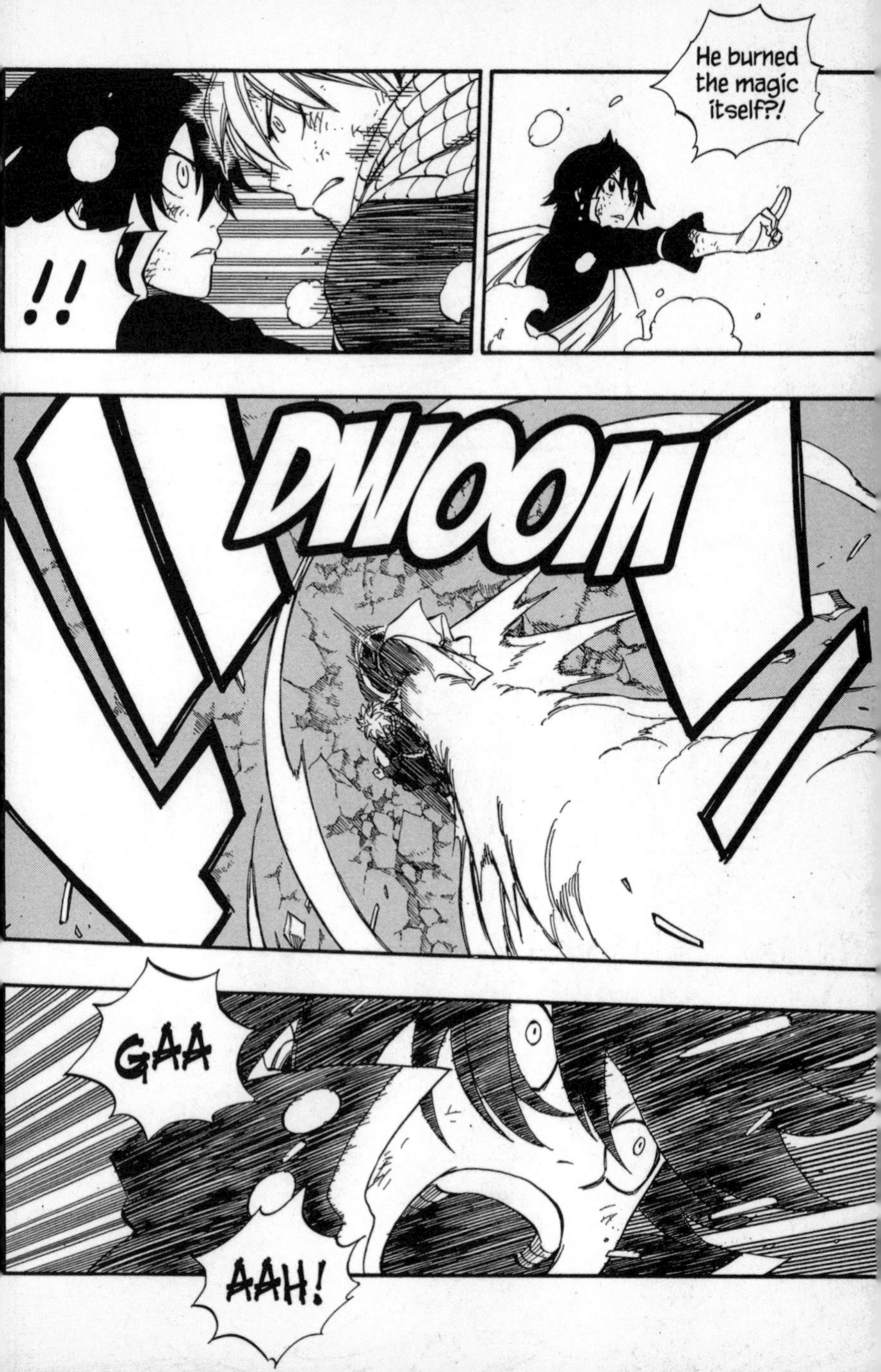
He burned the magic itself?!
!!
DWOOM
GAA
AAH!

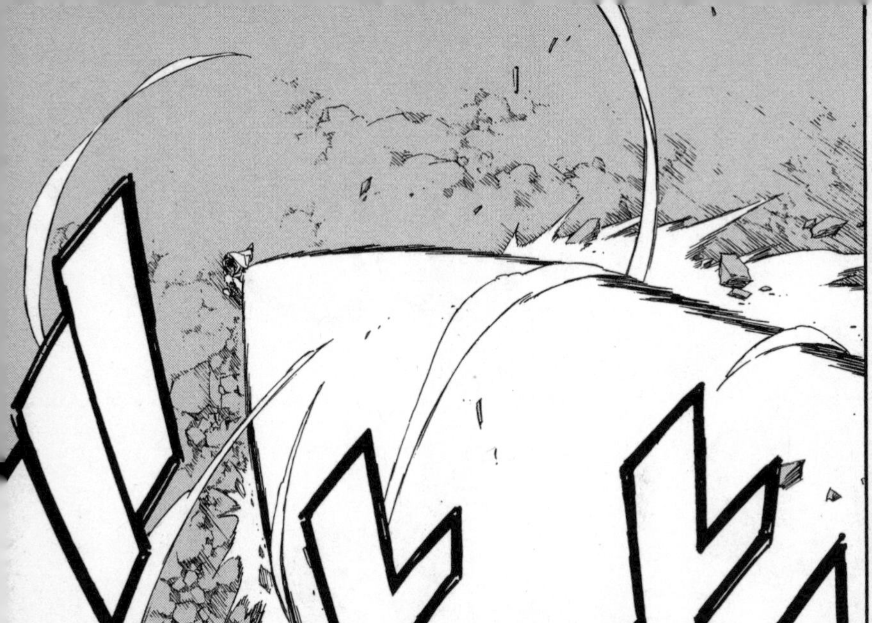
GWOOGH
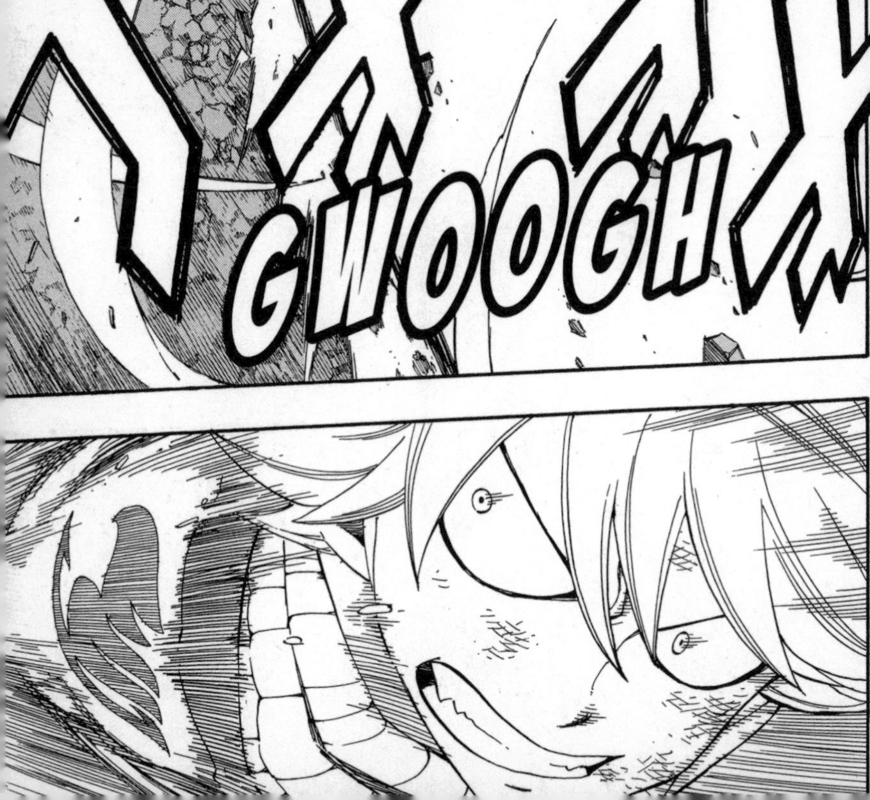

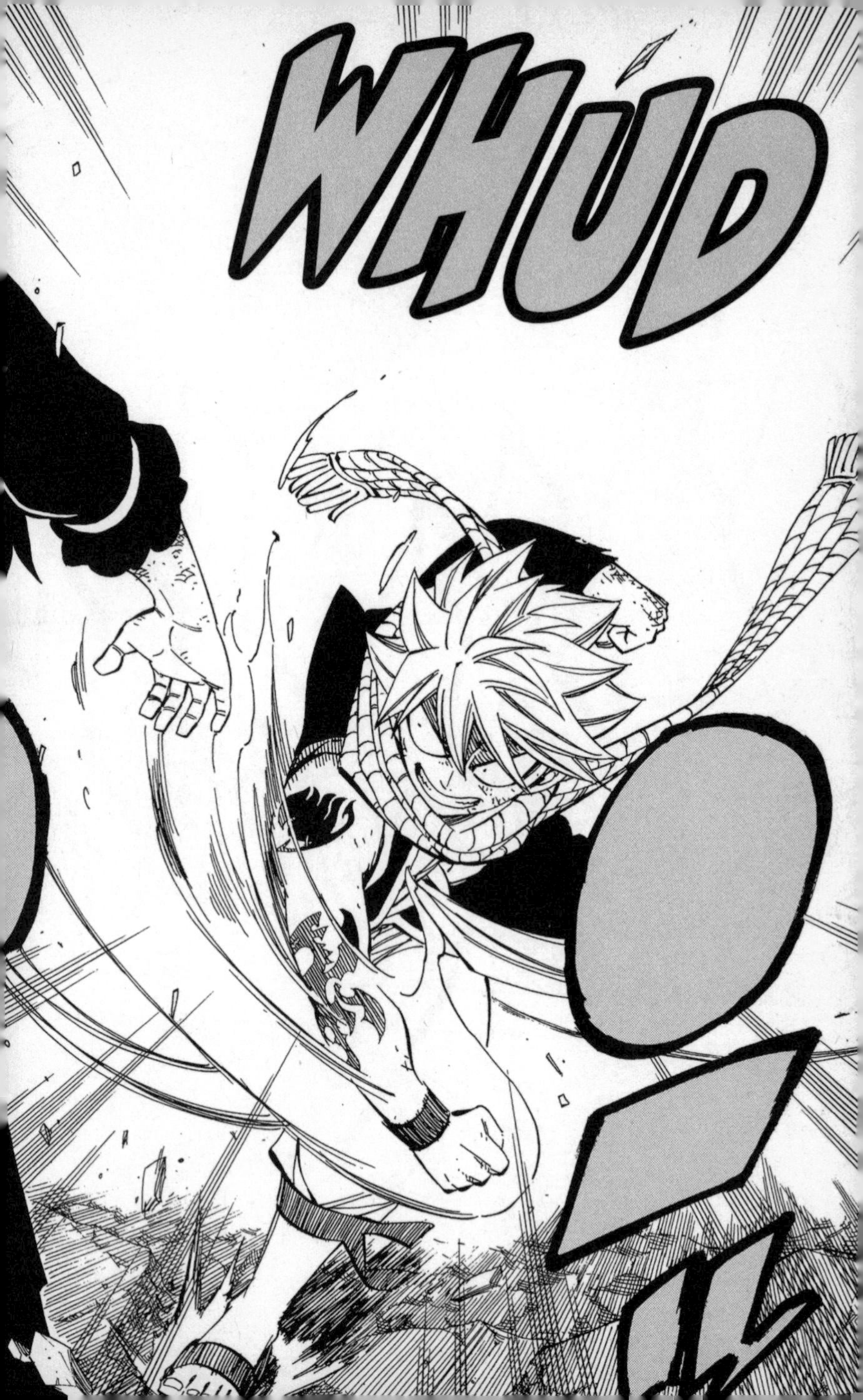
WHUD

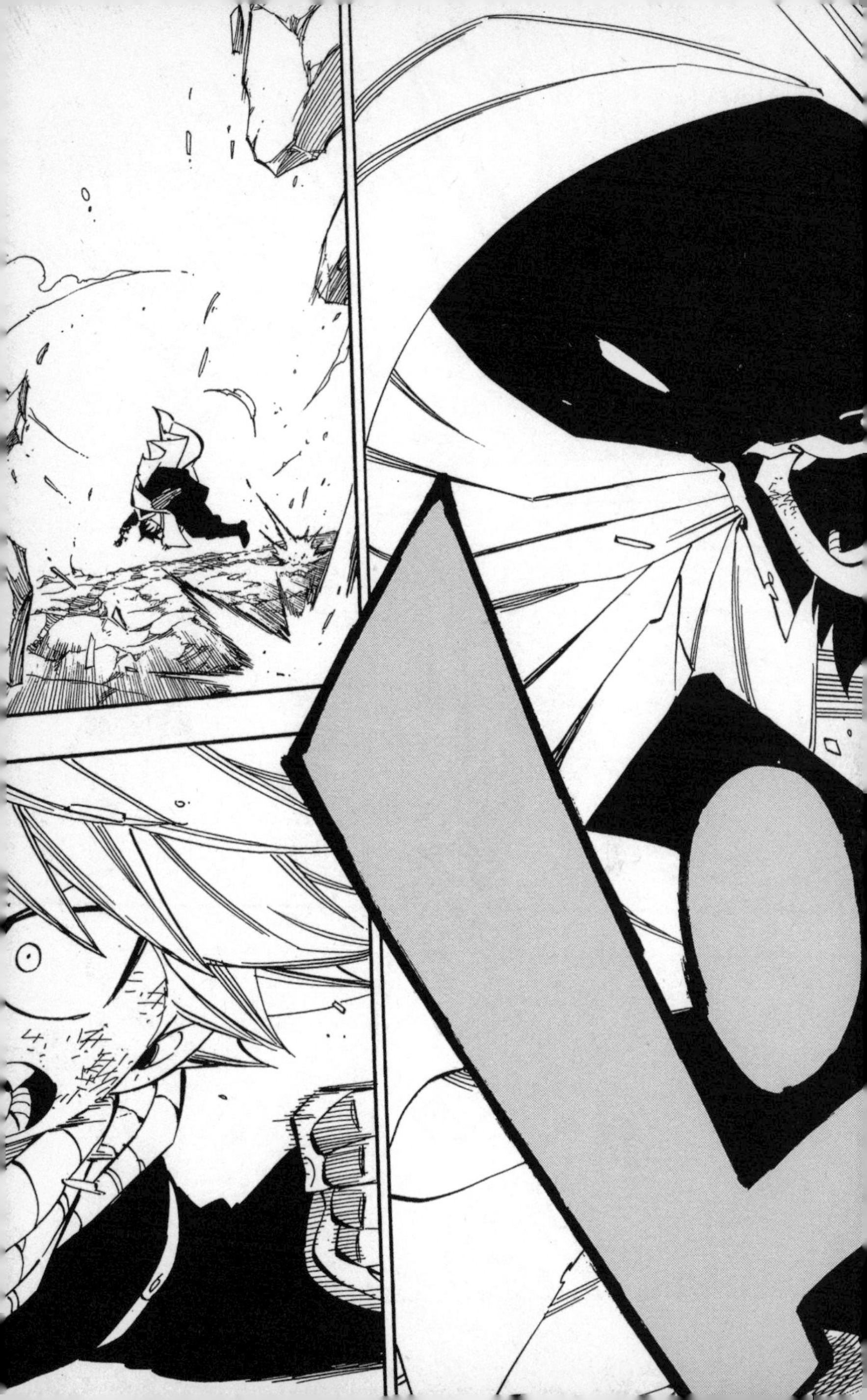

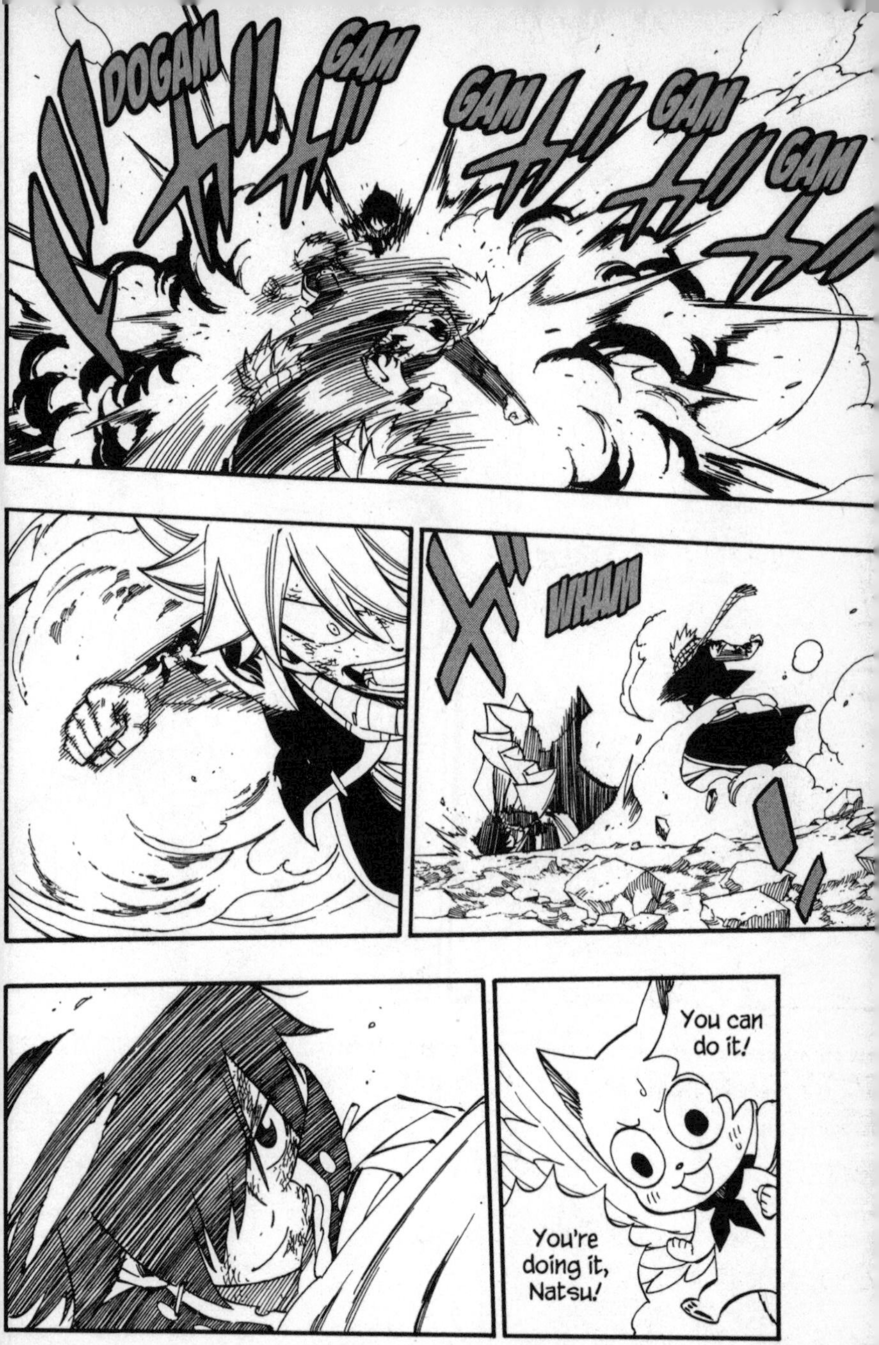
GAM
GAM
GAM
GAM
DOGAM
WHAM
You can do it!
You're doing it, Natsu!

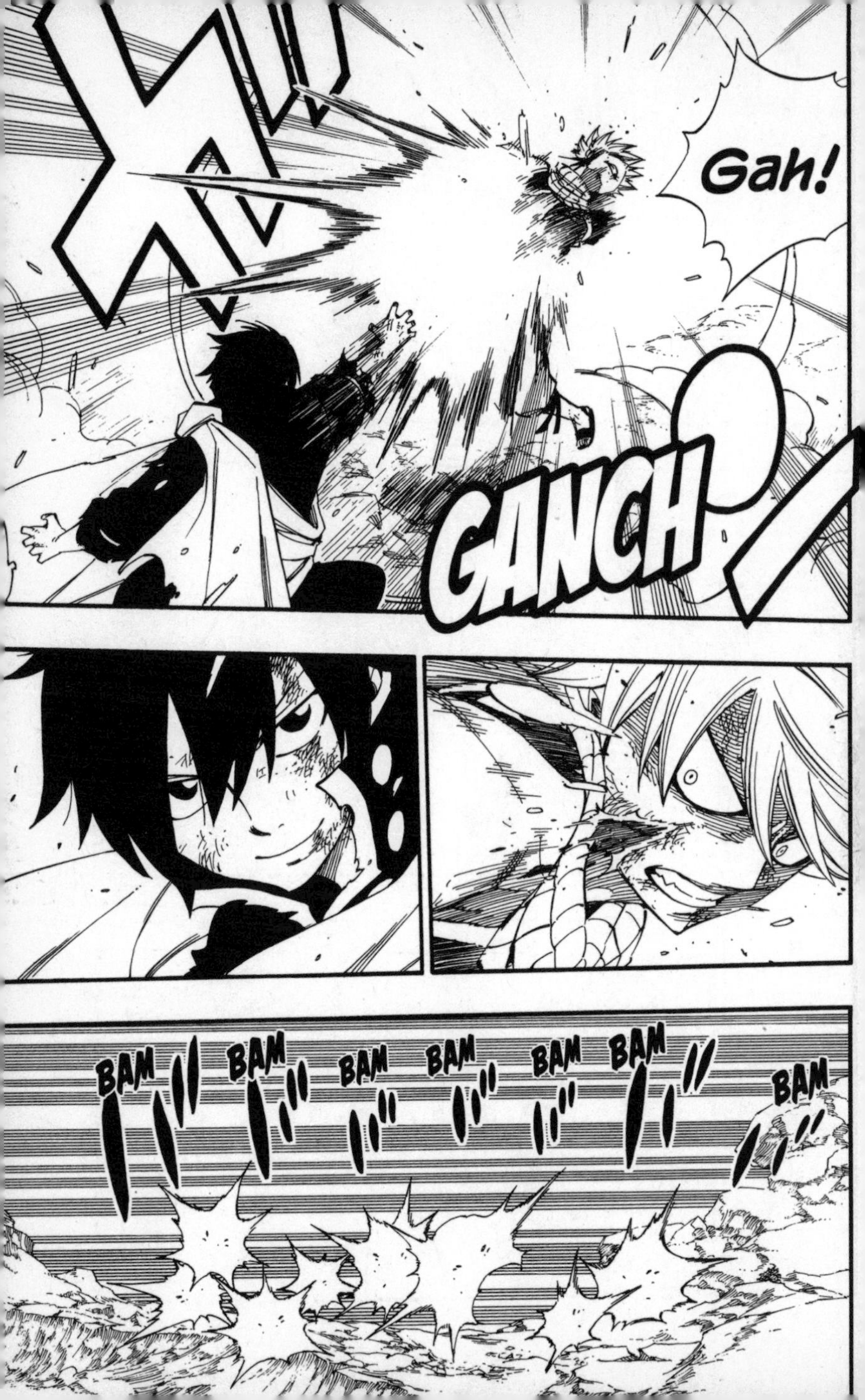
Gah!
GANCH
BAM
BAM
BAM
BAM
BAM
BAM
BAM

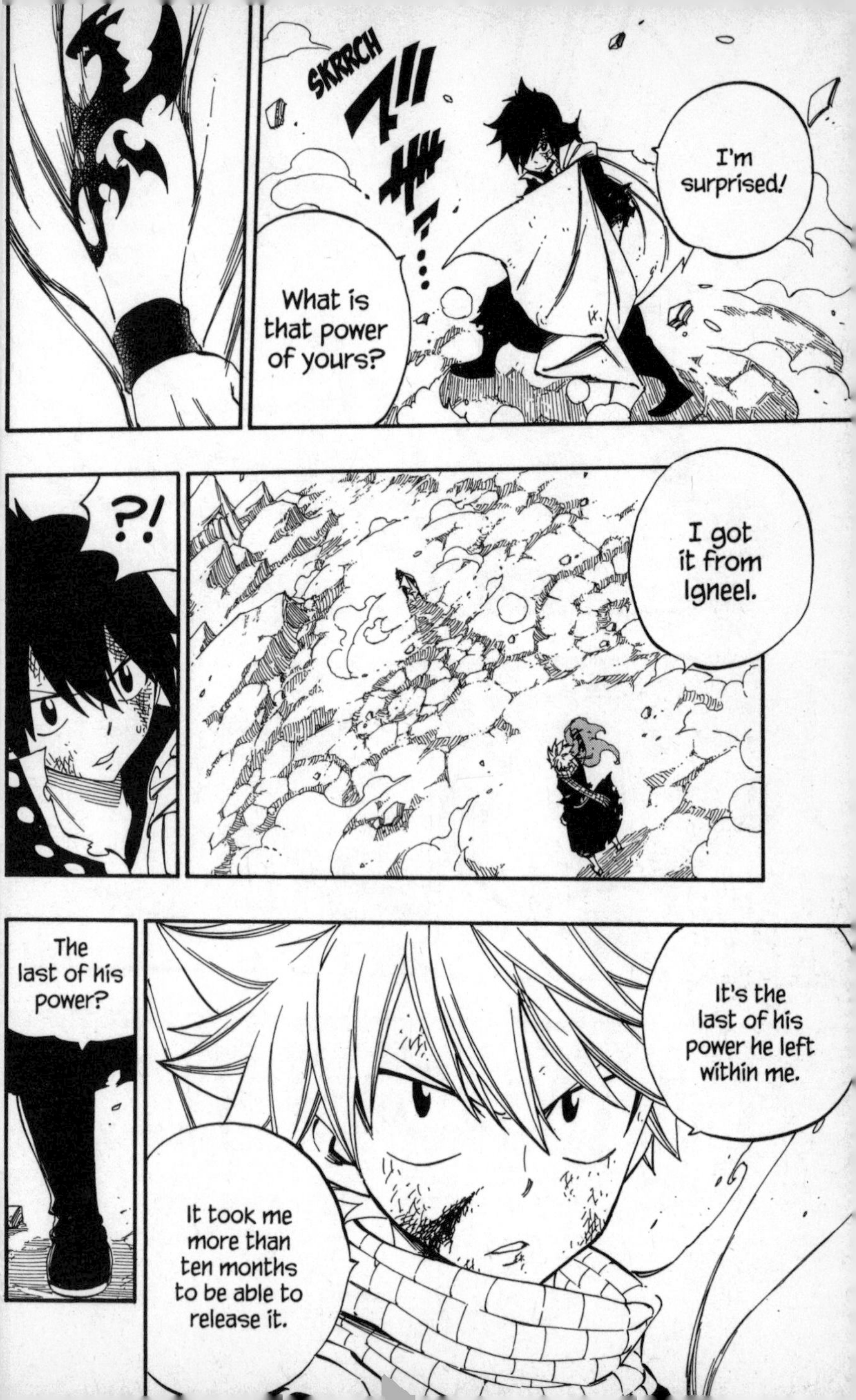
SKRRCH
I'm surprised!
What is that power of yours?
I got it from Igneel.
?!
It's the last of his power he left within me.
It took me more than ten months to be able to release it.
The last of his power?

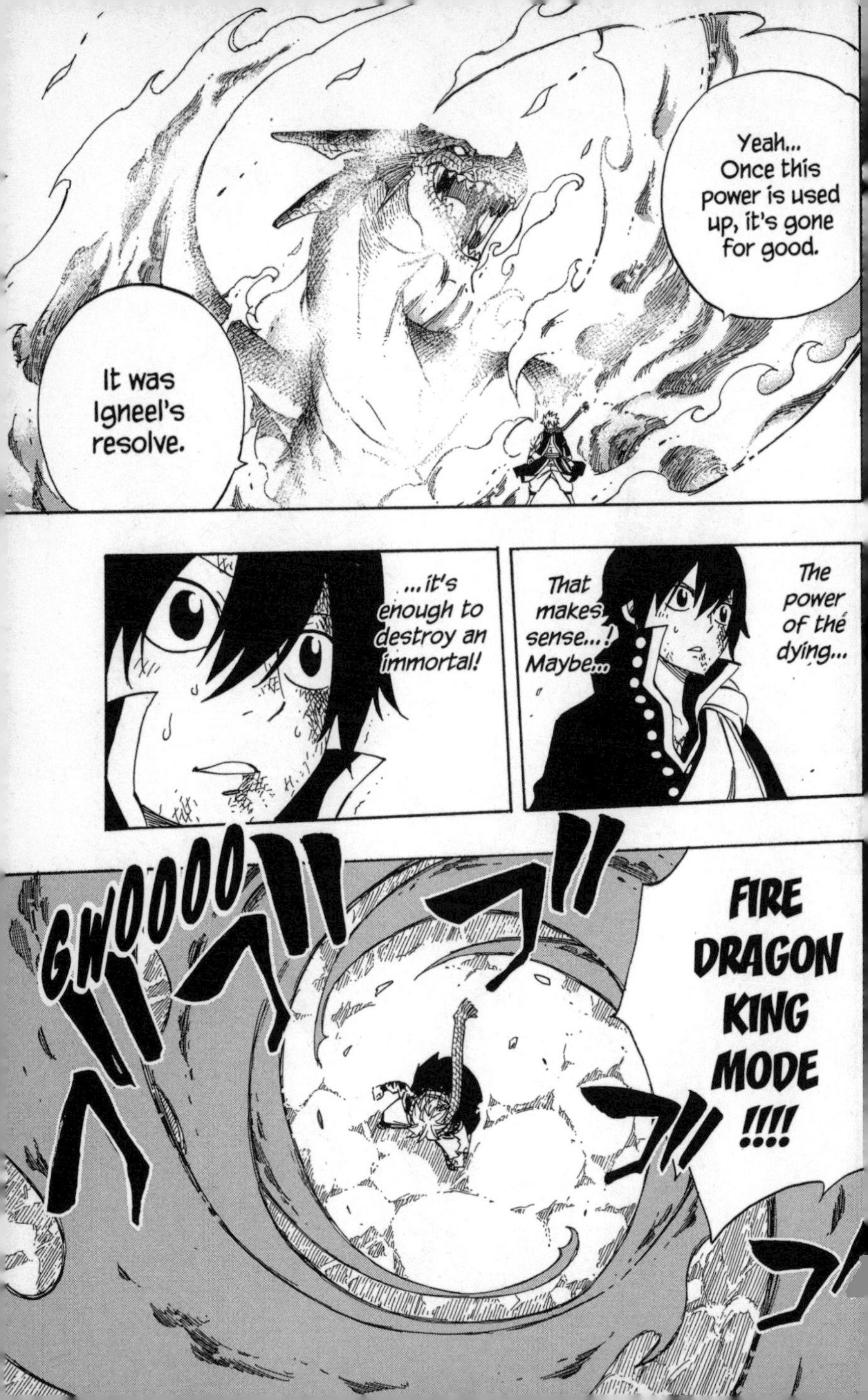

Yeah... Once this power is used up, it's gone for good.
It was Igneel's resolve.
The power of the dying...
That makes sense...! Maybe...
...it's enough to destroy an immortal!
FIRE DRAGON KING MODE!!!!
GWOOOO

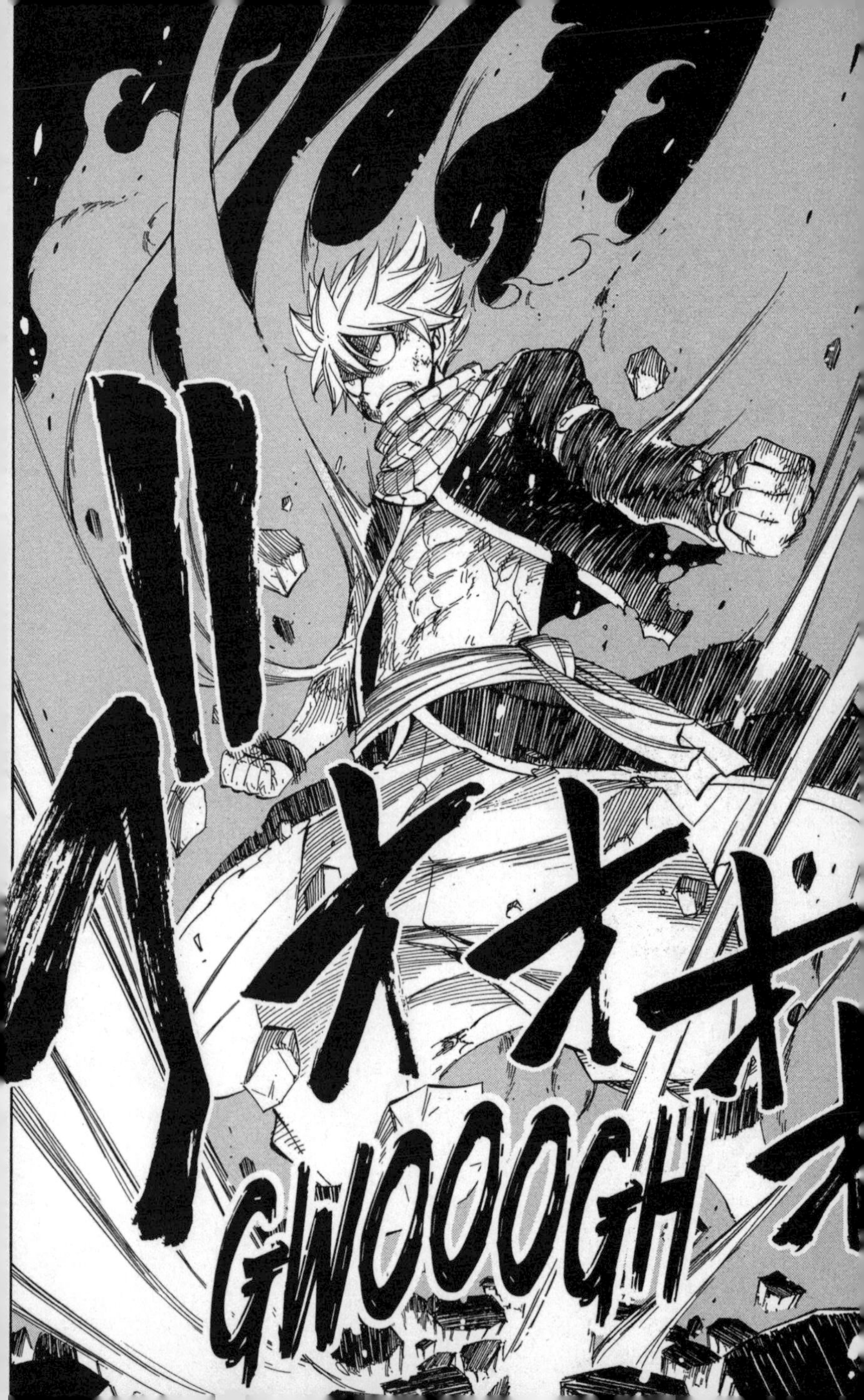
GWOOOGH

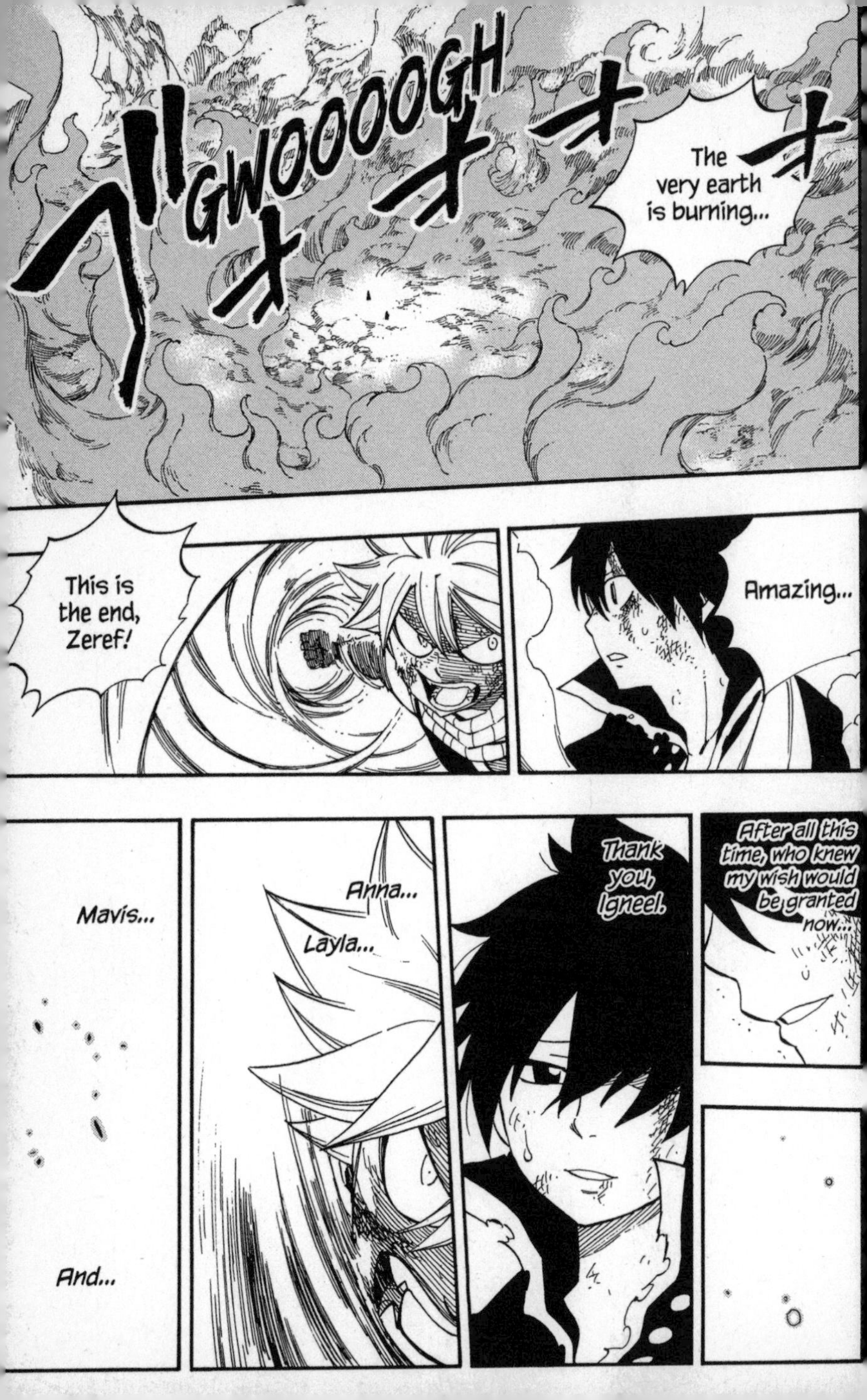
The very earth is burning...
GWOOOOGH
Amazing...
This is the end, Zeref!
After all this time, who knew my wish would be granted now...
Thank you, Igneel.
Anna...
Layla...
Mavis...
And...

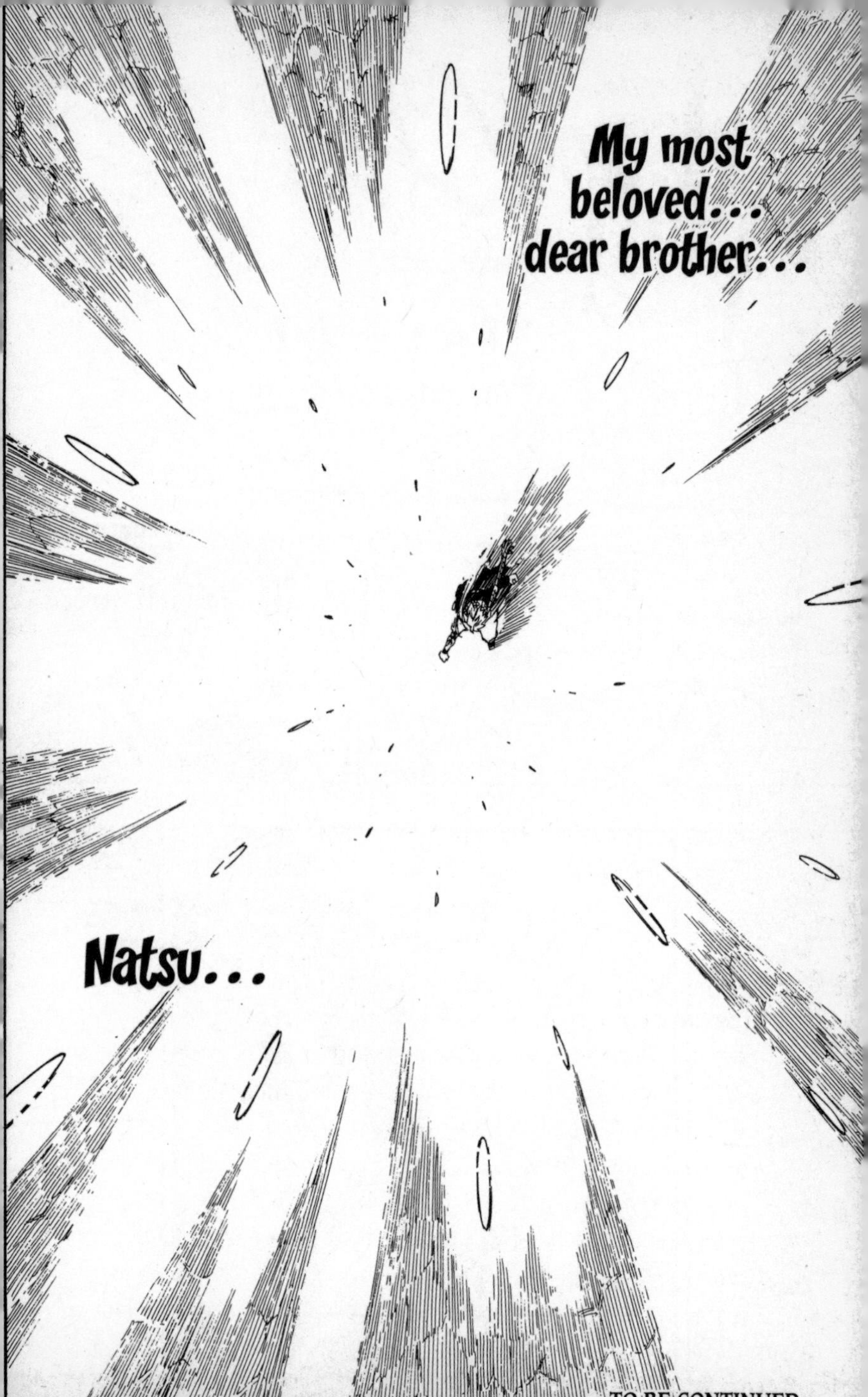

My most beloved... dear brother...
Natsu...

TO BE CONTINUED

あとがき

Afterword

Sorry to keep you waiting. It looks like the next volume, Volume 55, will be able to be released in Japan in a special edition that features an original animation DVD (OAD). I'm glad to say that this makes the lucky seventh Fairy Tail OAD made so far! The story of the anime will be based on a Fairy Tail short story that appeared in **Magazine Special** called "The Fairies' Penalty Game." It came out quite a while ago. It takes place sometime around the Grand Magic Games when Fairy Tail was divided up into the A team and the B team. The team that lost the tournament had to do some embarrassing things. But in the end, both teams had to combine into one, so things ended a bit vaguely. But in this one, the true winner is revealed! It's a mixture of funny and suggestive scenes, but in the end, it turns into an nice little story, so I hope you're looking forward to it!

And, of course, there will be original scenes in the anime!

Now, my current situation… Well, I've had to do all kinds of approvals on the OAD I just mentioned (including checking the original story over again), writing the script for the movie, and doing character designs, checking the novels and drawing the illustrations within them, checks on the spin-off manga, and checking on some projects that I can't talk about yet, so I've been so busy it made me dizzy. As the number of works based off my stuff increases, so does my workload. But as rough as it is, it's really fantastic, too! Hey, I know I'm not as young as I used to be, but recently a lot of people have been urging me to look after myself. I'm still pretty darned healthy! Actually, I'm grateful my body is doing as well as it is!

TAIL d' ART

The Fairy Tail Guild is looking for illustrations! Please send in your art on a post card or at post-card size, and do it in black pen, okay? Those chosen to be published will get a signed mini poster! ♪ Make sure you write your real name and address on the back of your illustration!

Tokushima Prefecture, Toshihiro Miki

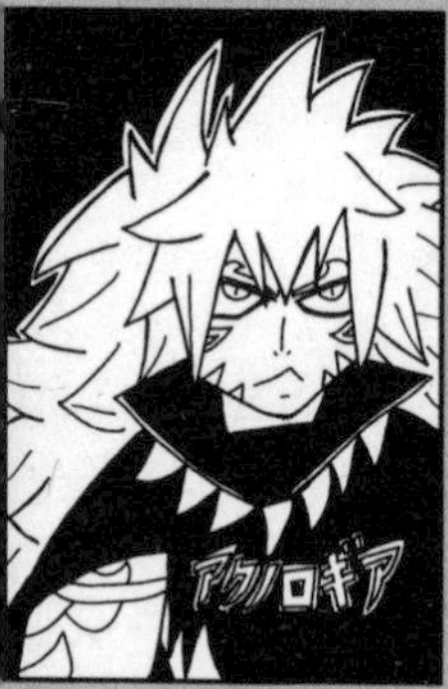
アクノロギア

▲It's Acnologia!! He's going to play a big part in the main story pretty soon.

▼Hey! Art from Fairy Tail ZERØ! If you want to know who Zera is, check out Fairy Tail ZERØ!

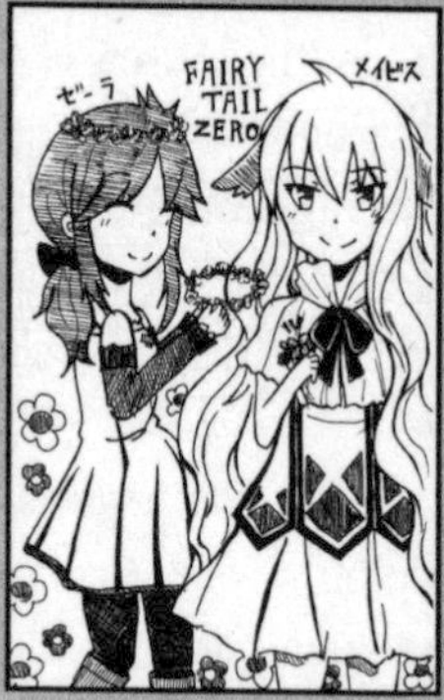
ゼーラ
FAIRY TAIL ZERO
メイビス

Tochigi Prefecture, Nori

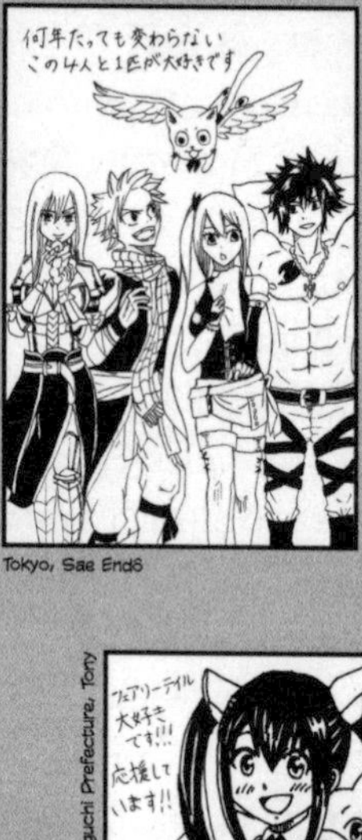
何年たっても変わらない
この4人と1匹が大好きです

Tokyo, Sae End6

Now◀ this is well done! Everybody's expressions are really nice!

Yamaguchi Prefecture, Tony

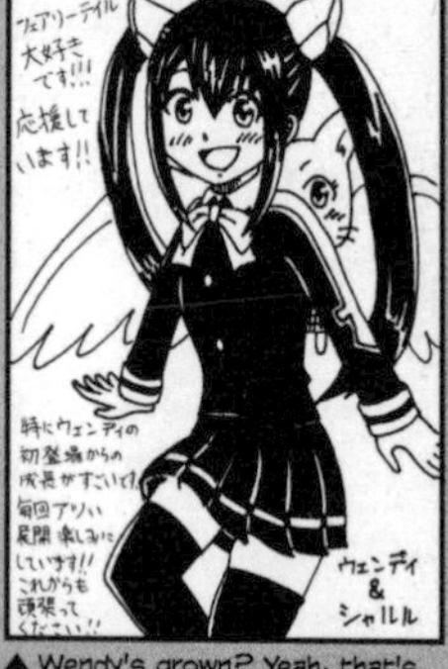
フェアリーテイル
大好きです!!!
応援しています!!
ウェンディ
&
シャルル

▲Wendy's grown? Yeah, that's true. She's gotten stronger, huh?

Okayama Prefecture, Kiminori Namba

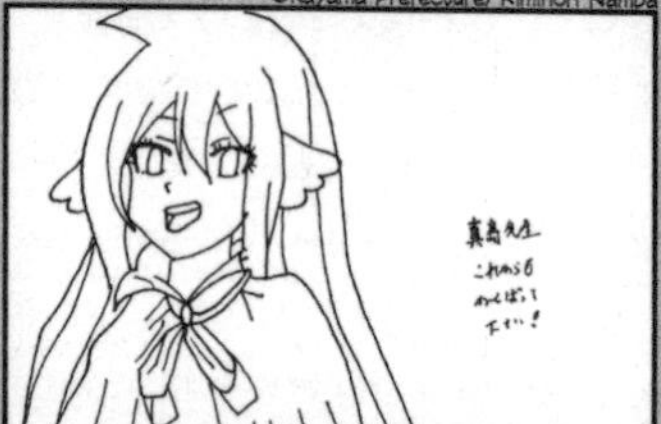

▶I'm giving it my best!! Thanks for the message!!

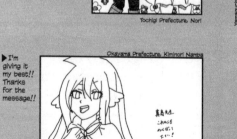

Send to Hiro Mashima, Kodansha Comics
451 Park Ave. South, 7th Floor New York, NY 10016

FAIRY GUILD

Kanagawa Prefecture, Akane Yamada

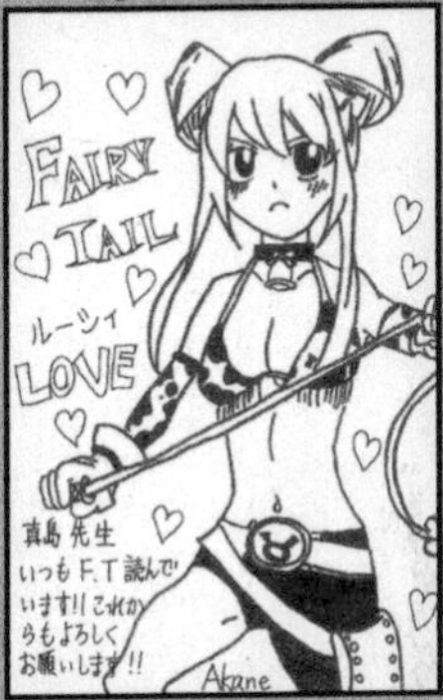
FAIRY TAIL
ルーシィ
LOVE
真島先生
いつもF.T読んでいます!! これからもよろしくお願いします!!
Akane

▲Taurus Form!! I actually, really like this design!

▼Zeref and Mavis... How will their confrontation go in the end?!

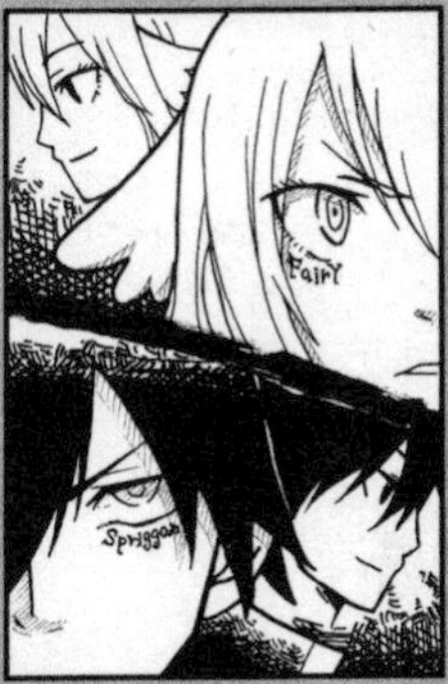
Fairy
Spriggan

Aichi Prefecture, Banka

As ◀ you'd figure, there are a lot of people who love these three people(?)! I love them, too!

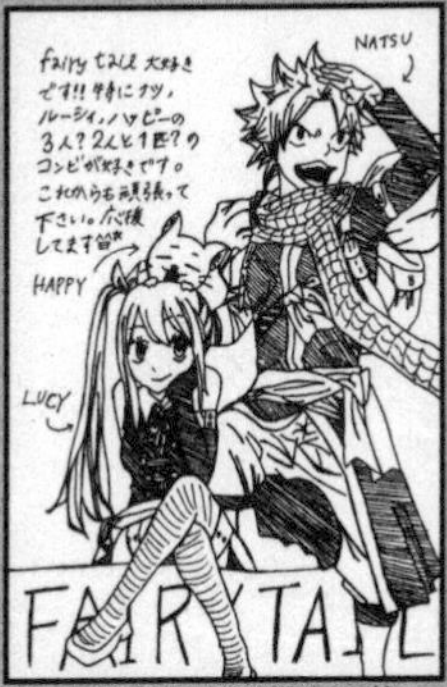
fairy tailは大好きです!! 特にナツ、ルーシィ、ハッピーの3人? 2人と1匹?のコンビが好きです。これからも頑張って下さい。応援してます!!
NATSU
HAPPY
LUCY
FAIRY TAIL

Ishikawa Prefecture, Yui Nakabayashi

This is ▶ a rare pairing. Extremely rare!

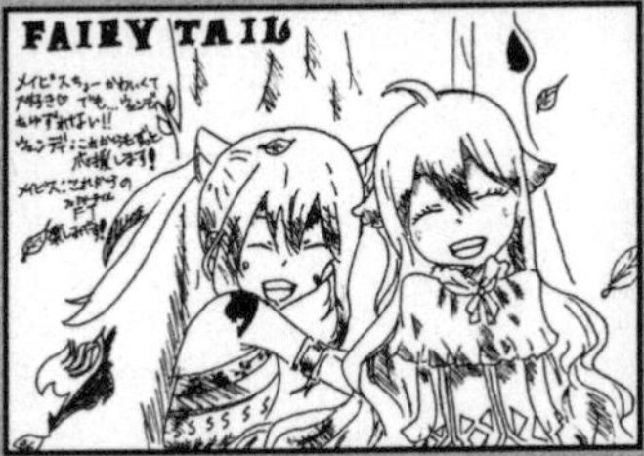
FAIRY TAIL

Saitama Prefecture, Misora Sekine

REJECTION CORNER

I know you asked to not be rejected, but... Sorry. ▶

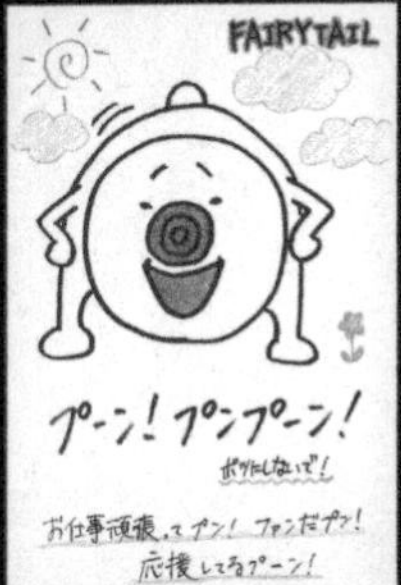
FAIRYTAIL
プーン!プンプーン!
ボツにしないで!
お仕事頑張ってプン! ファンだプン!
応援してるプーン!

Gunma Prefecture, Mamoozu Meeeen!

By sending in letters or postcards, you give us permission to give your name, address, postal code, and any other information you include to the author as is. Please keep that in mind.

FROM HIRO MASHIMA

Fairy Tail is becoming a stage play!

When I first heard the idea, I thought, "Huh? How are you gonna do magic and stuff?" But the answer they came up with was pretty incredible! As the opening night draws closer, my anticipation grows!

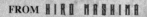

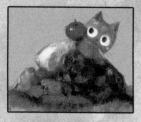

Original Jacket Design: Hisao Ogawa

Translation Notes:

Japanese is tricky language for most Westerners, and translation is often more art than science. For your edification and reading pleasure, here are notes on some of the places where we could have gone in a different direction with our translation of the work, or where a Japanese cultural reference is used.

Page 60, Nakagami Asterism

This is the same as the Nakagami attack found in Volume 38. As previously mentioned, Nakagami, also known as Tenichijin or Tenitsujin, is the chief of the 12 Generals of Heaven found in the esoteric astrology of the famous Japanese spiritualist Abe no Seimei. An asterism is a star picture (like the big dipper) that isn't an official constellation.

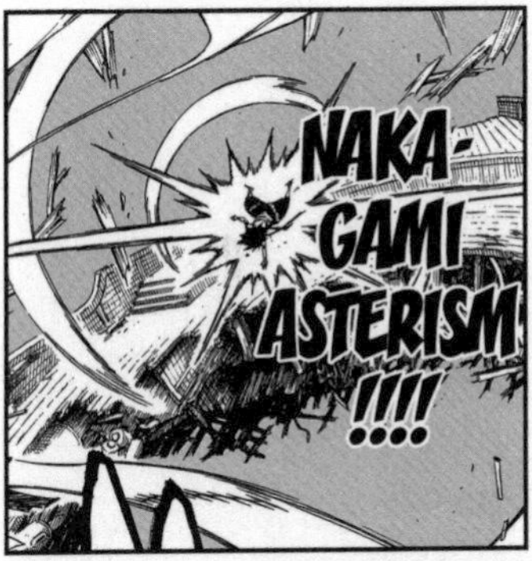
NAKA-GAMI ASTERISM!!!!

Page 81, Fairy dust

Evergreen's fairy dust seems to be derived from the scales on the wings of lepidoptera, an order of butterflies and moths. These scales on the wings can provide camouflage, or warning colors indicating that they are toxic (mimicking actual toxic animals). Since the wings can easily be shed, they provide a defense if they are trying to escape from a predator's nest or web.

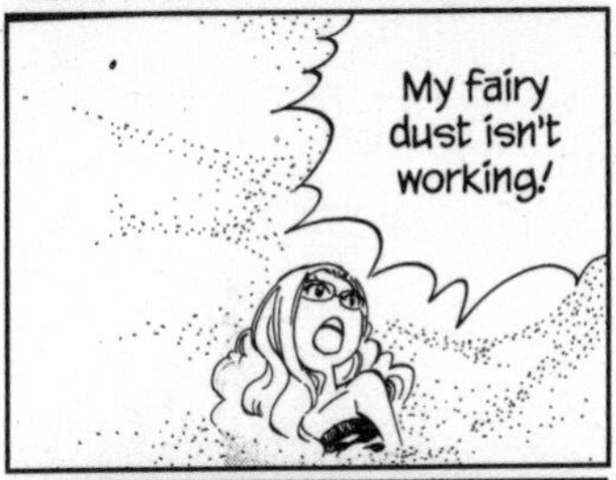
My fairy dust isn't working!

Page 104, Dark Écriture

As mentioned previously when Fried first used the attack in Volume 14, écriture is French for "writing," so Fried wrote the spell to enact it.

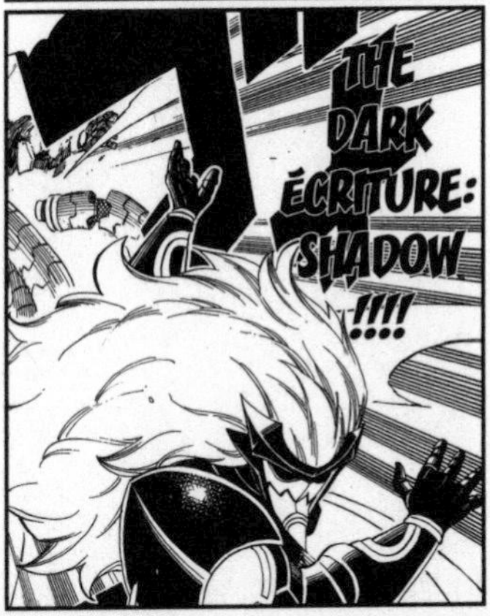
THE DARK ÉCRITURE: SHADOW!!!!

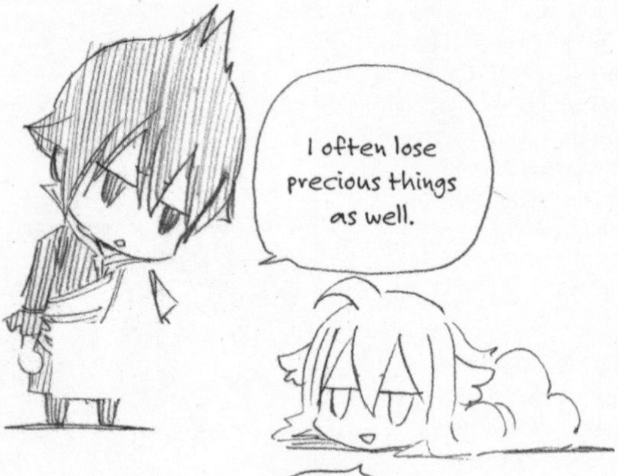
I often lose precious things as well.
Oh really?

Huh...? What, again?!

真島ヒロ HIRO MASHIMA

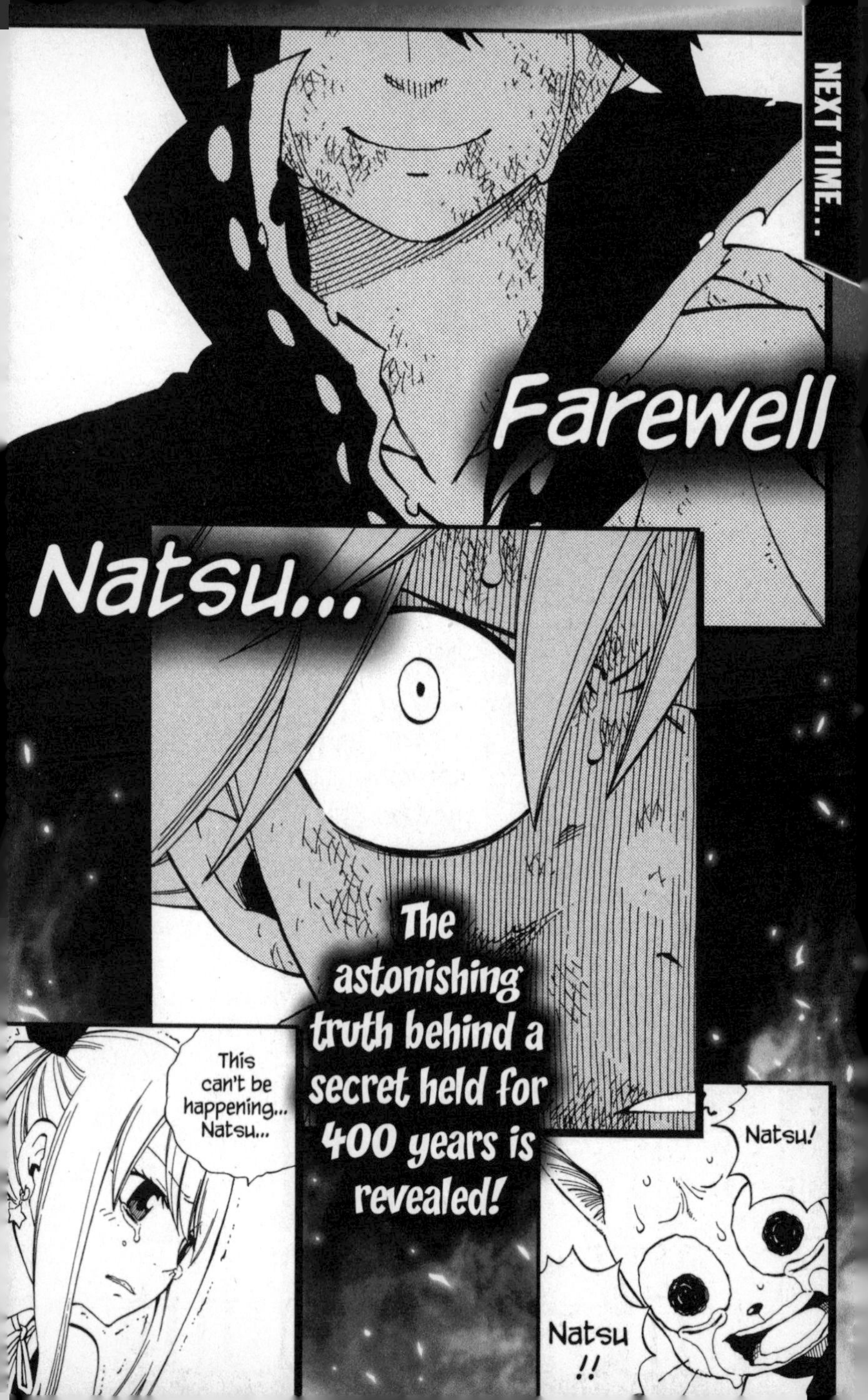
NEXT TIME...
Farewell
Natsu...
Natsu!
Natsu !!
The astonishing truth behind a secret held for 400 years is revealed!
This can't be happening... Natsu...

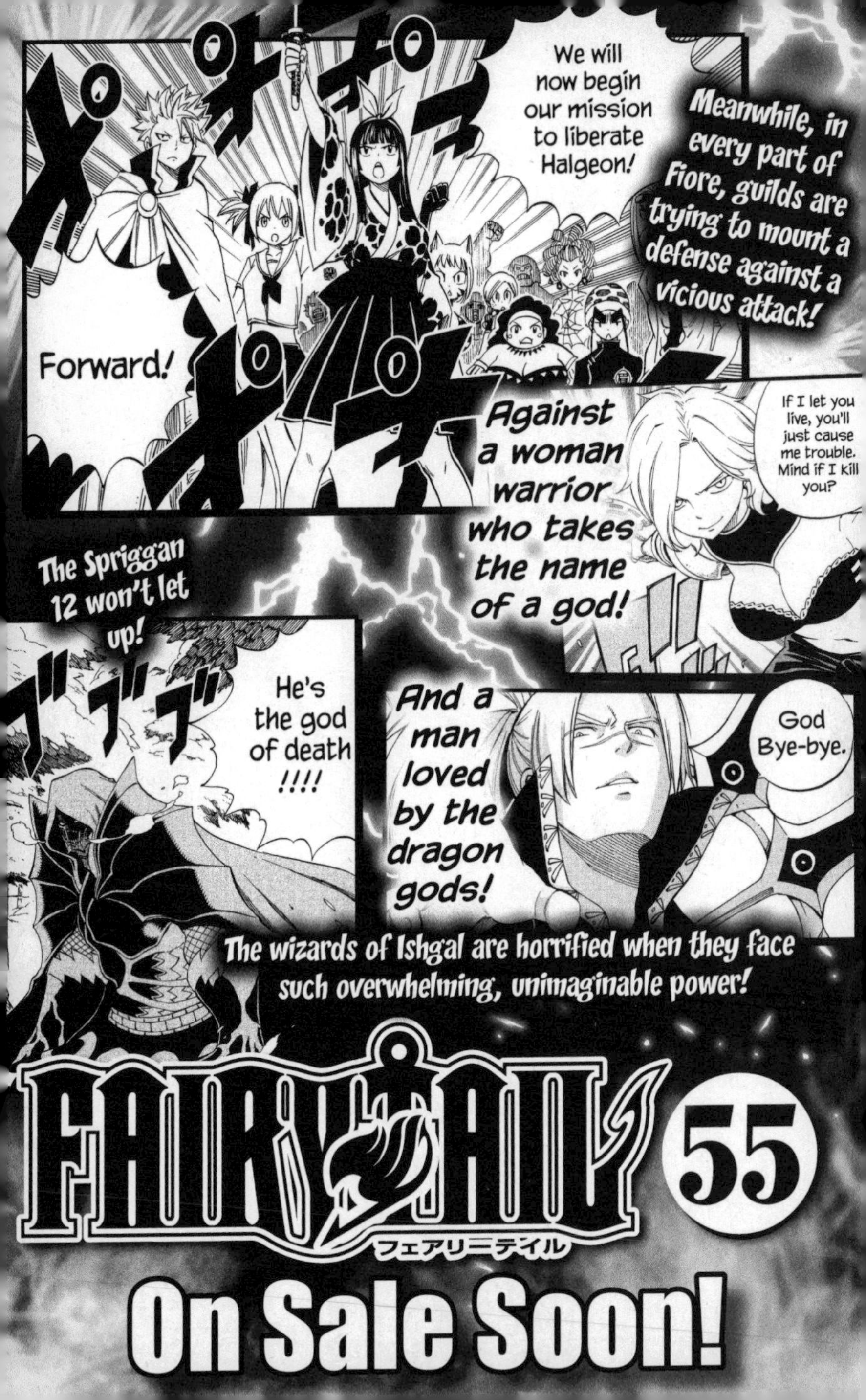
Meanwhile, in every part of Fiore, guilds are trying to mount a defense against a vicious attack!
We will now begin our mission to liberate Halgeon!
Forward!
If I let you live, you'll just cause me trouble. Mind if I kill you?
Against a woman warrior who takes the name of a god!
The Spriggan 12 won't let up!
God Bye-bye.
And a man loved by the dragon gods!
He's the god of death !!!!
The wizards of Ishgal are horrified when they face such overwhelming, unimaginable power!
FAIRY TAIL
フェアリーテイル
55
On Sale Soon!

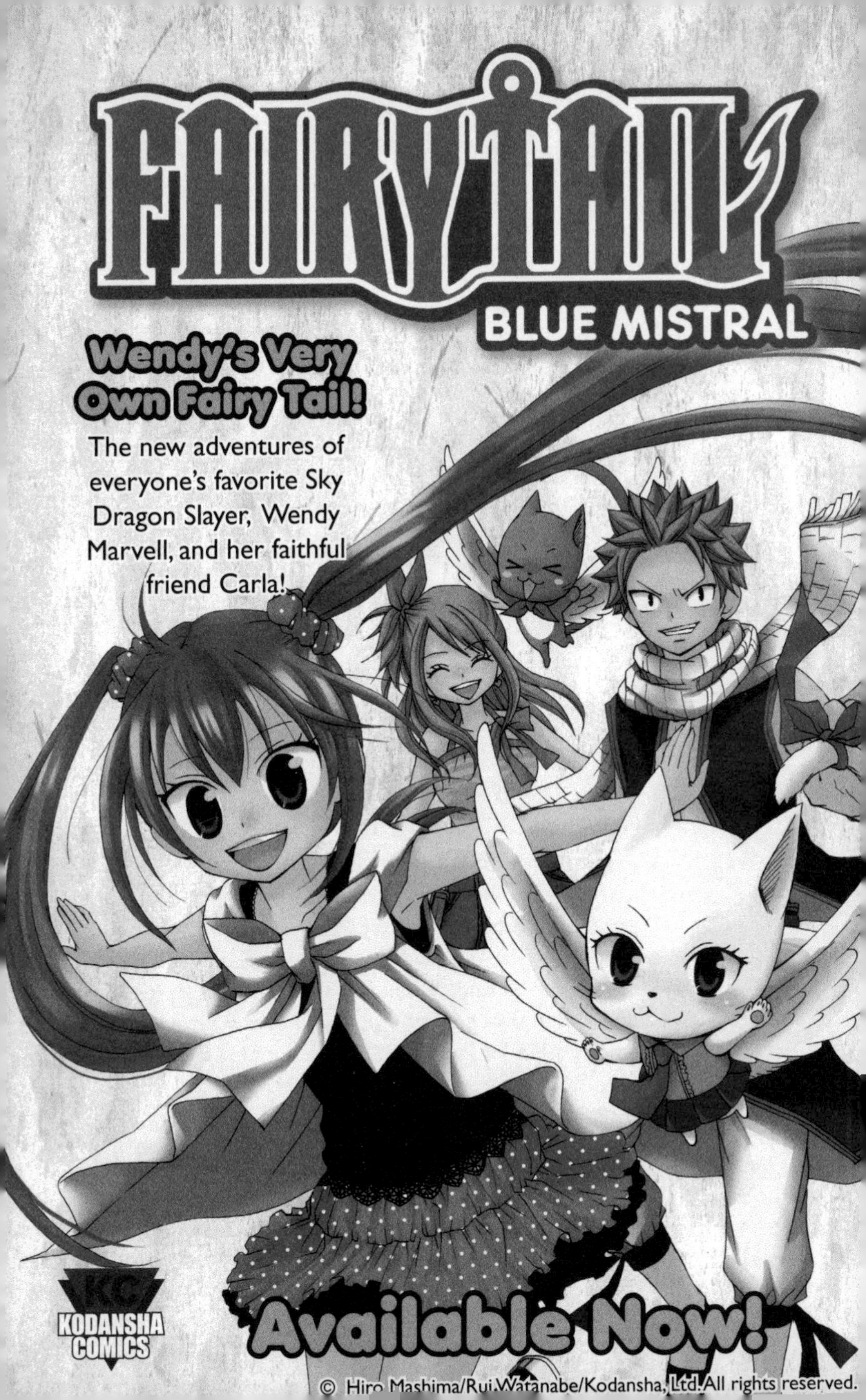
FAIRY TAIL
BLUE MISTRAL
Wendy's Very Own Fairy Tail!
The new adventures of everyone's favorite Sky Dragon Slayer, Wendy Marvell, and her faithful friend Carla!
KC
KODANSHA COMICS
Available Now!
© Hiro Mashima/Rui Watanabe/Kodansha, Ltd. All rights reserved.

Yamada-kun AND THE Seven Witches

"A very funny manga with a lot of heart and character."
—Adventures in Poor Taste

SWAPPED WITH A KISS?!

Class troublemaker Ryu Yamada is already having a bad day when he stumbles down a staircase along with star student Urara Shiraishi. When he wakes up, he realizes they have switched bodies—and that Ryu has the power to trade places with anyone just by kissing them! Ryu and Urara take full advantage of the situation to improve their lives, but with such an oddly amazing power, just how long will they be able to keep their secret under wraps?

Available now in print and digitally!

A Kodansha Comics Trade Paperback Original.

Fairy Tail volume 54 copyright © 2016 Hiro Mashima
English translation copyright © 2016 Hiro Mashima

All rights reserved.

Published in the United States by Kodansha Comics, an imprint of Kodansha USA Publishing, LLC, New York.

Publication rights for this English edition arranged through Kodansha Ltd., Tokyo.

First published in Japan in 2016 by Kodansha Ltd., Tokyo
ISBN 978-1-63236-215-5

Printed in the United States of America.

www.kodanshacomics.com

9 8 7 6 5 4 3 2 1

Translation: William Flanagan
Lettering: AndWorld Design
Editing: Haruko Hashimoto
Kodansha Comics edition cover design by Phil Balsman

TOMARE!

止まれ
[STOP!]

You're going the wrong way!

Manga is a completely different
type of reading experience.

To start at the *beginning*,
go to the *end!*

That's right! Authentic manga is read the traditional Japanese way—
from right to left, exactly the *opposite* of how American books are
read. It's easy to follow: Just go to the other end of the book and read
each page—and each panel—from right side to left side, starting at
the top right. Now you're experiencing manga as it was meant to be!

FAIRY TAIL

54

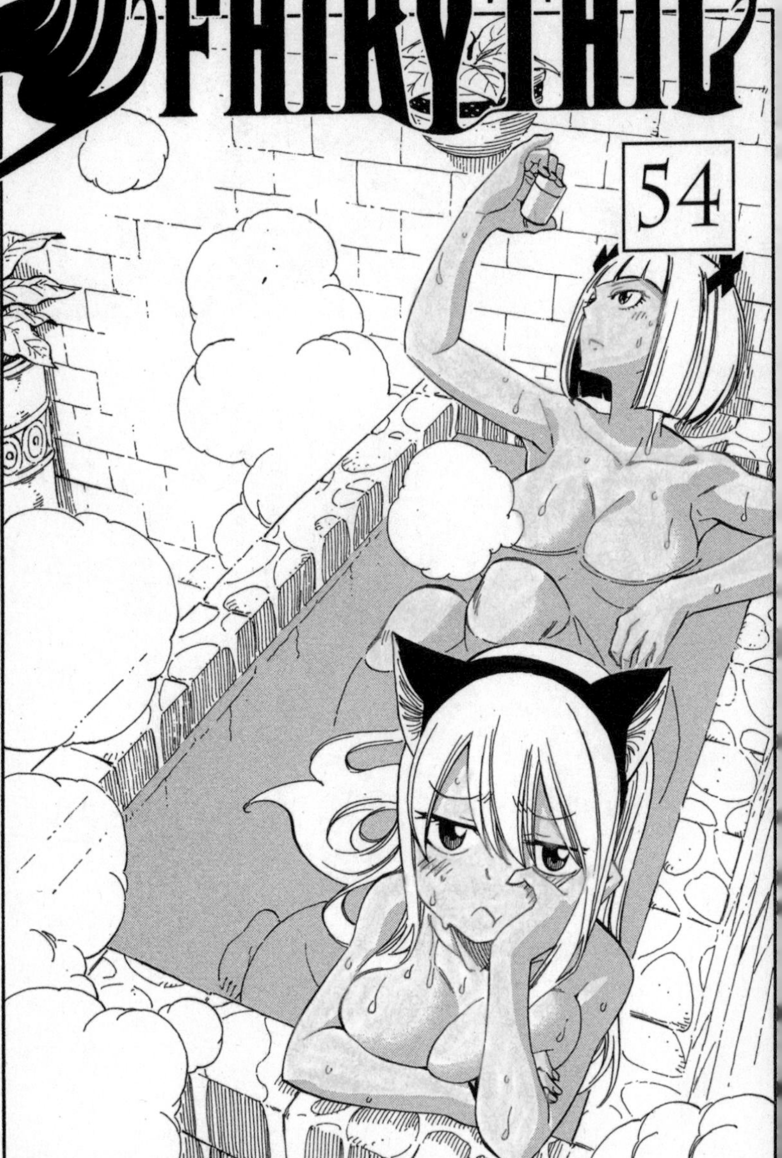

HIRO MASHIMA

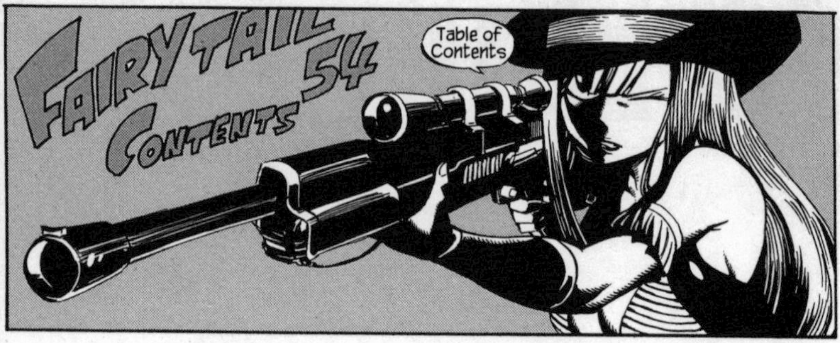
FAIRY TAIL
CONTENTS 54
Table of Contents

FAIRY TAIL
フェアリーテイル

Chapter 456: Orders

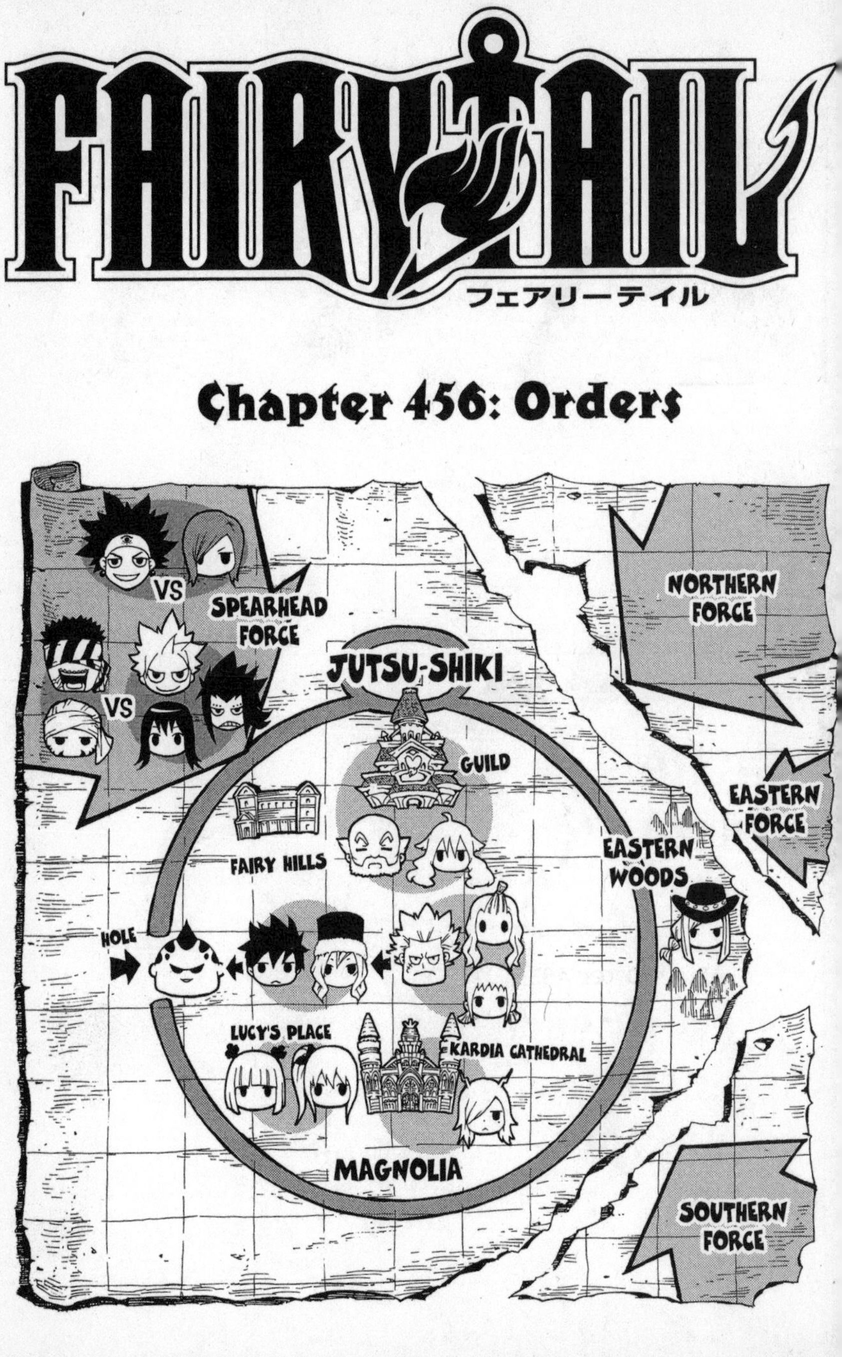
VS
SPEARHEAD FORCE
VS
JUTSU-SHIKI
NORTHERN FORCE
GUILD
EASTERN FORCE
FAIRY HILLS
EASTERN WOODS
HOLE
LUCY'S PLACE
KARDIA CATHEDRAL
MAGNOLIA
SOUTHERN FORCE

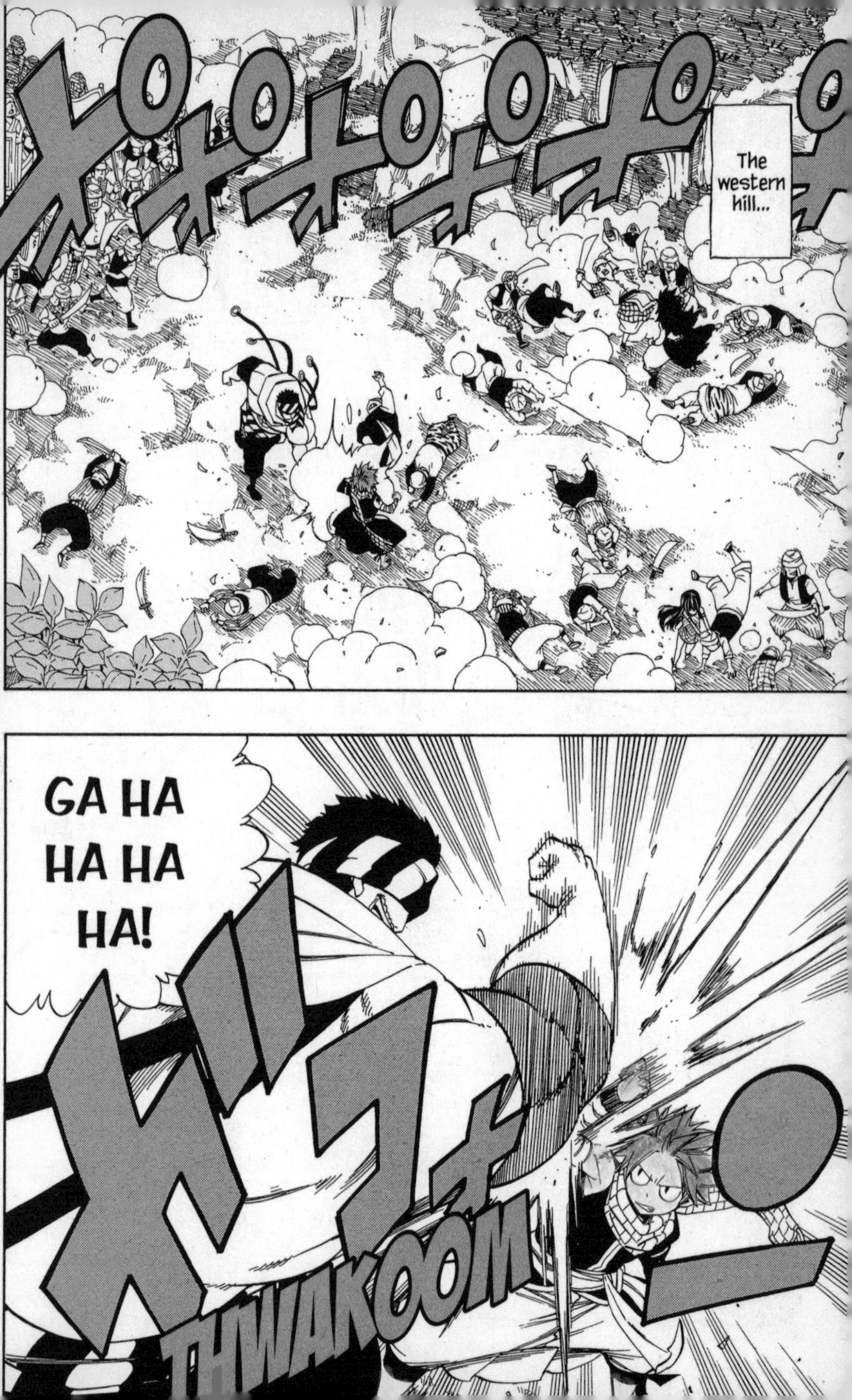
The western hill...
GA HA HA HA HA!
THWAKOOM